"This book is a wonderful mixture of autobiography, history, and politics. It is both riveting and very moving. Salman Abu Sitta weaves very skilfully his personal story with the broader story of the Palestine tragedy. Underlying it all is the terrible injustice that the Zionist movement has inflicted on him, his family, and his entire people. His book conveys eloquently and powerfully his own experience of dispossession and exile as well as his unflinching determination to map his return. . . . A really outstanding Palestinian memoir which deserves the widest possible readership."—Avi Shlaim, author of *The Iron Wall: Israel and the Arab World*

"An extraordinary engineer and scholar."—Edward Said

"Abu Sitta has ensured that the keys to the Palestinians' stolen homes will inevitably reopen the never forgotten doors."—Al Jazeera

"Salman Abu Sitta writes about a personal experience, but he also tells the story of a people and a nation. A highly recommended work from a well-known scholar that will appeal to anyone seeking to understand this story."—Dina Matar, author of *What It Means to Be Palestinian*

"Abu Sitta's memoir conveys a still burning sense of outrage at the injustice of the dispossession of the Palestinians and the denial of their rights—a personal and collective Nakba without end."—Ian Black, *The Guardian*

"The spirit of Dr. Abu Sitta's Mapping My Return: A Palestinian Memoir mirrors precisely the dynamic quintessence and will of its creator—in a word, sumoud—a compelling steadfastness to his homeland Palestine and to the right of return of every Palestinian."—Vacy Vlazna, *The Palestine Chronicle*

"This book is a valuable and unique addition to the genre of Palestinian autobiographies in English."—Rochelle Davis, Center for Contemporary Arab Studies, Georgetown University

"In a life lived intensely, with unflagging curiosity and vocal outrage at the injustices that have beleaguered his people, Salman Abu Sitta is to be celebrated for his tenacity, intelligence, and ability not to lose heart despite all the odds. This accessible and informative book describes all that he has lived through as a Palestinian, both on his own land and as a refugee. It also presents very clearly the fundamental need for the 'right of return' to be enshrined in any just and lasting peace in the region."—Selma Dabbagh, author of *Out of It*

"The events of 1948 have been told elsewhere, but rarely with the immediacy and poignancy of this child's-eye view. . . . All of Abu Sitta's research has led him to the conclusion that, far from being 'full up,' Israel has plenty of land available for the rehousing of refugees in and around the towns and villages depopulated in 1948. He envisions a state of peaceful coexistence, after the demise of a racist ideology that bears the seeds of its own destruction."—Hilary Wise, *Middle East Eye*

"Especially since less has been written about South Palestine than about other parts of the country, Abu Sitta's account is a valuable contribution to Palestinian political and social history. "—Sally Bland, *The Jordan Times*

"There is much debate about the origins of the quotation that Palestine was a land without people for a people without a land, but no doubt at all that it was Golda Meir who said that 'there is no such thing as a Palestinian people.' Palestinians remaining there and the diaspora scattered worldwide have totally disproved these statements in the hundreds of books and histories and mapping that have been published since the Nakba. Many are feats of great scholarship. Salman Abu Sitta has the broadest experience and longest tale to tell of any Palestinian I have ever met and this comprehensive history and geography of the land and its people should be on everyone's bookshelf. Everyone, that is, who seeks to understand fully the greatest injustice of the 20th century and how it affected the Palestinian people who still have not given up the hope of return to their homes in Palestine. Nor should they."—Baroness Jenny Tonge

Mapping My Return

A Palestinian Memoir

Salman Abu Sitta

The American University in Cairo Press
Cairo New York

This edition published in 2025 by
The American University in Cairo Press
113 Sharia Kasr el Aini, Cairo Egypt
420 Lexington Avenue, Suite 1644, New York, NY 10170
www.aucpress.com

First published in hardback in 2016

ISBN 978 1 649 03435 9

Library of Congress Cataloging-in-Publication Data

Names: Abu-Sitta, Salman H., author.
Title: Mapping my return : a Palestinian memoir / Salman Abu Sitta ; with a new afterword.
Identifiers: LCCN 2024049134 | ISBN 9781649034359 (trade paperback) | ISBN 9781617977077 (epub) | ISBN 9781617977084 (adobe pdf)
Subjects: LCSH: Abu-Sitta, Salman H. | Israel-Arab War, 1948-1949--Personal narratives, Palestinian. | Israel-Arab War, 1948-1949--Refugees. | Refugees, Palestinian Arab--Biography. | LCGFT: Autobiographies.
Classification: LCC DS126.97 .A287 2025 | DDC 956.9405/5092 [B]--dc23/eng/20250121
1 2 3 4 5 29 28 27 26 25

Designed by Amy Sidhom

To my parents, Sheikh Hussein and Nasra,
the first generation to die in exile

To my daughters, Maysoun and Rania,
the first generation to be born in exile

Contents

Preface

It is customary in the preface to a memoir to describe the book as the military exploits of a general or the achievements of a retired politician. These memoirs are neither. They are the experiences of an ordinary Palestinian refugee. Even at that, they do not chart the most tragic, painful, or traumatic fates of the hundreds of thousands of Palestinians made refugees in 1948. There are Palestinians who saw loved ones machine-gunned down before their eyes, others who fled into the darkness under the thud of bombs from tanks and planes, families who were decimated by explosions while having dinner, mothers who left in a hurry carrying with them a pillow instead of an infant, and children who were lost in the long marches of people seeking safety, crying for their mothers.

I have been spared much of the intensity of these experiences but I share with my fellow Palestinians the great pain of being uprooted, the loss of identity, and the struggle to reverse this nightmare.

I became a refugee at the age of ten. What stands clearly in my child's mind was the identity of the invisible enemy who destroyed my life. What did he look like? Was he a human or a beast? Why did he make me a refugee? What did I do to him? Where did he come from? What language does he speak?

I vaguely heard adults talk about Jews, brought by a British man called Balfour. They started to attack villages near Jaffa, far away in the north. I had never seen a Jew before, let alone a Jewish soldier with a gun.

This strange situation took hold of me. My life's mission became to try to put a face to this invisible enemy, in particular, the Zionist soldiers who attacked and burned down my home. I wanted to find their names, photographs of them, their origins from all over the globe, and their military formations. I wanted to understand their hatred for us, their desire to make us refugees and destroy our country, Palestine.

This led me on an endless quest: to discover how they destroyed my homeland, what became of our landscape that they left in ruins, its villages and towns, its people's lives, their folklore, their geography and history. My ultimate ambition has been to pick up the pieces of the debris and painstakingly reconstruct the destroyed landscape. If that could be done, would it then be possible to return to our homes? Using the planning and engineering experience I gained in later years, was it possible to recover the elements of this stolen patrimony? Could we shake off this terrible nightmare and be normal again, living in our country like the rest of the world?

Becoming a refugee coincided with two momentous dates in the history of the Nakba. The first was when news came from the north of Jewish massacres and the headmaster of my boarding school in Beersheba instructed us to go home and be safe with our families. That was in early April 1948 when Plan Dalet to conquer Palestine was implemented. The second made me a lifelong refugee, when Zionist soldiers attacked my own home and burned and destroyed everything they found on 14 to 15 May 1948. That was the day the disastrous British Mandate formally ended, the day when Ben-Gurion declared his state on Palestine's soil and the day when Arab regular forces came to save us, but failed.

Hence started my journey. This journey took me to Egypt, Kuwait, England, Canada, and a multitude of other places. None of them was my destination; they were stations on the route of return. The final destination, my home, remains my only target.

Unlike the birds that would fly out of their nests in our well and hover in the skies before landing back down again, I have made nine flights, from one exile to another, without landing back in my home. There are still three more flights to make before I reach my home to settle down forever.

It is not easy to put this experience into meaningful prose. It is as painful to write as it is to remember. The first attempt was a letter to my daughter Maysoun, studying in Canada in 1988 and heading a university group to explain Palestine, to tell her who she was and where she came from. She is the twelfth generation of my family, but the first not to be born in al-Ma'in, my birthplace. A second attempt was when my daughter Rania convinced me in 2010 to accompany her new family on a vacation in the Mediterranean. Here the solitude broke the mental barrier I had put up for myself and I started to write.

This tells the story of the long journey of a refugee trying to return home. There were no guns or tanks. There were no secret missions. It was simply a quest for a right to be restored, a truth to be unveiled, and a patrimony, lost in a moment of historical aberration, to be regained. That is the fuel which sustains all Palestinians in their long struggle. It is now close to a century of struggle since the First World War, through three or four generations, with no sign of them giving up.

It is my firm belief that Zionism's ill deeds in Palestine will come to an end. Regrettably these deeds have indelibly marked the history of the Jews forever, more than any other event in their history. Every chapter in history tells us that injustice is short lived. In Palestine, this is no exception. Our task therefore, in fact the task of every human being with a conscience, is to bring about the day when justice prevails and rights are restored, as soon as possible and without killing, suffering, and dispossession. These pages describe the work done which could serve as a road map to the return to our homeland, if not in my lifetime, then by the young generation who did not see their patrimony with their own eyes but have kept it well preserved in their minds and hearts.

There are expressions in the book which may not be familiar to the young generation; I have tried to explain them as they come. For the same reason I introduced footnotes to explain some historical events or references for those who wish to learn more. The Arabic transliteration of names follows the simplest in current use.

The words 'Jews,' 'Arabs,' 'Palestinians,' 'Zionists,' 'Israelis' follow the contemporary use of these words. During the British Mandate, the words 'Arabs' and 'Jews' were in use, in official documents and the press. The word 'Zionism' refers to the ideology of the settlers. From the 1950s, the words 'Palestinians' and 'Israelis' gained currency, although the phrase 'Arabs of Palestine' was common.

The maps in this book are a product of the long-standing work of mapping Palestine. The photos are all dated after 1948, except one, which is on page 14. This single picture, dated around 1944, is cherished because it is the only one that survived the Nakba, as all our homes and property were destroyed and burned.

This is not a research book drawing on many archives and libraries. Nevertheless, there are people who helped a great deal in writing this book, to whom I am immensely grateful. Yazan al-Saadi, a promising writer and a journalist, typed the whole manuscript and in doing so was my first critical reader. Hilary Wise read the first chapters and made valuable comments, particularly regarding British readers. The response of friends who had read selected chapters encouraged me that my message has been understood. They include Amira Howeidy, Inea Engler, and Asad Bushnaq, among others. Middle East scholar Rochelle Davis read the whole manuscript and made a thorough review, which was the basis of significant improvements in the flow of the story. Nour Joudah went through every page with care and diligence and, as a Palestinian-American young woman, was a perfect sample for the target readership.

I am fortunate that AUC Press have taken on the task of publishing this book. Nadia Naqib nursed the project from the start and helped in its development. Nadine El-Hadi went through every paragraph with careful editing, having in mind the young generation who are not familiar with names and events. The whole staff of AUC Press were enthusiastic supporters of publishing this memoir.

To all those, and others I did not mention, I am truly grateful for their advice, support, and help.

My deepest regret, however, is that my parents, my brothers and sisters, and my wife, who witnessed many of the events in the book and were an integral part of my life, have passed away. I wanted them to read the book and tell me if I described our life together as they saw it. Maybe they would find some solace in recounting the life that passed. I am sure they hoped the future would be much better.

But it is the young generation that I hope will find the story inspiring. My daughters Maysoun and Rania witnessed, and sometimes participated in, the last chapters and heard me talk so many times about the parts they did not see. My grandchildren, too, were listening. I hope some of what they heard will sink into their memories. To this young generation I say: do not forget, and struggle to recover the stolen patrimony. Let your motto be 'we persevere.'

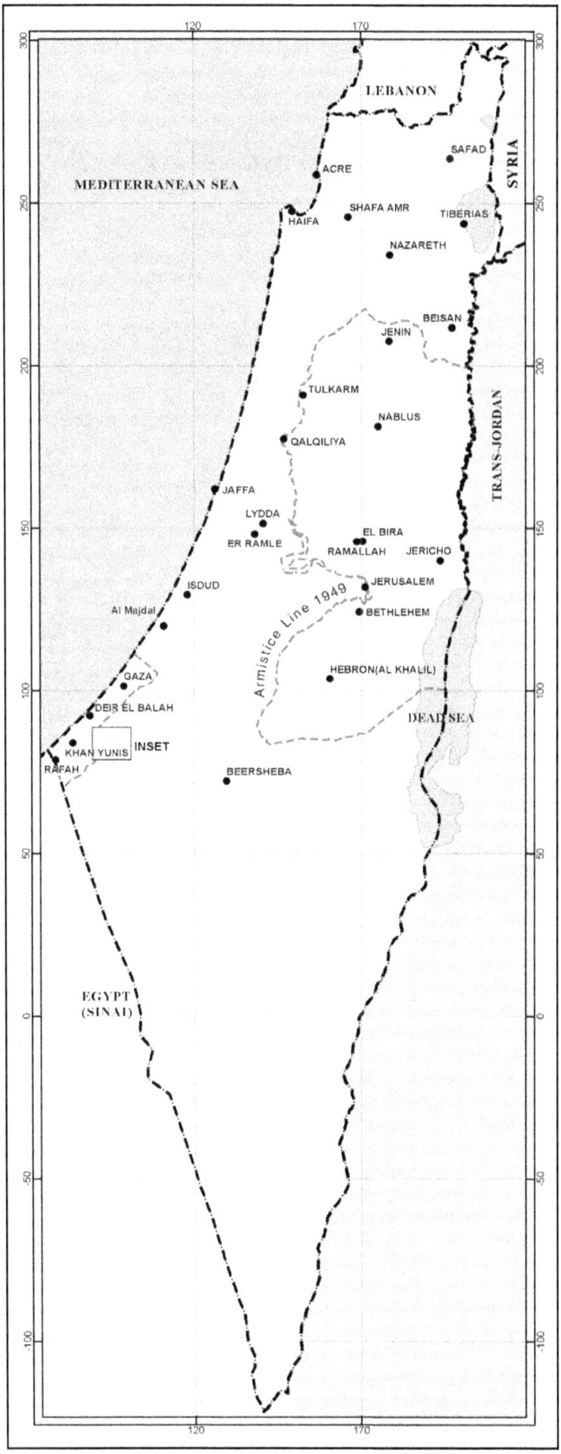

Map of Palestine, 1945–48.

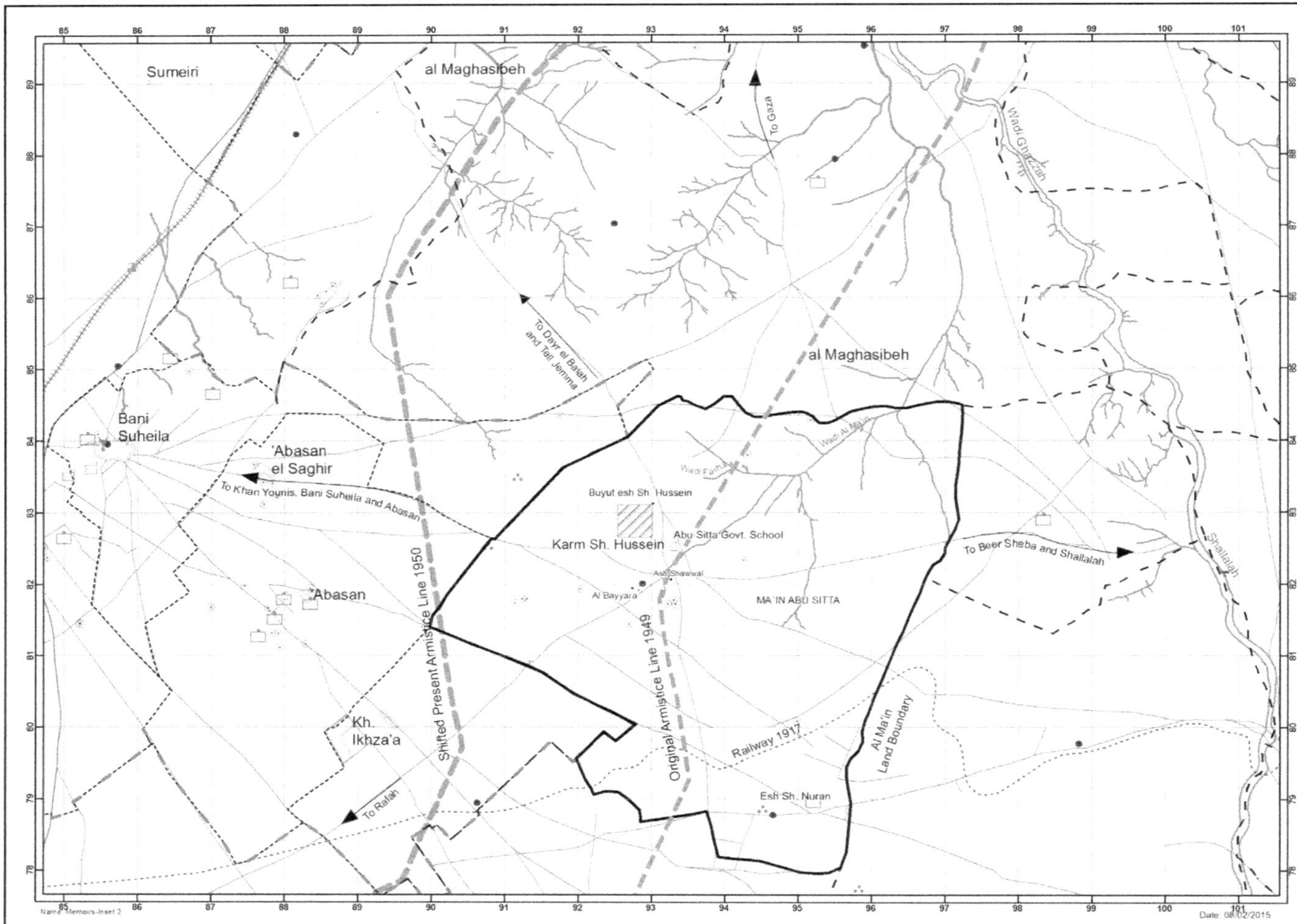

Map of al-Ma'in, 1948–50, showing the Armistice Line.

1

The Source (al-Ma'in)

I woke up from my afternoon nap at the sound of distant thunder. I rolled out of my bedding on to the floor and ran outside. There I could see the rolling meadows and gently sloping hills clothed in their autumn colors. To the north, dark clouds were taking the shape of a knight on a galloping horse or a thirsty cow rushing to a watering trough. In my childish imagination the swirling clouds, black and white, looked like the clashing forces of good and evil, slowly melting and reforming in the sky above me. These same images told our farmers a different story: they indicated whether it would rain tonight or tomorrow and whether or not it would be a good year.

Nearby, our farmhand Sa'id was plowing the land, preparing it for the winter. The plowshare, drawn by a camel, dug deep into the rich soil, forming an ever-widening pattern of straight furrows. Sa'id plowed all day, hoping that in the evening he would be able to boast in the *shigg* (my father's ceremonial seat or *diwan*) that he had covered more hectares than any of the other farmhands.

I followed in the path of Sa'id's plow, the freshly turned earth uncovering worms, which the birds picked up eagerly. Sometimes Sa'id let me hold the plow, urging me to push down hard so the blade would dig deeper.

The thunder grew louder and more threatening. The wind, blowing from the north, became stronger. The imaginary figures in the clouds grew more frightening. Spellbound, I found the land speaking to me, in its upturned earth, beautiful birds, and graphic cloud formations. Sa'id packed up his plow and left. I returned home to a worried mother and her usual refrain, "Where have you been?"

Home to my mother was *bayt al-sha'ar* or *bayt* for short (a spacious tent with rooms), which she had made over many summer months, weaving and dyeing the sheep wool. She refused to live in our stone house *(dar)*, which was sparsely furnished but spacious and comfortable. When I asked her why, her predictable reply was, "This *bayt* I made myself. That *dar* was built by fellaheen. It may fall on my head."

My father was frequently absent from our home village of al-Ma'in in Beersheba District, where I was born sometime around December 1937. I was never really sure of the exact date. My father used to go regularly to Beersheba, Gaza, or Jerusalem to deal with government officials. My brothers were away at boarding schools in Jerusalem or at university in Cairo. My eldest sister was married. That left my mother, my sister, and me at home.

At night, the wind grew stronger. It whistled through the *bayt*, which was flapping and shaking in the wind. My mother woke up my teenage sister and instructed her firmly, "Come on, help me. Tighten the ropes." Soon the flapping ceased; I could still hear the wind blowing but the roof over my head was firm.

We went back to sleep. I woke up later to find water dripping near my bedding and hear the sound of rain drumming overhead. The little gully that my mother had dug around the base of the *bayt* was overflowing, and the fabric of the roof had become very tight as it had absorbed water and shrunk. It might be ripped to pieces at any moment. My mother instructed my sister again, "Loosen the ropes," and they went out into the darkness and the pouring rain and loosened the ropes. Thanks to my mother's vigilance and traditional experience, we stayed safe.

In the morning, the sun was shining. The land was saturated and puddles glittered in the sunshine. The little ravines were flowing with water and filling the big wadi, a dry stream bed, several kilometers long. There was fear that the water in the wadi would grow into a flash flood. Yet everybody was smiling. This season was promising to be a bountiful one. The fields sown with wheat and barley seeds, extended over six thousand hectares, and would produce a very good yield.

No one was more pleased than Zeer, my father's chief foreman; he could see there would be a good harvest. He supervised the work of all the foremen, in plowing, harvesting, and storing. He was both loved and feared, depending on your position. Tall and heavily built, he was called "Zeer" or "Zeer Salem," due to his resemblance to a legendary folk hero of the same name. Zeer was known to slay his enemies with one stroke of his lance, and he was distinguished by his Turkish-style handlebar moustache.

Zeer was a kind man with a kind of childlike innocence. He once turned back from a dawn trip to the Khan Yunis market to sell a camel because he came upon a bad omen. In the early-morning mist, he saw the silhouette of a man squatting in the road to answer the call of nature. For Zeer, this was a sign that this day was not the day to do business.

Zeer's real name was Salem Abu Khatir Abu Jami'. He hailed from the village of Beni Suheila, only three kilometers away. He had divorced his first wife and brought his teenage daughter to live in al-Ma'in. She was the subject of attention of many young men, an attention that she reciprocated. She used to squat on the floor and cuddle me by holding me between her soft thighs. She seemed to enjoy that—as did I. Zeer married again—this time, to a plump, childless woman with fair skin and a ready smile.

There were other people from the nearby villages also earning a living in al-Ma'in. My mother owed a great deal to one of these women. After my youngest sister was born, my mother was worried that she could not have any more children. This woman gave her advice which worked and for which my mother was forever grateful. I was conceived four years later, the last of my brothers and sisters. Like many others from that time period, I do not know the exact day I was born, but I was always told that it was at the time of the general strike, or the Arab Revolt.[1]

We had two shopkeepers from nearby villages. The oldest and best known was al-Shawwal. His shop was strategically located in the center of al-Ma'in, where seven roads branched out heading to Gaza, Deir al-Balah, Khan Yunis, Abasan, Rafah, Nuran, Imara, and Beersheba.

Al-Shawwal was blind, but he compensated for that with his keen senses of smell and hearing. He would always catch little boys trying to steal a handful of sweets. He could recognize the intent of the young men who pretended they were talking to him but were actually addressing his pretty wife or two daughters. His wife was a good cook, and al-Shawwal used to send my father some of her best dishes.

The next day, after the rain, with the sun shining and the earth glistening, I ran outdoors barefoot, wading in the muddy water, chasing the birds, and admiring their beauty. On the trees in our *karm* (orchard), the birds were celebrating the rain, hopping from branch to branch. The sheep and cows seemed to be frolicking in the muddy puddles. I could see the cheer and hope in the weather-beaten faces of people in my family, the plowmen, helpers, and others. We all seemed to be in unison, loving and blessing this earth.

My joy was greatest when I was running free. I returned home only when driven by hunger. My mother would rub my frozen toes and cover me up with a second layer of clothes in spite of my protestations. During the cold winter days and nights, the hot bread baked by my mother and her helpers had an unforgettable taste and aroma. When I had a cough, she used to put a cover over my head and make me breathe the vapor of boiled chicken and bread, which instantly made me feel better.

Rain was the predominant subject at the *shigg*, where men gathered most nights. Zeer was planning to repair and reline the *mutmara*—the semi-circular hole dug deep in the ground and lined with hay to store wheat and barley. It ended up in the shape of a huge ball, half of it above ground. Zeer counted in his head how many *mutmaras* he had to prepare for this season.

All the wells were full with water, so much so that large pools had formed at their mouths. We children were warned not to paddle in the pools lest we fall into a well. We depended on these wells for drinking water, and we took the additional precaution of filtering the water through a piece of gauze to remove any floating hay.

In the early 1930s my father, with his cousin Abu Ibreisha, dug a ninety-five-meter well, where they struck good ground water. They installed a diesel-operated pump and a flour mill, bought from Jaffa. On the rare occasions when the pump gave trouble, a mechanic was brought in to fix it. Apart from getting his pay, the mechanic required that the well be blessed, which could not happen without slaughtering a sheep; the mechanic, of course, was the main beneficiary of its meat. A flourishing grove of date palms and other fruit trees grew on the spot. The *bayyara*, an orchard irrigated by a motorized well, was a busy place: people came to fill their earthenware jars with water and bring their grain to make flour. It was also a place where young men and women glanced at each other discreetly—an impromptu meeting place for lovers.

At about this time in the 1930s, my father brought seeds and sample plants from Tulkarm, where my brother Mousa was studying at the agricultural school. With Zeer's indispensable help, my father planted figs, grapes, almonds, and apricots in a new *karm* next to our house, barn, and store.

There was nothing like the spring on our land. The meadows were like a carpet of green as far as you could see, dotted with all the colors imaginable. The rolling landscape, with its curved, folded terrain, brought forth crimson anemones, scarlet poppies, yellow daisies, and yellow-and-white chrysanthemums—a vast bouquet created by the good earth. Birds were everywhere—sparrows, larks, starlings, bulbuls, and storks. My favorite was the *qerqizan*, with its long blue tail and its majestic walk, moving its head as if nodding to an invisible audience.

The wind sent ripples across the sea of wheat, which stretched across the valley and up the slopes of the hill two kilometers away. I would run out into these fields, the fresh breeze on my face—and I was alone. There were very few children of my age, and I was the youngest in my family. The nearest *bayt* was about one kilometer away. We played when other children came to visit. The best game was hide-and-seek in the maize *(dura)* fields where the maize would grow to a man's height—a cover that wheat fields could not provide.

Shepherds took the sheep to pasture in the spring and went their separate ways every morning and came back in the evening carrying newborn lambs in their arms. Understandably, the shepherds were all smiles, as they had a stake in the new lives.

Cows' milk seemed especially delicious. When it was available, my mother would give me the warm milk in a big jug and watch me gulp it down greedily. The evening hustle and bustle continued until well after sunset. The sheep had to be counted and tethered, and the cows had to be treated with great care, fed, and milked. Horses, ever the noblest creatures, were cared for by men alone and, mostly, by their owners. As darkness fell, the day's work came to a halt.

An hour or two after sunset, all was quiet. Fires were put out. All were fed and went to sleep—all except men in the *shigg*. There the kerosene lantern and the fire burning in the hearth, where pots of coffee were boiling, illuminated the rugged faces of the men. They exchanged anecdotes, news, future plans, hopes, and fears. My father served coffee in the place of honor, and then he explained what he had seen and done in Beersheba, Gaza, and Jerusalem. I would sit in his lap, holding his newspaper, and pretending to read it.

The spring also brought forth the beauty of youth. Girls seemed to be prettier and they paraded themselves, leading small flocks to pastures nearby. They were not professional shepherds, of course, but it was a token help, a little recreation, and it provided them a chance to meet young suitors, away from prying eyes. One noted beauty was Fatima. She walked like a gazelle. In poetic lines, suitors likened her beautiful eyes to white china cups filled with black coffee. Like other girls, she wore a long *thobe* (full-length dress) embroidered with blue geometrical shapes, birds, and flowers, as was typical of southern Palestine. The color of the embroidery changed from blue to red when the girls were married.

Fatima tied her *thobe* at the waist with a tight cummerbund. She pulled her *thobe* above the cummerbund in front to accentuate her ample bosom and left it loose at the back to accommodate her well-endowed derrière. She also pulled her *thobe* up at the sides to reveal her ankles. She would then walk with a swaying, rhythmic gait, kicking up her *thobe* front and back as she went. She hid her hair under a cap ornamented with old coins, including Maria Theresa[2] dollars and gold English sovereigns. The cap was held in place by a band passing firmly under her chin while her braids dangled over her chest down to her waist. Her *aba* (cloak) covered her body loosely, but not her face, allowing a suitor just a glimpse. Although her attire was typical of the local girls, she was quite a sight for the young men. In the end, she made an ordinary marriage, though she must have enjoyed her spring while it lasted.

The spring brought much more work for my mother. Not only did she have to feed my family, but also a dozen or so shepherds and a similar number of farmhands. However, she had a lot of help. Attached to our family for generations (nobody knows how many) were about eight families of Africans, about thirty people in all. They were Muslims, spoke Arabic as we did, and their names were registered as "Abu Sitta." They could seek other employment if they wished. Their women helped my mother in all the household chores.

The men made coffee at my father's *shigg* and looked after his horses.

In the old days, they were personal guards for the heads of our family. In the early eighteenth century, when the name "Abu Sitta" (literally, father of six) became the accepted name for my family, the legend goes that it was because my earliest ancestor, the founder of the Abu Sitta family, was accompanied wherever he went by six of the Africans as personal guards *(fedawiya)*, three on each side.

They never received a regular salary, but they were given everything they needed, such as food, shelter, and clothing. When a young man or woman got married, my father covered all expenses. They were afforded full protection and the prestige of belonging to our family.

The summer brought heat and harvest. Nobody cared more about the wheat crop than Zeer. This was his day of delivery to show the fruits of his labor. He would shade his eyes and scan the horizon for sheep straying into *his* wheat. No sooner did he see a stray sheep than he would yell out a reverberating "Heeee," audible on the hillside opposite, and the errant shepherd would run in fright to round up his flock.

The wheat and barley crops on our vast territory were so plentiful that our helpers could not cope with them alone. Dozens of harvesters came in from nearby villages, Abasan, Khiza'a, and Beni Suheila, and even from eastern Sinai. Young men and poor women seeking food for their children would be allotted areas by the indefatigable Zeer. He organized them, putting them in charge of squares, and they piled up the sheaves at each corner. He would reprimand them for leaving any long stalks behind.

I walked around the fields, not feeling the stubble under my feet. The poorest women would follow the harvesters, gleaning any remaining ears of wheat. One of them was a determined woman who went about her work diligently, however hot it was. Her labor eventually bore fruit: her son became a distinguished doctor with a strong political mission.

Zeer piled up the sheaves of wheat on the threshing floor. Every pile was trampled on until it was compressed into a manageable thickness. Camels and sometimes oxen pulled the winnowing plate around and around in circles until the thickness of the pile was reduced to a few centimeters. I was allowed to sit on the plate although my weight was not much help.

I watched from the windward side when men were tossing the wheat in the air with pitchforks. The hay would blow away and the grain would fall on the ground. Zeer and his helpers would collect both separately and the wheat would be stored in his already made *mutmara*.

The wheat and barley crops far exceeded our needs, even though Zeer stored to his heart's delight. The British Mandate government bought the surplus through its agent, Steele Company. The government needed the wheat, especially during the Second World War, and the barley was used for making beer.

Steele Company trucks with their long flatbeds were loaded with red-lined sacks of wheat. Zeer, ever careful, would count the sacks while using an incantation to avoid the evil eye. He did not count "one, two." Instead he would chant while counting, "Allah wahid, malu thani" (God is one, has no second). I used to run after the last loaded Steele Company truck and jump onto the back bumper, until the truck gathered speed and I fell rolling on to the dirt road.

In the mid-1940s my father decided to use a mechanical harvester to cope with the volume of harvest. The harvester was a combined tractor and a tray with rotating arms that cut down the wheat and gathered it into sheaves. When the tray was full, an operator pushed a pedal and the tray dropped the sheaves on the ground at intervals. I persuaded the operator to let me have a go at it. It was quite easy to push the pedal when the tray was full; however, the experiment failed. The harvester left ten to fifteen centimeters of the stalks uncut. That meant a loss of hay and a need to clean the fields afterward. The ungainly looking machine, with its roaring engine, left the field amid the cheers of the joyful human harvesters.

Such a large yield required more storage than the *mutmara*s could provide. We had huge barns built onto the back wall of the *dar* (house). From a door wide enough for a loaded camel to enter, you could see the vast interiors with their straw-clay (wattle-and-daub) walls and wooden roof supported by railway sleepers, in place of steel beams.

I can visualize its details to this day. First, to the left, there was the main barn, several spans of three meters each wide, where hay was stored. Next to it there were five large sheds for storing ropes, various implements, and red-lined sacks. In the courtyard you could tether and feed fifty camels. Horses and cows were never kept there. We used to play and hide in the hay barn. On winter nights, the shepherds slept there. If it was raining, the shepherds would bring the camels into the barn and share the shelter with them.

The harvest in May was not the only highlight of the summer. In the summer, we grew red and yellow melons and maize. As the weeks went by, the melons grew into round, green balls strewn all over the fields. It was a feast for man and beast.

My brothers, back from school, would compete in finding the most delicious melon. They would break one open, taste it, and eat a slice before trying another one. If a melon was found to be not red or sweet, it was thrown to the camels. Poor harvesters from Sinai, who lingered on after the wheat harvest, would devour the discarded melons eagerly.

Late in the summer, the grapes and figs were nearly ready to be picked. I loved figs and could not wait for them to ripen. I ate them although the white juice oozing from them stung my lips. The grapes too were sour before they ripened, and venturing to extend a hand to grab a bunch was dangerous for a child. I often saw a snake hidden in the leaves, too close to the inviting bunch. The cactus fence bore fruit too, but the fruit was protected by an outer layer of thorns. We pulled the cactus fruit down by grabbing them with a metal cup on the end of a long stick; they were then washed or brushed to remove the thorns, then peeled and eaten.

I used to run around in the fields and among the trees, exploring, tasting, and observing. Like other children, I learned to paint a twig with the sticky sap we tapped from trees. I then put the twig on a tree and waited patiently in the shade, but mostly in the scorching sun, until a bird landed on it. I would rush to catch the bird if it was not strong enough to fly away. If I was successful, I would examine closely its colors, its long and varied feathers.

At midday I returned home, sweaty and tired. My bare feet were aching from the burning earth. My mother would be appalled to see me and tell me sternly, "Look at your face, black as a slave." Forced to wash, eat, and take my usual nap, I then enjoyed the reality that life went on afterward as if nothing had happened.

In the late afternoon, I amused myself with a number of steel barrels with two heavy rings. I used to slide into one of them and turn around while the barrel was rolling, my head sticking out to steer it. I also found bicycle wheels without tires. These wheels I made into a small car, and another time, I pushed the metal wheel by a long handle, which was hooked to fit the wheel.

As I grew older, my brother tried to teach me to ride. He put me on a horse and trotted ahead on his horse as I followed on mine. Barely able to feel my light weight, my horse promptly threw me to the ground and followed the other horse. My riding lessons came to an abrupt end unintentionally, as the events that overtook Palestine prevented me from ever taking revenge on that rebellious horse.

The summer was usually the time when my mother visited her family. She would ride on her donkey, with me riding behind her, for a distance of about five kilometers. My uncles had more than one *karm* on Wadi Selqa. Its grapes and figs were so delicious that I usually slid from the donkey as we approached and rushed to investigate the trees and eat from them.

My mother had two brothers: Mahmoud, the farmer, always making faces to make me laugh, and Muhammad, the serious, quiet uncle and head of the family. My mother had a younger sister, almost a copy of my mother in her looks. The visit to my uncles was always a joy. The warmth of my mother was reflected in all of them. We returned loaded with all kinds of gifts.

There were popular poems about the men of my mother's family, known to be fierce, daring fighters, coming to the help of the weak and not tolerating wrong deeds.[3] My mother's character was a good reflection of that trait. She was extremely devoted to her children. Once she rushed off toward Jaffa, where she had never been, on account of a rumor she heard that her son Ali had drowned there. She returned when she was told that someone had seen him alive and well. God knows where she thought she was running to find her son. Also, she was not interested in idle gossip as her neighbors were and was careful to do her social duties, such as visiting other families on special occasions to celebrate a wedding or to express condolences.

While she had a deep respect for custom, she had a keener sense of justice and would never give up her claim if she felt wronged. On some nights, I awoke to hear her pleading her case with my father about some domestic matter. The test case came in the mid-1920s. There was a rumor that my father had received an offer from a man who wanted to marry my twice-divorced and childless aunt, in exchange for my father marrying that man's sister (in what was called a *badal*, a common form of marriage exchange). A female servant of the prospective bride was sent to explore the situation. My aunt warmly received her. My mother got wind of this and set up an ambush for the marriage broker. As the woman was returning from her mission at dawn, riding half asleep on her donkey, at a deserted spot just north of us, near Wadi Farha, she was terrified to find my mother emerging from the darkness, forcing her down to the ground, and threatening to finish her off with a short sword. The woman swore she would never set foot on our territory again and promised to report the terrible fate awaiting the bride if she came near us. Although my mother was actually as frightened as she was, the threat worked and that was the end of the story.

The summer was also the time when we visited our *bayyara* in Deir al-Balah, a coastal village, just west of Wadi Selqa. As its name implied, the village was known for its rich groves of date palms. My great-grandfather Saqr built this *bayyara* in 1844. It was the only land we owned that I saw firsthand as a child, other than al-Ma'in. I never saw our other lands in al-Dammath, al-Mu'allaqa, or Egypt. The *bayyara* was almost half a kilometer away from the Mediterranean, separated from it by a ridge of sand dunes. When we visited Deir al-Balah, our land partner and its caretaker from the village, with the Turkish title of al-Tawashi,[4] made a delicious lunch and we returned laden with dates.

I rode behind my brother on his horse and we climbed the ridge. Unable to see anything ahead, I could hear a tremendous roar in the background. Leaning sideways, I could see nothing but a vast blue horizon and pounding waves advancing toward the shore like soldiers marching to war. I had never seen anything like it. My fright was so great that I found myself jumping off the horse and running as fast as I could in the opposite direction.

Summer nights were special. Boys and girls gathered in a circle under the shining moon. We played a game called Utham Mrah. The player threw a small stick or a stone behind someone. The rule of the game was to search for it behind you without turning around before the player completed one circle.

The big event in the evening was Samer, the harvest festival, especially when it coincided with one of the religious holidays. Two rows of young men and women faced each other and one singer recited lines of popular poetry. Both groups responded as a chorus, while dancing toward each other and then retreating. In the moonlight, some girls carelessly dropped their veils. On such nights, many marriage matches were made.

Young men also competed for the attention of the girls in a famous horse race held regularly, usually in the summer. A large white handkerchief, known as the *gurra*, was placed on a pole. One of the horsemen would grab it and race toward the finishing post. The winner was the one who could snatch the *gurra* from him and pass the finishing post, amid the shouts and cheers of the waiting crowd. I remember my brother Ibrahim winning the *gurra* one year.

All of these events, like everything else in our lives, revolved around our precious land.

2

Seeds of Knowledge

Like the earth, the mind too can be cultivated and made fruitful. My father built the first school in our region in 1920, less than half a kilometer from our *karm*, before his eldest son was born. It was one spacious room, built of stone said to have been brought in on the backs of camels from the ancient site of Khalasa, fifty kilometers away. He hired a teacher from Gaza to sleep in and teach at the school from Saturday to Thursday. My mother used to send him milk, eggs, and the occasional chicken. On the weekend, he rode home to his family, he and his donkey having been well fed during the week away.

The first few years, teachers were paid by my father and the pupils' parents, who usually did so in the form of agricultural produce. In the mid-1920s, the British Mandate government listed the school on its roll and began paying teachers from taxes collected in Palestine.

Pupils used to come to school from as far as ten kilometers away. Some came on foot and others rode on donkeys, which they tied up near the school. Some pupils were old enough to carry a sword, the mark of reaching sixteen years of age. As if to allay the fears of the timid teacher from the town, one of these grown-up pupils would jokingly say to him, "Do not be afraid of me, sir. Punish me if I do wrong."

The schoolroom was divided into four sections where the four different classes were held. On the blackboard, the teacher would write out the lesson for the first-year pupils while the others were doing tasks he had already assigned. Then he did the same with the second year, and so on. My father planted a eucalyptus tree in the schoolyard, which grew to a tremendous size by the time I was a pupil at the school. I used to climb its branches and stay up in partial hiding, savoring its aroma. Over the years, visitors to the remnants of the village told me that it was still there, a silent witness to the presence of its absent family. When I visited many years later, its scent was my guide back to my destroyed schoolhouse.

The only surviving picture from al-Ma'in. Taken in 1944, it shows Abdullah (seated) after return from exile in Cairo, his daughter on his right, and me on his left, wearing a tarboosh. Back row from left: Suleiman, Ali (with tarboosh), and Mousa.

My mother decided that it was best for me to go to school at an early age, to absorb what she thought was my excessive energy and to satisfy my apparent desire to read the newspaper. I did well at school, to the point that two boys came to my mother and asked her what she was feeding me to make me learn so easily. They wanted the same food. She laughed and said it was not due to the food I ate; it was because I was born on the blessed night of Laylat al-Qadr, toward the end of Ramadan.[5] Over the years, she came to firmly believe that the timing of my birth was the reason for the rapid progress I was making in my education.

During the height of Second World War, a senior official—either the British district commissioner or the high commissioner in Jerusalem, I do not remember which—came to visit our school. The teacher picked me to answer questions in front of the important visitor because he thought showing off his best pupil would gain him credit as a teacher.

On the wall hung a map of the world and the inevitable pictures of King George VI and Queen Elizabeth. The teacher gave me his pointer and asked me questions about the people in the pictures and some world capitals on the map. Then he asked me to indicate the four points of the compass. I jabbed the air, waving energetically in a northerly direction, where the commissioner happened to be standing, and I nearly caused a disaster. The pointer almost scored a direct hit in his eye. A nimble military man, he retreated just in time.

My memories relating to that school and our education are some of the most vivid of my childhood. During the long summer months, I used to sneak into the school by prying open the wooden window and squeezing between the bars. Alone in the school, I lived in the fantasy world of the stories, pictures, and new words in the books spread about on the desks. I filled the blackboard with shapes and scrawled drawings. On one occasion, my teenage brothers, back from their college in Jerusalem, opened the school door and started fooling about in the classroom. They were dragging each other across the desks when my brother Suleiman fell and gashed his eyebrow. Afraid to tell anyone, they asked me to run and bring coffee powder to stop the bleeding. I ran and snatched the coffee pouch from the *shigg*. Behind me, I heard cries from some family members who saw me: "What's going on? That naughty boy again!"

Luckily, the bleeding stopped and my brothers kept out of sight for the rest of the day.

As the youngest of my brothers by some years, I learned a great deal from them by watching, listening, and tagging along. At the time, their main ordeal was passing the arduous matriculation examination, which granted the highest school certificate in Palestine, qualifying them for university entry in other countries. The examinations were set in London, and the head of the education department was always British, although the senior staff members were Palestinians. The students who reached that level were only a select few, usually the brightest in Palestine. They were so few—three or four dozen annually—that later they naturally became the leaders in various walks of Palestinian life.

My four brothers and two of my cousins went through this education system in the 1940s. For that number of students from one family to be studying in Jerusalem was remarkable by any standards. My cousin Hamed, for example, obtained six distinctions on his matriculation certificate. Given that he had to escape his father's summons to help on the farm by hiding and studying his Latin in an abandoned shallow well, it was quite an achievement.

I recall hearing my brothers talk about the strange expressions they studied in mathematics and chemistry. But the most enjoyable was to hear them, in the summer evenings, compete in Arabic poetry where each competitor had to recite a line starting with the last letter of the previous line.

The colonial Department of Education of the British Mandate saw fit to impose Roman history and Latin on the Arab students' curricula at the expense of Arab and Palestinian history. Nevertheless, hearing such names as Shakespeare, Julius Caesar, and Dante enriched my early years of education at our school.

I cannot forget hearing one of my brothers reciting over and over again something that had a pleasant and intriguing lilt. I learned it by heart and parroted it repeatedly, to my mother's confusion at such gibberish. She was not to be blamed. Who would expect an Arab boy to recite, "at tuba terribili sonitu taratantara dixit?"[6] Who would expect the famous lines of the father of Roman poetry to be recited in southern Palestine? But perhaps it was not so strange. After all, Palestine had more and longer-running cultural, political, and commercial links with Rome (and Greece) than England had.

My brother Ali, the youngest of my teenage brothers, was very inventive, which led him, and me in his footsteps, to be an engineer. He made a windmill and fixed it onto the roof of our *dar*. This contraption had a rope and a bucket, and it was my job to fill it with sand. He would shout from the roof that an empty bucket was coming down, which I promptly filled. The bucket was very small but it was exciting for both of us to see it hoisted up by Ali's invention.

Then, there were the inventions of the time that made their way to our village. In the early years of Second World War, the British were keen to win the propaganda war against Germany, as the advancing German army was about to invade Egypt. They distributed wireless sets to the region's notables. Government workers came and set up two long poles, stretched a wire between them, and installed a radio in the guest room in the *dar*. There were two fixed radio stations: Jerusalem and the (British-run) Near East Station from Cyprus. Ali, ever curious, turned the box upside down and, fiddling with a screwdriver, found the knob that turned the tuner. Hearing a babble of languages, strange music, and all kinds of odd noises he ran out excitedly, throwing up his arms, declaring, "I've found the whole world!"

Preparing for his sons' education, my father spoke to the district commissioner and suggested he make a recommendation to grant us a scholarship to study at Oxford or Cambridge. The commissioner replied, "Why, Sheikh Hussein? Your sons will be sheikhs, like their father and grandfathers before them. Do you want education for your sons so they end up as clerks in a government office?"

"No," my father replied. "I want education for them because it is education which brought you from a faraway land to rule over us!" It was very unusual to be so keen on education beyond the elementary level in Mandate Palestine, especially in the rural south.

What made my father such a pioneer in education? He was eager to know more about the world around him and about a time period that would forever alter it. In his younger days, he taught himself to read and write. He would sit by and listen for a month or two to Sheikh al-Kuttab, a lay teacher, and then move on to another sheikh. Later in life, he became an accomplished speaker, writer of letters and petitions, and an avid reader of leading Arab writers such as Abbas al-Aqqad, Ahmed Amin, and Taha Hussein.

My father was born in the early or mid-1880s in al-Ma'in. When he grew up, he heard people speak of *Hawjat Urabi* (the Urabi Revolt) in 1881, in reference to the demand for reform by Egyptian Nationalist officers. These officers were protesting against the prejudice by the Turkish and Circassian ruling class against home-grown Egyptian officers. Khedive Tewfik, the ruler of Egypt, sought British help to put down the revolt. Waiting for just such an opportunity to take control of the Suez Canal, the British sent their fleet in 1882. They destroyed large parts of Alexandria, and their army defeated Urabi at Abu Kabir, near the Suez Canal.

Bilad Ghazza, or the Gaza Region, in southern Palestine had close links with Egypt. Gaza was one of the main stopping places on the road between Cairo and Damascus. There was a brisk trade with Egypt as caravans from Egypt sold their goods in Gazan markets and vice versa. Some of modern Gaza's merchants originally came from Egypt. Fugitives from Khedive Abbas's tyrannical rule sought refuge in Palestine. One particular Egyptian family, al-Tahawi, escaped to Palestine after Khedive Abbas took their sons hostage. They stayed with us for a while and we maintained friendship with them well into the twentieth century. The learned religious men in Gaza graduated from al-Azhar University in Cairo. It was not surprising therefore that those preachers in their Friday sermons supported the Urabi Revolt, praised his deeds, and prayed for his victory. Their national compass was correct. The British set up their largest base in the Middle East in Egypt from 1882 to 1952, from where they advanced to occupy Palestine in 1917.

In 1908, my father first set foot in Egypt to recover land belonging to his grandfather (but that is another story). He was impressed by the bustling life in the streets of Cairo with so many people milling about, talking, shouting, and selling their wares. He would sit in a coffee house in Opera Square for hours, opposite the equestrian statue of Ibrahim Pasha, reading the *Al-Ahram* newspaper and meeting friends. Seeing the hurrying crowd, he would exclaim, "Where are the Egyptians going?" We repeated this cliché often.

My father also read about Muhammad Abdu, the late nineteenth-century Islamic reformer. As he told me once, he realized that learned people had eyes to see, while ignorant people did not. Learned people took charge, he believed, led people, and did (mostly) good things. He would frequently recite the well-known Arabic poem: "Knowledge builds houses from broken stones / Ignorance destroys once glorious houses."

Building a school at his expense was his first educational effort. As he became the sheikh of our clan during the First World War, he undertook many more projects in education, agriculture, and politics as paramount sheikh of the Tarabin tribe and chief judge at the tribal court in Beersheba. He also made frequent trips to nearby Gaza and Jerusalem to participate in national conferences on the Balfour Declaration and Jewish immigration.

Naturally, as a child, I looked on these trips and duties a little differently. I would always know when he returned from Beersheba. Beyond Sheikh Nuran hill in the east, I would see the billowing dust of his bus rise on the horizon as the bus moved along the dirt road. I would alert everybody to this smoke signal. Somebody would take my father's favorite horse to meet him at the bus stop. He usually brought delicious things from the town: kebab, *kunafa*, and, of course, newspapers and his documents. At night, the men of my extended family would meet and discuss the progress of the war and the possible fate of Palestine.

Having finished four years at our school by the time I was eight years old, I was sent to finish my primary education at the boarding school at Beersheba, generally reserved for the sheikhs' sons. Most of my brothers had been there before me. My father ordered the list of clothes prescribed by the school. After having said good-bye to my mother and sister and having been exhorted to eat properly, bathe, and cover myself well when asleep, I started off with my father on this new journey with a heavy heart.

He entered the headmaster's study with the customary salutations. I felt apprehensive meeting Abdullah al-Khatib with his air of authority. I could not bear my father leaving me there, although he promised to see me once a week when he came to court. He gave me a shilling (five Palestinian piasters) and told me to collect one shilling a week from a particular shop in town where we were allowed to go twice a week.

The school building was built in 1908 and was a magnificent Turkish-style stone structure. It was a military hospital just before the end of the First World War, when the Mandate government converted it into a school. The ground floor was for classes and the first floor consisted of the dormitory, with the dining hall and bathrooms behind the main building.

There were about three or four dozen boarders. Day students from the town shared the school with us in the morning. I liked the classes and the teachers, but I hated the boarding aspect of the school. I was one of the youngest students and missed my mother and my family. The school was regimented: classes by day, dinner at six, and homework until nine. The food was terrible. We carried our plates to the kitchen hatch where a lump of food was dumped on them.[7] There was occasional excitement when we bartered with each other, exchanging the odd banana or apple for the rest of our food.

During the spring holidays, my mother fed me well and supplied me with a large bag of boiled eggs for my return to Beersheba. After many days, the teacher in charge smelled a foul smell. He traced it to my locker and reprimanded me for not reporting it.

On Fridays, we had to take a full bath. There was no actual bath, only a showerhead with a thirty-centimeter barrier on the floor to keep the water in. One day I slipped and hit the back of my head on that edge. The teacher saw my head bleeding and declared the cut was not serious. But left untreated, the wound became infected and the infection spread. Luckily for me, the next school holiday was near. My mother was appalled at my condition. She applied a powder to the infection and it did the trick. In a week or ten days, my wound had healed.

The highlight of my week was my father's visit when he came to court on Mondays. Every week I waited, glancing at the central hall from my classroom window. As soon as I saw his imposing and dignified figure passing by the window on his way to the headmaster's office, I knew that at any moment the headmaster's office clerk would call me. Sure enough, he soon came in and asked the teacher for me. I greeted my father politely, kissing his hand and raising it to my forehead. As soon as we left the headmaster's office, I would ask him how my mother and sister were and if he had visited my brothers in Jerusalem. During the break, he took me for a tasty kebab lunch followed by fruit for dessert. These meals somewhat compensated for the dreary ones in the dining hall.

My days at the boarding school came to an abrupt end with the news of the Jewish takeover of Palestine.

3

The Talk of the Hearth

Evenings sitting in my father's lap as a young boy in the *shigg*, listening to people talk of the old days, was a fascinating and warm experience. We were surrounded by members of my family and frequent guests. Abu Freij, one of the servants, lit the fire in the hearth and made fresh coffee, pouring it from one pot into another until it attained a special aroma and texture. Sipping their coffee, friends and family exchanged tales of their own past and stories of their ancestors.

In addition to the fantasy world I had built from my school days and summer months in the schoolhouse, the stories I had heard at the *shigg* as a child also created in my mind a world of heroes and villains, with real horses galloping on the ground and imaginary ones taking shape in the clouds. As was the case with oral tradition, the stories had no fixed time reference, other than "a long time ago" or "in my great-grandfather's time," and no identifiable location, other than "far away from here," "a month's ride," except, of course, when referring to well known places and landmarks.

Naturally, some of the guests were well known for their storytelling skills. One such storyteller, Hammad Abu Tawila was a member of my extended family. He acquired the nickname "Abu Tawila" on account of his height. He was a tall, gaunt man with big feet. His appearance and attire were rough and uninviting. He compensated for all that when he started talking of the old days in such detail that you would think he had been there himself. He raised or lowered his voice according to the gravity of the situation. He waved or gestured to emphasize a point, sometimes shaking his hooked, foot-long smoking pipe. All those present were spellbound by his narration, although many had heard the story many times. Of all those present, I was sure I was the most mesmerized by his storytelling. That night, I would vividly relive the talk of the hearth in my dreams.

Through my travels over three decades later, I found in the libraries of London, Paris, Berlin, Cairo, Istanbul, and other places, official documents or travel books, all written by travelers from faraway lands. They shed light on the stories I had heard, sometimes closely corroborating them and always giving fixed time and place references.

Often, these stories at the hearth were the way we learned about our family histories. Genealogy *(nasab)* was of the highest importance to us. Not only was it important for our identity and self-respect to be able to recite the names of our ancestors (as a boy, I could recite the names of twelve generations), but it was an essential tool for delivering justice. For example, nothing was more horrible than the crime of murder. It was mandatory to exact revenge *(thaar)* on the criminal's family, however long it took. A well-known proverb chides the haste of the one who takes revenge after only forty years. The wronged could take revenge on any member of the criminal's family up to the fifth generation.

My extended family *(ashira)* belonged to the Tarabin, the largest, wealthiest, and strongest tribe in southern Palestine. Before the establishment of physical barriers such as the Suez Canal, built in 1869, and political boundaries such as the Administrative Line of 1906 between Egypt and Palestine (the latter being part of Syria before Sykes-Picot carved it up), various branches of the Tarabin could connect throughout the land. Although the largest part of the tribe was in Palestine, another major branch lived in central western Sinai, on the Gulf of Aqaba at Nuweiba al-Tarabin (now just Nuweiba); others lived at Ras Sidr near Suez and as far west as Basatin, in the Cairo suburb of Maadi on the eastern bank of the Nile. Before the Suez Canal was built, movement of people across Arab countries in that region was unrestricted. Since all wars or clashes with other tribes were over disputed ownership of land, the Tarabin were able to come to each other's aid from as far away as Cairo.

By most accounts, the name "Abu Sitta" became current around 1730. There are tales of a link with the al-Saqr, the strong tribe of the Beisan region, southwest of Tiberias.[8]

What we know beyond doubt is that the Tarabin in the late eighteenth century consolidated their control over their land in Palestine; the area was bounded in the north by Qanan al-Saru,[9] just north of the Gaza–Beersheba road, in the west by the lands of the coastal Mediterranean villages, and in the south by a line passing through al-Auja Hafir and the town of Beersheba.

Map of Ma'in Abu Sitta, before 1945. Owners of the land: 9,000 refugees.

The land of al-Ma'in, owned by my family, extended over sixty thousand dunums (about six thousand hectares) and was bounded in the east by Wadi Ghazza at Shallalah and in the west by the villages of Beni Suheila, Abasan, and Khiza'a. We also owned land in al-Mu'allaqa (twelve thousand dunums), in Dammath (two thousand dunums), and the *bayyara* in Deir al-Balah, in addition to our land in Egypt.

My great-great-grandfather, Dahshan I, consolidated his strength by good judgment. Once he solved a bloody dispute between two families in Khan Yunis, the al-Agha and the al-Astal. The Sataris, who lived in Satar, near Qarara, accidentally killed one of the Aghas. They had to flee to avoid bloodshed. The al-Astal and al-Agha fought over the land left behind. They asked Dahshan I to judge the issue. He rode along on his horse saying, "The land on my right is for the al-Astal and on my left for the al-Agha."

"What about you, Sheikh Dahshan?" they asked.

"I have the seven waves of the sea," he replied.

There was a conflict between him and the Turks on authority over the area. This was a constant source of friction between the distant central government and the local leaders. He was forced at one time to retreat to Rakhama, south of the town of Beersheba. When his wife died, he carried her body a long distance, some seventy-five kilometers, to bury her in our cemetery at Beni Suheila. He had to travel by night to avoid clashing with the Turkish soldiers.

His son, my great-grandfather, Saqr, was the one who established the family's power and reputation from Transjordan to Egypt in the nineteenth century. According to Peake Pasha,[10] the commander of the Transjordanian police force, Abu Sitta forces attacked al-Shobak castle after Ibrahim Pasha's Syrian Campaign ended (1831–40).[11]

When the raiding party headed east toward al-Shobak, Saqr, barely sixteen at the time, followed them at a distance. They refused to take him on this expedition due to his young age. However, he persisted. While he was riding alone behind them, marauders attacked and robbed him. They left Saqr lying wounded in the open desert. Vultures pecked at his wounded back, leaving a permanent scar. He was saved by a passing caravan of the al-Ruwwad family, whose home was east of the Jordan River.

They nursed him for a long time until he was well. Knowing who he was, they took him back to al-Ma'in. Everyone had assumed he was lost or dead, so great celebrations were made when the al-Ruwwad unexpectedly turned up with the son of Dahshan I. This good deed *(husneh)* was rewarded for almost a hundred years, until the 1930s. Al-Ruwwad made annual visits to us and always returned with loads of grain and gifts.

Saqr rose to lead all of the Tarabin in war and to advise them in times of peace. Naum Shuqair, the British Army historian in Egypt, relates how Saqr organized three armies from the sea, center, and east to defeat his enemies decisively at al-Maksar southeast of al-Arish.[12]

Saqr was deeply rooted in our ideals of retributive justice, so it was not surprising that when his brother Salim was murdered he avenged the death, and that we would go on to tell the story for over a hundred years after him. Salim was on a trading trip to Cairo to sell a herd of camels. On his way back, thieves were stalking him. At Salhiya they tried to strip him of his money, he resisted, and they killed him. When the news came to Saqr, he gathered the elders and they decided to punish the murderers, who were identified as the Ma'aza, an Egyptian tribe. Saqr led a small band of his people to Egypt through the province of Sharqiya up to Giza, south of Cairo. He clashed with the Ma'aza wherever he found them and burned their houses. On the way back, he was feted by the chief of the Tumaylat.

It was no small feat for Saqr to travel from Palestine through Sinai to Egypt along the Nile with a small band, which they called a *jaish* (army), in order to exact revenge for the murder of his brother.

The Ma'aza complained to Egypt's ruler Khedive Ismail about the attackers who had come from Barr al-Sham (Syria). Khedive Ismail imprisoned the Tumaylat chief for giving hospitality to Saqr. When Saqr heard of this, he went back to Egypt, accompanied by his uncle Hussein, who was nicknamed "the warrior" because of his size and ferocity. The story of his return to Egypt was told so often around the evening fire that it became a legend. It was said that Saqr met Khedive Ismail (or more likely one of his senior aides) and asked him to release his innocent host, the Tumaylat chief.

"Here I am. It is I whom you want. Release my host," Saqr demanded.

"Are you not afraid to return from your country and face me?" the khedive asked.

"I came so that people will not say that men of honor are dead," Saqr replied.

"And I forgive you, so that people will not say that men of generosity are dead," the khedive responded. "Stay with us, and bring your people."

If the details of the story are fiction, the result is well documented. The khedive ordered that Saqr be awarded an estate. Saqr accompanied the government surveyor and chose pieces of land near the lands of those who had welcomed him or those whom he knew from their trading trips to Gaza. The khedive offered him two thousand *feddans* in the Sharqiya province. His uncle Hussein refused to take a share in this land. He had enough in Palestine, he said. The wiser Saqr thought of a more creative way to administer this land.

Sometime in the first half of the nineteenth century, a rebellion of Tarabin and others from the coast took place against the cruel Turkish rule, and some of government officials were killed. One of the victims was the tax collector al-Kashef. He left a widow and daughters. Al-Kashef was from the Si Salem family in Gaza who trace their ancestry to the noble al-Idrisi family of Libya.

Saqr married one of these widows or daughters and she bore him a son, Hammad, a town-bred boy who learned to read and write. Who better than the urban Hammad to go to Egypt and administer the land there?

Hammad took to his task with excessive zeal. An entourage of willing Egyptians gathered around him and arranged nights of pleasure, drinking, and belly dancing for him. In short, he acted as a minor lord. This lifestyle, of course, needed money, so he started to sell pieces of the land, often under fraudulent circumstances. (The rumor that he traveled to Cairo in a private train was probably an exaggeration.) It is likely that, given his loyalty to the new Khedive Tewfik, he did not support the revolt of Urabi Pasha. He died at the beginning of the First World War, sad and disillusioned. In his last days, he wrote letters to his mother's family in Gaza saying, "My dear uncles! Why have you forsaken me?" By this time, he had squandered much of the land by real or fraudulent sales. What was left of the land is what my father went to recover in 1908 when he first set foot in Egypt.

The stories about Saqr are among the many stories whose details have been corroborated during my travels. In the nineteenth century, European scholars, spies, priests, travelers, and survey officers descended upon Palestine, the Holy Land, to discover or verify biblical stories or to prepare plans for eventual takeover of the region when the so-called sick man of Europe, the Ottoman Empire, died.

One of these men was Victor Guérin, a French Jewish scholar who visited Palestine several times in the period 1852–88. Guérin wrote about the identification and history of archaeological sites, referring to passages from the Hebrew Bible and Greek mythology. I was reading one of his seven volumes in a quiet corner of l'Institut du Monde Arabe in Paris in 1991 when I suddenly jumped up from my chair. Guérin was describing his encounter with my great-grandfather, Saqr.

Guérin wrote that he had proceeded one morning from al-Nuseirat (near Deir al-Balah) going east with a local guide, one Nabhan from Hanajera. He related in his journal for 6 June 1869:

> Near one of these mounds, there was a small ravine that flows into Wadi Ghazza near waterfalls, bearing the same name of Wadi Shallalah. By the time we were on our way again [after watering our horses], we were joined by the chief sheikh of Tarabin, rich and substantial character, owner of many [things: land, cattle. . . , etc.], but whose countenance was far from breathing the comfort and the loyalty that shone on the face of Nabhan sheikh. His name was Saqr Abu Sitta. He was accompanied by several horsemen with weapons, and he wanted to know who the foreigner who traveled in his territory was.[13]

Perhaps the description is not very complimentary, but it confirmed Saqr's authority over his territory.

For almost a century after his death, there were memorials of and testimonials to Saqr's leadership. Because he solved a dispute between the al-Zawaydeh and al-Tawashi families in Deir al-Balah, the families rewarded him with a share of al-Tawashi's land. He built a *bayyara* and dug a well there. Inscribed on the foundation stone is the following:

> In the name of Allah, the Merciful, the Compassionate.
> This was built by the paramount Arab Sheikh *[sheikh mashayikh al-urban]* Saqr Dahshan Abu Sitta may God bless him and his parents and his companion Ali al-Tawashi.
> Completed on Friday 26 Sha'ban 1260 Hijri [6 September 1844].
> Al-Fatiha.

The stone remained visible and in good shape until the chaotic conditions of the mid-1990s in Gaza buried it somewhere.

Stories about Saqr intrigued me and I wanted to know more. In later years, as I searched the Royal Geographical Society map room, I found that the German engineer from Haifa, Gottlieb Schumacher, who belonged to the Templar Society, drew a map of the coastal region south of Wadi Ghazza in June 1886. On his map, he marked "Abu Sitta" on the *bayyara* site. This map went beyond the southern limit (Wadi Ghazza) of the *Survey of Western Palestine* (SWP),[14] conducted by the Palestine Exploration Fund (PEF). I became a member of the PEF, where a treasure of maps, photographs, and documents about Palestine in the nineteenth century was located. Here Saqr appeared again.

By the beginning of the twentieth century and the demarcation of the first Administrative Line between Egypt (under British domination) and Palestine in 1906, the Turks, sensing the threat posed to them in Palestine by the British presence in Egypt, turned their attention to the southern district. Since this territory was largely self-ruled, the Turks planned to assert the control of Istanbul's central government over the district and do this through the *mutassarif* of Jerusalem. Saqr was one of the key figures whose local authority challenged the influence of the central government. Istanbul sent a telegram to Cairo to lure Saqr to Jerusalem, indicating that "he was needed there immediately." Saqr was then in his *dawwar* (seat) at his property in the Sharqiya province in Egypt. The ruse worked. He rode to Damietta (Dumyat), sailed to Jaffa, and then rode to Jerusalem.

We do not know exactly what happened in Jerusalem except that there was a rumor that he was put in chains and jailed. A report in the *PEF Quarterly* indicated that "the famous Saqer Abu Sitta" was "captured" in 1887.[15] He died two years later. The death of Saqr was a grave blow to my family and the Tarabin. It created a vacuum that lasted until the First World War when a new age and new people appeared on the scene.

My grandfather, Dahshan II, found it hard to follow in his father's footsteps, though his life was eventful as well. When he was wanted by the Turks, he traveled to Transjordan and became a guest at al-Zabin camp. It was the custom not to inquire about the name of the guest or where he was heading during a three-day period of hospitality. The guest might be a passer-by or an ordinary traveler in need of food and shelter. Dahshan woke up one day and found the male hosts had gone and only women remained. It was the custom too that since the guest was under the protection of his host, the guest was not expected to defend his host in case of danger.

Dahshan found that his horse was tethered with a lock. He surmised that his hosts had gone to recover their cattle from a raiding party. He insisted that the woman of the house give him the key to untie his horse or he would shoot the lock open. She did so reluctantly. Dahshan sped on his horse and found his hosts fighting the Ruwalla, who were a large tribe in eastern Syria and Transjordan and who were known to raid their neighbors. The Ruwalla were the ones who had seized his hosts' cattle. Dahshan was armed with a *wirwir*, a pistol with a six-bullet magazine, unknown to his guests or the Ruwalla at the time. The continuous shooting, without pausing to arm the gun with powder, must have startled the raiding party. They fled shouting, "The fire has eaten us!" and they left the cattle behind.

The Zabin returned with their cattle and expressed their gratitude to their mysterious guest. Pressured to stay on and declare his name, he stayed on for a while. They suggested he stay permanently and marry their daughter Qutna. He politely declined.[16] My grandfather returned to al-Ma'in but was distrustful of the Turks, who wanted to capture him. He paid nocturnal visits to his home but kept moving around in Sinai, Rafah, al-Arish, and al-Auja Hafir.

I have discovered another witness to Dahshan's wanderings as well. Not far from al-Ma'in, he met Professor Alois Musil, who was unquestionably the most learned European scholar of Arabs and Islam at the time.[17] Musil was a great traveler and a prolific author. He wrote about the Arabs in Syria, Transjordan, Hejaz, Palestine, and Sinai, and he included information about their customs, habits, numbers, wars, and conflicts. He also wrote about their homelands and territories. Musil spoke fluent Arabic and had knowledge of the various dialects.

Musil was a scholar and a spy for the Austrian Hapsburg dynasty, which wanted to carve out a part of the Arab provinces of the Ottoman Empire for their empire. He almost succeeded in forging an alliance with Nuri al-Sha'alan, the great emir of the Ruwalla, who, after Ibn Saud, the sharif of Mecca, and Ibn Rashid of Arabia, was the prominent power in the region extending from southeast of Damascus to north Nejd, which is today part of Syria, Jordan, and Saudi Arabia. Musil visited the shrine of Sheikh Nuran on a hill in al-Ma'in.[18] He could not have traveled to these parts without meeting Sheikh Dahshan. He related the encounter:

> Here [at Rafah] we met the brave and generous sheikh of the Abu Sitti [*sic*] Tarabin tribe. He is a great friend of Egypt, just like all

> the tribes in Arabia Petraea. He did not want to fall in the hands of the Turkish government. He sometime stayed in Egypt and in the northern Hejaz. Finding about the land of my proposed trip, I understood he knew it well and had many friends. I asked if he was inclined to accompany us. Then he advised me about the great dangers of a journey between the wild, small tribes of the Araba, especially this year.
>
> The first person who saw us [in our trip] praised Allah, who sent him guests. As the popular Abu Sitti was with us we should be entertained with meat and bread. Because Abu Sitti was the first person who was everything to him, he presented the boiled goat and all the bread to him. He shared everything with us and we gave food to our men and the newcomers from the Bedouins.
>
> While we were eating cooked rice in the courtyard, a young man with squinting eyes and thick lips, dressed in Egyptian dance dress, with a long stick in his hand, began to sing in a falsetto voice. The people present watched him in awe, while Abu Sitti could not conceal a mocking smile.[19]

These were the last days of the nineteenth century. With the start of a new century, a new era dawned: the reemergence of the European domination of the Holy Land after a seven-hundred-year absence. Unbeknownst to us, those travelers, spies, and priests were charting our future and deciding our destiny.

I wondered what our people made of those foreigners when they saw them, in their peculiar dress, accompanied by a dragoman, a guide perhaps, a mule to carry luggage, wandering around in our land, taking notes, charting routes, and asking discreet questions. What did they carry in their luggage? Very likely letters of introduction, writing materials, books, maps, instruments, medicines, currencies of different countries, and some kind of special food. Their luggage must have been like a mobile secret embassy. Our people never knew at the time, the names of those travelers or the stories they wrote in their books. For some, these foreigners must have seemed like stray travelers seeking solace and contemplation, or pilgrims and scholars looking for ruins or treasures of bygone years.

As the fire glowed in the hearth at my father's seat, its reflection on the wrinkled faces of the narrators of old stories gave an aura of mystery to their past deeds. The hearth's stories were something I believed in and adopted as part of my personal history, a history that I learned to cherish, honor, and live by. Above all, these stories registered in my heart the pledge that I shall never do anything to blemish their memory.

My faith in this lived history was reinforced by the dry, often convoluted, and certainly prejudiced writings of these travelers who visited my country. Seated on the hard seats in the libraries of Europe without a hearth or fire, I read their narration, saw their maps, and pondered their "discoveries." As I recalled the stories I had heard at the hearth, told by my people, I imagined those wrinkled faces nodding in agreement with some of those travelers' writings or frowning in disapproval of others, confident that, in the end, it is those storytellers at the *shigg* who are the real source of our history.

4

Europe Returns to the Holy Land

The beginning of the twentieth century marked the end of an era in Palestine and the whole Middle East. Having been largely secluded from foreign influence for many centuries, the region found itself alone no longer. These years of seclusion were by no means marked by stagnation, since during the nineteenth century much had happened in the way of modernization. Some of the most prominent figures in the history of the region pushed the boundaries of political reform, Arabic literature, and technological advancements.[20] During the second decade of the twentieth century—one hundred years after Napoleon's failed attempt to control the region and seven hundred years after the ill-fated Crusaders' campaigns—Europe sent its soldiers to the region again. Instead of coming as feudal lords carrying their lances, their prejudice, and religious zeal, the new Europeans came armed with diplomatic intrigue and modern armies. Since their arrival, the region has not seen a moment of peace. As events unfolded in the next one hundred years, European colonialism, spearheaded by Britain and its Zionist ally, brought death, destruction, and dismemberment to the region. The first and the longest-suffering victim was Palestine.

In 1914, there was a Turkish call to eliminate the *Inglizi*, or British, threat to Greater Syria as a province of the Ottoman Empire. It was a Muslim call to defeat the invading infidel and was heeded as such. Of the almost 1,500 Beersheba District horsemen who responded to the call, several hundred gathered at Shallalah Springs, about halfway along the length of Wadi Ghazza, three kilometers east of al-Ma'in, as one meeting point for the three assembled groups.

The paramount Tarabin sheikh was Sheikh Suleiman Saqr Abu Sitta, my father's uncle. A man of imposing stature, wearing a Maghrebi-style burnous, he rode back and forth before the Shallalah group, exhorting the assembled horsemen to defend their country from the *Inglizi* attack. My father, a young man in his early thirties, was among them. When the three groups had assembled, they proceeded to al-Arish, then to Qatiya, where they clashed with British forces composed of British, Indian, and Sudanese troops on 15 November 1914. They defeated them on the first day.

On the second day, the British brought reinforcements and machine guns. What could a horseman, on his noble horse, charging with a sword high in the air, do against machine guns? Suleiman was killed instantly but his horse refused to leave his body. My father looked around and through the dust of battle saw his uncle bleeding, lying on the ground with his horse beside him. He laid his uncle on his horse and returned home to bury him in the Tarabin cemetery in Beni Suheila. The martyrs of this battle were remembered in a prayer in al-Aqsa Mosque in Jerusalem in January 1915. I remember seeing my father, on several occasions, wearing the medal of bravery awarded to him by the Turks. A contemporary folkloric poet described the event:

> At the first wave fell Suleiman,
> The bridge on which people relied,
> As of now and of old battles.
> The Mitrailleuse sprayed death,
> With its deadly blue nose,
> And death showered from the skies.[21]

In the following year, in 1916, Sharif Hussein of Mecca arrived at a different agreement with the British: the Arabs would fight the Turks alongside the British on condition that the Arab provinces became a single independent Arab state after victory over the Turks. With no intention of keeping the agreement, two colonial diplomats, Mark Sykes of Britain and Georges Picot of France, huddled secretly in a room over a map of the Middle East and conspired to divide the Arab provinces of Turkey between them after the war. To help maintain the fiction of independence, Allied (British and French) planes dropped leaflets on Gaza and Beersheba, promising the Arabs total independence and freedom once the Turks had been defeated with their help. The promise, thought to be genuine, ignited the Arab Revolt of 1916 under the leadership of Sharif Hussein of Mecca.

One of those who wished to join the revolt was Ahmed 'Aref al-Husseini, the mufti of Gaza, and his son, Mustafa, an officer in the Turkish army. Afraid of detection, they left Gaza at night and sought refuge with Sheikh Ahmed Saqr Abu Sitta, who had replaced his martyred brother, Suleiman. According to the customary code of honor, they were afforded hospitality and protection.

However, informers led the Turkish authorities to their hideout. Mufti Ahmed was hanged; Mustafa, as a military officer, was also executed; and Sheikh Ahmed was banished to Qunya in southern Turkey. Sheikh Ahmed's nephew, Abd al-Aziz, was a cadet at the military school in Istanbul for the sons of tribal leaders.[22] When the school closed at the beginning of the First World War, he returned home and on the way stopped at Qunya to look up his uncle. Abd al-Aziz found that his uncle was dead and reported the news to us. How he found his uncle's residence is a mystery. It must have helped that he recognized his uncle's belongings; noticeable among them was a special sheepskin he was known to wear. Abd al-Aziz took his uncle's remaining belongings and returned home.

As winter rains swept southern Palestine in January 1917, British forces crossed the border from their base in Egypt. Bearing the ironic name of the Egyptian Expeditionary Forces (EEF), they planted their first headquarters in Palestine near Khan Yunis in what is known today as Gaza Strip.

Cries of "The *Ingliz* are coming!" were heard in our neighborhood. Sandwiched between the advancing British forces and the strong Turkish defenses supervised by the Germans in Gaza, my family decided to evacuate the battlefield to a place called Khuweilfa, northwest of Beersheba. My mother, a young bride at the time, described that flight to safety and how hungry Turkish soldiers asked for *ekmek* (bread). My father went straight to Esmet Bey, the garrison commander of Beersheba, and told him that the invaders had taken over our land.

As the British had been defeated twice in Gaza, after incurring heavy losses, General Archibald Murray, the commander of the British forces in Palestine, was relieved of his duties and General Edmund Allenby was appointed in his place. Allenby assessed the situation and took the advice of his Australian generals to take Beersheba in a long sweep from the east, while pretending to attack Gaza for the third time. The Australian Cavalry archives in Melbourne describe their base in Abu Sitta, Nuran, and Tell al-Far'a. They extended the railway line and carried the Nile water right up to our land.

In the last days of October 1917, Allenby launched a surprise attack on Beersheba. The British Forces marched at night along Wadi Ghazza, Beersheba, on the eastern border of al-Ma'in, sleeping in the daytime and hiding out of sight at the bottom of the valley. How did they find this circuitous route and surprise the Turks? Priests and officers had participated in months of intelligence gathering.

A priest at l'École Biblique in Jerusalem, Father Antonin Jaussen, known locally as the man of "white robes," traveled extensively in Transjordan. His skills exceeded delivering religious sermons and speaking in Arabic dialect. He was an accomplished spy, traveling to Aqaba and al-Arish, scouting for Turkish positions prior to the First World War, and coordinating with British intelligence in Sinai. A.C. Parker, the British inspector of Sinai and nephew of the famous Horatio Herbert Kitchener, assumed the position of civilian intelligence chief for Allenby's campaign in 1917. Parker gave Jaussen a safe-passage certificate to roam where he wanted. Jaussen was seen in al-Arish sending messages by carrier pigeons.[23]

Parker had recruited Sheikh Freih Abu Middein for the reconnaissance of the countryside to locate the unusual route to take Beersheba unexpectedly. The contact between Sheikh Freih and Parker was Abu Zikri, a camel-transport contractor in al-Arish and Parker's agent. While everyone evacuated the area before the advancing British forces, Zikri advised Sheikh Freih to hide in his house until the British arrived. Parker sent emissaries to my father to persuade him to cooperate with the British on the eve of their invasion of Palestine, but my father refused.

In spite of his authority, Parker, or "Barkal" as the Arabs of Sinai called him, was the subject of satire. An unknown folkloric poet composed these popular satirical lines about him, which were still recited more than a half-century later:

> "Your donkey will have his tail cut off if it trespasses on my maize field.
> Pray tell me his description so I can stop him in time."
> "My donkey walks on two legs, sometimes four,
> If he saw she-donkeys, a whole tribe could not restrain him.
> If he brays in al-Arish, Gaza hears him.
> His penis is like Barkal's stamp which he prints on his papers."

At Beersheba, Esmet Bey was uneasy. Sensing the danger and not believing the German assessment that the British would not venture to sweep around Beersheba, he asked my father and two other sheikhs to bring arms and supplies from Damascus to arm the people for the defense of our land. "We proceeded to Damascus with great hopes," my father told me the last time I saw him, when he was well into his eighties. "On the way we heard that Beersheba had fallen. So we returned."

Apparently, Sheikh Freih, acting as a guide for the British forces in their surprise attack, was very useful.[24] Beersheba fell at 6:00 p.m. on Wednesday 31 October 1917. Esmet Bey barely had time to retreat on horseback. The 4th Australian Light Horsemen, which penetrated the Turkish defenses and were the first to enter Beersheba, lowered the Turkish flag and raised the British flag, ending fourteen centuries of Muslim rule.

Two days after the fall of Beersheba, the British foreign secretary, Arthur James Balfour, issued a letter to Zionist leaders, known since then as the Balfour Declaration, which aimed to facilitate the establishment of a "national home for the Jewish people" in Palestine. It was a promise from those who do not own to those who do not deserve, in the absence of the rightful owners of the country. The declaration has, to date, ushered in more than ninety years of bloodshed and suffering. As the Palestinian jurist Henry Cattan observed, "the Balfour Declaration was legally void, morally wicked, and politically mischievous."[25]

Following Palestine's conquest, the British military handed over Palestine to a civil authority, headed by the Zionist British High Commissioner, Herbert Samuel, in June 1920. Samuel's plan was to allow Jewish immigrants to settle in Palestine in accordance with the Balfour Declaration, whose clauses were incorporated in the

Mandate terms under the influence of Zionists. In his five-year term (1920–25) Samuel laid the foundations for the future state of Israel. He passed laws which created a separate legislative body for the Jews, separate education, banking, public works, and energy, regulations facitiating Jewish immigration and land acquisition, and more fatally, separate armed units, which became Israel's army thirty years later. All this was against the wishes and rights of the Palestinian majority population. The greatest immediate threat to them was the influx of Jewish immigrants to Palestine.

The first riots in Palestine caused by Jewish immigration took place in Jaffa in May 1921 between the people of Jaffa and the Jewish immigrants who just landed there. These people were Bolsheviks from Eastern Europe who had espoused communism. To the people living in Palestine, the newcomers seemed foreign: they had a foreign way of life and different values. They posed a threat to Palestinian life in their country. A British committee, the Haycraft Commission of Inquiry, investigated the cause of the riots, treating them as a civil disturbance, not as a threat to the majority (over 90 percent) Arab population. Although it called Jewish immigrants "colonists" and listed the Arab grievances, it blamed the Arabs for the riots.

Like many more commissions of inquiry afterward, it diagnosed the disease of colonial rule and sometimes prescribed the cure of limiting Jewish immigration. However, political expediency and intrigue always prevailed and buried their recommendations.

Just two months earlier, Winston Churchill, then colonial secretary, had convened the Middle East Conference in Cairo to sort out the conflicting promises that the British had distributed liberally in Iraq, Transjordan, and Syria during the First World War. Above all, Palestinians demanded the fulfillment of the promise of independence. They soon discovered that the British-appointed Herbert Samuel as high commissioner with the intention of making Palestine a Jewish national home. The deliberations in Cairo went on from 3 to 23 March 1921. Subsequently Churchill decided to investigate the riots in Palestine, which Samuel had encountered in his first year in office, in 1920.

Churchill took the train to Palestine accompanied by Samuel. His first stop in Palestine was Gaza, where crowds were waiting at the station, waving, chanting, and shouting. Churchill appeared at the window and waved regally in response to the welcoming crowd. Perhaps nobody dared to tell him that the crowds were not welcoming but cursing Britain and Balfour and demanding independence. In the following days, he made speeches and held meetings with the dignitaries of Palestine, including my father.

After the war, the British, with their usual diplomacy, confirmed my father as sheikh although he had never cooperated with them during the war. He assumed his duties with vigor. My father had a pleasant appearance and a commanding presence; he was well-spoken and persuasive. He chose the pursuit of justice without belligerence, an approach befitting his role as a judge. In the years to come, he would play an important part in the Palestinian national movement.

The last time I saw my father, in July 1968 in Amman, I asked him about that first meeting with Churchill:

> "Sheikh Freih Abu Middein and I stood on the balcony of the Government House in Jerusalem, representing southern Palestine."
> "Did you ask him for peace in Palestine?" I asked.
> "No, he asked us. Peace and security in the country was in our hands, not his," he said. "That is why he asked us to keep the peace under the British Mandate."
> "Did he offer you anything?"
> "Yes. He said the government recognized our laws and customs, our freedom and our property."

A government statement was made to confirm that undertaking.[26]

The first test of who actually controlled the country came eight years later. In 1929, the Bolshevik Jews staged a demonstration at the Western (Wailing or Buraq) Wall of al-Aqsa Mosque, calling for the rebuilding of the temple and installing permanent structures, all contrary to the status quo which had been maintained in Jerusalem for centuries. There were clashes between the Bolshevik Jews and the Palestinians. "Al-Aqsa under attack" was the call heard all over Palestine. Hundreds of Beersheba horsemen prepared to charge toward Jerusalem.

"While we were preparing to group, a word came from Aref el-Aref, the district officer or *qaymaqam*, that the situation in Jerusalem was now calm and the district commissioner cabled from London that he was returning to Palestine and would give satisfaction to all," my father said.

It did not take long for the situation to flare up again. By the mid-1930s, the British Mandate had allowed in an alarming number of European Jewish immigrants (comprising about 30 percent of the population in 1936 compared to 9 percent in 1917), which prepared the ground for the great Arab Revolt that lasted from 1936 to 1939.[9]

When the general strike was declared at the start of the Arab Revolt, national committees were formed in every region of Palestine to fight the British (and the Jews) in order to stem the flood of Jewish immigrants, which threatened the survival and independence of the Palestinian people.

Hajj Amin al-Husseini, the acknowledged Palestinian leader, approved national leaders of the regional committees. He asked my father to let one of his sons lead the revolt in southern Palestine. Abdullah, his nephew, was the perfect choice.

My paternal uncle had died just after the end of the First World War, leaving behind a widow and a young son, Abdullah. As was the custom, my father married his brother's widow to keep his nephew within the family, and he sent Abdullah to al-Rawda College in Jerusalem. This college, established by Hajj Amin al-Husseini, was called "the school of patriotism," because its education focused on Arab history and culture, with particular focus on Palestine, something which government schools under the British neglected.

At the age of eighteen, Abdullah left al-Rawda College and took his position as the leader of the southern front, which covered the vast district of Beersheba. The freedom fighters (known in Arabic as *thuwwar* and in the British lexicon as 'bandits') laid mines under British trains and ambushed their convoys. Abdullah's fighters were from the Beersheba District and southern coastal villages and towns such as Khan Yunis and Gaza. In addition to Abdullah, leading the revolt in Beersheba, other leaders included Abd al-Halim al-Joulani of Hebron. Others supported the revolt politically; among them were Yacoub al-Ghusain of Ramleh, Mustafa Bushnaq of Nablus, and Muhammad Ali al-Taher, writer and journalist.

I recall my family talking about Abdullah's nocturnal visits to us during his secret work, sometimes arriving with people we did not know and then disappearing for days on end. The blowing up of railways led the British to make Palestinians human shields by tying them to a wagon that ran ahead of the train. The *thuwwar* cut the telephone lines. The British rounded up the farmers of the land where the telegraph poles were pulled down and held them until they informed the British who the fighters were.

British armored vehicles came to our land in al-Ma'in one day, looking for Abdullah. He was not there, naturally. My father was away too, but he had left a box of important letters with my mother. It was not difficult to have an early warning of their arrival; we could spot a stranger quickly. My mother gave the box to my sister, a child barely seven years old, and she told her to run away with the box. British soldiers searched the whole place, *dar* and *karm*, shouting, "Where is Abdullah? If we do not find him we shall blow this place up."

Terrified, my sister sat paralyzed on the box and started to cry. She could not run as my mother had instructed. Her tears and her age saved her from being searched; and the box, covered by her clothes, was also saved.

The greatest victory of the revolt in the south was the capturing of Beersheba town and liberating it from British rule for a whole year. Combining forces with Abd al-Halim al-Joulani of al-Khalil (Hebron), who commanded the surrounding hills, Abdullah's group attacked the town. The British left and some Arab policemen remained.

This is the way the British described the event in the fortnightly report of the district commissioner to the high commissioner:

> On September 9th [1938] Beersheba was attacked by rebels who captured 86 rifles, a Lewis gun and 10,000 rounds of ammunition. The wireless station, the quarantine station, and the Post office were burnt and British Sergeant Landers was murdered. The British Police were withdrawn from Beersheba after this attack.
>
> On the 20th a further attack of the rebels was made on Beersheba, when the Governorate and the documents it contained were destroyed by fire, and the police barracks were likewise gutted.
>
> On September 23rd, the abandoned Police Post at Imara was burnt.
>
> On September 24th a highly organized attack on the railway line between Yebna and Khan Yunis put the line out of action for seven days. The attack seems to have been organized from Hebron, but a very large number of the villages in Gaza Sub-District took part. The centre of the actual operation was Majdal town.

> The railway stations at Gaza and Majdal were burnt during the month. There are now no railway stations remaining in the Gaza Sub-District.[27]

Abdullah told me later about it: "We set up a national, independent rule in Beersheba for a year, complete with its administration and courts."

My brothers told me that they had taken arms from the government depot in Beersheba town. The district of Beersheba, an area equal to half of Palestine, was liberated. British reports at the time stated that government authority was limited to police forts on the coast.

Aref el-Aref (1891–1973) had an important though ambiguous role in the revolt. As Beersheba district officer, he was extremely influential in the district from 1929 to 1939. However, he was much more than an official. El-Aref was an Arab nationalist who had a knack for steering the Palestinians through the hostile British waters. He was a frequent guest at our house and my father saw him on government business at least once a month.

During his ten-year tenure in Beersheba, he had become very popular. He went by the name of Abu Sufyan, according to the Arab tradition of calling a man by the name of his eldest son. I do not recall seeing him at this time, but I visited him at his home in Ramallah in 1966 where he showed me many photographs with my father. That was invaluable for me, as all our pictures and documents were stolen or burned by the Israelis in 1948.

El-Aref had had a distinguished career. He was an officer in the Ottoman Army and the Russians incarcerated him as a prisoner of war (POW) in Siberia. He was able to escape from his Russian capture and eventually found himself in Salt (in Transjordan) where he made peace with the British, while remaining loyal to Hajj Amin al-Husseini, the popular Palestinian leader.

Aside from these experiences as a military man, he also dabbled in the humanities. One notable example was his literary talent, which blossomed when he edited a newsletter entitled "God's Camel" *(Naqatu Allahi)*, in reference to a story in the Quran in which God gave the prophet Saleh a she-camel that produced fresh milk in the desert. The newsletter title was an interesting departure for a confirmed secular person like el-Aref.

The British Mandate government utilized his exceptional abilities in administration, but the British were not entirely sure of his loyalty to their policies. They were correct on both counts. El-Aref had very good relations with the sheikhs and carried out the first census in Beersheba in 1931. My father told me thirty-eight years later that el-Aref approached him first, as a distinguished and enlightened sheikh. My father agreed to the idea. The census found that the Abu Sitta family numbered 660 at the time, a pure coincidence that the number six *(sitta)* would be so prominent. Other sheikhs followed.

At the end of the 1936–39 revolt, informers told the returning British Mandate administration that el-Aref was secretly supporting the revolt in Hebron, advising and providing information on when to strike. When the British resumed their control of Beersheba in the summer of 1939, they ignored these accusations. They gave el-Aref a warning, however, not to repeat the offense!

The British abruptly transferred el-Aref from Beersheba to Gaza in July 1939. During his first year there, he kept a diary containing some critical remarks on the subservience and collaboration of certain Gazan notables with the British administration. In his unpublished diary, which I accidentally found, he alludes to the British accusations that he supported the revolt but does not refute them.[28] He refers frequently to Dr. Suleiman Saleem of Beersheba, whom he loathed, as the person inciting informers to report him to the government.

What was also of interest to me in his diary were el-Aref's meetings with exiled leaders of the revolt, including Abdullah who took refuge in Cairo after the revolt, during el-Aref's holiday in Cairo in April 1940. That was an act quite contrary to his role as a British Mandate official.

El-Aref also recalled in his diary a big party, which my father hosted on 28 August 1940 for the British District officials and a large crowd. It was after Britain had announced the White Paper, partially accepting Arab demands to stop Jewish immigration and promising independence. At this party, my brother Ibrahim, a high-school student, and Hussein Abu Hassan, "our orator" as we called him, praised el-Aref, the outgoing *qaymaqam*, for his dedication, efficiency, and wisdom. He took this praise in his absence as vindication of his standing after the British had removed him from Beersheba.

El-Aref wrote in his diary that Gawain Bell (later Sir Gawain Bell), the district officer, hated the Arabs and they hated him, although Bell knew them best and was the best Arabic speaker among the British. I heard the name repeated in our household, as he was a frequent visitor, one of many British officials.

After a long search and correspondence, I located Bell in 1991. I told him I was Sheikh Hussein's youngest son and wished to ask him about the old days. He invited me to lunch at the St. James Club in London. Bell was the young British colonial officer who had restored government authority in the Beersheba district after the revolt. At twenty-eight, he told me, he had toured the whole district for eight days by camel, which he had learned to ride in Sudan. He was accompanied by Arab gendarmes, assuring the sheikhs of British goodwill and respect for the promises they had made and persuading them not to ignite a new revolt.

After lunch, we had tea in my apartment, where I interviewed him on video. I asked him about el-Aref's role in the revolt. He said they had received several reports from informers and his enemies, but they had not taken any action. I think the British thought he could be more useful as an official on their side than a loose revolutionary. When I asked what good deeds Bell had done for the district, the answer was, after long hesitation, "Lining up walls of some wells." The priority was to pursue government policies. I inquired whether pursuing them was more beneficial to the Arabs or the Jews. He said that many of the British Mandate officers in Palestine thought that the Arabs got a raw deal, but they could not do anything. If they left or resigned, someone else would do the job. London made the policy and we had to obey, he explained.

As it was getting late, I offered to take him to the station. He lingered on and we kept talking until after seven. In the cab he explained he had a train ticket which was only valid for late trips, after rush hour. I was amazed. Here was a man who was Sudan's government secretary, political agent in Kuwait, and governor-general of Nigeria, and yet he could not travel on the train any time he pleased. In another country, he would be rolling in money. His mission was to serve the British Empire. Like thousands of others, he did it; that is how the empire lasted as long as it did.

During these difficult times of British oppression of Arabs and bias in favor of the Jews, my father attended practically every national conference in Palestine organized by leaders of the Palestinian national movement led by Hajj Amin al-Husseini. At a critical conference, the National Committees Conference in Jerusalem that debated the future of Palestine during the revolt in 1936, some *effendi*s counseled calling off the strike in response to British promises. My father rose from his seat and said loudly and clearly, "The jihad cannot be postponed."[29]

My father's cousin, Abd al-Razek, the son of Hammad who was sent to Egypt in the nineteenth century to manage our land and property, came from Egypt to join the struggle. He formed the Beersheba Society in 1936 and rented a house for its headquarters in the town. He often received visitors and preached to them about their duty to their country. He accompanied one of the Egyptian ulema (scholars from al-Azhar University), traveling with him all over Beersheba District. The al-Azhar sheikh preached that hell was awaiting those who sold their land to Jews. For emphasis, Abd al-Razek carried with him a camel's skull and clapped its jaws to demonstrate the sound effect of the hell awaiting the offenders. Either the preaching was effective or was not needed in the first place, as by the end of the Mandate, the Jews had managed to purchase less than 1 percent of the district.

At the beginning of the Second World War, the British bent over backward to gain the Arabs' support. Australian troops came to defend Palestine in case the Germans took Egypt and crossed over to Palestine. To improve relations and to make the Arabs forget Balfour, temporarily at least, the British arranged joint functions for the Australians and the Arabs. These were camel and horse racing—what else! It was a roaring success. Both groups were excited at the races and the winners were acclaimed all over the district. My father's portfolio of photographs, copies of which I found with el-Aref, showed many of these functions. There was even one with Major General Arthur S. "Tubby" Allen, the commanding officer of the Australian forces.

The Australians were mostly down-to-earth farmers, good-natured, simple people. They demonstrated their fair share of drunkenness in public, which was severely punished. Rape cases were rare, and the British were aware of the severity of this crime, especially in the eyes of conservative Arab society, and of the damage it would cause to their reputation in Palestine.

The appearance of the Australians in Palestine for the second time in nearly twenty years was different from the first. In 1917 they were soldiers on horseback—the last cavalry charge in modern history. They had no contact with the population and brought to an end 1,400 years of Muslim rule in Palestine. The second time, in the early 1940s, they attempted to befriend the Palestinians, competing in the horse and camel races. Those young soldiers were probably unaware that an older generation of Australians had marched from the same point, Sheikh Nuran, heading in the opposite direction to conquer Beersheba town.

We encountered the Australian soldiers when, one day, a column of them appeared suddenly in al-Ma'in. At the head was my brother Ali. "Why did you bring them here?" my father shouted angrily.

"I did not. They wanted to go to Gaza. I told them: this way."

I watched them through the rising dust and heard the distant thump of feet. One platoon of approximately thirty soldiers appeared, followed by another, then another. The Australian soldiers were marching on foot from the direction of Sheikh Nuran to Gaza town. They were most likely performing a drill.

I followed them at a distance, fascinated by their distinctive Australian slouch hats, khaki shorts, and backpacks. They looked young, tired, and slightly bewildered. Most conspicuously to me, they had very *Inglizi* red faces. They then stopped for a rest. I watched as they sat on the dirt road, still in loose formation, taking swigs of water. I had never seen so many soldiers in uniform. From a safe distance, I watched their every move in awe and admiration. To my great astonishment, one of them leaned sideways and farted. The others did not take any notice and continued chatting. For an Arab boy, this act was unbelievably rude. I ran a little farther away in fear of another surprise.

In the same period, an interesting new player came to the fore in the Palestine arena. He was not quite new, but the British took notice of him when the fate of Palestine was being decided—King Abd al-Aziz Ibn Saud, the founder of the modern Kingdom of Saudi Arabia.

This attention given to a leader of the Arabian peninsula is not strange in the context of the history of this region since the beginning of the twentieth century. Aqaba and southern Sinai were located along the Egyptian Pilgrimage Route (Darb al-Hajj al-Masri), which was part of Hejaz province (Wilayat al-Hijaz). So was Ma'an, a town now in Jordan, which also belonged to Hejaz. King Abd al-Aziz had his eye on extending his rule to these territories.

The agreement on establishing the administrative line between Palestine and Egypt was signed in October 1906 by Hejaz province on behalf of the Ottoman government on one side and by Shibh Jazirat Tour Sina (the Sinai Peninsula) on behalf of the British-controlled Egyptian government on the other.[30]

When Winston Churchill created Transjordan in 1921 in partial compensation for the British betrayal of the Arabs (not keeping to their promises to support Arab independence), Ma'an and Aqaba were not included, as they belonged to Hejaz. When the British annexed them to Transjordan, Ibn Saud made it clear that he did not relinquish his claim to the southern regions of Palestine, Jordan, and Sinai. In their deliberations about partitioning Palestine after the Second World War, the British were acutely aware of these claims and thought of ways not to antagonize King Abd al-Aziz. Ibn Saud's political maneuverings manifested themselves in opening a consulate in Jerusalem with Abd al-Aziz al-Kahimi as his consul. There was only one other Arab consulate, that of Egypt.

That was of course above my head at the time, but I was aware that my father announced in July 1945 that the consul of King Ibn Saud would be our guest. As the news spread, it was exaggerated, until word got around that Sheikh Hussein's guest was the king himself.

Although my father received a long stream of distinguished guests, this one was a special case. This guest was the emissary of an Arab king who controlled a large peninsula extending as far as Palestine, Jordan, and Egypt. Furthermore, he was a senior Arab figure, not a British government functionary, however high. He knew what Arab hospitality and etiquette meant, so no lapse of protocol could be allowed to happen.

My father brought in caterers, cooks, and servers from nearby Khan Yunis and Gaza. Servants and other helpers stitched together ten long tents, open to the east and closed at the west, like a grandstand. Carpets and pillows were spread along the length of this marquee about a hundred meters in length. A few days earlier, my father had sent horsemen to invite Beersheba sheikhs and *mukhtar*s of the southern villages to attend the event. I watched the upholsterers at work, wearing their long robes *(gumbaz)* with a broad cummerbund and tarboosh as they prepared the seating.

On another site, there were several butchers skinning calves and many sheep. The blood gushed out of the slaughtered animals, each of which was hanging from a tripod. It was a disgusting sight. The soil was soaked with blood, turning it red. Two of my brothers, Mousa and Ali, could not eat meat afterward. Mousa recovered from this shock many years later, but Ali never ate meat again, only chicken and fish. I, on the other hand, was not deterred by this bloody sight.

In one corner, huge pots filled with water to boil meat were laid on stones, and fire was stoked under them, waiting for the meat to arrive. Other pots were filled with rice. Zeer presided over another site where servants filled smaller pots and jugs with water, sugar, and some red powder to make *sharab* or sherbet. Lumps of ice were added at the last minute to make a cool drink. At yet another location, a little removed, there were a dozen fellaheen women baking bread under my mother's supervision. Although they had started preparing the dough the day before, they baked the bread just before lunch. It was an exciting time for me, observing what everyone was doing.

Local guests began to arrive. Helpers met them before they dismounted and took their horses to be tied and fed. Guests slowly filled the edges of the seating toward the center, which was reserved for the main guest and other notables. Someone shouted, "Here they are!" I looked to the west toward Khan Yunis and saw a cloud of dust rising on the near horizon. Soon, about two dozen horsemen emerged, flanking a small convoy of cars. They were sent there to escort the consul on his arrival.

My father and the leading guests greeted the consul. The mounted escort and many others started to display their prowess and gallop in the field before the guests two to three kilometers on either side of the main guest reception, as a show of horsemanship and celebration. Welcoming speeches were given. The guests admired the performance of the speakers although their content was predictable: they warned against the impending danger of Zionism and emphasized Jerusalem as the first qibla and the third holy shrine of Islam. No doubt someone talked about the British betrayal of the Palestinians. Not a single British officer was invited.

I was not allowed to go near the main guest but I could just about hear the speeches and I was old enough to understand them. The most eloquent speaker was a cleric by the name of Ali al-Najdi. He had studied at al-Azhar University and was of Egyptian origin. His speech was punctuated by long quotations from the Quran, which pleased the audience. It was also a message to the consul of the king, who held the title "the Servant of the Two Noble Sanctuaries"; Jerusalem was the third. Then al-Najdi moved from his speaking place and exhorted the large audience to follow him in the noonday prayer. I felt reverberations of awe, reverence, and pleasure in this spectacle.

After the conclusion of prayers, there was no better reward than a sumptuous lunch. A dozen or more servants carried on their heads large trays, which each held a mound of rice, bread, nuts, and meat. They placed the trays in front of the guests in order of importance. As was the custom, my father stood by his guest, handing him choice morsels. It was his duty to make sure his guests were welcomed and well fed. He would not sit to eat unless pressed by his guest to do so.

It was an impressive sight. Although my father had taken me with him to less important occasions, I had never seen so many people sitting and eating all at the same time. There were around two hundred guests, but relatives, close neighbors, helpers, attendants, and others increased the crowd of people eating to many more.

The procedure reversed after lunch as farewells were made, cars driven away, horses saddled. By sunset, the scene looked like a deserted battleground.

At dusk, I could see slowly moving figures cleaning pots, packing supplies, and putting things in order. The air was still filled with the smell of meat. It was quite likely that no one within walking distance had failed to taste meat that day.

The British district commissioner was not amused. His eye was on the waning British influence, which it was his imperial duty to preserve. This display was too close for comfort and he wrote scathingly about it in his fortnightly report:

> The party given by Sheikh Hussein Abu Sitta to the Saudi Arabian Consul was attended by about 200 guests but it does not appear to have either enhanced the host's position or to have stirred political feelings or activates . . . [missing] A touch of [word unknown] was

provided by a religious notable of uncertain mental stability who insisted on boring the assembly with a rambling and disjointed speech. Later he persuaded, with difficulty, most of the guests to follow him in prayer.[31]

Sheikh Hussein Abu Sitta (seated) on a visit to Egypt in 1945 to see his sons (from left: Mousa, Ibrahim, and Suleiman) studying at Cairo University. During the trip it was planned he would meet King Abd al-Aziz of Saudi Arabia.

I understood later that Kahimi, Ibn Saud's appointed consul in Jerusalem, had earlier invited my father to meet King Abd al-Aziz, who was supposed to visit Egypt in February 1945 to meet the American president, Franklin D. Roosevelt. My father traveled to Cairo to see his sons studying at Cairo University and perhaps to see the king too. However, King Farouk was not favorable to the meeting between Roosevelt and Abd al-Aziz taking place in Cairo, probably due to a conflict between King Farouk of Egypt and the Saudi king. Instead, Roosevelt met Abd al-Aziz on board the USS *Quincy* on the Suez Canal. The agenda of the meeting, not surprisingly, covered the Palestine issue, and the king explained his position in no uncertain terms.[32]

To give him credit, Kahimi, the Saudi consul, did not forget my father's hospitality. After the Nakba, he repeatedly offered to receive my brothers and give them (especially Mousa, the agriculturist) high offices in the Saudi government. My brothers went to Kuwait instead.

The sequel to the story includes a visit to my father, two years later, by Kermit Roosevelt, Jr., the grandson of the U.S. President Franklin D. Roosevelt, and then a senior member of US intelligence, the precursor to the Central Intelligence Agency (CIA). He wanted to hear the opinions of my father and other Palestinian figures regarding the future of Palestine. He was accompanied by the young Nicola Ziyada, who became a noted Palestinian historian. The telegram about their intended visit did not reach us and so when the two arrived, they found no one to receive them except my brother Ali, a high-school student. The conversation between the two guests and my father would have been interesting had it taken place. Kermit Roosevelt, Jr., however, wrote an interesting article after visiting Palestine, in which he assessed the situation. He concluded that US support of Zionism, if it followed the British policy, was damaging to US interests in the region.[33]

How right he was. Even by the late 1940s, people still remembered the ruthless British suppression of the 1936–39 Arab Revolt, which left many killed, wounded, or imprisoned, dismantled the fabric of Palestinian society, deported its leaders, and left Palestine easy prey for the Zionists in 1948. The revolt ended when the Arabs accepted British pledges to curtail Jewish immigration into Palestine. The leaders of the revolt did not trust British promises, so many of them sought refuge in Egypt. Abdullah, my cousin who led the revolt in Beersheba, was among those who went to Egypt. He returned to Palestine two years later, in the early forties, when things had calmed down and Britain was preoccupied with the Second World War. His return was a cause for quite a celebration. He even enlisted me as a soldier, buying me a khaki shirt and shorts from Jaffa, and a gun that popped a cork instead of bullets.

In the late 1940s he quietly resumed his fighting activities soon after his return. His old comrade in the revolt from Hebron, Munir Arafa, a.k.a. Abu Nimr, used to visit us at night. I once saw them walking in the dusk amid the trees discussing matters earnestly. Abu Nimr asked me to recite a verse from the Quran and reminded me of verses about al-Aqsa Mosque and Jerusalem. He asked what they meant, for which I had no answer, and, like a very good teacher, he explained to me that it meant that we had to defend our country and protect our people from their enemies.

During the Second World War years, there was an eerie silence and a sense of foreboding in Palestine. Every night, men gathered at my father's seat listening to the one station we could get, run by the British propaganda department. Some hoped that Britain would restore Arab rights after the blood and destruction the Arabs had suffered during the revolt. Others warned that the worst was yet to come. However, no one was fully aware of the extent of the Zionist preparations, which, as it turned out, included the training of thousands of Jewish fighters and the amassing of weapons in preparation for the conquest of the country.

When the war ended, news trickled in of Jewish terrorism in the north. The Jews turned against the British—their erstwhile benefactors—and between 1945 and 1948 committed several terrorist acts against them and against Palestinians. They bombed the British headquarters in the King David Hotel in Jerusalem, hanged British soldiers in trees, and kidnapped a British judge. To curb terrorism and to protect their own troops, reinforcements of British army regiments returned to Palestine. For us, though, all this was distant news. We had no Jews in our area. However, unlike many, Abdullah sensed the imminent danger that loomed on the horizon.

By late 1946, people in the south started talking of seeing Jews in our area. They spoke of a Jew speaking Arabic scouting for land to purchase. This smooth-talking Jew, who would say "*sawa sawa khabibi* [we live together, my friend]," feigning devout friendship, went around with a man from Khan Yunis, Muhammad (Abu Hilmi) Jeratli, looking for a piece of land to buy. When my father's cousin, Abd al-Razek, heard of this, he rode with several men to look for this man. The next day, the group returned and told us that the Jew had run away and that the man from Khan Yunis had pleaded for mercy at swordpoint, swearing that he would never do it again. Indeed, no one dared to sell so much as a hectare plot to Jewish buyers in our area.

However, as we would soon discover, the Zionist forces in Palestine were much bigger, better equipped, and more organized than we were. At the end of 1946, they set up eleven military posts in the Beersheba district to influence the expected partition of Palestine.[34] All of them were far away from us in al-Ma'in.

People started talking about the Jews in jeeps with machine guns, running patrols between their isolated posts in the Beersheba district. They also brazenly extended water pipes across Arab land without permission or approval. The British, who only a few years earlier had imprisoned a Palestinian Arab for life for possessing a pistol, turned a blind eye to the Jews' machine guns and mortars. Occasionally the British made feeble attempts to disarm the Jews, who responded by sending a convoy of locally made armored cars loaded with arms to fortify their isolated posts.

Back in my boarding school in Beersheba, older boys were voicing anger at the British who had "created this monster among us." Some boys wanted to volunteer when the terrible news came in late November 1947 that the western powers in their council in New York had proposed to give away more than half of our country to the Jewish immigrants who had just waded onto our shores.[35] There was total disbelief. The majority of people scoffed at this astonishing idea and did nothing. Others saw the danger clearly and started to prepare.

A British base was next door to my Beersheba boarding school on the main Gaza–Beersheba road. British army soldiers frequently passed in front of our school, and sometimes the sentries stationed at the fence between the school and the government building talked to us, and we talked to them out of curiosity and to practice our English.

We also threw stones at their passing trucks, as a protest against Balfour's betrayal and his flooding our country with colonizers. Our teachers made half-hearted attempts to stop us, but we were able to continue expressing our protest day after day. One day I noticed a soldier who was a sentry at a post at the edge of the school. He did not seem angry at our throwing stones and asked me, "What is your name?" I did not answer. "Mine is Patrick." Intrigued, I said the word I knew.

"Battery?"

"No, P-a-t-rick." I repeated it after him.

The next day, he asked if I remembered his name.

"Pat-rick," I said.

"Patrick Payne."

"Pain?"

"No. P-a-y-n-e," he said, spelling it out for me.

He gave me a bar of chocolate. Patrick Payne was Irish. He did not seem to mind us throwing stones at the *Inglizi* soldiers. He probably would have liked to do it himself.

More ominous news continued to come from the north. Zionists were attacking and killing Palestinians, burning their villages around Jaffa and along the northern coast. We knew this from Gazans who had business selling or buying goods in and around Jaffa. They packed up their goods and returned as clashes increased.

Abdullah's activities intensified. He gathered his old comrades and recruited new ones. He went to Qatana in Syria for officer training and to Egypt several times to purchase rifles. My eldest brother, Ibrahim, joined him. By then, Ibrahim had graduated from the Faculty of Law at Fouad I (later Cairo) University. Many members of my extended family and men from the whole district joined Abdullah.

The Zionists got bolder again. The British ignored instances when they attacked the Arabs, but rushed to their rescue when they complained that Arabs were surrounding and threatening them. It was true that the Zionists were surrounded, holed up in a few military posts, each one thirty men strong, within an Arab population of over one hundred thousand. However, they had thousands of guns, ammunition, and armored cars, which they had manufactured themselves. They had a central command, wireless communication, light planes, and later fighter planes, and an embryonic navy. We Arabs, who "surrounded" them, had none of this.

There are two stories which I heard many times and which illustrate the situation at that time. In both cases, Abdullah and Ibrahim miraculously escaped being killed by Jewish forces. The Jews had established a base in the sand dunes near the Egyptian border, twenty kilometers away from us (which at that time meant four hours away by horse). From that base, they ran patrols, becoming notorious for their aggressive manner and actions. They ran the Second World War British jeeps with one driver and two soldiers pointing machine guns forward and backward. They blocked the roads, terrified farmers in their fields, and shot at any potential threat, real or imagined.

In February 1948, Abdullah came back from one of his forays to bury one of his comrades. He had clashed with one of these patrols and destroyed it. With their efficient communications, Jewish reinforcements had arrived quickly and surrounded Abdullah's group. With no outside help, Abdullah's group faced certain death. They were within sight of the Imara police station where my cousin Hassan was the wireless operator. He sent an SOS to British headquarters that it was the police station that was being surrounded and attacked by Jewish forces. Soon, British forces arrived and the Jews quickly retreated to their base. One of Abdullah's comrades had already been shot in the head, and had fallen on his shoulder, but Abdullah was saved by British help, although that had not been their intention.

Thirty years later, my brother Ibrahim told me about the other incident in which he and Abdullah narrowly escaped death. He recounted it as follows:

> I remember it vividly as if it were yesterday. We were in a convoy of three cars traveling on the main road from Beersheba to Gaza. In the first car, a passenger saloon, there were two volunteers: Dr. Taher al-Khatib of Jerusalem and Lieutenant Abd al-Mun'im al-Najjar, an Egyptian volunteer officer. I was in the second car, an armored car we had won from the Jews. There were four of us in it: the driver, a German given the name Anwar; a German gunner named Abd al-Aziz with a Boys anti-tank rifle; me with a Browning machine gun; and a relative of mine, Korrayem, who also had a rifle. The third car was a

> jeep; Abdullah was driving and with him was a German, and both had machine guns. The three Germans were volunteers who had come from Cairo, presumably released POWs, to assist the Palestinians. On the road to Gaza, a narrow bridge at Shar'ia (Abu Irqaiq) had been built to cross a deep wadi. Immediately afterward, toward Gaza, the road rose and then dropped again. When the convoy approached the bridge, the saloon car went through and disappeared beyond the mound. When the armored car was in the middle of the bridge, it was hit by a hail of bullets and a grenade. The source was three Jewish armored cars blocking the road.
>
> I looked from the back window and saw Abdullah's jeep burning. We kept firing at the armored cars blocking the road.
>
> "Open the back hatch and reverse," Abd al-Aziz shouted in German at his German comrade. Anwar reversed up to Abdullah and his German companion, who crawled into the car. Anwar then drove slowly forward while the shooting on both sides increased in intensity. Suddenly the Jewish tanks moved apart, opening a gap in the road. The occupants of the surrounded armored car were shooting with all they had. Ibrahim said that in the heat of battle he experienced an eerie feeling of calm. The roof of their car was open and they were shooting from the hatches on the sides.

Ibrahim saw the German bleeding from the forehead and Abdullah from the neck. He felt himself bleeding from the neck. Then they saw Zionist infantry shooting at them from both sides of the road. Ibrahim thought the Jews planned to kill or at least capture them, and told Abdullah: "We are done for." "*Ma'lesh*, never mind. Our lives are for our country," Abdullah replied.

It was not the first time Abdullah's life was directly threatened. In March 1948, the Haganah, the Jewish militia, planned the assassination of Palestinian political and militia leaders in Operation Zarzir and ordered all units to kill them without further approval and make it look as if Arabs were killing Arabs. Abd al-Qadir al-Husseini and Abdullah Abu Sitta were among the ten names disclosed.[36]

Anwar drove slowly toward the gap—or trap—left in the road. Then he revved up the engine with all his might and dashed toward it. "Go for it," shouted the other German. The hail of bullets and grenades from the Jewish forces on all three sides increased in intensity.

The German driver pushed through the Jewish blockade and sped on toward Gaza. They were free.

In the distance ahead, they saw armed men in trucks coming from Gaza to help them, headed by Dr. al-Khatib. He had raised the alarm and returned with help. By this time, the Jews had withdrawn to their posts. The wounded were taken to hospital, but their wounds turned out to be superficial, caused by grenade shrapnel.

"The main lesson I learned was that if we Palestinians had been trained in military warfare, like those German volunteers, we would have defeated the Jewish attack on our land. We only had the will and steadfastness. No arms, only a few old guns. No training. No central command. That was how they defeated us," said Ibrahim.

Ibrahim did not know at the time that the Jews who had tried to kill them were the Palmach, who were veterans of the Second World War with immeasurable war experience compared to us. The Palmach would strike again. Their victims, instead of a few wounded, became the whole population of Palestine.

5

The Conquest

The fears of the older boys at my boarding school grew and they started to speak of the terrible things that they thought were about to happen. We did not know what exactly would happen or where, but many talked about volunteering when the school year ended.

One day we heard a shot and cries of pain. We rushed to see what had happened and saw that one of the senior boys, Khalil Abu Rubay'a, was lying in a pool of blood. His friend Abd al-Qadir Abu Ruwa' had apparently acquired a rifle and was showing him how it worked. Abd al-Qadir Abu Ruwa' had accidentally shot his friend. The sadness that we had lost one of our schoolmates in such a tragic accident—the shock of seeing death first hand—was traumatic for us to witness at such a young age.

News started to trickle down from the north, particularly Jaffa and Tel Aviv. Those who had work or relatives in the north started to return home. They said that Jews were attacking more and more villages, blowing up buses, burning houses, and expelling people.

Who were these people? They were not our neighbors and certainly not our friends. People said they were a motley assortment of Jews imported from across the sea. They called them "vagabonds of the world." What did they look like? Those who had seen them close up said they wore a variety of odd uniforms, quite unlike those in the British army. They did not all look the same: some were blond, some swarthy, some dark, and some looked *Inglizi*. They spoke a babble of languages—English, French, Russian, Hungarian, Romanian, and

Spanish, to name but a few. Sometimes they used what was thought of as a secret language, like a code or cipher; it was *ibrani* or Hebrew.

Those who came from the north said these people were not *awlad Arab*, or Arab Jews, who spoke Arabic like us. They were ruthless, unruly, and vicious, and they hated the Arabs. They did not know the country, but they always carried with them detailed maps, no doubt obtained from the British.

All the fears we had, and worse, came to pass. One day, in early April 1948, the school headmaster, Abdullah al-Khatib, spoke to all the pupils during the morning procession: "The Jews have attacked our villages and towns in Jaffa, Jerusalem, and Haifa. We will terminate the school term. Day-school boys: return to your families in town. Boarding-school boys: you have two to three days to pack and go back to your families while you can. I cannot protect you here."

Where should we go? The Jews with their machine-gun-mounted jeeps were blocking the roads to Gaza and Khan Yunis. We grouped ourselves according to our destinations. There were three boys who were about ten years old: the brother of Abdullah's wife, a boy related to my mother's family, and me. We packed our things in sacks and waited.

With the Jewish blockade and attacks, people drifted to the nearest town. Somebody came from Jerusalem via Hebron and said that Jews had butchered men, women, and children, ripped open pregnant women's bellies with bayonets, and cut off their fingers and earlobes to get their jewelry. This had happened in a village that had signed a peace pact with them. The village was called Deir Yassin.

Two of my relatives, Hazaa and Mahmoud, aged eighteen or nineteen, were schoolteachers in rural schools, north and south of Beersheba. They came to Beersheba to find a way home and I was relieved to see them. We thought of the best way to reach home, some forty-five kilometers away.

The town of Beersheba was in a state of confusion. New people from nearby areas were drifting in, disoriented and frightened. Others dashed out into the unknown, never to be heard from again. The British were still there, but with a reduced force. They were busy packing, glad to return home. They had little interest in the fate of the people they were leaving behind, defenseless against the immigrants they had brought to Palestine.

Hazaa found a man to take us to safety. We knew him only by the name Shutti. He had a red pickup and I remember the color vividly. He was a dubious character; I did not like him. His reputation preceded him: he alternated between being a patriot, fighting on Abdullah's side, and being a detested seller of land to Jews in a faraway region. However, he agreed to haul us in the back of his pickup along the Gaza–Beersheba road, but only when a British convoy was going to Gaza, escorting stranded civilians to safety.

We waited. Every day Hazaa looked for Shutti. "When are we leaving?" we would ask Shutti.

"The British convoy will leave tomorrow afternoon." We sat on our sacks, which we used as pillows when we slept. Hazaa chased after Shutti the next day.

"No, they are not going today," Shutti would say.

"When?" Hazaa would implore.

"I don't know."

Suddenly, Shutti came in a rush one morning: "Hurry, hurry. The convoy just left. We can catch up with it." We scrambled onto the back of the pickup. The old machine rattled us along the asphalt road. We went down a depression, then up a mound. Looking toward the horizon, there was no sight of the convoy. Perhaps after the next hill, we thought.

Another depression and another hill. And still we could not see the convoy. The sound of the engine quietened down. "We are going back. We've gone too far and are alone. It is too dangerous," Shutti announced. Our spirits and the sound of the old engine sank. Dejected, we could not sleep that night. We were trapped.

The next day he came with the same exhortation: "*Yalla, yalla!* I am told on good authority that another convoy has just left."

We piled again onto the back of the pickup. Looking hopeful and shaking his head in defiance, Shutti bent over the steering wheel, his foot pressed down hard on the accelerator. No sign of the British convoy. We couldn't even hear its distant roar. Up and down the road the car went and, with it, our spirits. Shutti halted and proclaimed gravely, "This is it. I cannot go any farther. We are near a dangerous Jewish colony. They will kill us all."

"What are we going to do?"

"You get off here and walk through the fields westward. You have to walk home."

"What about you?"

"I am returning to Beersheba before it gets dark."

We don't know what became of him, but he dropped us near the bridge where the Jews had attacked Abdullah, Ibrahim, and the German volunteers. Three children and two young men, not yet twenty, stood there alone on the deserted asphalt road.

"Let's head west, away from the main road," Hazaa said. We waded through the fields of ripened wheat.

"If you see Jewish jeeps, just squat down. They will not see you," Hazaa advised.

"If they come too close, rub dirt on your face and pretend you are locals working your land," Mahmoud added.

We walked through the fields with heavy hearts, carrying our light sacks and pausing at intervals to listen for the distant hum of Jewish jeeps. By the end of the day we were tired and hungry, having walked for hours.

"I recognize those people," Mahmoud suddenly cried. We came across farmers, still in their fields. They were distant relatives of Mahmoud's mother.

They gave us a drink of water and some bread. We left our sacks with them for safekeeping. I was sad to part with my schoolbooks, as I wanted to show my father my good marks. After a short respite, we resumed walking. I did not see those people again for probably two years, when I came across them in a refugee camp.

After the aborted pickup ride, it was at least another thirty kilometers to home. That meant brisk walking all night. We weren't sure we would make it and did not know the way, just the general direction. Evening came and with it we felt a coolness in the air. Worse, the landmarks which Hazaa and Mahmoud claimed they would know had become unrecognizable in the darkness.

I read, many years later, that soldiers do not feel fatigue during war. They are busy with the business of war itself. In my small war, this was true. I did not feel fatigue; it was masked by the determination to survive.

Moving shadows appeared to pop up in the dark. When we came close, we recognized them as branches moving in the wind. The deep, long howls of wolves, or perhaps abandoned dogs, hung in the air, sending a chill down my spine. We talked to each other in soft voices for encouragement.

The terrain changed and we came across a broad wadi.

"That is Shallalah," Mahmoud said. That was good news, but we still had to walk another ten kilometers. The headlights of a vehicle and the roar of an engine pierced the darkness.

"Jews!" someone whispered. We froze in our tracks and hit the ground. As the object came nearer, Mahmoud jumped up.

"It's Abu Swelim." He ran toward the light and we followed cautiously. "Come on! It's Abu Swelim!"

Abu Swelim was returning home, driving our tractor and plow after charging the radio battery at Imara police station. It was the same radio the British had installed at my father's house in 1940 to listen to British war propaganda.

We climbed up onto the sides of the tractor, feeling a temporary sense of safety, but unsure of what could happen next until the familiar sights of our home became distinguishable in the darkness.

Undoubtedly, someone had alerted my family. I saw my father waiting and my mother in her quarters. They did not know how to express their joy and surprise at our sudden arrival, or shock at what we had been through. Thankfully, they had been spared the anguish of knowing that the school had been closed and that we had been stranded alone in Beersheba.

By this point, my adrenaline had run out and was replaced by the ache of the journey. I spent two or three days in bed, with my mother hovering over me. I soon recovered from this, but a major tragedy was still waiting for all of us.

The harrowing tales of massacres and mass expulsions of Palestinians by Jewish forces reverberated in Arab capitals. Citizens in Cairo, Baghdad, Damascus, and other Arab cities held huge demonstrations, pushing their reluctant governments to come to the rescue of Palestinians. There was news of the savage massacre of Deir Yassin, on 9 April 1948, in which more than one hundred villagers, mostly women and children, were murdered in their houses in cold blood by gunfire, daggers, and axes. The few survivors were paraded in Jewish neighborhoods among the cheers and curses of the jubilant crowd. This was followed the day after by the great loss of the resistance leader, Abd al-Qadir al-Husseini. These two tragedies struck in one week and inflamed Arab people everywhere, including the students on the Fouad I (later Cairo) University campus, who led a major demonstration. One of the demonstrators was my cousin Hamed, who was in his third year of engineering. Hamed addressed the student crowd: "This is not the time to study. Our country is being taken away from us. What purpose will our study serve if we have no country? We must go to Palestine to fight."

With that, Hamed took a box of matches and set fire to his books. A young man approached Hamed and said in an Egyptian accent, "I'll come with you." It was Yasser Arafat.[37]

Hamed and my brother Mousa took the first train to Khan Yunis.

"What brought you back?" my father said in surprise, finding them walking from the station.

"We want to defend our country," they replied.

"You will defend it better with an education," my father remarked.

As Jewish attacks on the coastal areas intensified, members of the Muslim Brotherhood began to arrive. They were dedicated and brave because they believed in their cause. They were probably no more than 150 volunteers, mainly from Egypt and Palestine, but some from Saudi Arabia and Libya. A few of them were army officers who had been granted leave. They spread out across the predominantly Arab southern Palestine. Although there were only small numbers of Jews holed up in colonies in that region, they were well armed and trained, ready to pounce when needed.

Abdullah cooperated closely with these volunteers and informed them about the terrain and the location and strength of the Jewish colonies. However, there was no central command for all these diverse volunteers and defenders. Among Palestinians, young defenders in each village rushed to help an attacked village when they heard the news, in what was known as *faz'a*, a call for help.

By mid-May of 1948, the British started to leave Beersheba district without much ceremony and with their tails between their legs. Comparing the British arrival in 1917 with their abrupt departure three decades later is one of history's most shameful episodes. In 1917 the British arrived as victors and allies with the promise of their "sacred trust of civilization" to prepare Palestine for independence. Now they withdrew surreptitiously, without a word of good-bye, leaving behind their Arab charges, defenseless in their own country, to the mercy of the Jews, who were preparing to take it over.

The British took most of their supplies and equipment—what they thought essential—but turned a blind eye when Arab policemen did not hand over their rifles, claiming they were lost. However, a few ignored, lost rifles were insignificant compared to the well-stocked British military bases left—either through bribery or in collusion—for the Jews.

As the British left Beersheba, the Palestinians were obliged to defend themselves with what they had. They formed a National Committee headed by the mayor, Shafiq Mushtaha, the longest-serving previous mayor, Tajeddin Shaath, Abdullah Abu Sitta, and others.

The Arab Higher Committee (stationed then in Cairo where Hajj Amin al-Husseini was given refuge) appointed Abdullah as the local leader of the defense for the district, under General Suleiman Abd al-Wahid, an Egyptian professional soldier appointed by the Arab League for the defense of southern Palestine (Beersheba and Hebron). Abd al-Wahid did not keep his post for long. All these arrangements were titular in nature with no enforceable chain of command behind them.

The weapons available to the defenders were meager. They consisted of the rifles left in the hands of the Palestine police and the rifles they had bought from Egypt with the little money they had collected from the people. These rifles were Italian made, of doubtful quality, and ammunition was scarce.[38]

In the Imara police station nearest to us, my cousin Hassan unscrewed his wireless set and handed it over to the Muslim Brotherhood members in Khan Yunis. The police station was now empty and policemen joined the defenders elsewhere.

Hamed, with about half a dozen volunteers, set up his defense post at Imara. One member of his team was Abu Khudeir, an expert in making mines. Hamed's post was about ten kilometers away from us. He found this place indefensible so he moved closer to Wadi Shallalah, digging trenches and burying mines on the possible route for the Jewish tanks. He used to gallop around at night and fire shots here and there to give the impression of a large force.

The Jews wanted to test our defenses. They attacked our land in al-Ma'in on 8, 10, and 12 May 1948. About a dozen fighters with rifles, one machine gun, and one Boys anti-tank rifle, held them off;

meanwhile the Zionists burned piles of harvested wheat and killed cattle. Their main target was to cut off the railway line at Deir al-Balah Station, which was located near the Kfar Darom colony. The planned date was 15 May 1948: the end of the British mandate and day that the Egyptian forces were expected to enter Palestine. And of course we did not know it at the time, but the day before, on the afternoon of 14 May, had come the unilateral declaration of Israel's statehood.

Meanwhile, the planned attack on the railway would not only cause major disruption to the Egyptian forces, but it would have been a huge embarrassment to King Farouk who was about to visit his forces. To cut off the railway, the Jews had to conquer al-Ma'in first. They were well prepared and knew that al-Ma'in was a Palestinian stronghold.

In the late hours of 14 May, Hamed, in his observation post, saw row upon row of headlights advancing toward us. Surprised, he fired one shot from his flare gun to warn us. A green light rose on the horizon: the wrong signal. He corrected himself by sending two red ones into the air. Hamed's contraptions delayed the Jewish troops for some hours, but in the end they detonated his mines and crossed over his ditches on planks.

On the ridge, facing us four kilometers, away lay the shrine of Sheikh Nuran, a venerated *weli*, a revered saint. Wadi Shallalah, where Hamed was stationed, was beyond Sheikh Nuran's shrine, on low-lying land. When Jewish troops had passed the temporary obstacle of Hamed's mines and trenches, they ascended the Nuran ridge and came into full view.

"Oh my sons, the Jews are coming to take you. The Jews are coming," cried Abdullah's mother. An old woman and a light sleeper, she was overwhelmed by the sight of a long line of lights probing the darkness. There, on the near horizon, we saw the headlights of twenty-four armored vehicles approaching us. A monster with forty-eight eyes faced us, with the ominous roar of its engines.

About fifteen young men, including Hamed, assembled quickly and fired their rifles toward the advancing column, without much effect. The main force of about a dozen men was stationed at the school, forming the second line of defense. The men at the school were armed with rifles, but Mousa had a Browning machine gun and Ibrahim a Boys, which could penetrate an armored car. These were the most powerful armaments we had. The defense party was on high ground facing the Nuran ridge. Their hail of bullets, especially the threat of the Boys, stopped the advancing Jewish armored vehicles in their tracks for a while as they assessed the situation. Then the Zionists split into two groups: twelve armored vehicles veered toward Nuran ridge and the remaining twelve advanced directly toward the defense party on my father's land, where the school, the house, and the farm stood.

At the school building, Salman Abu Suleiman, my father's cousin, recklessly stood on the roof and started shooting his old rifle. Mousa, with hardly any experience, kept his finger on the trigger of the machine gun until it overheated and jammed. Ibrahim, on the Boys, must have hit at least one tank, or so the confusion of the headlights indicated.

The tanks had overrun Hamed and his small group, but they, our first line of defense, kept shooting at them from behind, moving from one side to another. Women and children ran in a northerly direction. Mothers tried to locate their children in the darkness. They tried hurriedly to pick up things their children needed: milk, blankets, and the like. In the background, the threatening lights, the hail of bullets tracing arcs in the sky, the hurried confusion, the agonizing cries, and the shouts for a missing child heightened our fear of impending death.

My mother led my sister and me in the darkness. "Where are you?"

"I am here," I cried back.

"Where? Where?" she pleaded.

All the women and children knew where to go. They all headed toward Wadi Farha, a deep ravine and a dry riverbed in the summer. In the winter, its bed carried rainwater that filled the wells. I knew this wadi well; it had steep sides that were several times my height. It was a place where I often hid and went on wild adventures, with galloping horses, monsters, and demons. But that night—or dawn—was different. It was not a flight of childish fantasy. The thud of Zionist bombs, the crying children, and the frightened mothers were the elements of a real nightmare. Women splashed dirt on their faces to discourage rape.

Our schoolteacher, Muhammad Abu Liyya, was an affable young man, liked by everyone. A man of learning, he did not carry a gun. He fled to the wadi. Finding himself among women and children, he felt ashamed and ran for safety toward the village of Beni Suheila, leaving his wife behind.

On the way, he ran into the grand old man, Hajj Mahmoud, Hamed's father, on his horse, returning from Beni Suheila.

"Ya Hajj, *al-yahud!* The Jews!"

Hajj Mahmoud was hard of hearing. "Huh?"

"*Yahud! Yahud!*"

"Huh?"

Abu Liyya sped on his way, repeating the same warning. Hamed's father continued on his way toward the battle site, unaware of the danger ahead. When he came closer, he realized what was happening. Hamed had not yet emerged from the battle and was assumed dead. Later the next day, he saw Hamed in terrible shape, but alive. The grand old man wept. "I had never seen him cry before," Hamed remarked later.

During the night in the wadi, we were worried about what had become of the men, our fathers and brothers. With the first light, we could recognize objects. Someone peered out of the ravine: "Look at the smoke!"

"Oh, that's the school. It's gone!" A column of smoke was billowing from the direction of the school that my father had built in 1920. I felt a bomb explode in my guts. There was another explosion and a column of smoke rose up.

"That's the *bayyara*," someone shouted.

Our house, all the homes, had gone up in smoke. Columns of smoke, announcing the destruction of our landscape, were rising into the sky. Their peculiar shape and distant smell filled us with grief. Still, the concern was for the people. Women started wailing and beating their cheeks in anticipation of bad news.

By midday, the shooting had stopped. Twelve tanks continued westward toward Deir al-Balah. We remained hiding in the wadi. Half of the Jewish tanks were still there. A light airplane was hovering overhead most of the day. It seemed that the destruction of the Zionist convoy at Deir al-Balah had been reported. The remaining convoy that had stayed in al-Ma'in retreated to its base, leaving only the smoldering remains of their work.

Slowly we emerged from our hiding place and began inspecting the charred ruins. My brothers Ibrahim and Mousa emerged, to our joy, alive and well.

They told us about how they had been surrounded. They had retreated to the *karm*, my father's orchard, with its cactus fence. The enemy thought they had them cornered inside the fence, but the defenders escaped from the other side of the *karm* through hidden gaps in the cactus fence. Still, we had lost a number of fighters, and found many in a ditch, dead. My father was not in al-Ma'in; he had gone to Khan Yunis. Abdullah had gone two days earlier to the Egyptian border to meet General Mawawi, the commanding officer of the Egyptian forces, coming to save us.

We found corpses here and there. The two shops owned by al-Shawwal and Abu I'teim stood wide open, their shelves empty. Near the *bayyara* we found Muhammad Abu Juma lying dead, spattered with blood. Poor man, he was a simple, peaceful young person, who never carried a gun or even knew how to use one.

We spent the following night and day taking in the shock and contemplating what to do. My father and Abdullah, whose direction and counsel we were waiting for, returned. Abdullah said the Egyptian forces had now entered Palestine and "our rescue was imminent." He told us that when he offered to join the army with his group, General Mawawi replied, "Leave the business of war to the professionals."

"We can show you the way. We can be the front line. We can keep an eye on and surround the colonies," Abdullah insisted. He received no response from the Egyptian general.

My father told my brother Mousa to return to his university and urged Hamed to do the same, leaving the fighting to 'the professionals'. I stood there looking helpless. My Beersheba school was out of bounds, my old school destroyed. My father came up with the solution: "Take your brother with you," he instructed Mousa.

We bade a tearful farewell to mother and father and the few family members who were still there. It was a subdued good-bye, without the anticipation of expected adventure that would normally accompany a journey like this, or the assurance that those whom we left behind would be there when we returned.

Hamed, Mousa, and I rode to the Khan Yunis railway station. I rode behind Mousa. We carried nothing with us, no clothes, no papers, just the few pounds my father had slipped into Mousa's hand. I looked back at the smoldering ruins, at the meadows of my childhood, golden with the still-unharvested wheat.

I was engulfed by a feeling of both anxiety and serenity: serenity because we were still alive and an anxiety that was never to leave me. I wanted to know who this faceless enemy was. What did they look like, why did they hate us, why did they destroy us, why had they had literally burned our lives to the ground? What had we done to them? Who were these Jews anyway? I thought to myself that I must find out who they were: their names, their faces, where they came from. I must know their army formations, their officers, what exactly they had done that day, and where they lived later.

I scanned the horizon behind me, recalling the places where I was born, played, went to school, as they slowly disappeared from view. My unexpected departure did not feel that it would be such a long separation—it was simply a sojourn in another place for a while. If the future was vague for me at that moment, the past that I had just left behind became frozen in my mind and became my present forever.

I never imagined that I would not see these places again, that I would never be able to return to my birthplace. The events of those two days catapulted us into the unknown. I spent the rest of my life on a long, winding journey of return, a journey that has taken me to dozens of countries over decades of travel, and turned my black hair to silver. But like a boomerang, I knew the end destination, and that the only way to it was the road of return I had decided to take.

6

The Rupture

We arrived at the subdued Khan Yunis streets. The railway station was deserted.

"When is the next train coming?" we asked someone passing by the station.

"Train? What train? They stopped coming. Go to Rafah. They may be running from there."

We started walking on the tracks toward Rafah, silent, fearful, and anxious. We were fearful about the tragedy that had befallen, not knowing the extent of what had happened, having left our home too soon to find out. We were anxious about what the future would bring. Mousa always had a sensitive stomach; he threw up on the tracks. The stoic Hamed marched on. I did too, not yet able to understand the full impact of the past few days, but reassured by the presence of my brother and my cousin.

We arrived at the dusty Rafah station, the first one built in Egypt, its yard full of people jostling each other, struggling to board the train. Some were carrying sacks while others had nothing at all. Many were wearing *gallabiya*s, the typical Egyptian dress, while others were wearing shirts and trousers. Although the station had a military air, lots of uniformed persons, police, and the like, I did not see signs of the Egyptian army that we had all expected. Perhaps they had crossed to Palestine the day before, or perhaps they had come from another station. Most of the people I saw were Egyptians returning home, most likely to al-Arish, the next train station.

Hamed pushed his way through, followed by Mousa, and then me. I remember only the train wheels clicking in rhythm on the old tracks, but not whether we found a seat or remained standing. I saw the palm dates of Rafah slowly disappearing, replaced by the vast Sinai sand dunes and the Mediterranean waters shining in the distance.

"Papers," demanded a young Egyptian sergeant.

"We have none," Hamed replied.

"What? How come? Why did you board the train then?"

"We are Palestinian students returning to university."

"University? You do not look like university students. Look at yourselves."

"We were volunteers defending our country. The Jews destroyed our homes, our papers, everything. Now that the Egyptian army has arrived, we are returning to study."

In spite of his and our shabby appearance, Hamed was able to persuade the young official, who agreed to hand us over to the al-Arish police station. That way, he would get rid of us as his problem.

In al-Arish, passengers were met by joyous relatives, thanking God for their safe return from Palestine's troubles. We were met instead by policemen who escorted us to the town's police station.

A wiser, older police officer listened to our case several times. His verdict was to detain us for the night until he received a reply from Cairo. Hamed's main argument was that if we reached Cairo, we could prove that we were registered university students. As they led us to the prison, a notable from al-Arish came to the room. He inquired about our problem and the officer filled him in.

Turning to us, he asked the customary question, "*Intu awlad meen*? Which family are you from?"

"We are Abu Sitta."

He turned to the officer and said, "Oh! These are respectable, well-known people. Upon my guarantee, release them, and I am sure they will be back here tomorrow morning." The kind man offered to host us for the night. Hamed thanked him and suggested we go to a hotel. The 'hotel' was a building under construction *intended* to be a hotel. Many rooms did not yet have windows or doors. Then again, we were not looking for comfort. The alternative was a dirty prison cell.

The next morning, we boarded the train, accompanied by a policeman and an arrest order for delivery to Cairo police headquarters.

We all, including the policeman, sleepily dozed off to the sound of the rickety tracks. On the long journey, we went first to Qantara on the Suez Canal. It took several hours to get that far and I woke up from time to time to see patches of palm dates receding in an ocean of sand dunes; their frozen waves stayed etched in my mind as a changing pattern of black-and-white shadows. In contrast to the hours of monotony on the train, the palm dates appeared full of life, like ships sailing in this ocean of sand. Along with the clusters of palm dates I noticed a lone camel or two led by their owners, or a group of straw or half-built houses huddled together. I saw rugged and sand-pitted station signboards carrying strange names, where the train did not bother to stop.

Palestine felt far away. The unknown became closer to reality. As we sped toward Qantara, our official status had changed from Palestinian students with a known family name, admirably fighting a just war, into suspects under arrest to be handed over to Cairo authorities. We were people no more. We were names and numbers printed on an arrest order. When I say "we," of course I mean just Hamed and Mousa. Thank God nobody bothered to question whether I, a person who had not even finished primary school, was a university student.

At Qantara, our Egyptian police escort handed us over to the police station. It had a detention center right inside the station. The three of us were held in a fairly wide, relatively clean room, with the door not firmly closed. We knocked on the door and a policeman would slowly leave his comfortable chair and open the door.

"Here is a piaster and a half. Please buy us bread and a slice of *halawa*. And this is for you." There was no obligation on the Egyptian government to feed us, but the policeman smiled at the tip and called another to keep an eye on us until he came back from an errand. The hardship was not being in detention; it was the waiting. Nobody could tell us what was going to happen and how long we would stay in detention.

At night, when the lights were out, sounds took on a different, inexplicable character in my mind. What was their meaning, I wondered, in this strange place? There is a language of sounds in any place. In familiar places such as al-Ma'in, I knew the sounds; I could recognize cooking pots clanking, my father's horse neighing, which dog was barking, or a lone wolf howling in the wadi.

The strangest of sounds came from the adjacent detention room. It was some form of chanting, wavering between the strength of an anthem and the weeping sound of mourning. Strangest of all was the language: it was bizarre, unfamiliar. It was not an Arabic, either Palestinian or Egyptian. Night after night, this wailing rose to triumph and then fell to despair.

We asked the policeman delivering our bread and *halawa* about our neighbor.

"This is an Egyptian Jew being deported to Palestine, where he wants to go."

Deported? This young man was Egyptian. Why would they send him to Palestine? To fight us, no doubt. Was he one of the "invisible faces"? I never actually saw him, but I had the horrible feeling that he was going to live in my house and on my land, and that I would never see my home again. The "enemy" was so close, ready to take over my birthplace to make it his own. That enemy could be Egyptian, one of the people among whom we were seeking refuge. He may be willing to shed his Egyptian identity and go to kill us and kill his fellow Egyptians, in order to force his way into a home not his own. The wailing eventually stopped. He had gone. I can only assume that he succeeded in joining the army that had burned down my home.

We were told that we would leave for Cairo on the following Wednesday. The weekly train from Port Said to Cairo carrying criminals and convicts, a train specially armored and guarded, was to arrive on Wednesday, and we would be on it. Orders from Cairo. The last vestiges of treatment for respectable university students had gone. We had become criminals.

The train arrived at midnight. There were no passenger cars, only closed boxes, each with one high, barbed window. We were shoved into one of them. The stench was unbearable. The looks on the faces of the other prisoners, their dirty tattered prison uniforms, were grotesque in the dim light. My cousin and brother stood around me like a shield, near the window. It was hot and sweaty. The smell was awful. I could not breathe. I gasped for air. Hamed and Mousa took turns in lifting me up and pushing my nose up to the bars so that I could take a lungful of fresh midnight air from the speeding train.

The train stopped at the next station, loading more 'criminals.' I was thirsty. There was no water. Then we heard the cries of an enterprising soft-drink vendor at the platform. Mousa called the vendor and slipped him a coin between the bars. Hamed carried me as the vendor opened a bottle (of Coca-Cola, I think it was) and fed me through the bars like a baby. The train started to move. The vendor prepared to disengage.

"I have not finished. I am still thirsty."

Hamed and Mousa shouted at him. The vendor held the bottle for me, running beside the train. He ran as the train sped along until the high platform abruptly ended. I could see him receding from sight with the unfinished bottle held high in his hand.

At dawn, we finally arrived at the grand railway station of Cairo. It was deserted, except for policemen standing in a long row the length of the platform. At the front of this row, officers stood with their fingers on triggers. Their chief, a short, fierce-looking officer, stood out in front and, as a warning, raised his pistol in readiness to shoot.

"Get out slowly." They repeated the order along the platform. "Stand in line. Turn right." We filed in a single line. "March slowly." The long line started to move. "Stop. Squat on the ground." As we did, an officer started to count. "Stand up. March. Stop. Squat." Again.

It took a good part of an hour to cover the few hundred meters of the platform. The early morning breeze outside the station brought welcome relief. The officers ordered us to mount a flatbed truck with a flimsy rail bordering its sides. We were crowded on board, with hardly enough space to stand. I was sandwiched between Hamed and Mousa.

The trucks drove at terrific speed through Cairo's empty streets, escorted by police cars. On the tail of the police cars, the truck drivers swerved around the bends and the junctions at the same speed. As the trucks turned, we were thrown to one side. Finding no safety in the flimsy rail, we quickly devised a system to grab each other in the opposite direction of the curve, so as not to fall from the speeding truck onto the hard asphalt. When the truck turned around another bend, we grabbed each other in the opposite direction. The bulk of the bodies, struggling for dear life, moved as a solid jelly from side to side against the truck's movements.

We finally arrived. The trucks were emptied into a prison cell, complete with all the stench, dirt, and foul language one could expect. As usual, Hamed and Mousa made themselves a barrier between me and the prisoners. We had to endure the heavy, concentrated stench in the small, packed cell for what seemed like an eternity until the morning.

The officer in charge came in at 8:00 a.m. We were presented to him. Hamed made an impassioned speech that we were university students doing our sacred duty to defend our land. The fact that we had no papers, no belongings, no money was proof—not lack of proof—that we were part of this just fight. The Zionist enemy had destroyed and burnt our homes. That was the reason we had nothing. We were returning to study, now that the Egyptian forces had entered Palestine to save us from the Jews. "You, Mr. Officer, have only to check our papers at the Ministry of the Interior."

The officer seemed convinced and prepared to move us. "Handcuff them, soldier."

A policeman handcuffed Mousa and Hamed, and me. Innocently I slipped my hand out of the handcuff.

"I could not handcuff him, this one, sir," said the policemen as he saluted and stood to attention. The officer looked at me. I was not much taller than the height of his desk.

"Hold him by the hand, soldier."

We went out to the sunny bustling street. So this is Cairo, I thought, of which the Holy Quran says, *And they will be told to enter there* [Egypt] *in peace and security* (Surat al-Hajj, 46). We did enter it officially at about 9:00 a.m. on 27 May 1948.

Hamed, never someone to give up, took the guard to one corner and whispered, "Do you think it is right and proper that we, educated university students, should board a bus or a tram with handcuffs? I ask your conscience, is it proper?" Without waiting for an answer, Hamed continued, "No, I do not think you accept it. Let us take a taxi. We do not have much money, but we will take a taxi. Just take the handcuffs off and we will sit next to you in the taxi so you are assured. After all, we are going to the ministry building. There, you can handcuff us again."

He agreed and did not handcuff us again.

At the ministry, Hamed pleaded his case once more. University records were brought in and names checked. Hamed now felt elated; he was sure of the result. We were ordered to wait in the corridor. Hamed's good spirits made him reckless.

A policewoman in civilian dress passed carrying papers. "Inti bolisa? Are you a policewoman?" he asked in slang.

She looked at him in disdain, telling him off in Egyptian slang. "Flirting while in custody? Wait till you get out."

Our release papers were prepared. "Sign here." Hamed and Mousa signed jubilantly. "These are only two. Where is the third?"

Hamed said, "He is a child, and so cannot and should not sign." This caused a legal problem: I would have to be registered as a refugee, which would mean being taken to a refugee camp, unless . . . Hamed intervened and proposed, "Yes, he is a refugee but he is under our care."

They agreed and Hamed was given a piece of paper to sign: "I solemnly guarantee to provide the above-named person shelter, food, education, and health care." For years after, I reminded Hamed, when we met in Beirut, Damascus, or Cairo, of that pledge. Teasing him, I would say, "Hamed, I am hungry. I want a good lunch now."

We left the building, free people, but with a heavy heart, fearing what was to become of our homeland.

We knocked forcefully on the door. My brother Ali, followed by my brother Suleiman, opened the door. There were hugs, shouts, and cries. I was standing near the door. When the noise subsided, they saw me. "And you too?" There was lots of talk, hunger for news, questions to be answered.

In the small students' flat, there was little food; the biggest prize was half a chicken. There was no money and, worse still, there was no expectation of receiving money any time soon. The struggle for domestic survival had started.

The first thing my brothers and cousin did was to take stock of the new situation. Emptying their pockets on the table did not yield much. There was no hope of borrowing money because all those we knew were in the same situation or worse. There was one remote possibility: help from Hajj Abdullah, an affable man, and the brother of my father's cousin Abd al-Razek from the Egyptian side of our family. Hajj Abdullah and Abd al-Razek were the sons of Hammad who was sent to Egypt in the nineteenth century to manage our land and property there. Although he owned some of our Egyptian land and rented the rest from the family, he was broke most of the time. In good times, we had helped him financially. He more than compensated for his chronic shortage of money with a charming personality, being always full of stories and anecdotes, telling them with animation, and seemingly without a care in the world.

It was agreed that Hamed would go to see him, not only because he was persuasive, but also because Hamed's father was the richest landowner in the family. My father invested in education; Hajj Mahmoud, Hamed's father, invested in land.

The second thing was to make a list of Palestinian students who were cut off from their families, especially those who had come from coastal towns and villages such as Jaffa, Haifa, and Acre, which had been attacked and conquered by the Jews. These students knew nothing about the fate of their families, but had heard of people killed in their homes or driven away. They did not know of the fates of their own families but knew people who had drowned in small boats that capsized in Jaffa, gotten lost in the rocky hills of the Galilee, or died of exhaustion on the trek to Lebanon.

Some weeks later, a number of Palestinian students got together in our small flat. They decided to make presentations to the Arab League and the Egyptian government. They formed the Palestinian Students Union, which developed later into the General Union of Palestinian Students—GUPS—and become an international force to be reckoned with. My brother Suleiman was elected as its first president after the Nakba.

One day, we had a visitor, a Palestinian with an Egyptian accent.

"Are you alone?" he asked.

"It's only me and my brothers," Suleiman answered.

The visitor took a piece of paper from his breast pocket and started to read, "You are in grave danger. You are being watched. Take care. . . . Do you have a match?"

We gave him one and he burned the slip slowly. The visitor was Yasser Arafat.

I always sat in the background, listening to the anxious deliberations of the budding union. For the first time, I met Palestinians from Jerusalem, Haifa, and Jaffa, and listened to their city and rural accents. I ran errands from time to time: fetching tea or bringing chairs.

Those were the years when few could afford university education in another country, usually in Cairo or Beirut. They sold their expensive watches and clothes. I recall a student who used to wear breeches and a hat in the manner of the English gentry, ending up wearing an ordinary shirt and trousers. Students moved from their individual serviced flats, usually run by a Greek woman, to shared, sparsely furnished flats that housed many.

It was summertime and there was no school. And the bad news kept flowing in. More and more Palestinian towns and villages had been attacked and conquered by Zionist militias. Meanwhile, growing streams of refugees flowed into the neighboring Arab areas that had not yet been conquered. Jaffa refugees came to Cairo, first by boat to Port Said and then by train. They were herded into the Abbasiya camp in Cairo. Those who managed to slip away told us about the horrors of what the Jews had done, and bit by bit the stories formed a larger picture of what was happening around us.

By July 1948, the military situation was in a state of flux. Palestinians were waiting for liberation by Arab forces, but there were no signs this rescue would materialize.

My father traveled back and forth between Egypt and Palestine—at least to the parts that were still accessible, namely, Gaza and Khan Yunis—to discover the whereabouts of his scattered family. In these trying times, which we could never have imagined, my father wanted to be sure we held on to our values. He gathered us around him in our small Cairo flat: "Listen to me. Do I find in you people who will choose the right path and take their father's good advice?"

We all nodded. He started to read from a palm-sized note he held in his hand,

"Do not commit anything God has forbidden. Diligence at work will get you your desired objective. Wasting money spoils the spirit. Follow good counsel to the fullest extent to see your path clearly. Keep your faith and hold on tenaciously to your patrimony. These are the essence of your dignity."

We stood up, kissed his hand one after another, and raised it to our foreheads in the traditional manner. I still keep the palm-sized note with me.

7

The Carnage

By midsummer of 1948, a second truce had been declared between the Israeli militia and the Arab regular forces. The first (11 June to 8 July) and second (18 July to 15 October) truces were declared by the UN and agreed by the parties. Arab regular forces who entered Palestine after 15 May to rescue Palestinians after massacres such as Deir Yassin were: Egyptians in the southern half of Palestine; Jordanians, assisted by Iraqis in and north of Jerusalem (today's West Bank); and Syrians in the northeast around Lake Tiberias.[39] Although the Jews had conquered more land, we were hopeful that we would recover what had been lost. Ultimately, this truce proved to be the longest lasting.

My father decided that I should return from Cairo and continue my education in Khan Yunis. I was admitted to the seventh (final) primary grade at Khan Yunis school. As my father was traveling between Egypt and Palestine, my mother stayed with my eldest sister and her husband, and I was not sure where exactly. That summer we rented a house on Galal Street in Khan Yunis. My father instructed my brother Ibrahim, by now a budding lawyer, to look after us. Under his wing were my teenage sister, me, and our servant, the kindly Umm Ali. She was the wife of Abu Freij, one of our servants who used to make coffee at my father's seat. The living arrangements were my father's decision. He wanted his unmarried daughter and young son to be under his elder son's protection.

Umm Ali was a loving, ever-smiling woman. She looked after my sister and me. She used to bathe me and sing songs. When she rubbed my body, I had a strange sensation and was embarrassed if she noticed my awkwardness. I told her that I was now big enough to bathe myself.

On my return to Khan Yunis, I was bewildered to see how the small town (or rather, large village) I used to know had changed in this short period. Masses of people had flooded the whole area from Gaza to Rafah. They sought shelter in mosques and schools, under trees, in empty patches of land. People from hundreds of depopulated villages in southern Palestine headed toward Gaza by boat or on foot, walking along the shoreline or deserted roads.

Everywhere you turned, you found families separated. Mothers were looking for their children. Men were looking for their scattered families. The bonds of family and kinship had held them together for so long, and now they had to find a way to preserve it, needing it and each other more than ever. People recognized one another by a variety of markers, such as the traditional embroidered dresses worn by women that signified their original villages, or by the slight differences in accent. The magnitude of this calamity became more obvious when people exchanged stories about their experiences. It was not a personal tragedy; it was the obliteration of an entire nation on an unimaginable scale. Despite this, there was no way people would beg in the streets. Their pride would not allow it.

With little supervision from my brother, I had lots of time to roam about, see people, and listen. I saw on the corner of one street a man who put out a small table, with a single dish of hummus for sale. He was unsightly, in scruffy clothes (although that was no longer a novelty), and seemed to have lost his sight in one eye. Around him were his five children, squatting on the ground with their mother.

The next day as I passed, I saw him preparing two plates. Apparently, his business was improving. Then, he installed a large table in front of a closed shop. One of his children used to help. He brought in more pots and pans. Several weeks later, a handwritten sign was posted on the shop behind him, "Jaffa Restaurant." He managed to rent the very shop where he had installed his lone table. This Jaffa man stood proudly in front of his shop, smiling and energetic. Similar stories of perseverance and adjustment to a new life as refugees could be found everywhere.

* * *

On a sunny afternoon, I was walking along the sandy road leading to the school when some people in the street shouted in agitation, "Look, look!" In the sky, over the Mediterranean, we saw three silvery objects approaching us. Nobody knew what they were.

As they veered toward us and descended, someone shouted, "Jews!" No one believed it at first. Then a huge barrel was dropped from the plane and it exploded a few hundred meters away from me with a big thud and a cloud of dust. We heard cries, screams, and shouts for help. I ran back home thinking that this would save me from the bombs falling from the sky.

It was late October. Israeli air raids were a new phenomenon, which caused a great many casualties and much panic. As terrible as they had been, the Zionist ground attacks using jeeps with mounted machine guns, armored vehicles, and tanks were at least visible, even if they were faceless. But this? Death showered from the skies? This was new and terrifying.

It continued with a vengeance. In the last week of October 1948, Beersheba town fell to the Jews. Early in November, al-Majdal fell too. The Egyptian forces, under the command of General Mawawi, retreated quickly in a state of panic from its farthest point north, Isdud, back to Gaza town. As a child I was not supposed to know what was going on but of course I overheard things, and have since learned in more detail, in particular, what happened in southern Palestine.

All the villagers in southern Palestine, from a total of about 250 villages, poured into the Gaza area—now dubbed the Gaza Strip. The retreating soldiers and the terrified refugees flooded the small piece of land, increasing its population from eighty thousand to about three hundred thousand, practically overnight.

Misery was etched on the faces of these masses, who filled every inch of the small Strip. I saw more and more women and children walking aimlessly, small families huddled under trees, sheikhs and *mukhtars* (local leaders) looking submissive and distraught as they tried to retain their dignity and authority over their people.

What before August was a flood, became a deluge after October. The air raids continued. A family we knew from al-Jura (old Asqalan), which had been a village of fishermen, told us harrowing stories. A family of eleven—a grandfather, his children, and grandchildren—were having supper on their farm when a bomb dropped on them. They were all killed. Their limbs were found hanging on tree branches; heads had been torn from their bodies; and a woman and her child became a pile of unrecognizable flesh, a headdress without a head.

The horror of the air raids was indescribable. People could not understand or predict when they would come. They could hear the roar of the approaching tanks. But air raids brought sudden, violent, and widespread death. You did not know when and from where the raids would come. You did not know whom they would hit. You could be killed but the person standing a few paces away might be safe. You could die at any moment. You could be out to get some food for your family and never come back.

By the end of December 1948, when the land war was about to end (if you can call a one-sided attack a war), the bombing intensified. It was clear to us that the bombing was for the sole purpose of terrifying people and discouraging them from ever contemplating a return to their homes. There cannot have been a military reason for the bombing because the targets were all civilians.

The International Committee of the Red Cross arrived to distribute food. They set up a distribution center in the main square in Deir al-Balah. Hundreds of family heads and young men gathered in lines waiting for their turn to receive food rations. At midday, in January 1949, at peak distribution time, "Israeli" planes, as they were now called, dropped bombs on the center. Blood and limbs and corpses were strewn everywhere, mixed with the flour and spilled oil. Even for the Red Cross team on the site, fresh from the agonies of the Second World War, this was too much. The team described it as "unbelievable horror."[40] Eyewitnesses counted 225 corpses that day.

One of those corpses was Muhammad, my uncle. He was doing his ablutions at the mosque when the planes hit the crowd. Muhammad was a favorite brother of my mother and the head of her family. She always relied on him. She took pride in her brother and found in him moral support when she needed it.

This raid on what was obviously a civilian food center was no accident. In the following days, the raids expanded to the Khan Yunis and Rafah food centers, and to Gaza's clearly marked hospitals.

* * *

When I returned home one evening, my sister Nadia took me aside and whispered, "I have a plan. Do not tell our brother."

"What is it?" I asked, my curiosity perking.

"You and I are going to our mother. I will not stay here any more."

We did not know where our mother was, not exactly. We knew she was safe and was with my eldest sister and her husband and children somewhere near al-Arish, some fifty-five kilometers away. With them were other members of my extended family. It was a crazy idea, of course. A boy and his teenage sister marching into the unknown, without the knowledge or approval of their elder brother, was a foolish and dangerous act.

I do not recall if we were afraid of what the journey would entail, or only slightly apprehensive about the wrath we would face from my brother, and later my father, at our sudden disappearance. We sneaked out of the house, telling Umm Ali that we were going out to get something. We did not have luggage. We headed west to Rafah. The excitement overcame any feelings of tiredness. It was after Rafah, in Sinai, that the risk of our adventure became clear.

On the wide, level, sandy plain, we saw hundreds, maybe thousands of refugees heading west as well. There was no clear road. They were marching, ten abreast along a wide front, with nothing in common except the direction they were going.

As we approached Sheikh Zuweid, a man looked at us suspiciously.

"Don't take any notice. Keep going," Nadia said.

The man kept looking. Then he came nearer, at a respectable distance.

"*Ya walad*, boy, what is your name?" I did not answer. "Whose son are you?" Again, no reply. I would not talk to a stranger or reveal my name. "Are you Abu Sitta?"

I looked at him in surprise. "Yes." I felt more assured, but my sister pushed me away.

"I thought so," he said. He looked as respectable as could be expected under the circumstances. He noticed us, among the marching crowds, only because he felt he knew us, I thought.

"I am the son of Sheikh Hussein," I gave a belated answer.

"Where are you going?"

"My sister and I are going to my mother in al-Arish, I think."

"Alone?" he said in surprise. "Does your sister have jewelry?

There are desperate people who may attack you." He told me, with my sister listening, that he was from the al-Smeiri family, our neighbors; their sheikh was a friend of my father's and a frequent guest.

"Very soon, we'll reach Sheikh Zuweid. I'll get a car to al-Arish and I'll take you there." That was good news as this would be by far the longest part of the journey. This man was entirely reliable; he was as good as his word. When we arrived at al-Arish, he asked if we knew where to go. We thanked him and started looking for my mother.

Looking back on those days, I am amazed by the total trust we felt in other Palestinians. We always felt sure that in our catastrophic and unprecedented dispersion, we were bound to know someone from another family or from another village and to whom we could relate.

We made inquiries about refugees. We were told there were many camping on the outskirts of al-Arish. We walked toward the sand dunes surrounding al-Arish. It was an entirely different scene from our rich brown land in al-Ma'in. We walked among fellow refugees, some in shacks, some in tents, and others in neither. We saw children playing, going up and down the sand dunes.

My sister was the first to recognize our family in the crowd. When we came closer, they noticed us and then came running toward us; others ran in the opposite direction to tell everyone else. There were about a dozen Abu Sitta families there. I saw grown-ups, men in their white *gumbaz* and women in their black garb looking, then shouting, and then hurrying toward us. In the approaching and welcoming crowd, I saw a worried and anxious figure rushing toward us. It was my mother. Amid the prayers thanking God for our safety and the scolding we received—mainly directed at my sister—I felt relieved and safe.

In the next few days, I started to learn a new language, the language of the sand dunes. The other boys and I spent the days rolling down the slopes covered with sand, starting at the top again and again in an endless race. I knew which sand dunes were hard to walk on or soft enough to roll over. Isolated trees, depressions, peculiar and different waves created by the wind in the sand, were the alphabet of the sand dunes' language. I don't recall how long I stayed there.

I knew that my brother had naturally discovered our escape the day we had gone missing and sent word to my father, who was in Egypt at the time. Once they had established our whereabouts, my father, worried about my education (I had attended Khan Yunis primary school for only two to three weeks), sent Hajj Abdullah's son to take me to him in Cairo. Hajj Abdullah's son was an Egyptian who could cross the border without questions being asked. At the end of 1948 or the beginning of 1949, I entered Egypt again, this time without handcuffs, and this time I would stay there for ten years.

Even throughout my school years in Egypt, I was never far away from events in Palestine. In the summer holiday of 1949, I took the dusty train, cranking along on its First World War tracks, to Palestine, or more accurately to the Gaza Strip, which remained unoccupied by the new Zionist state.

I was eager to see what had happened to my family after my first long absence in Egypt. I was united with my mother, my eldest married sister Harba, and my younger sister Nadia (my companion in the escapade to al-Arish), who were now all in Khan Yunis. Abdullah had taken a house for his family, and my brother Ibrahim had started his law practice.

My father went back and forth to Egypt to oversee his affairs. His main concern was to provide for his three sons who were about to finish their university education; my burden was light in comparison to theirs. It was a blow to my father's prestige that he had lost his land and the income from it. The prospect of finding means to continue the education of his sons, who were on the threshold of graduation, was daunting.

Back in Khan Yunis, I sat and I listened to the stories of my extended family whom I had left behind on 15 May 1948. When the Jews withdrew the remainder of their tanks from al-Ma'in on 15 May, the men of the family returned to examine the debris and damage done to their property, as well as to harvest the wheat. Some women returned too, but cautiously for fear of the mines the Jews had left behind, especially near drinking water and well-trodden paths. The Egyptian Border Guards *(haras al-hudud)* were stationed at Sheikh Nuran and Tell Jemmeh, both high points, at the eastern and northern extremities of al-Ma'in.

Emboldened by their successes on other fronts in Palestine, the Jews, by that time calling themselves "Israelis," attacked al-Ma'in again on 5 December 1948. The lightly armed Egyptian police force could not stop them and called for help. The Egyptians sent forward two columns of light tanks, called 'locusts.' These were small, fast tanks recently procured in Europe from some dubious source. Egyptians thought the surprise of their appearance would win the day. One column advanced toward Sheikh Nuran and the other toward my father's *karm*. The Egyptian force came down from Asluj in an overnight journey of eighty kilometers. They arrived in the early morning, tired and disoriented. They had no detailed knowledge of the terrain. Their communication equipment was faulty and had no operating batteries. One column did not know what the other was doing.

I listened to the young men in my family describing the bloody scene. The Egyptian force suffered heavy casualties and retreated toward the coast, making the safe strip even more crowded. The Jews settled on our land and could not be dislodged. We were now officially refugees.

The Israeli success at al-Ma'in and other villages encouraged a Zionist attack on al-Arish in Sinai. British intervention forced them to withdraw from Sinai. Nevertheless, they concentrated a massive force to split the crowded coastal strip, occupy it, and decimate the remaining Egyptian forces in Palestine.

In the Gaza Strip, there were, at that point, eighty thousand inhabitants and two hundred thousand refugees huddled under trees, in schools, and in mosques. In an area you could drive the length of in thirty minutes, and the width in ten minutes, almost three hundred thousand civilians were surrounded by their enemy on all sides, and hemmed in by the sea.

In November 1948, the inept General Mawawi, the commanding officer of the Egyptian forces in Palestine, lost almost half of Palestine to the Israelis before being relieved of his duties. The Egyptian Command appointed General Ahmed Fouad Sadek as the new commanding officer. Sadek was a tough soldier of Sudanese origin. He reviewed the desperate situation and decided to put up a determined fight.

The Israelis gathered a massive force of tanks and infantry in Shallalah and al-Ma'in. Eyewitnesses said they saw a huge array of lights, moving and realigning on the far horizon. The Zionist commanding officer was a tough Russian general, just released from the Red Army at the end of the Second World War. Sadek, on the other hand, was concerned that his relatively small force, demoralized after a series of reversals, would not be enough for the expected battle. He gathered all available Palestinian volunteers but the Egyptian government had other plans. Sadek was ordered to withdraw completely from Palestine and save what remained of the Egyptian forces. In a memorable cable, recounted endless times by the refugees, Sadek replied:

> My military honor does not permit me to see my brothers and sisters, defenseless civilians, cornered in this small strip of land and let them be slaughtered like chickens by the Jews.

Sadek went a step further. He sought help from the Muslim Brotherhood volunteers detained in prison in the Rafah camp. The Egyptian government had assassinated their leader, Hassan al-Banna, in February 1949 in retaliation for the assassination of the Egyptian prime minister Mahmoud al-Nuqrashi. They banned the Muslim Brotherhood party and imprisoned their members. The government ordered Sadek to put their volunteers in a detention center and not to send them back to Egypt. The leader of the Muslim Brotherhood's volunteers in Palestine, Kamel al-Sharif, told me later in Amman, in 1994, that Sadek came to the detention center and told them, "The Jews are massing a large force to attack us. You know how many innocent people will be killed. We need your help. Come and fight with us."

"And then?" Sharif had asked him.

"I take you back to prison," was his reply.

They agreed. The battle took place at Sheikh Hammoudeh or Hill 86, on the northern extremity of al-Ma'in, on 25 December 1948. It was a fierce battle, probably the fiercest battle the Egyptians had fought in Palestine. Each side put its full force into the field. The Egyptians employed flame-throwers for the first time.

The Israelis were crushed. Their Russian general was killed. They left behind arms, wrecked vehicles, pools of blood, and the tracks of their dead, whose bodies they dragged back with them.[41] The Gaza Strip, the remainder of Palestine, was saved.

The Muslim Brotherhood volunteers were taken back to prison. Sadek visited them. They stood to attention as he pinned medals of honor on their chests. Reprimanded by Cairo, Sadek replied that it was his prerogative to decorate soldiers who had served under his command.

Meanwhile, away from the military front, the life of the civilians was no less dramatic. I tracked down our schoolteacher, Abu Liyya, who sought refuge in the Deir al-Balah camp, wanting to see what had happened to him. When he had run from al-Ma'in, Abu Liyya was met only by more bad news. His relatives, now refugees in the same camp, told him that two days before the attack on al-Ma'in, his own village, Burayr, was the scene of a terrible massacre, on 13 May 1948.

They told him that the Jews cut off the area around Burayr from three sides, the west, east, and south, leaving the north open. They bombed the village with artillery from al-Wakr in the east. Tanks advanced from the south and the west, toward the school where Palestinian and other Arab volunteers were stationed. The defenders fought bravely to the last bullet. They were all killed, thirty-eight in total. The tanks then advanced into the village. Families were huddled in their houses. Jewish soldiers kicked doors open and lobbed grenades at the families cowered in the corners of their houses—fathers, mothers, and children. Their blood was splattered on the walls. Since the houses were stacked with hay, the whole village went up in flames in no time.

Others in the village, hearing the attacks on their neighbors, were helpless. No family knew when their door would break open. They heard terrifying screams but hoped they would be spared. The village fire, its ashes, and the stench of burned human flesh were described by a few daring young men who returned two days later to inspect the village, to find if a relative was left behind, or to fetch some supplies or valuables.

Abu Liyya, a man with a soft heart and quick tears, listened to his relatives reciting the names of those who had perished, all 125 of them, trying to recall a face or a memory when each name was mentioned. He also heard stories of earrings ripped from earlobes, fingers cut off for rings. There was a whisper about rape cases, but no one would admit it publicly.[42] It seemed he, like so many others, had grown much older than his thirty years in those days after the massacre.

The story of the Burayr massacre did not attract much attention from the early historians of the period, including the Palestinian chronicler Aref el-Aref. The Israeli narrative did not admit the massacre at the time, only casualties of war. Instead, David Ben-Gurion mentioned the victory of his soldiers over the largely unarmed villagers of Burayr. Twenty-four hours after the Burayr massacre, on the afternoon of 14 May, Ben-Gurion, together with the European Zionist elders, met in Tel Aviv to declare the State of Israel. He read the Declaration of Independence (which did not specify independence from whom) in which he presumably addressed the people of Burayr and other Palestinians and appealed to them to cease "the onslaught launched against" the Jews when he said:

> We appeal—in the very midst of the onslaught launched against us now for months—to the Arab inhabitants of the State of Israel to return to the ways of peace . . . on the basis of full and equal citizenship and due representation in all its bodies and institutions.[43]

8

Life as a Refugee

Historians, writers, and storytellers speak of battle scenes, soldiers, and guns. Very few describe the landscape left behind when the soldiers have gone and the dead are buried.

Consider Khan Yunis, the town, a large village really, with its small, mud houses, palm trees, and serenity. It was hidden from the Mediterranean by three kilometers of sand dunes. In the summer months, people walked or rode on donkeys to reach the shoreline and set up summer huts among the palms trees in al-Mawasi, where you could find sweet water by digging a shallow pit by the seaside.

In 1949, everything had changed. Long lines of white tents strung one next to the other in winding rows up and down the dunes covered the once-barren area. These wretched lines of tents were crowded, but were certainly considered a step up, as people had previously found themselves living under trees and in mosques and schools. The tents could be differentiated in people's minds by the nostalgic character, represented in so many ways, of the home village they had left behind. Here or there, a cluster of houses became the refuge of people from Burayr, al-Jiyya, or Barbara. They were uprooted people, robbed of their land, but not of their identity and least of all their familial cohesion. Groups maintained their social structures, complete with the village *mukhtar* and sub-*mukhtar*s (heads of *hamula*s, extended families). The *mukhtar*s maintained their influence, stamped papers, solved disputes, and represented the village before the authorities.

Of course, there was a price to pay for the crowding. The tents were so close that their pegs and ropes intertwined. There was no privacy to speak of; even a whisper could be heard at the next tent. So it was inevitable that scandal would erupt in this conservative society. I remember once, a young man and woman were caught in an indecent act. The judge scolded them for their unforgivable behavior.

"Have you no shame? In these trying times, you make improper advances toward your neighbor?" the judge asked the young man.

"Judge, sir, our tent was crowded. There was no room to sleep. My leg stretched out of the tent at night. Apparently she also had the same problem. Our legs got mixed up. What could I do?" the guilty man pleaded.

The first relief organization to arrive in Palestine was the Red Cross.[44] They set up an office in Gaza and focused mostly on the dead and wounded, as well as facilitating prisoner exchanges. However, the real relief work was undertaken by the American Friends Service Committee (AFSC), or Quakers, who arrived a little later. They were a dedicated, sincere, religious pacifist group. The sheer size of the human tragedy overwhelmed them. They were somewhat surprised to meet Gazan Christians who had held on to their faith for the last nineteen centuries. In spite of their short stay, from winter 1948 to spring 1950, the Quakers had, by far, the largest impact on the refugees in Gaza. They transformed old British army camps in Maghazi and Nuseirat into the refugee camps we know today, and they created new ones on the Gaza shoreline *(al-shatt)*, in addition to camps at Deir al-Balah, Khan Yunis, and Rafah.

I will never forget "Mr. Marshall," as everybody called him, a tall young man who operated the Khan Yunis camp. Marshall Sutton was active and resourceful in solving problems related to bureaucracy with the Egyptian authorities. I saw my relative, Hussein Abu Hassan, coming and going with him, translating and explaining. The young Hussein was lively and communicative, and he had oratorical skills. He was a land surveyor with the Palestine government of the British Mandate and made himself a de facto refugee spokesperson before the endless parade of foreign visitors. The latter came to watch the spectacle of a people uprooted from their land by 'the brave few who defeated the savage majority,' as they were called.

Marshall was adept at his task, but he was also aware of the dimensions of this unprecedented tragedy. In the mid-twentieth century, at a time before the communication technologies of today, and coming from a western culture, it was remarkable that Marshall and his colleagues so quickly grasped the essence of Palestinian suffering. This was not a standard case of victims displaced by war. It was, they soon found out, not food and shelter the Palestinians wanted, but something much more fundamental.

Almost half a century later, in February 2002, I traveled to Philadelphia to visit AFSC headquarters. AFSC gave me Marshall's telephone number and I called him. A frail voice came on the line: It was his wife and she told me he was in Washington.

I wondered what was this man, well into his eighties, was doing in Washington.

The next day, I called again: "I am Palestinian. My name is Abu Sitta. You do not know me, I was a small boy when we met. But I know you."

After a short silence, his voice came on the line, old but firm, "Yes, yes. I knew Abu Sitta, when I was in Gaza."

"I want to thank you very much for what you have done for the Palestinians. I am sorry it is fifty years late."

"I am sorry too that the problem is still there, getting worse every day. I was in Washington yesterday talking to a member of Congress about the worsening situation in Gaza."

I couldn't find the words to reply. Humanity was alive and well. On that trip to the United States, I spent a week at AFSC headquarters. I saw the original correspondence between the officers in Gaza and their head office in the US. I learned how they set up their operations, how they created new camps, and how they overcame the immense hurdles of importing supplies and transporting them through webs of bureaucracy.

For me, one letter in particular was worth all the searching through files. The letter, dated 12 October 1949, could have been carved in stone for how timeless it remained. It is as fresh now as it was six decades earlier. The letter was from AFSC's Gaza Unit to Clarence Pickett at AFSC headquarters in Philadelphia.

> Dear Clarence Pickett:
>
> With the rainy season about to begin, and the nights already growing

colder, the Unit in Gaza wishes to write you this special letter about the current attitudes and thinking among the refugees of the Gaza area. It is not, and indeed cannot be a reflection of the attitudes of refugees other than those for whom we work. It is no way a reflection of our own attitudes toward present and coming problems concerned with continuation, participation, registrations or diet cuts. Please use this letter in any way you see fit which will help alleviate human suffering. Primarily, however, it is for you, to provide background material upon which Committee decisions might partially be based.

Since it is very difficult for refugees here to communicate with the outside world, we feel we have an obligation to cover what we can of their opinions and thinking at the present time. They feel strongly that the United Nations are responsible for their plight, and therefore have the total responsibility to feed, house, clothe, and **repatriate** them. This is in addition to the feeling of many of them that the Arab governments have also let them down; some even feel that left alone they could have, and even now might reach a solution with the Jews. Accordingly, the relief we bring them appears to them to be their right, and in no way an act of humanitarian charity on the part of the United Nations. There is some sentiment that once the United Nations leaves the area, the matter could be finished by war: "therefore, why don't you leave us"—runs this line of thought.

Above all else, they desire to go home—back to their lands and villages which, in many cases, are very close. Apparently they do not hesitate to go back to the changed culture which is growing in Israel. This desire naturally continues to be the strongest demand they make; sixteen months of exile has not diminished it. Without it, they would have nothing for which to live. It is expressed in many ways and forms every day. "Why keep us alive"—is one expression of it. It is as genuine and deep as a man's longing for his home can be. In the minds of refugees, resettlement is not even considered.

They realize that their skills are deteriorating. They recognize the erosion of the soul which their situation is fostering. No daily run of report or statistics can adequately convey the hurt and injury done to family life, to young people with no normal hope of work or school. A culture just on the threshold of progress—by western standards—has been set back a generation. Violence and criminality, always close to the surface here, move closer. One of us was told the other day upon leaving, "Remember us in your heart"—the implication being that no concrete help would be forthcoming.

It takes no expert to notice that their living conditions are becoming worse. Tents are ripping and burlap roofs rot. They see that they are being barely kept alive in a world that, apparently, has no place for them. The marginal diet which we administer is resented by them, and we are gravely concerned by talk of loathing it. Babies of a year and under do not receive the kinds of nourishment which might give them reserves of health for the winter. They appreciate the health services, and increasingly use the camp clinics. Clothing, never adequate by our standards, is a constant item requested by them of us, but unfortunately we have no stocks of clothing sufficient for a distribution to those in need. As they become colder and more hungry, **the refusal of the outside world to make decisions which could relieve their suffering creates more and more bitterness. Their hope for help is more pathetic because they cannot see who is [*sic*] their real friends. They feel that the bigger nations have created a situation which they are now abandoning in some part.**

Through you, we hope this interpretation may be brought to those whose duty it is to make the necessary rapid decisions, as well as in an indirect manner, before the conscience of the public. The refugee asks not for long range solutions, important as we know them to be, but for some practical token of justice and good will in the immediate future.

American Friends Service Committee
Gaza Unit
[Bold added for emphasis]

In Gaza during the summer of 1949, bundles of used clothing were distributed to families in a haphazard fashion. The color, style, and even the appropriate season of the clothing were a matter of luck. A respectable, bearded Arab man could be seen walking solemnly, wearing a shirt or a coat with the words "Brooklyn Dodgers," "Boston Red Sox," or "Washington Senators" on his back, or a young man wearing a woman's pink overcoat. It was outlandish, even comical, but nobody paid it much attention.

Meanwhile, al-Jurani fishermen started to ply the waters from Gaza to al-Arish and provide abundant supplies of fish to the market.

Refugees from al-Majdal, known for their distinctive textile industry, restarted their work. I saw, in the dusty streets of Khan Yunis, sticks fixed in the ground and rolls of weaving bundles strung over them for hundreds of meters, with no fear of damage or loss.

The people of al-Majdal continued their well-known textile tradition while in exile. Here, they spread their material along the streets of Khan Yunis without fear of damage or theft. (Photo by the author, ca 1951).

In subsequent summer holidays, I saw schooling improve. Instead of attending classes under trees, children went to a tent school with improvised desks. Due to the overcrowding, they took classes in shifts, in the mornings and afternoons, well into the summer. The thirst for education was insatiable. It was the only "territory" Palestinians could capture and hold, with no fear of conquest or occupation. In late afternoons, I saw boys pacing up and down the only asphalt road, learning their lessons. With no possible space in the tent, they had to do their homework in the open air. When darkness fell, they sat under the few lampposts lit by kerosene, finishing their homework. Without a blackboard, they solved algebra problems using soft stone as chalk, writing on the tarmac.

My relatives, Hazaa and Mahmoud, who were my companions in the Beersheba trek, became schoolteachers at the refugee schools. While we were sitting together in the evenings, they told me harrowing stories about children arriving hungry at school, fighting over a sandwich, or bartering it for an errand or a small job.

At first, teachers were paid in sacks of flour and cans of oil, by way of a salary. This was not enough, of course. One enterprising young teacher made sweets and would take trays of them to sell in the afternoons among the Gaza villages: Beni Suheila, Abasan, and Khiza'a.

One day he heard shouts. "Stop. Do not move." The local people were worried. "Are you crazy? Where are you going?" The young man was recklessly crossing the imaginary cease-fire line where Jews had planted a forest of mines.

He was a talented artist. He saved enough from his sweet-selling earnings to buy drawing paper, crayons, and pencils. He drew to get his feelings out on paper. His experiences in the Nakba and from his life as a refugee in Gaza provided an immense reservoir from which he could draw.

He was from Lydda, a survivor of the death march in which seventy thousand people, the inhabitants of Lydda, Ramleh, and neighboring villages, were expelled at gunpoint on orders by Yitzhak Rabin, chief of operations of the Israeli army, following a major massacre at Dahmash Mosque in Lydda.[45] Many died on this march and he and his family ended up in Khan Yunis. As the months went by, he and his cousin set up a photo shop on the main street, opposite the most popular coffee house.

My brother Ibrahim asked him to draw a portrait of my father. The young artist took a picture of my father, and my father sat for him several times until he had had enough. He finished his work from the photograph. The portrait now hangs in a prominent place in my drawing room. The signature and the date are clearly visible: "Shammout, 1950."

Ismail Shammout became *the* Palestinian painter. His work became the chronicle of the Nakba, the suffering of dispersion *(shatat)*, and the longing for return. His works hang in every Palestinian house, even in the shacks of the refugees around the world. A lifelong friend of my brothers and me, he was always true to the bond he maintained with his homeland, preserving that same air of humility and nobility of character.

Sheikh Hussein Abu Sitta, as painted by the foremost Palestinian painter, Ismail Shammout, in 1950, one of his earliest paintings.

Ismail Shammout (left), his wife Tamam al-Akhal, and me, on the occasion of restoring my father's portrait, painted by Ismail in 1950.

"We Shall Return." One of Ismail Shammout's earliest, most famous paintings of refugees.

At that time, *mukhtars* of the neighboring villages would visit my father's seat (which he had reestablished in Khan Yunis) to discuss our future, hanging on to hope and nothing else. No one could comprehend the dimensions of the tragedy.

Older men talked of the era of Ottoman rule by the Turks, when an oppressive governor would punish a whole village, and the men would disappear and hide in the mountains for a while. They talked about the flight of people evacuating their homes in the face of the advancing British soldiers for fear of the bombs that showered Gaza and Jaffa. When hostilities subsided, they all returned home. But this? Some felt there was no light at the end of the tunnel and perhaps no tunnel at all. On an almost monthly basis, Israelis raided the camps, killing and wounding people while they slept. It was no comfort to them that blue-eyed, blue-helmeted United Nations (UN) officers came, took notes and photographs, counted the dead, and then left. Nothing happened to ensure their safety, let alone to give them hope that justice was coming.

The inevitable happened: Palestinians turned to politics. Young men discussed what they should do. In this traditional society, it was natural to turn to Islam. The reputation of Muslim Brotherhood volunteers—brave, courageous, and dedicated—was cited as an inspiration. Although the Egyptian members of the Brotherhood had left Gaza, the presence of Palestinian members was noticeable. They held meetings and made speeches throughout the Gaza Strip.

Perhaps to give a new perspective, since I was coming from a high school in Cairo, I was invited by Khan Yunis High School to give a talk in 1951. I was fourteen at the time. The school hall, where the meeting was held, was packed. Nothing I said was new to the audience, but the oratory probably lifted their spirits:

> If you get thirsty, you will not find but the water of your homeland to quench your thirst. If you are hungry, only the goodness from your earth will feed you. If you get sick, only the fresh air of your homeland will cure you. If you have a longing, you will only satisfy it by walking on the soil of your homeland. If you despair, you will only find serenity and tranquillity in your home.
>
> Prepare for that day. The engine that will propel you to reach these objectives is but one word, one word alone: faith. Do not lose it.

I was encouraged to write articles for the newspaper, *Gaza*, a modest four-page bulletin aiming to fill the information gap in Gaza. One surviving article, published on 2 October 1956, one month before the Suez Campaign, referenced the refugees' suffering:

> The refugee receives nutrition equaling 1,600 calories a day, half the world standard. Is he expected to lie down and wait to die so as not to consume these precious calories? Tell me the name of a refugee whose rations are not consumed in the middle of the allotted period. But Palestine's Nakba is not alleviated by keeping the refugees on the edge of starvation. It is alleviated by one thing only: returning home. The western donors can then pack their rations and leave.

I spent the long summer months reading. With my small allowance, I bought books. That did not go far enough for me. I arrived at an arrangement with the owner of a second-hand bookshop that I would pay him all my allowance against borrowing books, reading, and returning them—a dream deal for me.

Over several summer holidays, I read Arabic translations of William Shakespeare, Victor Hugo, Leo Tolstoy, Jean-Jacques Rousseau, and others. I also read our great writers of Arab literature—Taha Hussein, Mustafa al-Rafi'i, Mustafa Lutfi al-Manfalouti, Abbas Mahmoud al-Aqqad, Ahmed Amin, and others.

I read the latest political books of the time with keen interest and curiosity. Sayyid Qutb and Khalid Muhammad Khalid charted a vision of Islamic rule. By contrast, the Arab Nationalist Movement was not as prominent as the emerging communist ideology. There was no lack of an Arab identity—which, if anything, was taken for granted—but it was not yet articulated in a political program. The Egyptian Revolution and the rise of Nasser dramatically changed this situation.

Sheikh Muhammad Awwad was a frequent guest at my father's seat and Abdullah's constant companion in the refugees' political activities. He was an energetic, patriotic man, imprisoned frequently by the British Mandate government for his patriotic activities. During the Mandate, he was stripped of his position as mayor of Faluja village (thirty kilometers northeast of Gaza city and the site of important battles in 1948 ended by the so called 'Faluja Pocket'), but was later reinstated.

He and the people of Faluja, as well as those of the neighboring village of Iraq al-Manshiya, were expelled in circumstances very different from those of the majority of the refugees.

Sheikh Awwad told us that after the Israeli attack on Beersheba and Gaza, and the Israeli foray into Sinai, the Israelis surrounded and outnumbered the Egyptian forces in Faluja. The villagers and the Egyptian soldiers, who came to save them, had to live together under Israeli siege. They shared flour, water, and the occasional chicken and eggs. The women baked bread daily and cooked whatever vegetables were available, all the while being bombarded by air and artillery, but refusing to surrender.

Nicknamed the Black Leopard on account of his Sudanese background, the commander of the Egyptian forces, Sayyid Taha, remained resolute in his decision not to back down. His next in command—a young officer by the name of Gamal Abd al-Nasser—stood at his side with the same resolve.

When the armistice agreement was signed on 24 February 1949, one of its conditions was that the people of Faluja and Iraq al-Manshiya villages stay in their homes, unharmed and unmolested. Israel assured the United Nations that it would guarantee the safety of their life and property; the assurance formed part of the agreement endorsed by the United Nations.

There was a tearful good-bye to the Egyptian soldiers, who withdrew with their weapons, from the villagers, while Cairo greeted them with a victorious reception, for their courage, refusal to surrender, and honorable withdrawal.

Of course, as experience would show, agreements, assurances, and the like, when given by Israel, are meaningless. In the following three to four weeks, Israel subjected the population of these two villages to curfews, harassment, looting, arbitrary shooting, and attempted rape. In the end, with no protection, the villagers were carted away to Gaza in trucks supervised by the Red Cross.

On 23 July 1952, not long after the armistice agreement and its betrayal, and while I was in Gaza for the usual summer holiday, King Farouk's corrupt regime was toppled by a group of army officers, known as the Free Officers, that included Gamal Abd al-Nasser. Nasser had quickly concluded that the source of the Egyptian defeat in Palestine was the corrupt and inept governing regime in Egypt. To fix this weakness, the regime, from the top down, was to be cleaned up. Egypt should not be ruled by a king but by the people.

A new era had begun, one which called for the Arab nation (from the Atlantic Ocean to the Arabian Gulf) to rise and be free from occupation and colonialism. Nationalist feelings and the common bond between Arabs gave rise to Arab nationalism. One speech by Nasser, at times of crises or war, could, and did, stop all supplies to ships of hostile countries at ports everywhere in the Arab world.

How strangely history works. Only thirty years earlier, thirty kilometers away, a similar scenario had unfolded. I recall my father's talk about the fall of Beersheba in October 1917 at the hands of British forces led by General Allenby. Esmet Bey, the Turkish garrison commander in Beersheba, fled on his horse at the last minute to avoid capture. He immediately contacted his friend and fellow officer, Mustafa, who commanded the Turkish garrison in Nablus.

Like Nasser three decades later, these two officers concluded that reform should start from their capitals, not in the outlying battlefields. Their military defeat wasn't from lack of courage, but due to an inept government system that needed to be changed.

These two officers, Mustafa Kamal, later named Atatürk, and his friend Esmet Inönü, brought about dramatic changes in Turkey. Turkey would no longer be ruled by a sultan; it would become a republic with a government elected by the people. Atatürk became the first president of the Republic of Turkey and Esmet Inönü the second.

In the mid-1980s, I told this story to friends of mine in Istanbul. They suggested I contact Inönü's son, who was then a physics professor at Ankara University. We exchanged correspondence and he sent me his father's memoirs about Beersheba. In his book, Inönü described the Beersheba battle. Unlike his German allies in Gaza, Inönü believed that the British would be able to sweep to the east to surprise the Beersheba garrison.

These two dramatic historical events in the twentieth century took place in Palestine, very near my home. We were distant witnesses to them and, indeed, victims of their results. Both were responses to the European colonial invasion of Palestine.

9

Crossing the Line to Return

No one ever questioned the idea of returning home. The refugees discussed only "when." Hope was a plentiful commodity and still is. In the house we rented in Khan Yunis in the summer of 1948, my father reestablished his seat, where family members and leading sheikhs and *mukhtars* would gather every night to discuss the developments of "the Palestine Question."

Every night, they would listen attentively to the news on the radio and discuss what was meant by the statements by Trygve Lie, the first secretary general of the United Nations. They hoped he would bring justice to Palestine. They were not aware that he was actively working against them.[46] They heard about the comings and goings of another group with a strange name: The United Nations Conciliation Commission for Palestine (UNCCP). This was part of the famous UN Resolution 194, which became the single most affirmed resolution in UN history. UNCCP was given the primary task of repatriating the refugees.

There would be much debate. One person would say, "That is it. The UN will do it. Didn't they say that in their decisions?"[47]

A voice from the end of the room would disagree, "No. I do not believe that. They are friends of the Jews. The Jews brought them *here*."

"Yes, that's right. Didn't you hear what the American ambassador in Cairo said: 'Israel is here to stay.' Yes, to stay in our homes and you will remain here, useless refugees."

We were fluctuating between hope and despair, and the subject of discussion never changed. In the corner of the room, I listened most nights as my brother Ibrahim, the lawyer, and my distant cousin Hussein Abu Hassan, the orator, added their sophisticated take on things.

During my early high-school years, as I decided to be a journalist, I spent most of the day listening to the radio. I wrote summaries of the news bulletins on a sheet that I hung in the *diwan*. When everyone assembled in the evening, I read out the news of the day. It would be this summary that launched conversation for that day.

Not everybody was satisfied with endless talking and lamenting our fate every night. Abdullah, the veteran fighter, was one who wanted action. He built a house at the entrance to Khan Yunis, to which we all moved later on. My father's *diwan* also moved to its palm-branch-covered roof. While my father received refugee *mukhtars*, notables from Khan Yunis, and others, Abdullah assembled his old fighting group and added new recruits. Finding recruits wasn't difficult. Many young people, now branded refugees and living on charity rations, were burning with the desire to be a part of a group taking action to kick out their homeland's occupier and return to their homes.

It was still relatively easy for them to cross the armistice line (as they knew where to go and what the risks were) and return to the home villages. The Israeli occupier had not yet digested the immense expanses of conquered land. Most areas, especially in the south, were very sparsely guarded; a few military posts, each thirty men strong, were erected at key locations on hills or at crossroads. These developed into kibbutzim, essentially military centers, although they claimed to be agricultural settlements. To compensate for the shortage of manpower, the Israelis planted mines at locations where they thought Palestinians would return: wells, grain stores, and houses that remained intact.

However, the refugees, unlike their new occupiers, knew every corner of their land; they knew shortcuts in the roads, where to hide, and when to move. The Israelis did not move at night but ran patrols during the day.

Refugees would go back for several reasons: to fetch an older relative who had been left behind in the heat of attack, to feed the cattle, to water the trees, to bring some food supplies to live on, and so on. Others went armed for the explicit purpose of defeating the invader. They had guts and a few arms, but completely lacked anything resembling a master plan. I noticed Abdullah disappearing most nights, driving his old jeep. Sometimes mysterious visitors would show up. One of them was Abd al-Mun'im Abd al-Ra'uf, one of the Free Officers headed by Gamal Abd al-Nasser who had led the coup against King Farouk in Egypt in 1952. He had split from Nasser's group and returned to Palestine to fight the conquerors. With his moustache and proud countenance, he reminded me of an Osmanli officer.

One night, unable to sleep, I got up and wandered around the house in the darkness, where I saw half a dozen figures with Abdullah. They had moved the parked jeep a few paces from the garage and removed a false floor with a pit dug underneath. They carried rifles and machine guns one by one, loaded them into the jeep, and disappeared into the night.

These men, who crossed the new border and defied the occupation of their land, were the fedayeen, risking and at times sacrificing their lives for their country and people. They went on nocturnal raids into the occupied land; some returned the following morning, and others hid for several days and operated at night. The secrecy of their operations was not primarily for security against enemy intelligence but for fear of the Egyptian authorities, who administered the Gaza Strip, getting wind of them. Both during King Farouk's regime and in the early years of Nasser's reign, the fedayeen, if caught, would be jailed.

A relative of mine, Hassan Madhi, whom I remember as full of life and hope, smiling as if he didn't have a care in the world, was a fedayee. A few younger members of the extended family took Hassan aside to a corner and asked him to tell us what it was like in al-Ma'in. He said our land was still empty. "They cut down your *karm* trees," he told us. "They tried to cut the cactus but it is still there at the north end. I saw them plowing our fields in the opposite direction to our way, probably to confuse us. They are building a new road."

Hassan Madhi told us how he had crept, one evening, so close to the Israeli soldiers, to below their window, that he heard them chatting. He kept silent until they slept. He attacked them with grenades. In the confusion, he collected their identity cards and other objects to show proof of the raid. Hassan Madhi said they were better organized than we were and that they compensated for their loose hold on the land with an efficient wireless communication system so they could call for help.

"If we attack multiple locations at the same time, they cannot cope," he explained.

We asked him if they ever found themselves cornered or surrounded, and he went on that they were, many times:

"We soon learned that the Jews would rush to obstruct our return to the Gaza Strip. So, instead, we advanced in the opposite direction, deep into the occupied territory. We hid during the day and resumed operations the following night. If that plan was too dangerous, we headed farther and farther east until we reached al-Khalil [Hebron]," he explained.

"I told you, our land is empty," he continued. "On Sheikh Hussein's land, they built a prefabricated cluster of houses, and called it Nirim [the old name of Dangur colony, later called Nir Yitzhaq]." Hassan turned to my brother Mousa, the agriculturist. "They cut all the trees on your farm down. They stripped the motor in your *bayyara* and took it away."

Abu Gheith, our cousin, was with us, listening attentively, and asked, "What about our land at Sheikh Nuran?"

"They installed an observation post on the hill and erected a few shacks around it. Otherwise, everything is the same as you left it, including the debris and ashes of our houses."

On one of his trips, Hassan stepped on a mine and died. We lost fifteen martyrs from my family alone in the early 1950s.

The four kibbutzim built on our land were Nirim, Nir Oz, Ein Hashlosha, and Magen. Far from being agricultural settlements, they became the staging points for Israeli attacks on the Gaza Strip. From these alleged agricultural settlements, Israelis killed thirty-eight Egyptian soldiers in their barracks at the Gaza railway station in February 1955. From there too, Ariel Sharon, the commander of the notorious Unit 101,[48] proceeded to Khan Yunis in August 1955 to demolish its police station and kill seventy-two Palestinians.

***

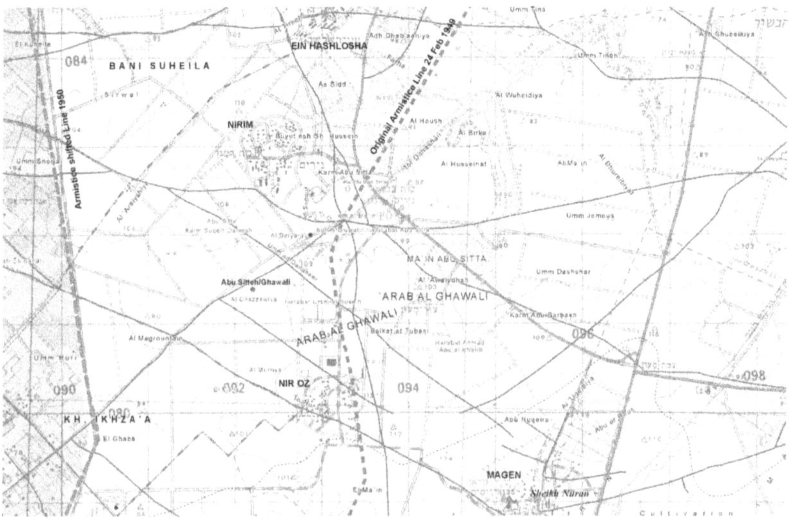

Map of Ma'in Abu Sitta, after 1948, with original place names and roads. Occupiers of the land: 1,000 settlers, in 4 kibbutzim, Nirim, Ein Hashlosha, Nir Oz, Magen.

The imaginary line separating us from the enemy on our land was blurry during the 1950s. During my research many years later, I looked at the armistice agreement, signed between Israel and Egypt on 24 February 1949, and compared it with the current maps showing the Gaza Strip boundary. The current line is two to three kilometers deeper into Gaza, reducing an already small area. I was puzzled. I spoke to an elderly man, the *mukhtar* of Abasan, Hajj Muhammad Abu Daqqa, whose land was on the armistice line.[49] "Yes, the Israelis moved the line. And I fought them with my neighbor al-Najjar, the *mukhtar* of Khiza'a."

Abu Daqqa was a grand old man, born before the First World War. He was rich with plenty of land and children. When the Egyptians came, he made many friends among them, in particular Mahmoud Riyadh (who was to become foreign minister under Nasser) and Salah Johar, members of the Mixed Armistice Committee. He told me that one day he saw UN jeeps and Egyptian and Israeli officers demarcating the armistice line on the ground. Neither the Egyptians nor the Israelis were interested in protecting our land, he insisted. The people in the villages of Abasan and Khiza'a came out in force, screaming, shouting, and yelling, shooing them away. They pushed them east to the edges of the village's land.

In the 1990s, I sent a relative to get the testimony of Khiza'a's *mukhtar* on that incident. He confirmed Abu Daqqa's account. As was the case with so many stories, typical of Israeli deception and coercion, further confirmation came from the Israeli archives themselves: an Israeli photographer had taken pictures of the incident.[50] The Israeli negotiator in the picture was Abraham Shakarczr, a kibbutznik from Mashabbah (or Be'eri) colony. Shakarczr is another name to remember.

The official armistice agreement limited the Israeli presence to one platoon in al-Ma'in's center. It also stipulated that the line ran about one kilometer east of Nirim (at al-Shawwal's shop in central al-Ma'in) and passed through Tell Jemmeh and Wadi al-Hesi until it met the Mediterranean. Thus, the area of the Gaza Strip was 555 square kilometers in 1949. So how then did it shrink to 365 square kilometers by 1950?

The Israelis found plenty of underground water at Wadi al-Hesi in the north end of the Strip and planned to take it. They convinced the Egyptian officers—by means that are unclear and fraught with rumors—that frequent border incidents required setting up a temporary line, as a buffer zone, until things cooled down. A secret agreement between Egypt and Israel (made in February 1950, one year after the original armistice agreement of 24 February 1949), unknown to the Egyptian and Palestinian peoples and named "Modus Vivendi," was signed in al-Auja Hafir, to move the line two to three kilometers to the west "on a temporary basis." The temporary line became permanent, complete with electrified barbed wire and physical and electronic observation systems.

The first attempt at demarcating the armistice line started in 1950. The armistice agreement stipulated clearly that the line does not confer or grant rights to any party. It was a temporary line aimed at stopping the fighting. For the people, the line was a vague notion established by the United Nations. For the Israelis, it was very important as a measure of the land they had conquered and now claimed as their own, and thus, they wanted to demarcate the line permanently—to establish it as a fact on the ground. The Suez Campaign (known also as the Tripartite Aggression, in which Israel colluded with Britain and France to attack Egypt and topple Nasser) was a manifestation of their intention to transform the armistice line into Israel's borders. Israel would then be able to attack Palestinians who were crossing the line under the pretext of retaliation. In turn, the Palestinians would not be able to cross the line in the opposite direction to return to their homes.

For their part, Palestinians, undeterred by Israeli mines and the threat of sudden death, kept returning to their homes. "Why am I barred from my home by a fictitious line created by foreigners?" they kept asking. Whether the line was marked on paper or by barrels (as it was), it did not mean much to the people of the land. How could it tell them that their life experience was a mirage or that the stories of their fathers and forefathers about how they had lived and died on this soil were mere delusions?

Where was this line anyway? Nobody knew where it was. It kept moving, reducing the Gaza Strip each time. At first, it was marked by the presence of blue-helmeted Danish and Colombian United Nations truce observers. Then it was marked by empty barrels that could be kicked away. Then it was marked by a ditch plowed by an Israeli tractor. And today it has become an electrified wire with sensors, monitored by patrols along a military road.

This armistice line meant nothing to my maternal uncle, Mahmoud. I remember him clearly as the kindest of my uncles. When my mother took me to visit her family, he always gave me more than my share of his time. I recall his longish face and unkempt beard; he had a smile like sunshine. He made faces and imitated animal sounds to make me laugh or wonder in surprise, and would bring me bunches of grapes or figs from his farm. He tended trees in his *karm* with delight and devotion, as if they were his own children. He had a round growth on his forehead and used to let me play with it with patience. When I returned in the summer holiday of 1950, I said I wanted to visit him. There was silence. I was then told the painful story of his last days. He continued to tend his trees as usual. When told that the armistice line passed through the middle of his *karm* and that he should abandon it altogether, he responded,

"To those Jews out there? This has been my *karm* before we ever heard of them!"

He kept going every morning and returning in the evening. One evening, he was late. As the night wore on, his sons and relatives were worried. In the morning, they set out to search for him, but Jewish jeeps with their mounted machine guns were too close for comfort.

By the late afternoon, they crept into the *karm* and found him under one of the trees, tools by his side, his body pierced by several bullets. He had been shot mercilessly by Jewish soldiers—an old, unarmed farmer, whom they saw as an infiltrator.

The irony must have escaped the UN truce observers who reported such killings. They were not aware, or did not care, that the killer, a Romanian or Hungarian Jew who set up a house on our land, was the real infiltrator.

Many families were struck by similar tragedies. There was hardly a single family that did not send one of its members back home to fetch or tend to something. In the summer of 1949, the inhabitants of the Palestinian villages near the virtual armistice line were hit by a particularly ugly tragedy, for which they exacted a corresponding revenge.

Two brothers and their teenage sister took off to fetch some of their supplies from their land east of Sheikh Nuran. On their way back, an Israeli patrol intercepted them. The Israelis killed one young man, the other fled, and they held the girl captive.

The returning young man told the village people that his brother had been killed but that the girl had been captured alive. This crime was beyond considering any compromise; a swift revenge had to be exacted. A dozen young men went to the occupied land and killed any Israeli soldier who came in sight. I do not know how many were able to return safely. I am sure the vengeance would have been even more severe had the victim's family known what actually happened to their daughter.[51]

In the early 1950s, Israelis became bolder in dealing with the returning refugees. They were not satisfied with shooting and killing returnees, with their take-no-prisoners doctrine. They started to cross the line into Gaza to attack refugees in their camps, not only with air raids, but also with tanks and machine guns.

It seemed Israelis preferred summer for their raids and wars, perhaps because of clearer skies and drier roads. Although I spent every school year in Cairo, I was able to see during the summer, or at least hear firsthand, much of Israel's war against the refugee camps.

My mother's family found refuge in the central refugee camps of al-Bureij, Nuseirat, and Maghazi. At the end of August 1953, as I was preparing to return to school, terrible news came from al-Bureij camp. The Israelis had attacked the camp, a few hundred meters from the armistice line, and had blown up refugees' homes while they were sleeping, killing at least seven women, five children, and thirty-one men, and wounding twenty-two others.[52]

My mother's sister, terrified, came to stay with us for a few days—not that Khan Yunis was more secure. But there was comfort in being together with the family, something she desperately needed. Almost two years later to the day, in August 1955, I witnessed an even more devastating Israeli attack, this time on Khan Yunis.

As I was settling down for the night, I heard shooting. The shooting was not strange in itself, but its intensity increased and the sounds changed into a variety of sharper sounds and heavy thuds. They were very close, coming from the direction of the Khan Yunis police station. The station was about two hundred meters away from our house, separated by a thin line of trees. Gunfire and bombs lit up the sky. We cowered beside the nearest wall. Women started sobbing—softly, for fear of being heard—and in fear of terrible news to come.

"It's the police station. It's been blown up," someone shouted.

In the flash of bullets and bombs, I could see behind the trees the smoke and dust rising, billowing into the dark sky. If they reached us, we would be finished. Did they know Abdullah's house? If they did, his family, children, my parents, other relatives in the house, and I would all be gone.

The fear of the next bomb gripped us. I heard my mother reciting the Quran in a low voice. I felt a strange kind of serenity, completely detached from reality. I wondered whether I would see my school again. It was due to reopen in two weeks. I do not know how long the attack lasted. It must have been several hours, but it felt like an eternity. When the shelling subsided, there was an eerie silence. No one felt safe.

"Have the Jews withdrawn?" No one was sure. Perhaps they were hiding somewhere, or perhaps they had laid mines everywhere. With the early rays of the morning sun, people wandered out of their homes to see what had happened.

The majestic police station, commanding the entrance to Khan Yunis, was a pile of rubble. People looked for their relatives. They found many bodies buried under the rubble. The sounds of wailing women looking for their brothers and husbands were mixed with cries for help. There was no serious medical aid, no ambulances; nothing except the traditional gathering together at a time of crisis.

Seventy-two bodies were buried. Others survived to tell the story. One of them was my cousin Hassan, the wireless operator.[53] His grief over losing his friends and comrades was great. They were policemen whose job was to keep law and order. With their rifles and a mere five bullets each, they could not repulse an army with tanks, explosives, and machine guns. They were Palestinian policemen keeping law and order under an Egyptian officer from the Egyptian administration for the Strip.

Days later, I packed my bag and returned to school in Cairo, but my heart and mind remained in Palestine.

Efforts by Abdullah and others to fight the occupier were not limited to armed resistance. In 1953, he and the leading personalities of the southern villages in Palestine held the first conference for the refugees in Gaza. Their demand was clear and simple: "We want to return home. We do not want your [UN] food and shelter."

Abdullah was elected general secretary of the Executive Committee of the Refugees' Conference. The committee was tolerated by King Farouk's regime and then encouraged by Nasser. The members of the committee met Nasser several times and participated in many international conferences. I still have post cards from Abdullah with various stamps from Asia and Africa.

The Asia–Africa Conference in Bandung, Indonesia held in 1955, from which the Non-Aligned Movement grew, was attended by delegates representing two-thirds of the world's population. The conference aimed to enhance goodwill and cooperation among Asian and African nations, to affirm national sovereignty, and to reject racism and colonialism. The stars of the conference were Chou En-lai of China, Jawaharlal Nehru of India, Josip Tito of Yugoslavia, and Gamal Abd al-Nasser of Egypt. The conference was a tremendous boost to the morale of oppressed people all over the world.

With the rise of Nasser's stature in the Non-Aligned Movement (formally founded in 1961), we received many distinguished visitors in Gaza. Nasser wanted to show the non-aligned world, which had just shaken off the yoke of colonialism, the new colonial project being planted in Palestine. Old family pictures show Abdullah with other Gaza notables receiving Che Guevara at a refugee camp, while another depicts Ibrahim receiving Jawaharlal Nehru.

Nasser's Stature in the non-aligned countries brought world leaders to Gaza. Top: Jawaharlal Nehru (left) and Che Guevara (right) meeting Gaza leaders including Abdullah and Ibrahim; middle: Gaza delegation visiting Nasser; bottom: Muhammad Naguib, first president of Egypt, visiting us in Khan Yunis.

To his credit, Nasser arranged for the first Palestinian refugees' delegation to attend the UN General Assembly session in 1961. This may sound quite ordinary now, but at the time, the Zionists had not only stolen Palestine, but had managed to erase the name Palestine altogether. We were simply "Arab refugees."

Schemes were floated to transfer the refugees from crowded Gaza, the last spot in Palestine. One of them was a joint UN (represented by United Nations Relief and Work Agency, UNRWA) and Egyptian government project in 1955,[54] that planned to settle them in the northwest Sinai desert. They saw this as completing their ethnic cleansing under the cover of a peace proposal. The Refugees' Committee and active political groups led the refugees in a large-scale demonstration, which included burning the UNRWA supply stores that fed them. Their only demand was to return home. Many arrests were made by the Egyptian authorities. One of those arrested was the famous Palestinian poet Muin Bseiso who spent eight years in an Egyptian jail in the Western Desert and wrote poems which later became popular songs.

The Gaza Strip was vibrant with political movements, especially in the second half of the 1950s. Secret societies of all shapes and colors formed: communists, Muslim Brothers, Arab nationalists, and others. Most of these movements found a voice in the first Palestinian Legislative Council, elected in 1961 in Gaza, again with the support of Nasser. All of these political movements joined the Palestine Liberation Organization (PLO) and its Palestine National Council (PNC), established in Jerusalem in 1964.

Refugees in the West Bank did not enjoy such freedom. They were absorbed into the expanded Hashemite Kingdom of Jordan. The Jordanian regime harshly suppressed any political movement by the refugees to claim back their homes in Palestine, although official media trumpeted adherence to the "sacred Arab rights" in Palestine.

10

Egyptian Days

By the end of 1948, my father faced the painful realization that the war would continue for longer than expected. I had lost almost half a school year and my father wanted me to complete my primary education as soon as possible. He had sent Hajj Abdullah's son to fetch me from al-Arish, where I was, after my escape from the Khan Yunis air raids with my sister in October 1948.

I was eleven years old at that time, and he decided to put me in the care of the family of Muhammad Saleem Abu Tama'a, a friend of his and an *umda*, head or mayor of a village or clan. Abu Tama'a was one of the Egyptian sheikhs with whose family we had had relations since long before the Suez Canal was opened.

My father and I went to his house, a comfortable villa at the edge of Helwan, a small upscale suburb of Cairo. Abu Tama'a welcomed my father warmly and assured him that his young son would get all the care and attention possible. After a tearful good-bye, I let go of my father, assuring him I knew how to look after myself.

There was a train that went from Bab al-Luq (in central Cairo) to Helwan, with day-trippers occasionally filling the train cars for the short half-hour ride. Helwan was on the edge of the desert; it was renowned for its clean, fresh air, to the extent that even a tuberculosis sanatorium was built there. Its natural underground spring also attracted many visitors for its health benefits. It was not crowded; its streets were straight and usually empty, and its houses were small villas, pleasant but not ostentatious.

At the home of Abu Tama'a, the head of the family had a special entrance, leading to the guest-reception room and his personal quarters. The rest of the family entered from a back door, leading to a large central hall, with bedrooms on either side and the kitchen and bathrooms in the back.

The family had three boys and one girl. I never saw the eldest son, Helliel. I was told he was studying law at the Sorbonne. It was most unusual for men of means to send their sons to France at that time, and Abu Tama'a's stature in his locality did not require this added prestige. The mother, Umm Helliel, was a very kind woman. She hugged me and told me that I was like her son.

I felt, in spite of the warm welcome, that there was an air of sadness in the house. I slowly found the reason for this sorrow. The eldest son, their pride and joy, had died in Paris. I did not know how or when, and nobody wanted to speak about it.

The daughter, in her late teens, was well groomed and ready to get married. She was attractive and took a lot of time over her looks, constantly combing her hair, changing dresses, or putting on different kinds of jewelry. She was waiting for the day when an Arab knight in shining armor would plead to her father to give him her hand in marriage.

Muhammad was my age or a little older but much bigger and taller. We shared a room with a bed and desk each. Muhammad was friendly but did not know what to make of this stranger. He kept busy playing football in the street after school. The third son was a toddler.

I was registered in Muhammad's school, Helwan Primary. When we returned from school, we would have a meal, and then I'd start my homework. One afternoon Umm Helliel put her head in the room and saw me studying. "Where is Muhammad?" she asked me.

"I think he is out."

Muhammad returned, sweaty and dirty after a game of street football. His mother was waiting. She scolded him for being lazy and careless, among other things. Then she pointed to me, and said, "Look at this poor boy, after a long arduous journey to get here, while his family are far away, and the Jews attacking them and burning down their houses, he sits here studying."

He promised her, yet again, to finish his homework. When she turned her back, he looked at me angrily: "Where the hell did you spring up from?" In spite of these words, Muhammad did not bear a grudge and we would go for walks and play together. All was fine as long as the subject of study did not come up.

In the evenings, Umm Helliel would sit and sip her cup of tea in the hall. This poor woman, who surely did not need more sadness to contend with, would ask me how it was in Palestine, where my mother and sisters were, and she wondered aloud how worried my mother must have been about me in a new country. "Safe, yes, but will he eat and sleep well?" she asked herself on my mother's behalf. I told her about the long trek from the boarding school to my home, the attack on al-Ma'in, the bombs from the sky, and the long walk along the Sinai coast. Occasionally, gentle tears streaming down her cheeks accompanied my words.

School was not a problem for me. The courses, especially English, with which I was already familiar, were a breeze. What gave me some trouble were the Egyptian courses in the history of the pharaohs and the geography of Africa, all of which was totally new to me. In the classroom, I would always be the first to raise my hand to answer the teacher's question.

The pupils in this small suburban school did not know, or care to know, much about Palestine. They knew I was different because of some tragedy out there in Palestine and my accent was a constant reminder to them of my outsider status.

In spite of the kindness and care of the family I stayed with, I felt homesick. Before I slept, I thought of my mother and my sisters. My brothers, though, were nearby, at university in Cairo, and my brother Mousa sometimes visited me on Thursday afternoons. When he knocked on the door, I rushed to meet him. We would walk in the streets nearby, and I'd ask him about everybody and everything. When he said good-bye, I tried to make even the farewell last as long as possible. As he headed for the station, I would sneak behind him, walking slowly. When he discovered me trailing him, he shooed me away on the promise he would return next week.

The Primary Education Certificate was a big thing in Egypt, especially for the majority whose schooling would end there. Only a few went on to a secondary school, and even fewer went to university. When I look back at a group picture taken at the end of the year, I see faces that became prominent in Egyptian life, such as the famous writer, Mahmoud Fahmi Howeidi.[55]

I obtained the coveted certificate, complete with ornamental frame and distinctive calligraphy. Though I did not rank first as I had in my previous years, I did rank 243 out of 11,974. Not bad for a homesick child in a three-month-long school year.

I said good-bye to my life in Helwan in September 1949, when I started at Saidiya Secondary School in Cairo. I moved to live with my brothers and it was a great feeling to be among the older boys in the school, some with moustaches, although I still wore short trousers. My brothers chose this school for me. Adjacent to the university campus, its buildings were indistinguishable from it. Saidiya was a prestigious school, built in 1908, the same year Fouad I University was established.

The school was more like an English public school, meaning private school. It had three main buildings for classes. The cream-colored walls and late nineteenth-century European architecture were impressive. The school had many other facilities not usually found in schools: a proper theater, a gymnasium, a prayer hall, and a full-fledged sports fields with tennis courts and running tracks. The school had a nice library, rarely visited by most students. It had green-covered tables, where Amm Abdu (Uncle Abdu) served tea and petits fours every day at 5:00 p.m. Judging by his waistline, it seemed he was the main beneficiary of the afternoon tea.

Its headmaster, who had been a colonial Englishman in the early days of the school, was addressed using the honorific title "Bey," and he lived in a villa on the grounds.

In the main hall, next to the offices of the headmaster and his deputies, there was an honors list of the names of Saidiya students who ranked in the top ten in the general final secondary-education examinations in Egypt. Many of these alumni figured prominently in Egyptian political, cultural, and financial life. Trophies, cups, and medals hung on the walls. As I went up and down the stairs in my first weeks, I marveled at this history, although soon, like the other students, I stopped noticing them.

My adjustment to the school was not smooth, but it was much less difficult than at Helwan. My accent was unmistakably Palestinian, but by then, I could converse in a passable Egyptian dialect. Plus, non-Egyptian students were not a total novelty at this school; there were the children of diplomats and political refugees from Arab

Me outside Saidiya School in 1953. The hall in the background housed trophies, prizes, and the honor list for top-ranking students in the general certificates of education.

countries colonized by Britain and France. One prominent leader, whose children were my classmates, was Muhammad ibn Abd al-Karim al-Khattabi, a Moroccan nationalist leader who fought a combined French and Spanish army and was then forced to seek refuge in Egypt.

The school's small class sizes, good teachers, and well-equipped laboratories enabled educational excellence. Three teachers stood out. First was my French teacher, a young Frenchman afflicted with a constant cold. Then there was my English teacher, an Egyptian, heavy at the waist with a tarboosh (fez) that sat slightly tilted on his head. His English pronunciation caused me great discomfort, since I came from Palestinian schools where we were taught English by British-educated teachers.

Our Arabic teacher was a gem and I was very enthusiastic in his classes, using the composition assignments to assert my growing sense of self. He was pleased with my enthusiasm and I learned from his gentle reasoning.

The students were generally too young to know about or be interested in Palestine. There was one student who was different: Mustafa Nabil was inquisitive and confident for his age. From time to time, he would ask me about Palestine, how it was there, and what brought me to Cairo. During breaks, we would chat about Palestine and he showed great interest in what I had to say. Mustafa Nabil came from a well-to-do family. His father was an engineer, a construction contractor, and they lived in a nice villa. Mustafa was far from typical for his family. His inquisitive mind led him to become something of a revolutionary.

We started to spend a lot of time together, reading, arguing, and debating. He invited me to his house. His mother was very welcoming. Like Umm Helliel, she genuinely cared for me, this refugee boy from Palestine who had traveled alone to study in Cairo without his parents. Mustafa was very independent and so his family gave him a room with a door that opened directly onto the street, allowing his many and diverse friends to come and go with ease.

My brothers and I lived in Manial in a sixth-floor apartment in the Eshmawi building, overlooking one branch of the Nile, and each of us had our own room. Suleiman was studying medicine, Mousa was studying agriculture, Ali was studying mechanical engineering, and I was in my first year of secondary school. Our rooms were sparsely furnished, with only a bed and a desk. The hall served many purposes: a dining room, a sitting room, and an extra studying space. The ornamental orange-and-black sofa and chairs survived ten years of use.

The bathroom was equipped with a large, tall, Primus pot for heating water and a large flat dish you sat in to bathe. Taking a bath was a ritual that took a lot of preparation. There were several foot-long loofahs for scrubbing. My brother Mousa inspected me before and after the bath to make sure that my neck and ears were clean.

We went to our respective schools in the morning and returned at odd times in the afternoon to have lunch and study. The constant occupant of the apartment was Abdu Khattab, the cook. He was a jolly man and sang while he worked. I remember his Hitler-style moustache and his smooth hair, also combed Hitler style. Perhaps it is a bizarre comparison given that I do not think he even knew who Hitler was.

Every morning I walked along the Nile, crossed Abbas Bridge, and then followed the other bank of the Nile until I reached the school. It was a good four kilometers, but I did not mind. It was a nice walk. Sometimes fellow students joined me on the way.

A Palestinian family, refugees from Jerusalem, moved to the apartment below. Unlike us, they were a complete family: parents, a son, and five lovely daughters. Romance was bound to blossom. I caught one of my brothers whispering to his lovely neighbor directly below in her balcony. and realized why he had maneuvered to get this particular room.

The romance was totally innocent, with a smile here, a word there, perhaps a letter. One of my brothers became interested in another of our neighbors, a young Egyptian. They found a meeting place on the roof where they hung the washing and hid behind the clothes. I was reading there one time and saw them, but they did not see me.

A row erupted between my two brothers when one of them saw the other sitting in the local cinema close to this young woman, a few chairs away from her, obviously by prior arrangement. The argument broke out about this "compromising" situation when we were meant to be struggling hard for a good education, while our country was in ruins. Socializing with a young woman, however innocent, was considered tasteless under the circumstances.

Indeed, we were struggling. My father had put four sons in university before the Nakba, when higher education in Palestine was very limited. It was so limited that the most prestigious college in Palestine, the Arab College in Jerusalem, had a graduating class with the matriculation certificate earned by only about thirty to forty students each year. My eldest brother, Ibrahim, graduated from Cairo (then Fouad I) University in 1946 as a lawyer. When the Nakba struck, three brothers were still at university, two or three years away from graduation. And I was yet to be added to the list.

While in Palestine, my father managed to pay the costs of his children's education from the proceeds of his land. Now that the land had gone, he had no resources left. It was very hard for him to face this situation; he felt helpless. A man who pioneered education in our family and the region, who invested in education while others invested in land and business, was distressed to see his project in jeopardy, but if anything, this tragedy confirmed that he was right: when the land had gone, education was an asset that could not be lost or stolen.

During one of his visits to see us, a small team from the Arab League came to register students for possible financial assistance. We and the League's social worker sat around the dining table, and my brothers filled in forms about the cost of our food, rent, any money we had, and any money we expected to receive. My father was sitting behind them in the main chair and I was opposite him, watching the exchange. When the discussion went into the details, I saw my father, this grand man, had moist eyes. He left the room. I had never seen him like that.

As a boy away from my parents, I sometimes received special treatment. I was invited to spend weekends with Salama Salem's family. They were friends of ours who invited my brothers for Friday lunch frequently, but I was the one who spent weekends with them.

The origin of Salama Salem was obscure. People said that, as a young man, drifted from Beersheba across Sinai to Egypt, where he struck good luck by buying scrap metal from the British Army in Ismailiya and selling it during the Second World War. He had a black car (it was a Dodge, I think), which was polished daily and parked in a garage a hundred meters from his home. He had a two-room office in Suleiman Pasha Street, the prestigious commercial street in downtown Cairo. He sat behind a big desk with a nameplate prominently displayed for all guests to see: "Salama Salem, Commission Agent." As if they did not know who he was.

Of all my brothers, I knew best how he and his wife lived at their home. They lived in al-Dhaher quarter, a middle-class neighborhood, home to many Egyptian Jews. His wife, Hajja Amina, a plump, short woman, was compassion itself. The couple was childless. Hajja Amina smothered me with attention: eat this, eat that, and more of this. She showed me old photographs of my family, showing our long friendship, and explained the origins of various souvenirs on the wall.

Their apartment was very small. It had a tiny kitchen, a dining room where we usually sat, a central room filled with objects, a guest (reception) room, which was never opened, and a bedroom. A huge four-poster bed made of brass, with a mosquito net hanging from its four corners, took up most of the bedroom. The bed was so high that a step was positioned below to climb up onto it.

On Friday mornings, Hajja Amina prepared our fresh breakfast: hot bread, *fuul medammes*, and tea. She lowered her basket from the tiny balcony to purchase the *fuul* from the vendor's cart below. They all knew each other. Housewives shouted their orders and lowered their baskets with the money, and up came the order and the change.

The visits were fun, filled with delicious food and heaps of kindness. But there was also a fear that permeated the whole weekend. I would sigh with relief when I left. The building was very old and each step of the worn-out stairs was just big enough to place a foot in. The stairs shook with every step. At every floor, I was terrified that we would not reach the next. Years later, when I read in the newspaper that a building had collapsed in that area, I always thought it might have been theirs. Luckily, the couple did not see it happen in their lifetime.

The other terrible fear I had revolved around the sleeping arrangements. There was no place for me to sleep, so they let me sleep between them. On Hajja Amina's side, there was peace and quiet. On Salama's side, there was a nightmare. He was a big, fat man. When he lay on the bed, I could not see beyond his fat, round belly. He snored in short bursts like a machine gun, and then he fell silent for a few seconds. At that moment I thought he was dead and that I was sleeping next to a corpse. But moments later, he roared again with a huge burst of air, followed by his machine-gun snoring.

The morning washed away the fear, when Hajja Amina, with her cheerful "good morning" and her breakfast basket, brightly ended my sleepless night.

The ritual of my return to Cairo at the end of summer holidays in Gaza illustrated how certain traditions and social customs were faithfully followed. Saying good-bye to a pilgrim to Mecca was a big event in which well-wishers for a safe journey visited the family of the pilgrim. A journey to Cairo in the early 1950s for year-long schooling was second best. Heads of families came to visit my father the night before, wishing me a safe journey and a victorious return with a certificate of education. The train would arrive early in the morning for the day-long journey to Cairo. Young men from the family did their part by seeing me off at the platform, coming to say good-bye in person, and carrying my bag to my seat.

My mother had her own way of welcoming me and saying good-bye. On my arrival, after inspecting my health, she would ask how long my holiday would last. I would tell her to enjoy my being back, rather than counting the days that I would spend during the summer with her. I was the youngest and thus the focus of her maternal affection. On the night of my departure, she repeated the same old advice to take care and recited, "How many gazelles will be grazing between us tomorrow?"—an expression she inherited from the old days to describe the growing distance between us. I would tear myself away and head for the station.

I waved good-bye to the young men who had carried my bag and seen me off. As the train moved, I watched the smoke rising from the houses announcing the start of the day and empty streets with nobody yet walking about. A little later, I saw a solitary figure in black walking toward the railway line and waving aimlessly at the train windows. I knew that she was my mother, and I waved back vigorously to acknowledge her and shouted, "Ma'a es-salama! Goodbye!" over the roar of the engine.

This ritual was repeated for every student's trip, but with time, as travel became less of a novelty, the young men who came to see me off were fewer. But my mother's ritual of waving at the train lasted much longer, until her legs were not strong enough to make the early-morning trip.

When I returned to school at the end of the summer holiday in 1952, I found a different mood in Cairo. A revolution had been proclaimed. King Farouk and his dynasty were gone. A new Egypt had been born. Young people were jubilant. Older people were not sure of the future. My friend Mustafa Nabil and I were hopeful of a better future. We recalled the Nakba, which was attributed in Egypt to the faulty and unsafe weapons purchased by Farouk's entourage. We hoped for a quick liberation of Palestine.

None of us expected the revolution so soon, although there were early signs of discontent. The previous January, I saw the charred buildings in Cairo's commercial district after a mysterious fire gutted them. I knew this area very well. When my father visited us, I accompanied him on his regular visits to the café, opposite a statue of Ibrahim Pasha, Syria's conqueror, sitting grandly on his horse. My father would sit at the marble-covered table at the café, order his coffee, and read the popular *al-Ahram* newspaper. Palestinian émigrés and refugees would congregate and discuss the cloudy future of Palestine. The émigrés included the writer Kamel al-Sawafiri, the colorful journalist and activist; Muhammad Ali al-Taher, a distinguished Palestinian; and Muhammad Abu Reida, professor of Islamic philosophy. They were part of the throng of stranded Palestinian refugees in Cairo.

More than once I accompanied my father when he visited the Palestinian leader, Hajj Amin al-Husseini, in his temporary residence in Heliopolis. My father had been loyal to Hajj Amin's political program since the early 1920s. I did not follow their conversation closely, but I was struck by Hajj Amin's countenance. He was handsome, soft-spoken, and aristocratic in his demeanor. He appeared careful and firm with his words.

With Nasser's revolution in July 1952, nobody was more optimistic than the Palestinians. The expectations were as high as the certainty of the justice of our cause. Many flocked to Cairo from Gaza. Faluja's mayor, Sheikh Muhammad Awwad, and a delegation from the village (where he was under siege by the Israeli army in Faluja Pocket) went to see Nasser, who warmly welcomed them. Scores of delegations led by young Palestinians, including Abdullah and Ibrahim, made regular visits to Nasser and the Egyptian leadership. One year after the revolution, Muhammad Naguib, the nominal leader of the revolution, also visited us at our rented home in Khan Yunis.

My school had its share of celebrations too. Traditionally, it celebrated its achievements annually on Saidiya Graduates Day. It was a big affair, held in its football stadium and attended by graduates who held prominent positions in government and society.

On the first anniversary celebration after the 1952 revolution, the headmaster asked me to deliver the students' speech. The guest of honor was one of the Free Officers, Kamal al-Din Hussein, as I recall. Choosing me to deliver the speech was a bit odd. This was an Egyptian celebration in an Egyptian school for an Egyptian revolution, and I was Palestinian.

My speech followed the usual line of condemning the evils of King Farouk and Muhammad Ali's dynasty. But I also could not ignore Palestine. I struggled with the right words, primarily not to upset or embarrass the headmaster. I concluded my speech by saying that the revolution was good for Egypt *and* Palestine, as the army now was ready to clean up Egypt and liberate Palestine. The guest of honor came forward, shook my hand, and even took my notes.

On typical days, I finished my homework quickly and still had much energy left to spend on extracurricular activities. I started publishing a class newspaper. It contained articles, news, jokes, and anecdotes. It even had graphics to separate the articles. No student in my class could miss it, as I hung the articles on the wall of the classroom next to the door. Despite this, I admit that I was its main reader. Very few students, apart from some curious ones, looked at it. The class teacher praised it, which encouraged me to issue the paper every two weeks. The publishing medium was glossy toilet-paper rolls lined side by side. The glossy quality was cumbersome for the written text but was very convenient for water-color graphics.

One day, I came across an advertisement from the Egyptian College of Journalism, an outfit housed in a small decrepit building. The ad promised to award a diploma of journalism by correspondence for a small fee. A small fee was all I could afford. After several lessons and journalistic assignments by post and one or two visits to the college, I received the diploma of journalism in my second year of high school.

This interest in journalism continued, and I managed to fit it in around my schoolwork so as not to damage my grades. I took over the school's radio station (which consisted of one microphone and a loudspeaker), where I broadcast news and held interviews during breaks. I gained both popularity and mild criticism, from jealous classmates. The biggest disadvantage as far as I was concerned was not having enough time to eat my sandwich during break. During the final year, I edited the school yearbook, the first printed work for which I can claim credit.

11

The Funeral Town

My friend Nadid was about my age. He lived in Khan Yunis with his large family. Impatiently counting the days and months to finish high school, he was eager to burst out of his family cocoon and embrace life at Cairo University, in Europe, and farther afield. His youthful energy was ready and waiting to be consumed in the business of life and love. He was ready to take risks, jump into adventure, work hard—all for the price of living a full life with all its challenges.

The only outlet he had for the expression of his bottled-up hopes was his letters to me in Cairo for three years. He had endless questions about the nature of life out there. He did not want to leave anything to chance. When he arrived in Cairo, he wanted to behave like a native from the first day. His father, Sheikh Hafez, was an Islamic cleric of wide repute in the town. He had studied at al-Azhar University for several years. He was an admirer of the Egyptian reformist Muhammad Abdu, and was something of a disciple of the Syrian reformist Ali Rashid Ridha, who was popular during his father's youth.

Sheikh Hafez built a large house on a main street in Khan Yunis. The house was distinguished by his study on the first floor, a single, elevated, red-roofed room. Most afternoons you could see him from the street, sitting in the balcony, reading and annotating books of Islamic jurisprudence. His wall-lined library was unequaled in the quiet, small town.

He felt his learned background was well above the level of the townspeople. He had mild contempt for their ignorance and self-importance. He refused to be the main mosque's preacher and was satisfied to be the Arabic and Islamic teacher in the school in the mornings, devoting his afternoons to study. He was of moderately short height with an extended round waist. He had a prominent jaw with slightly protruding teeth, a feature inherited by some of his offspring. On the rare occasions when he smiled, you did not know if it was a welcoming gesture or a threat.

He controlled his family by the authority he commanded, but also by his watchful eye. Sheikh Hafez's reception room, and above it his study, were the first observation stations from which he followed who was coming into and going out of his household. At the entrance, a high wall and a door separated the observation station from the women's and children's quarters.

Behind the wall, life flourished. There was a large living room, bedrooms, kitchen, and bathrooms. There was much noise, gossip, stories, the cries of children, cooking, washing, and young women hoping for love and marriage. In the women's quarters, there was an indoor garden with fruit trees. Beyond that, there was an unfenced large garden or small *karm*.

Sheikh Hafez married three times. His first wife was Egyptian; he married her when he was a student at al-Azhar. Very little was known about her. The second wife was from the well-rooted al-Idrisi family. She died around 1930, leaving three girls and one boy. The eldest of their children was Madiha, a bright energetic and well-spoken young woman, who became in her late twenties the headmistress of the town's girls' school. Her literary writings were published in *al-Risala* and *al-Thaqafa*, two prestigious Cairo periodicals, the closest equivalent to today's *New York Times Review of Books*. She also joined Palestinian women's secret societies during the British Mandate.

Next came Hassan, a jovial young man. While he obediently followed his father's wish to be an austere and serious graduate of al-Azhar University, another sheikh, he also savored the other side of life in Cairo, not missing out on having fun. His company was most delightful, full of anecdotes and laughter.

Next was Ni'ma, a beautiful blue-eyed girl. Before she was three, she was struck by an illness that affected her eyes. She was rushed to doctors in Jerusalem, but nothing could be done and she lost her sight. She compensated by acquiring a keen sense of hearing and by her sharp intelligence. Next was the youngest daughter, Nadida, a good-hearted girl who felt, more than her older siblings, the pain of losing their mother.

The third wife was a gentle woman from Gaza, who was expected to look after her husband's four children as well as her own. She did so with grace. Her firstborn was Khawla, a bright-eyed and beautiful girl with a feminine resemblance to her father. After Khawla, Nadid was born. Both were close to my age. Khawla did not escape my attention. She blushed in the fleeting moments I saw her face-to-face. Of the younger offspring, there were two boys and two girls. It was a big household, ten mouths to feed, to educate, and to release to the outside world.

My friendship with Nadid, along with my young age (I was around twelve years old), gained me a pass to the women's household, under the watchful eye of Sheikh Hafez. He could not see everything, of course. My brother Ibrahim, a dashing young lawyer, became interested in the young school headmistress, Madiha. He managed to slip her a few letters at her school. I do not know what was in those letters but they must have been typical of the period—a young man approaching a young woman with expressions of admiration and interest. The letter exchange was tricky: who would deliver the letters? What if the postman (or postwoman) was rebuffed or punished?

Ibrahim noticed my friendship with Nadid and my easy access to the forbidden women's quarters of the household. He entrusted me with delivering a letter directly to Madiha. I hid the letter in my clothes and during the rare moment she was alone, I whispered and handed her the letter. Surprised, she smiled, and in a second, the letter disappeared. A week later, pushed by Ibrahim, I went again with a facial expression that did not need explanation. Quickly, the reply was in my pocket.

I became the silent, trusted postman for the good part of a year. Not one word to anyone, not even to Nadid. They married, and in spite of wars, tragedies, imprisonment, and exile, lived the happiest of lives together for fifty-five years until my brother Ibrahim passed away in 2004 and she in 2011. They had eight children to testify to the fruitfulness of this happiness.

As for Nadid himself, he wrote letters to me for two or three years in the early 1950s, and they constitute a chronicle of a young man's hopes for life. Some extracts from these letters serve to illustrate this:

Khan Yunis, 6 September 1955.
This is Khan Yunis unlicensed Radio Station:
The news:

- The City Magistrate [my brother Ibrahim] returned from pilgrimage. Lots of well-wishers and sweets.
- The Reverend Sheikh Hafez is still on holiday at Khan Yunis Riviera.

End of news
The next news bulletin: God knows when.
Please send me ten beautiful postcards from Cairo. Do not forget. I would love to see them and send some to my pen pals.

Khan Yunis, 21 September 1955.
I found your letter sitting waiting for me at home. The house looked different as if waiting to receive a king. There it was, your letter, looking fat. I knew it must have the postcards you sent in it. I lie if I say I was happy with your letter more than the postcards.

You ask me how I was when [the Israeli] shooting took place. Luckily, I was out of town, on the beach, and then the club. At 8:45 p.m. just before the shooting, I was returning home, and found no one at home. I climbed the wall and looked over my father's balcony. A bullet buzzed past to my ear. I rolled down the stairs, almost unconscious and went out to the street. There was a wedding nearby and lots of women were there. They rushed out crying, wailing and sobbing. I found everyone congregating at Madiha's house. Among them was a girl, Jamila, and her sister. I started to talk and joke, as if I did not care [about the shooting]. My brother Hassan winked and said, Nadid wished the shooting to go on all night.
I cannot wait to join you in Cairo in your new apartment.

Khan Yunis, 15 November 1955.
The school news is, as ever, boring. I am up to my old tricks with the teachers. My father returned from his summer sojourn on the beach. He is in much better health. The evidence is clear. He paid a deposit for a radio, imagine! He will get repairs done to the house and buy new sofas for the guest room.

I forgot to tell you that I went to greet your father upon his return and I found him at the café with some old friends, listening to the radio about the latest [Israeli] attack.

My mind is filled with confused ideas, some linger for a long time. But I shoo them away one by one as much as I can with God's help.

Khan Yunis, 27 November 1955.
I am surrounded by my sisters, clicking their tongues, gathering my courage to tell them about your request for them to knit you a pullover. They are ready but with conditions. Ni'ma wants you to build her a palace in the year 2000 when you become a famous engineer. Nadida wants a present from Europe when you go there. Khawla shyly says she will do knitting like the others.

Nadida interjected and says: Shame on you; you ran away on a donkey to Rafah when the Jews attacked you in al-Ma'in [in May 1948]. You kept telling us Jewish girls carry guns and fight and you, young man, run away! Wait till I see you and tell you my mind.

My sisters say, in a chorus: Do you remember when you and I were watching the schoolgirls with binoculars from Hassan's balcony?

Alas! The great news of a new radio did not materialize. Still, we live on in the dream it is coming. When it does, we will steal the key from my father when he is asleep. Or make a new copy. My sisters fear that my father will "occupy" the room when it is time for "listener's request."

This has been a long letter but I want to tell you all that is going on here.

Khan Yunis, 8 December 1955.
I thought of Italy, how beautiful. Italian women . . . ah! They do not believe in love until it is consummated! How wonderful. When I go to the beach, on this side of the Mediterranean, I stretch my arms, take a deep breath, and gaze at the horizon toward the other side of the sea. I tell you, I can smell the perfume of women in Capri.

I wait and wait till my grand trip around the world. First to Istanbul, Athens, Belgrade, Vienna, Paris, then Rome . . . ah! Rome! Then to London, then I'll sail to New York, then by rail to San Francisco, then Tokyo, Moscow, (Oh! I forgot Berlin), then I'll veer east to Beijing, Delhi, Bombay, and then last to Cairo, on my way to my final destination—to the great metropolis by the name of Khan Yunis.

Khan Yunis, 26 April 1956.
Sorry for the late reply. I should have written to tell you about the present situation because you said you were worried about us [after the Israeli attack]. Thank God, Khan Yunis was not hit. But Gaza had it bad. The next day I went to see the damage. It needs no description. The dead were many. There were demolished houses. But the horrifying thing, which made my blood run cold, was when I saw the telephone wires: They were not damaged but I saw pieces of human flesh stuck on these wires from torn bodies.

Khan Yunis was hit by artillery randomly. I had a walk with a friend at the entrance to the town. The artillery shells were hitting the village of Beni Suheila. We heard thuds and saw smoke billowing. We could guess where each bomb exploded from the location of the smoke. As the shells became closer, we walked . . . no, we ran toward the town. We were safe. I am still alive.

P.S. Cannot wait for the day, no, the hour and minute, to go to Egypt [to the university]. On 26th of the next month, we will have the exam and my fate will be sealed. Am praying to God for success.

Khan Yunis, 6 May 1956.
It is Ramadan and I am happy that the Eid holiday will come before the exam. I will not read a word. We had a curfew after the recent [Israeli] attacks. The police came around, knocking on doors, shouting "Lights out." I immediately switched off the light and closed my book. Got fed up with reading. Nobody can blame me.

Khan Yunis, 4 June 1956.
We finished the exam for the final year. It was a tough exam for the new system. I did what I could, although I am not sure about the French. It is all in God's hands now. My exam seat number was 14,001. In three months I shall be in Cairo!! Please God. Please God.

Khan Yunis, 20 September 1956.
I am VERY worried. I have not yet received the university application form. Please expedite it. I am determined to come although my father objects. Enough for now. I am upset, miserable, and a nervous wreck.

> Khan Yunis, 3 October 1956.
> Where is the application form? I have not received it yet. The condition of this writer, as you know, does not need any explanation. Lots of thinking. Depression. I only pray that God alone, the only support I have, will fulfill my most earnest hopes.

Three weeks later, on 30 October 1956, I was on my way to classes at the faculty of engineering when I saw the news headlines: "Israelis attacked Sinai from the south and north, now proceeding to al-Arish."[56]

Another war, another occupation, another mass of people killed and wounded, another mass displacement. And this, after eight years of monthly, sometimes daily, attacks. The Tripartite Aggression, or the Suez Campaign as the western press called it, was launched by Israel on the pretext of "clearing fedayeen bases in Sinai," which never existed. It was a flimsy cover for the collusion among Britain, France, and Israel to topple Nasser. Britain wanted revenge for the nationalization of the Suez Canal; France wanted revenge for Nasser's material and political support for Algerian independence; and Israel wanted to eliminate the armistice lines, to expand their territory, to get de facto recognition of the destruction of Palestine, and to remove Nasser, an obstacle to these aims.

At a distance from Palestine, concerns and fears were magnified. The inability to participate or even witness events at close range gave me a terrible feeling of helplessness. Preoccupied by these thoughts, I was walking across the lawn to the classroom, when one of my classmates called me.

"What are you doing here? The Israelis entered al-Arish. Go and fight."

With the exception of Muslim Brotherhood members and a few well-informed others, the political awareness of Egyptian students was minimal. Four years of Egyptian rule under Abd al-Nasser's leadership were yet to seep down to young Egyptians.

I looked at him in disdain. "If you see al-Arish as an Egyptian town, then *you* should go and fight. If you see it as Arab, then *you* and I should go and fight. So you see, in both cases, it is you who should not be here today." I left him with a bewildered look on his face.

It did not take long to discover what happened. Streams of refugees from Gaza arrived at Cairo and with them the harrowing news. The

Israelis had attacked Sinai on several fronts. They did not bother to take Gaza in the first three days. They knew that if they took Sinai and sealed the Gaza Strip at Rafah, Gaza with its crowded population of helpless refugees would fall like a ripe plum. With their superior arms and number of soldiers, the Israelis overwhelmed the resistance and entered the town of Khan Yunis on 3 November 1956.

Nadid's family heard a hard knock on the door. "Open. Open. This is the Israeli Defense Forces."

Sheikh Hafez rushed to the door in his bedclothes. His wife stood a distance away by his side. There were Jewish soldiers with long beards and a scruffy appearance.

"Get out. All the men out. All the men. Now! Now!" shouted the soldiers.

Sheikh Hafez asked to wear his cleric robes and head cover. He pleaded, "We have no men here."

They shoved him aside and looked around. They kicked the door of the women's section. They could not see anybody. Huddled under the staircase were the terrified young women and many children, Nadid and his brothers and sisters and the very young children of my brother Ibrahim and Madiha (who were in Cairo at the time). They could hear nothing. One child squealed. They turned to the source of the sound under the stairs. They saw eyes full of fear and a dozen children and women.

"Out! Everybody!" they shouted in broken Arabic. One look at Nadid and the soldier shouted, "You! Come."

"He is a schoolboy," his mother pleaded.

"Come here." The soldiers dragged the boy out. His mother pulled him back.

"He is only a boy. I can show you the school card."

They dragged him across the floor, by the lemon tree in the small house garden. His mother was hanging on to him. A dozen children and young women were screaming, pleading, and wailing. The soldiers kept dragging him. Just past the separating inner door, opposite Sheikh Hafez's room, Nadid uttered a deep cry from his throat:

"*Yamma* [mother], I am very thirsty, very thirsty."

His mother pleaded with the soldiers as only a mother can. "Please, let me give him a drink of water!"

"Yes. OK."

There was silence for a moment. Perhaps this act of kindness may grow to sparing the kid's life. She brought a glass of water with trembling hands and approached the parched lips of her son, still held on the floor by the soldiers. Suddenly the silence was broken. The boot of the Israeli soldier kicked the glass of water. Takh, Takh!

The soldiers emptied their machine-gun magazines into the boy's chest. His blood, together with the splashed water, splattered on the floor and wall. With a victorious smile, the soldiers left.

The women sat motionless on the floor, unable to comprehend their grief. The children rushed to Nadid and tried to stop the bleeding, hoping this would bring him to life. They scraped the dried blood on the floor with bottle tops. His body lay on the floor, a sad testimony to the end of a young boy's long-cherished dreams and hopes for a better future.

The same knock could be heard on the house next door, followed by pleading screams, then bursts of machine-gun fire, then agonized screams, then dead silence.

Four buildings away, the soldiers climbed to the second floor where Nadid's brother Hassan lived with his wife and two children. They grabbed Hassan and took him away. "He is a schoolteacher. Look at his card." His wife, Afaf, ran after them, waving the card.

The soldiers rounded up all the men in the street, led them in single file, and lined them up against the wall of the fourteenth-century castle built by Sultan Burquq in the town's main square. As they gathered, the assembled teachers, the bank clerks, the shopkeepers, the tradesmen, and the farmers looked as ordinary as they would on any other day, in a reception line to celebrate a wedding, to greet a returning pilgrim, or to attend a town-hall meeting.

More people were dragged in. More soldiers came. Again there was silence—long, deadly silence, filled with hopes of survival, fears of violent death, or simple paralysis.

Then a jeep screeched to a halt in the courtyard. An officer stood in his jeep as if to salute. He looked from one side to another. The soldiers waited in half-hearted attention with their fingers on the trigger. The officer raised his hand high, and lowered it down quickly like a chopping knife.[57] Bursts of machine gun shattered the silence, on and off, left and right. The machine guns rang out in unison, then separately as if playing in an orchestra of hell, led by a devilish maestro.

The captured men fell to the ground, some lying flat, and some leaning against the wall. Their falling shapes wrote the randomness of sudden death, which had no time to express itself. The splattered blood drew an odd caricature of red lilies, climbing the wall. The flowing blood on the ground drew streams, as if trying to write the last words of victims.

There was a long silence in the town. The town had died. It became a town of widows hidden behind closed doors. The streets were filled with bodies strewn everywhere. There were not many men left, just those who escaped capture and who had disappeared into the sand dunes. A curfew was imposed, and meant instant death to anything that moved after hours.[58]

On the third day of the carnage, the old mayor found the courage to ask the Israeli commander permission to bury the dead on the grounds of "public health concerns." Women in black went out carrying blankets to collect the remains of their loved ones and bury them. Defying the tradition that only men go to the cemetery to bury the dead, resolute women went about the task quietly and firmly, sobbing silently. They did not perform the last rites. They did not mark where the dead were buried. They put the dead to rest and prepared for a long life of sorrow, trying to cope, along with their children, without husbands, fathers, or brothers.

UNRWA came a few days later and inquired half-heartedly about the situation, mainly to inspect the refugees' conditions. The UNRWA director included a paragraph in his routine report, six weeks later, saying he had learned from "trustworthy sources" that 275 people were killed in the massacre; many were refugees. It was so painful to hear the survivors recount the events of this bloody day. Even though, from my family, the elder men were in Cairo and the women and younger men were not close to the center, this bloodbath left everyone in Khan Yunis in mourning. It was not the work of rogue criminals, but followed a pattern ingrained in Israeli practice, as proved by those events. The brunt of the massacre on 3 November 1956 was borne by Khan Yunis town and camp and the neighboring villages of Beni Suheila, Abasan, and Khiza'a. But it continued unabated in the neighboring areas of Zanna and Qarara on 4 November, and on the Mediterranean beach at al-Mawasi and Tel Ridan. My friend, Abd al-Rahim Hussein, a refugee from al-Jura (Asqalan), a village of fishermen, told me about his experience:

> Sporadic killing went on for another two weeks. On 17 November Israeli soldiers led by an Israeli-Druze major by the name of Mansour came from the north, put machine guns to our heads, and questioned us. I was released as they saw my school card and my hands were smooth and did not show rough military training. Another group came from the south. They grabbed a number of people and questioned them. They took four to their armored car and shot them to death. We were able to bury them the next day. The killing spree went on till 23 November. A total of 22 men were killed on the beach.

A list compiled of those killed in Khan Yunis showed 520 dead, probably 275 from Khan Yunis town alone.[59] That meant there were around five hundred bereaved families.

Close to my family, the most painful were the cases of my sister-in-law, Madiha, who lost two brothers in one morning: Nadid and Hassan, the young teacher who did not live long enough to care for his two small children. The news of more massacres kept coming.

On 12 November, the Rafah refugee camp was the scene of yet another massacre. Israeli loudspeakers ordered all males between the ages of fifteen and fifty to gather at the government school. The Israelis shot and killed anyone who was late or walked slowly. By the time they assembled in front of the school, many people lay dead in the streets.

Then there was a new Israeli invention. A ditch was dug along the school wall. Just in front of it stood the Israeli soldiers, who then ordered those lined up to jump over the ditch to the schoolyard and started hitting them mercilessly with long heavy sticks. As the sticks came down on their heads, many could not jump out of the way and fell into the ditch. Israeli soldiers with machine guns were waiting for them; those in the ditch were showered with bullets. The ditch became an instant grave. Bodies were heaped on top of each other in the ditch. Those who crossed over the ditch were not far from death either. They were ordered to lie flat on the ground while Israeli soldiers, around them and on the roof above, fired close to their heads. After two hours, any male found out in the streets was shot dead.

The captured civilians remained without food or water for two days, huddled together, heads touching the back of the row in front. They endured harrowing interrogation, accompanied by kicking, beating, and swearing. When they were released, they had the task of collecting corpses from the ditch and streets and burying them. A longer and equally painful task undertaken by the survivors on their own initiative was to identify who was left from each family, and whether the head of the family or the breadwinner had been killed.

The pattern of killing continued in other refugee camps. Deir al-Balah was the next target, but their story ended unexpectedly. A six-year-old refugee from Isdud witnessed the gathering of his people in this camp. He wrote his story many years later:

> I was six years old when the Israeli tanks rolled into Deir al-Balah on 14 November 1956. My mother recognised the sinister sound and screamed at us to stay in the house. The refugees in Deir al-Balah had heard about the massacres in Khan Yunis and Rafah, and were paralysed with fear. We could hear the commotion outside as tanks and jeeps came to a halt in the middle of the camp.
>
> Ignoring my mother's whispered begging and her gentle attempts to restrain him, my father took down his handgun from the roof. We children stared at it in awe as he opened the bullet chamber; it was empty and he put it down on the table and went to a cupboard to fetch bullets. At that moment the door burst open and five heavily armed Israeli soldiers marched in. Realizing that if they saw the gun my father would be killed, my mother managed to cover it with a basket.
>
> It was one of the most nightmarish experiences of my life to witness those Israeli soldiers beating my father and being just a little boy unable to intervene or defend him. They hit him with their gun butts until he nearly fell, then they told him to get out of the house, pushing him with their rifles. We were all screaming and crying and we followed them, emerging into bright sunlight and a terrifying scene: my father, together with the rest of the men from the camp, being kicked and shoved towards the empty bit of wasteland where we usually played football. Then the soldiers ordered all the men to stop. "Put your hands above your heads," they barked in Arabic. The women were wailing and sobbing, some were on their knees pleading for mercy; they knew what had happened at other camps and that this was the end for their men.
>
> Out of nowhere, an Israeli jeep arrived at incredible speed and came to a screeching halt right by the firing squad. A young colonel

> got out and started talking to them. To our amazement the firing squad saluted, put their guns over their shoulders, clambered back into their tanks and jeeps and left the way they had come. We stood and watched them disappear in stunned silence until the clouds of dust from their vehicles had settled. It dawned on us that the men had been spared and we started talking, quietly at first. We raced over to my father, clinging to him and jumping up and down for joy that he had been spared.[60]

The little boy who witnessed this was Abdel Bari Atwan, who grew up to be one of the best-known Arab journalists, running his own newspaper in London and making frequent appearances on media outlets such as the BBC and CNN.

The story goes that it turned out that this 'Israeli' officer was in fact a Palestinian. When his family was evicted from their home in Nabi Rubin in 1948, they lost their twelve-year-old son, who was hiding from the attacking Israelis. A Jewish family found him and brought him up as one of its own. He knew his real family was in Deir al-Balah. When he knew the people of the town were being rounded up, he rushed to the killing fields and the shooting spree was abandoned. This incredible story ended by the officer's real family moving to Israel with him, although certainly not to Nabi Rubin.

Even if the story of the soldier's origin cannot be verified, it shows how human life could be laid to waste or saved at the whim of an Israeli soldier. I often wondered about the possible loss of Abdel Bari Atwan's talent as a star journalist, had an Israeli bullet been lodged in his head on that fateful day in 1956. And how many young men could have made a mark on this world had their lives not been prematurely terminated in these massacres? Would Nadid have become a good writer? Would Hassan have become a learned professor like his father? What if Edward Said's family had been living in Gaza at the time? Would we have been deprived of the fruits of his intellect?

Cairo was full of Palestinians who could make the long trip to the city. They were not idle. I regularly saw petitions and press releases signed by Abdullah as general secretary of the Refugees' Conference, my brother Ibrahim as the Khan Yunis city magistrate, and Qassem al-Farra as the Khan Yunis municipality secretary.

In March 1957, the Israelis withdrew from the Gaza Strip overnight. In the morning, people woke up and could not believe that they were gone: no curfews, no random shooting.

Thus ended the Tripartite Aggression. The United States was not consulted and felt deceived. Its president, General Eisenhower, threatened the belligerent parties, especially Israel, and demanded immediate withdrawal of all occupying forces. In a rare statement, never to be repeated for Palestine by a US president, Eisenhower declared:

> Should a nation which attacks and occupies a foreign territory in the face of UN disapproval be allowed to impose conditions of its own withdrawal? If we agree that armed attack can properly achieve the purpose of the assailant, then I fear we will have turned back the clock of international order.[61]

This river of blood that engulfed the Gaza Strip in 1956 was not deemed sufficient to earn even a page of coverage in a dozen or so of the western books on the so-called Suez Campaign. It was not mentioned in Moshe Dayan's *Diary of the Sinai Campaign*. UNRWA's director was satisfied to mention in his annual report the number of those killed and explained that it was in the process of "searching for arms." There was no serious investigation, no commission of inquiry, no International Criminal Court, no meeting of the Security Council, no media reporting of any scale.[62]

Israel waited another ten years before it returned in a larger campaign, one that led to the longest, most brutal occupation in modern history.

12

The Long Desert Walk

It is often said that the line between genius and madness is but a hair's breadth. Ghaleb was neither genius nor mad, but he came close to both, at least in the minds of people around him. To me, he was like one of the tragic figures of Victor Hugo's *Les Misérables*. His intelligence, his love of poetry, and his constant search for fulfillment could have earned him a stable and fruitful life, had it not been for his status as a Palestinian refugee.

Ghaleb is a slightly older, distant relative of mine. We first heard of his family in 1942 when they returned to al-Ma'in from the town of Salt in Jordan. It was not clear to me when his father drifted alone to Transjordan. He appeared suddenly in our midst with a wife from Salt, a number of children, and a new occupation, which no one had: a bus driver. All of it was strange for us. The wife from Salt was miserable. She could not endure this kind of rural life, fetching water and baking bread daily. Her women neighbors did not make her life easier, subjecting her to gossip, jealousy, and sneering.

Ghaleb's father found a job as a bus driver along the routes of Khan Yunis–Gaza–Beersheba. Ghaleb used to impress us by saying that his father could actually drive the bus while lighting a cigarette. He was very important, Ghaleb said, because he always sat in front. He even told everybody when to get on and off the bus.

Everybody in my family owned land and cultivated it. Everybody had the same occupation. When the government passed papers to register people in the late 1940s, everybody was puzzled about how to fill the space under "occupation." After a long discussion, they settled on a common description for all: "landowner–farmer."

Landowner, farmer, country gentleman, horseman, or even knight *(faris)* were possible and common. But bus driver? Never had any of us had such a job. Even if we needed a mechanic to fix our *bayyara* motor or flour mill, we brought someone from Gaza or Jaffa.

I kept in touch with Ghaleb for many years after the Nakba. Between his bouts of melancholy and despair, he displayed sparks of brilliance. Others laughed at him and called him crazy, to which he responded violently, confirming their opinion. His letters reached me in London and Canada sporadically over the course of several years, between 1961 and 1968, after my insistence that he should write his story. The letters were few, less than half a dozen, but they were lengthy and coherent. After long, desperate wanderings, he settled in Kuwait for some years in the 1950s and 1960s, where he at least had the blessing of a stable residence. That was the time he wrote these letters to me. He described his days at Beersheba school, the loss of his mother, and his travels after the Nakba. I drew a map of Ghaleb's wanderings and he must have covered 3,500 kilometers, mostly on foot. His odyssey as a Palestinian refugee, with no homeland, no papers, no job, no help, left us a record of endurance and determination. In spite of bouts of despair, he kept soldiering on, with the promise of the hope that would be found on the next corner.

In one letter he wrote of his journey from Gaza to Kuwait:

> Just after the Nakba, I decided that my life as a refugee in the Gaza Strip was unbearable. I was one of hundreds of thousands in this big camp who felt the same. But I decided to break out.
>
> I went with a group who knew the way. We crossed the enemy lines at night and kissed the ground as we passed through our now-occupied land at al-Ma'in. We hid during the day and traveled by night. It was not too risky. The Jews were very few. They could not control the vast land they occupied. They had few kibbutzim, and we kept away from their lights. The fear was of mines exploding under our feet. Our guide was clever and he knew his way very well.
>
> We arrived at al-Khalil [Hebron] safely. We felt free again as we passed the Israeli-occupied land. We split and I started alone on my journey to Amman.

Amman was a bloated town with so many refugees. It does not smile except for those with deep pockets. The desert is clean, smiling, and welcoming for any man, poor or rich, high or lowly.

I suffered in this unblessed town for days I cannot forget. Hungry, penniless, without friends, without mercy; it was hell. Without regrets, I started on foot into the unknown, until I reached al-Zarqa. Someone was kind enough to give me a lift to al-Ramtha on the Jordanian–Syrian border.

There, I found a group of Gypsies trying to cross the border in Syria. I mingled among them. As we were about to cross, one shouted, "He is not one of us," pointing to me. The officer sent me back. I pleaded with him.

"If the Gypsies disowned you, how do you expect me to consider you a reliable character?" he said.

I sneaked through Der'a to the Syrian side and looked for a job. The only job available was harvesting. How could I do such a hard job? I wanted to do something with my education. Although I had barely completed the elementary grades, I was well read and I loved poetry and philosophy.

I left the plains of Hauran, covered with wheat fields, just like our land, and walked without a specific plan until I reached Damascus.

Another terrible town, God help us and keep us from evil. Damascus, like Amman, is grim and unwelcoming for penniless people. I could not stay for a single day and I walked toward the Syrian Desert to a place called Adra, the seat of the Sha'alan sheikhs, princes of the Anaza tribe.

I stayed there for the night and headed toward a village called Dhamir. I was thirsty, hungry, and tired. I saw a woman and asked her for a drink of water. When she gave me water, she asked me where I was from. "I am a stranger," I said. She responded, "Only the devil is a stranger. You are here among your family and friends."

I thought for a moment about her response, something that you would not hear in a town, even from someone educated. The luxury and comfort of life in the town destroys man's natural instinct to do good and honorable deeds.

I left the woman and headed for the desert with the aim of crossing the great Syrian Desert to reach Baghdad.

At sunset, I found Arab encampments and looked for the biggest tent. I saw two boys, apparently the sheikh's sons, and their servant standing in front of a Dodge.

At the sheikh's seat, I did not find anyone worth talking to. The sheikh, Farhan al-Mu'jil, came. He was tall as a ramrod and he looked a lot like my father. I stared at him and he responded with a questioning look.

"I am sorry, sir. I am your guest, I should be polite. But your face and physique resemble my father's. He is a great man with a great mind who fell on hard times among ignorant people," I said.

"That is OK. When was the last time you saw him?"

"Two years ago, sir. I said final good-byes to him and he said, 'I entrust you to God.' What immortal words were these, sir. What a wicked and mean life we lead when a man has to let his son wander in the hands of fate after what we have been through, with the loss of our home and our land, to become refugees like this."

"What is your job?"

"I am a car driver and I am on my way to Baghdad."

"Baghdad? Do you know how far it is?"

"Yes, I do. It is 850 kilometers from here."

He suggested I drop the idea and stay with them and I agreed. Next morning, he stood by the car with his entourage and he ordered me to show him my driving ability. I had never driven a car before but I observed what drivers do. I turned on the engine and pressed the pedal hard. The car reversed violently, almost running over someone behind. I apologized politely and changed gear. As if it were a galloping horse, the car sped into the desert, leaving a cloud of dust behind. With no obstacles to to maneuver around in the open space my lack of skill was not revealed. I turned left and right and in circles.

Behind me, the sheikh and his friends were waving, cheering, and congratulating the sheikh for his luck in finding such a good driver in the desert.

I taught the sheikh's sons some of my poor English; I taught the older boy twenty words and the younger ten. The news of this learned stranger spread around among the family. Their beautiful girls gathered around me while I read for them the *Odyssey of Beni Hilal* and *One Thousand and One Nights*.[63]

There was a feeling of shy affection with the girls. The older boy became my very good friend.

One day, a group of Aleppo Bedouins stayed as guests of the sheikh. After dinner, they went to sleep, except for one.

"What are you doing here?"

"I am the sheikh's driver."

"How much does he pay you?"

"Nothing. I am happy living here."

"Why don't you come with me to Aleppo? You can work on tractors for the Ibn Mhaid clan. They have a good reputation and they will pay you well."

In the morning, I asked Sheikh Farhan to give me a paper to protect me from the police, but he refused because he wanted me to stay.

His eldest son told me about the Aleppo man. "This man, he speaks lie." I laughed at my student's attempt at English, this silly language that I claimed to know and traded as my expertise.

I said a warm and tearful goodbye to all, especially the son, Ubeid, and the girl, al-Labiba, and their mother.

Halfway to Aleppo, this man left me alone on the road with no money or friends.

I walked in the direction of Aleppo, totally penniless, because the sheikh did not pay me. (I was loyal. I returned a few years later, and I gave them some money, but the sheikh was not there).

I arrived at midnight in Aleppo and I slept in an abandoned truck. In the morning, I trotted out, walking in the desert alone, except for a single gazelle grazing in the distance. There was complete silence, only the gentle hum of the wind. I had nothing: no food, no water, no money, no clothes except those on my back.

A bus passed by me and stopped without me waving. The driver asked me where I was heading, I told him, Sheikh Faisal al-Nawaf al-Hadidi. He gave me a lift until I reached the village of that sheikh.

The sheikh received me with great warmth. He asked me about the purpose of my travel, I said I was looking for a job as a mechanic. "Well, good. We have a job for you. We have motors for the water well which need repair."

I started disassembling the motor and spread the pieces over a piece of solid ground. Tens of pieces were lined up in disarray. The sight frightened me. I was afraid of the sheikh's wrath when he found out that I could not even put them back, let alone repair the motor.

When everybody was asleep, I escaped and kept walking until the morning, when I came across another village. When I asked about it, it turned out to be the village of the sheikh's brother, Dahham al-Nawaf. The sheikh had relatives, friends, and agents in the whole region. I walked, no, ran really, for several hours until I had covered fifty kilometers and escaped from his territory.

I arrived at last at the camp of Sheikh Sufouk al-Murshid. He employed me to drive his tractor. Soon, the news of my hurried departure reached him from the agents of Sheikh Hadidi, whose motors I had taken to pieces.

They told him I was a very dangerous person, maybe even a political agent of some sort. I came close to being killed when they found me, to my stupid luck, wearing a western-style hat. They thought I was a dangerous foreign spy and a *kafir*.

I left Sheikh Sufouk, his son Faisal, and his slave Fayyad. I arrived at a lovely romantic-looking village called Kudtom, a place fit only for people of high spirits and noble thoughts. I stayed there for ten days. We ate gazelle meat and life seemed to have befriended me.

There, I heard about the Egyptian Revolution [of 23 July 1952].

I continued my travel to Deir al-Zour, then to Raqqa, then to Uyoun Eisa and stayed with Sheikh Nouri al-Mhaid who became my friend.

At first, Sheikh Nouri did not receive me well.

"Go find a job elsewhere. You are strange. The sunset sees you in one place and the sunrise sees you in another."

The news of my escape must have reached him over tens of kilometers. I walked on to Ras al-Ain and worked on a brand-new Oliver tractor. I drove it fast like a car. I was fired after five days.

I crossed the Iraqi border without realizing it, even without knowing where I was heading. I met some Shammar sheikhs but I continued my travels to Baghdad, then to Basra. There I met the honorable, generous man Rashad Ali Saleh. He was a man whose personality you cannot put to any measure nor can you ponder the analysis of his inner self. He rose to help me with his influence and generosity (he paid for me).

Due only to his great help, I survived and was able to pay for a ride on a camel until I arrived in Kuwait in 1952.

The journey from Amman to Kuwait took me four months, mostly walking, sometimes running, sometimes with a warm farewell, sometimes sneaking out in the middle of the night.

> But I achieved my aim. I found in Kuwait many friends and relatives. I learned to be a highly paid mechanic. I operated bulldozers, graders, trucks, and tall cranes. That is how I have had time and peace of mind to write these words to you.

In 1968, Ghaleb sought new adventures. He walked to Saudi Arabia, where the police caught him. After firing a scathing line of poetry at the police officer, he was promptly accused of sedition and was imprisoned for eight months.

He then walked to Qatar where he obtained, for the first time, official papers with his photo and a stamp identifying him as a specific human being. With that paper, he entered the Emirates (known as the Coastal Truce at the time) through a border crossing this time, rather than from the wilderness or deserts as he used to do. In the Emirates, he excelled as an experienced mechanic and operator of heavy equipment. He took jobs in all these emirates before they joined into one union. In about 1987, he returned to Amman, probably for the first time in nearly forty years, in a plane and with proper papers.

I lost touch with him after his last letter. In the mid-1990s, I met his brother in Amman and asked about his whereabouts. He filled me in with the missing details of that last twenty years or so and added that Ghaleb was near Amman.

"Please take me to him. But do not tell him I am coming."

Next day, we took a taxi on the road to Jerash.

"There he is," my companion said.

I saw a figure standing by the road. As I got out, he approached me.

"You are Salman, right?"

"Is it you, Ghaleb?"

The years had carved lines into his face, and he looked much older than his old age. Not always a neat person, Ghaleb appeared even more disheveled. His tattered clothes of mismatching colors drew a tragic figure at the end of his tether. We went to a deserted, semi-constructed house where he was supposed to be the watchman. I asked the others to stay in the car.

For over two hours we reminisced about the old days. More truthfully, he did the talking. He went back over stations of his life, laughing, frowning, exclaiming. His lined face expanded and contracted, and his eyes lit with excitement or dimmed with despair as he recalled his experiences. When he had discharged this painful load of memories, he fell silent for a long moment. Then he raised his head slowly and looked at me. "You know, I am angry with God."

Surprised, I asked, "Why?"

"Why is He treating me like this? Why? Why? What have I done to him to deserve all that?" His voice grew louder. His eyes lit up with rage. The lines on his face twisted as his face contorted. "He took away my mother, the fountain of kindness and love. He let the Jewish wolves eat up my homeland, and I became a destitute refugee forever. He let me wander as a vagabond in the wilderness for forty years, looking for a place to sleep and eat and be a human being with a photo and a piece of paper to prove it."

"But you overcame many of these obstacles. You survived against unbelievable odds."

"Yes, but I have an account to settle. I do not think I will live much longer. Then I will face Him and demand proper, just, and complete answers to what He did to me."

It did not take long for him to meet his Creator. In the cold winter nights, sleeping in this windowless room in the unfinished house, he tried to keep warm. Sparks from the primitive kerosene-lit heating device caught his clothes that were hanging on the wall. Heavily sedated by the medication he took, he was not alert as the fire swept him away in his sleep. The fire consumed him, his clothes, and whatever papers he carried, including the one of the photo giving him an identity. Only a skeleton and ashes were found on the floor the next morning.

He had started on his last journey to deliver his complaints to the Creator Himself. On this earth, only these notes about him and his memories remain.

13

My Battlefield

The Nakba, the uprooting from the homeland, the dispossession and exile were not a single tragedy that subsided with burying the dead and treating the wounded. No, it was an endless, relentless war on the victims. Refugee camps were attacked by land, air, and sea. The refugees were chased from exile to exile, refuge to refuge, with the aim of making them vanish from the face of the earth.

These events not only fueled my concern about my people from afar, but they spilled over to Cairo—right into my student flat—when my family members and friends came to stay with me, as stories of constant terror poured out of them. My school days in Cairo were pleasant and peaceful, but the distance magnified the smallest incident. The worry of who had been killed, wounded, or exiled was constant and it devoured the tranquillity of my life in Cairo.

Education was the only battlefield in which I was soldiering. My tanks and planes were my pen, paper, and school records. Like the thousands of refugees from Gaza, I discovered that education was the mission of our silent army and was filling Egyptian universities. Gamal Abd al-Nasser was our commander in chief, and had opened the doors of Egyptian universities to Palestinians, free of charge. Hundreds, thousands, and then tens of thousands of students flocked to Egypt. In the 1950s, they became the engineers, doctors, and teachers who built up the Gulf States during their endeavor to develop their countries with the newly found oil wealth. In the years that followed, this flow of students filled European and American universities as well. Education was the most brilliant manifestation of the refugees' human spirit, which elevated pupils from solving algebra on the tarmac to sitting in lecture halls at Harvard.

In Cairo, I had my own room, with a small bed and table, in our students flat. I needed some company in the room, but we did not even have a radio. I connected a crystal stone to a wire pin and then connected both to an earphone of an old, broken telephone. I kept the headphones on my head with bandages. The contraption worked and I could hear one station with no need for electricity.

Studying did not consume all of my time, even though I managed to stay top of my class. I played tennis with my friend Mustafa Nabil, and he admitted me to his rowing team. Rowing on the Nile and learning the unity of team action was a delightful experience. I also learned to draw and could produce decent pictures. I joined the Saidiya Theater group too, but it was a short experience as my accent was not thoroughly Egyptian. I landed the part of a dumb person who had to tell a long story by signs and noises. It was much easier to talk.

Mustafa and I had endless debates about the future of the Arab world, particularly Palestine and Egypt. Mustafa was not the kind who accepted the status quo. He had a revolutionary spirit that made him a celebrated journalist, editor, and an executive of the Journalists' Union in the years to come. But this spirit also earned him a jail sentence, which made him lose two years of education.

My secondary education had ended with two certificates. The first was called al-Thaqafa, the general certificate of education, which I obtained in 1953. The following year, I obtained the other, al-Tawjihiya, the particular certificate of education for the subject in which the student majored: the humanities, science, or mathematics. Both exams were held simultaneously in Egypt, Sudan, and Gaza, following the Egyptian curriculum.

The Thaqafa exam took place during Ramadan. I sat in the exam hall, fasting, anxious, and petrified, like all the students. We went through several days of exams, and I left for Gaza for my summer holidays. The results came in a telegraph from a friend and competitor in the class, Esmat.

"Congratulations, you came out number one."

Soon the news spread. The four-page paper, *Gaza*, ran the headline, "A Refugee Boy, Top Student in Egypt, Sudan. . . , etc."

Approximately forty thousand students sat the exam, out of a total Egyptian population of thirty million at the time.

The news came as a hugely pleasant surprise. It was uplifting for the Palestinians living in the wretched camps to talk of success and a yes-we-can attitude. Friends and acquaintances came to congratulate my father. When my mother went to the market and met other women, she dismissed the whole thing, for fear of the evil eye, saying, "All kids pass their exams. What is the fuss about?"

My name was placed on the List of Honor at Saidiya Hall. The Ministry of Education usually sent the top ten students of each school on a paid holiday. That year they canceled the plan for a trip to Lebanon, for reasons unknown to me. For the Tawjihiya exam, the following year, majoring in mathematics, I was the top student again, but only a few marks from second place this time.

It was a source of pride for our headmaster, Muhammad Ahmed Bannouna, to post on the Honors List the name of one of his students for the second consecutive year in the country's general exam. Bannouna was very kind to me. He wrote me a personal letter of congratulation and said he was very sorry that the trip for top students was canceled.

However, the impending higher cost of living as a university student soon dampened the joy of success. I applied to the Faculty of Engineering at Cairo University—no doubt influenced by my brother Ali and my cousin Hamed. I submitted my papers to the registrar and asked him about my chances of acceptance. He looked up with a smile and said, "Son, if we take only one student this year, it will be you."

Next came the problem of money. UNRWA started a financial aid program for Palestinian students. I received four Egyptian pounds every month of the school year, and though that was not enough, it helped a lot. My three brothers, now working in Kuwait, covered the rest.

My father objected to my brothers' sending me money and insisted they send money for him to distribute to the whole family as required. My father wanted to emphasize that it was his duty to educate his youngest son, and my education should not be a favor from my older brothers. Through all the years, until I finished university, he showed in his actions the worry that he might pass away before I, his youngest, received the same university education as my brothers.

I met fellow Palestinian students for the first time since the Nakba during the admission to my class at Cairo University. We were about ten Palestinian students from the Gaza Strip and the West Bank, the only regions of Palestine not occupied by the Israelis. We worked together as a group. Some shared the same flat. We of course discussed the situation in Palestine. The only Egyptian students who joined us or showed interest were politically motivated students, members of the Muslim Brotherhood, and the Arab nationalists. Pan-Arab nationalism, unlike the ideology of the Muslim Brotherhood, was encouraged during Nasser's regime.

One of my Palestinian colleagues, Kamal Adwan, a fiery and patriotic young man, became one of Fatah's three main leaders. He and two other Palestinian leaders were assassinated by Ehud Barak leading a group of Israeli commandos, dressed as women, in Beirut in April 1973.[64] Another colleague, Zuhair Alami, who was two classes ahead of me, became an executive of the PLO for a short while. The indefatigable Yasser Arafat had also graduated from the same department, though before our time.

It was during my second year at university that the Tripartite Aggression happened as Israel—supported by France and Britain—attacked Egypt. University students volunteered for the resistance. Mustafa, now a student at the Faculty of Commerce, and I both volunteered. We undertook two weeks of light training, learning to form lines, obey orders, and fire and maintain a rifle. We were not called to duty, but Mustafa and I decided to go to war.

We took the bus to Port Said. On the way, we stopped at a small café and had tea. The customers were simple fellaheen. We told them that we were going to fight. They did not know what we were fighting for. Questioning them further, I asked if they knew there was a war and that foreign soldiers were actually in Port Said. They were not sure but agreed there were some troubles over there. Mustafa, ever the Egyptian patriot, was angered by my questioning, thinking that I was trying to show up their ignorance. And in a way, he was right. We continued on our journey. At Port Said, we found the unoccupied part of the port full of regular soldiers and volunteers. The latter were lightly armed, but they had the advantage of knowing their way around the streets and alleys. We tried to find some office or military post to take us, but no one wanted two enthusiastic young people. We returned without medals of war, but with some satisfaction that we had tried.

The following summer, 1957, I decided to take the holiday to Lebanon that I was never awarded two years earlier. By this time, the Israelis had withdrawn unceremoniously from the Gaza Strip and Sinai, and the refugees resumed their life displaced in their own homeland, without Israeli guns on their streets and with the barbed wire limited to the border encircling them.

Two Egyptian friends suggested we go to Lebanon, to do youth work in the camps and stay at a youth hostel, in which we could do some service work for our food and lodging, leaving us with ample free time. One of them said he had names, addresses, and introduction letters.

We took the *Aeoliya*, a boat from Alexandria to Beirut, on 28 July 1957. I kept notes of my first-ever sea trip. Armed with a camera, harmonica, soap, food, notebook, and a little money, I started my journey at sea with my classmates as fellow passengers on deck.

The nights were very cold, but during the day, many passengers came up to the deck to take in a view of the sea. There were all kinds of people: travelers paying cheap passage, students, and tourists. The atmosphere and the whole experience were new to me. I enjoyed the tranquillity, suspended between the blue sky and the blue water, with no fear of falling bombs or of hearing the news of the killing of family members or acquaintances.

It was an ideal time to reflect, philosophize, and reorganize the world in an attempt to understand human behavior. I wrote in my small notebook:

> Human ingenuity led to scientific wonders, which we enjoy today. Although our way of life has changed a lot in what we eat, how we live, and do our business, human behavior did not improve much. On the contrary, it may have gotten worse. In olden times, the strong man killed the weak one. He stole, lied, deceived, cheated. Today, it is still the same, but with a difference. The primitive man killed one

> person by a stone pointed like a knife. Now, there is mass killing. Until today, we cannot even calculate the number of people who perished in Hiroshima and Nagasaki. . . .
>
> Those who stuck to their ideals suffered a great deal, but they won in the end. Do we not know what fate the prophets and social reformers met when they spread their ideas?
>
> The early Christians were left to be devoured by hungry lions. The early Muslims were burnt on the desert sands. Galileo, with his "wicked" telescope, insisted that the earth rotates around the sun. He was tried, punished, and forced to confess his guilt. But he left the court, murmuring to himself, "but it still rotates."
>
> The belief in your ideals and a strong will always make you win, no matter what the price is.

We arrived in Beirut, a busy port catering to sailors and travelers. Our leader, the young man who "knew" where we were going, made inquiries as to the location of the work camp, and even the hostel. No one met us at the boat, so we had to find our own way.

Night came and we still had no name and no address to rely on in this strange city. Finally, the news hit us like a thunderbolt: there was no camp, there was no hostel; both had been closed and the project canceled earlier that year.

We found dingy accommodation near the port, a place ready to receive whomever the ships spewed out. We started to count our money; would it last until the return date? We walked around, conspicuous as strangers. We passed by doors with women waiting. They waved to us. We debated the situation. One of us, the adventurous one, decided to go to a brothel. The other friend and I went to buy some food.

The hero returned and took most of the night to describe his exploits, exaggeration and all, and we listened with interest and a touch of excitement. We spent the rest of the days visiting villages in the lovely Lebanese mountains. My little camera did its job well. I photographed Baalbek and the sunset from the height of the mountains.

When we returned to Cairo, I wrote a long letter to Professor George Gardner, an American passenger on the boat, traveling with his family to Suq al-Gharb, a summer resort in Lebanon. He taught social science at the American University in Cairo. On the boat, I made heated comments about the US support for Israel which made me a refugee. He took my anger calmly and with gentle understanding. In the letter, I restated my feelings about American policy that unjustly sided with the Israelis, in no uncertain terms. With his reply, a lasting friendship started between the Gardners and my family. He wrote:

> September 13, 1957
> Dear Salman,
> I was delighted to receive your letter in Suq al-Gharb and to know that you arrived back in Cairo. Now, I have myself returned and I hope that you will be willing to come to see me either at the American University or here at home —even if I am an "American"! I enjoyed our conversations together, and I have something I would like to ask you.
> Cordially yours,
> George Gardner
> American University in Cairo

For the following fifteen years, I remained in touch with the Gardners. They had endured a taste of the hardships of war. George was in Greece during the Second World War when the American embassy instructed him to leave within twenty-four hours, in the face of an imminent German advance.

Mrs. Gardener came from quite a family line herself, related to Ernest Hemingway. Her husband was the professor, but she was the doer. In twenty-four hours, she packed the essentials of a seven-year stay in Greece and disposed of the rest. They were ready to leave in the nick of time.

Their life in Cairo's prestigious quarter, Zamalek, was tranquil. They invited me to dinner repeatedly, and when I could afford it, I invited them to tea at one of the well-known cafés on Suleiman Pasha Street. We also went to the theater and concerts together.

Then, months later, I received an invitation to attend a cocktail party in honor of the visiting president of the American University of Beirut. There were many diplomats and Americans of different occupations. It was a strange experience for me. Guests were standing, not sitting, as is our custom. They moved around, a glass in hand, from one conversation to another. I stood there, with my lemonade in hand, spoken to by those who wished to speak to me. This seemed a bit vulgar to me. I am used to guests sitting in a large room where everybody sees everybody else. The senior guests sit at the end of the room facing the door. Servants go around serving them tea and coffee. I noticed that after the party, I was followed wherever I went. It was not difficult to notice. The man wore the standard secret-police attire: *gallabiya* (long robe) and a black overcoat on top. At first, I was afraid. Then, thanks to the man's stupidity, I found I could have a bit of fun. Sometimes I slowed down to let him catch up with me. I gave him a bit of trouble when I went to have a glass of sugarcane juice and left through the back door without him seeing me. He must have been puzzled when I did not come out of the shop. I went around the block and stood a few paces behind him. He looked very relieved, an unspoken thank you on his face.

A Palestinian friend warned me to cut off any contact with the Americans. Nasser's Egypt had a strong intelligence service. He was right. I received a notice to appear before an intelligence officer. I got my first job offer as a spy.

"What is your connection with those Americans?" the officer demanded, with a stern look, sitting in his shabby office with worn-out furniture.

"Nothing."

"What do you mean, nothing? You attend their parties."

"They send invitations to professors and students and I got one. I went to see what it is all about."

"Ah! So we have the same aim."

"What does this have to do with me?"

"Very simple. Keep going and tell us who was there and what they were talking about."

"I wouldn't know how to do that kind of work."

"It is very simple. Just write us a page or two about what you see. You do not even have to enter this building. Someone will meet you in a café."

"Look, I study hard and get top marks. This will delay my studies and give me poor marks."

"So what? You can repeat the year. No problem. It is better than us canceling your residence permit and deporting you."

That did it. I could never contemplate lower marks, let alone repeating a year. I could not sleep that night. I thought of packing my bag. What were the alternatives? If deported, I could enter any other university; my three brothers in Kuwait could finance my education elsewhere. By the morning, I decided to ignore the so-called job offer. Let the officer make the next move. The man in the black coat still followed me, but less frequently. Then he disappeared altogether. I kept seeing the Gardners. They were so kind and understanding. I did not think they had the slightest intention of recruiting me or had any knowledge of others trying to do this. I never told them about the attempted recruitment by the Egyptian intelligence.

In the summer holiday, the Gardners wished to visit the Gaza Strip. They had an introductory letter to a relief organization, CARE I think. We took the dusty train across the Sinai to Gaza, a journey thoroughly familiar to me. There we took them around with the usual fuss accorded to foreign visitors. They met doctors, teachers, mayors, and of course, the orator Hussein Abu Hassan, my relative, who delivered speeches with the slightest provocation to explain our situation as refugees.

Naturally, the Americans were not popular because of their blind support of Israel. People did not need to be experts in foreign policy to feel the consequences of that support. They knew where they had lived in Palestine and where they were now, in refugee camps. They knew Israel could not do this without massive American help. They did not expect America to help them as refugees necessarily, but they hoped that America would not cause them more harm by voting against them on UN resolutions.

We visited the Jabaliya refugee camp. As we walked in the narrow alleys, George insisted that he choose which house to visit. We entered the house, or rather the shack, he selected. He found it very clean and tidy. He was visibly impressed by the numerous plants on the wall, in pots, and in a tiny patch of land, where familiar vegetables and flowers were grown—a replica of the dispossessed land in the villages. As we were leaving, I heard a woman say in her typical rural accent, "Here they come and go. They watch us like animals in the zoo and take our pictures. They are the source of all this evil."

George also noted that the family structure was still intact. He did not see boys loitering in the streets or vandalizing property.

He told me his impressions later as a sociologist. He compared the situation with what he knew in Europe after the Second World War, when crime, drugs, and broken families were common after the war.

I took him to the girls' school where Madiha, my sister-in-law, was the headmistress. After a tour of the classes, the girls sang national songs, and I was asked to translate.

"Our homeland is near but far, we shall not forsake thee. We will return home, no matter what," I whispered in his ear.

"But you did not translate the part where they say *yahud* [Jews]," he pointed out.

He was right. I skipped over: "We will defeat those criminal Jews, vagabonds of the earth, and exact our revenge for our Nakba, against them and their supporters [meaning America]." I murmured a few weak explanations, but he knew that these words fell right in the stereotyped "hatred of the Jews," not love of Palestine.

We kept in touch for years. Their daughter, Cynthia, blossomed into an intelligent, thoughtful, and decent young woman. We took a liking to each other and corresponded for several years. She visited me in England; I visited the family in the United States; and they, in turn, visited me later in Canada as well.

When another disaster struck in 1967, with the Six Day War, they were in the United States. John, their son, now a young man, wept when he heard that Cairo, his childhood playground, was bombed by Israeli planes. Cynthia was deeply upset and hurt. It left a lasting impression on her. Back in the United States in 1967, the Gardners invited me to speak to foreign-policy community groups regarding Palestine and the consequences of the Israeli occupation of land in Egypt, Syria, and the remainder of Palestine.

Studying engineering required hard work. We stayed up sometimes to the early hours of the morning to complete our projects. By contrast, those studying social studies spent most of their time at the cafeteria debating ideas. In reality, they were talking to the girls, of whom many studied social sciences. Few girls ventured into engineering. One of the few who did was my main competitor in gaining top marks. Another of our female classmates had an angelic, beautiful face and a lovely gait. All of us fell for her. She knew it, and she distributed smiles and nods sparingly in order to have the maximum impact and create rivalry among us. Her name, Balqis, fitted her description as it is the Arabic name for the Queen of Sheba—who seduced King Solomon. Our infatuation with girls did not go beyond little gestures and possibly a few private conversations. We did not have the time anyway.

I went to the university by bus. A common sight, especially during the crowded morning rush hour, was passengers clinging to a bulging bus by foothold and a hand clutching a window. I got used to this sight but for us engineering students, it required some acrobatic skills. We had to carry a T-square, a one-meter-long ruler for drawing. We did it with one foot on the step, one hand holding a window, and the other hand holding the T-square, which was flying in the wind. I managed, like others, to arrive safely. It was not much of an adventure, though; the journey was short and the bus slow. You could disengage at any time without harm.

I bought a bicycle. I strung my T-square across its length and placed my books in its rear bag. I lived on the third floor, and it was my helper's task to carry the bike daily up three floors and park it in the flat. The helper was sent to me by Hajj Abdullah, our Egyptian relative; he was a country boy who knew practically nothing of household chores.

Other non-Palestinian Arab students shared apartments or stayed in boarding houses that usually had Greek landladies. They were well off and and had plenty of spare time; they hired 'maids' to cater to all their worldly needs. Such maids hunted for clients of this sort, and called on them to offer their services. Our colleagues from Gulf countries in particular were much more privileged. They had generous scholarships. Few studied engineering or medicine. The majority studied humanities and either they were in the cafeteria or they did not show up at all. They were, however, politically alert and they embraced Arab nationalism in Nasser's Egypt as the only way for a better future for the Arabs. Some of them paid heavily for their political views when they returned and faced the traditional control of the ruling families. Others rose to very high positions in their respective countries, in spite of once harboring liberal views.

One Gulf peer of ours who was studying engineering had the habit of arriving late to classes. We had to come early because we were not sure we would find a foothold on the next bus. But he would arrive—to our amazement and endless remarks—in a taxi at the last minute and walk majestically to the classroom.

Our teachers were excellent. We were students in the best engineering faculty in the best university in the region. Many of the professors were graduates of European universities and had just returned. We were a small class, about 110 divided into four sections, and so had plenty of attention from the teachers. Still, I wanted more attention, and I visited my teachers' offices frequently. On occasion, when pressed for an answer, I would stop one of my teachers in the yard and both of us would squat on the ground drawing shapes and diagrams.

In spite of very high educational standards and teachers, my only regret on that front was that the emphasis was on reproducing the class notes in the exam, not on innovation and critical inquiry. While I frequented the empty library for extra reading and I debated with my teachers, students were not generally encouraged to question, analyze, or take a contrary line. That said, the professors responded warmly to my interruptions in their offices or in the yard—they tolerated me mainly because of my performance in class.

Social life within the university was very poor, however. There were one or two half-hearted functions per year. We never had a group photograph or a yearbook. I regretted that very much.

Our associations remained political. We, the Palestinians, together with a score of politically active Egyptian students (one of whom joined us after spending two years in jail), sat together and discussed current events. The political associations are clear in photos of the trip we took in our final year, when we toured Egypt from Alexandria to Aswan. In the photos, you can easily identify those politically active students and the Palestinians who were always in their midst.

I departed from Egypt after ten years of education; having arrived as a refugee boy, I left as an engineering graduate.

Now it was time to move on from a study desk for homework to a work desk for the real world. I was hired almost immediately for a job in Kuwait. My record got me a contract and a visa. By the end of the summer of 1959, I was on my way.

It was my first flight, and I took a vintage Second World War plane with propellers on the long journey across the Arabian Desert.

There was essentially nothing to see during the flight, but as we approached Kuwait, the plane flew over the coastal town in preparation to land. I saw an egg-shaped town, bounded by the Gulf waters and an ancient wall on the desert side, built to protect the town from raiders. It was very small (one-fortieth of its present size). As the plane veered, I took pictures of the boats and mud houses. The houses looked organically connected and neat, the results of centuries of adaptation to sea and desert life.

We landed outside the town wall *(sur)* on a stretch of land called Nuzha, now in the middle of Kuwait's metropolis. As the engines shut down, people waiting came forward and helped us carry the luggage from the plane's belly. A police officer in the crowd stamped our passports. It was a friendly and informal reception with my brothers waiting for me.

I stayed temporarily with my brother Mousa, who was a science teacher in a school recently built in Shamiya, outside the *sur*. The teachers there were provided with and stayed in new accommodation next to the school. "How was your trip?" asked Mousa, who had an aversion to air travel.

"Not bad. A little bumpy," I said.

Clearly surprised by my answer, Mousa asked, "Were you not afraid when the plane started to land?"

"No. I was taking pictures."

"Pictures? Are you crazy?" he laughed.

My brother arranged bedding for me in the sitting room until I received government accommodation. I spent my first evenings reading an Arabic translation of Hemingway's great work, *The Old Man and the Sea*.

I was nervous on my first day at work in the design section of the Public Works Department. Here was real work in a new country among colleagues who came from different countries. I shared the office with two others. The first, who became a life-long friend, was a Kuwaiti architect, a graduate of Oxford, and had recently married a young Scottish woman. The second was an Egyptian who had been in the country for some years and had adjusted his habits to suit the new locale.

There were others whose background was not clear to me. As expatriates, most of us were single, and our accommodation was at the edge of the town, some fifteen kilometers away. The group was diverse and included several German architects, one Italian, one Hungarian, and one Turk.

The Turkish architect, Altay, was a quiet man whose only job was to design mosques. The German architects stuck together and lived as a group. One of them, Fuchs, had an imposing figure and a brisk military walk; he looked much like a tank-battalion commander, which I had seen in war movies. He seemed to command the respect of his peers. His distinctive architectural work is still visible across Kuwait. Fuchs designed Kuwaiti schools, inside out, placing the corridors on the outside of the building.

The Italian architect, Negroni, was full of energy, humor, and the ability to undertake the craziest of tasks with ease. Every afternoon, he raced the Germans back to their accommodation. The road was newly built and three lanes wide, with roundabouts, instead of traffic signals every two kilometers to slow and divert the traffic. There was very little traffic and certainly no traffic policemen at the time. Negroni and the Germans sped at full throttle, and Negroni was always keen to win. When he approached the roundabout, he just cut across in a straight line over the curb and the roundabout—his rickety sports car shaking in the process—but he always won.

Practically all my Palestinian classmates in Cairo ended up working in Kuwait. The Palestinian community was growing rapidly, not only with new recruits to the workforce but also with new brides brought into the country by bachelors who were married during their summer-holiday visits back to Palestine. For the first time a new generation of Palestinians was born—far away from home.

The work was routine and I felt bored by it; despite the tremendous volume, it was not challenging. The country required so many infrastructure projects that design drawings took little time to be translated into construction. I told my brothers I wanted to pursue postgraduate education. Their response was, "You got what we have, as your father always demanded. If you wish to have further education, you do it yourself." I waited for that opportunity.

We expatriates were moved to a building more crowded than the single bungalow in which only five lived. We numbered thirty or forty, all Palestinians, mostly engineers. Someone had to look after our domestic affairs. We had a mess master and two cooks. The mess master was one of the residents and we paid him from our monthly dues to take care of the administration. He was elected, and the successful candidate was always Yasser Arafat.

Arafat's government job was as a supervising engineer, responsible for the construction of several sites. He was busy most nights debating with his friends what to do about Palestine. He continued that during the day. He managed to get away with his frequent absences (caused by his political activities) from work with the classic excuse of always being at "the other site."

I had a lot of free time on my hands in Kuwait. I visited the library of the British Council, which had opened in Kuwait several years earlier. The visitors were mostly Indian. The director was a chubby old colonial by the name of Onslow Tuckley. He had beady eyes and an instant smile, that soon disappeared, giving the impression that he concealed more than he showed.

I saw a notice of invitation for young Arab engineers to go to England for two years' training with British companies. The idea, of course, was the introduction of these promising engineers to British industry, materials, and specifications, so that these engineers would import the materials to their countries when they returned. I applied, sat for an interview, and was selected; though admittedly, it was not much of a challenge, as only a few applied.

I was not very enthusiastic about it. Who wants to provide cheap labor (we were paid living costs, not salaries) for British companies and upon our return to buy their products and increase their profits? But I took the offer, sold my second-hand Volkswagen, and pocketed seven hundred British pounds, now my total savings.

After less than a year in Kuwait, I was on my way to a strange new world.

14

Britannia Rules the Waves

It was a depressing sight. When the plane doors opened and we walked out onto the tarmac in London, in the gray autumn of 1960, I saw, in the dim-yellow caged lights, a barrack-like building ready to receive us. I went straight to the notice inscribed with my name and held by a man from the British Council, my only friend and host in England.

As I arrived at my designated accommodation, I saw the British dominions personified: black from Africa, brown from India, and yellow from the Far East. Though racist, these descriptions and appelations had been given to them by their colonizers at the time in the press, literature, and common use. It was bewildering for me to see this world of British colonies at one glance. The earliest memory I had of the British colonial regime was an Englishman, the British district commissioner who had visited our school a decade ago—the one whose eye I almost poked as I pointed to the large pink area of British dominions on the school map.

So here they were, in the flesh. Those victims of British imperialism, now beneficiaries of its generosity; we were in one huge hall together. The large hall had wooden dining tables with a serving kitchen at one end. On all sides there were corridors leading to two floors of rooms. When we were gathered for our first meal in the dimly lit hall, with unidentifiable lumps of food on our plates, I felt insulted, humiliated, and hurt. The site of the Empire's subjects gathered in one place brought to mind slave markets or captives dragged from defeated countries to show to the victorious emperor.

I could not bear this human circus in which I felt we were incarcerated. I went out to look for a decent meal in more pleasant surroundings. I entered a restaurant and asked for the menu. Although my university education was in technical English, it did not prepare me for this: the menu was a mixture of old English and affected French, pronounced with thick English accent.

I took the safe route of selecting something I knew: salad. Then came a huge bowl of salad, which I munched like a lamb eating grass. My idea of salad was a side dish of a delicious combination of vegetables, olives, hummus, and eggplant.

I had to wash it down.

"May I have coffee, please?"

"Black or white?"

I always thought coffee was black; we had it in small cups with its majestic aroma. Is it different in England? The waitress repeated the question.

"Black, please." I again went for the safe option. Then came a large teacup filled with this liquid they called coffee. That was not a good omen. My first adventure with English food was memorable in ways I had not expected.

The British Council gave me a list of homes ready to receive foreigners, and soon the question of where I would live was settled without much trouble. My random choice turned out to be a happy one, which lasted all my years in England. The home was on the edge of Blackheath in southeast London, with a huge plain and pleasant meadow where I spent many afternoons walking. The house had two bedrooms (the smaller was mine), a sitting room with a TV, a kitchen with a hatch where we had our breakfast, and a small dining room, never used.

My landlady was Margaret, a cheerful, pleasant woman in her early forties. She worked as a telephonist in a city bank, using the switchboard with headphones. Her association with the bank gave her accent a polish, concealing her working-class origins.

Ray was her second husband, whom she married as a poor replacement for her first (the man she truly loved and respected), who had passed away and had been a clerk. Ray was a soldier in the British Army at a base on the Suez Canal. He exhibited his knowledge of Arabic by repeating to me the words he had learned, which were vulgar words he picked up from camp followers. Ray aspired to social promotion by reading the conservative *Daily Telegraph*. He examined the creases of the newspaper every day to see if I had looked at it before he did.

During my first week, Margaret watched my every move discreetly from the hatch when I had my breakfast. She saw me handle a knife and a fork and that I sipped my tea without a slurp. Thankfully, she refrained from asking me, as others did, whether my (European) suit was comfortable for me, having shed my Lawrence of Arabia *thobe* in a hurry.

When she scrutinized my gestures, handshakes, and reception of new guests, she secretly decided I must have been an Arab aristocrat. She was amazed that I knew expressions like "vice versa," "quid pro quo," or "indubitable," and laughed when I spoke English translated literally from Arabic, saying things like "fish thorns" for fish bones and "foot fingers" for toes.

Margaret regularly attended séances of clairvoyance sessions, probably in search of the soul of her beloved first husband. She lit candles for him every Friday night. Despite my scepticism, she convinced me one night, several months into my stay, to accompany her to one of the séances. She must have rigged the séance proceedings, as the master pointed at me, in this hall packed full of believers.

"The gentleman in the gray suit. You are worried about people far away. You will get a letter with foreign stamps carrying good news."

The amazed British audience turned to me in awe of such precise prediction. Apparently, the clairvoyant's powers were not confined to the British Isles, but extended overseas.

"Thank you very much," I replied.

In spite of my reluctance to believe in clairvoyance, Margaret was extremely understanding and sympathetic toward me. Because my constant talk of wanting to improve my accent, she arranged for me to have elocution and dancing lessons. The elocution lady was insistent.

"Repeat after me: home, home, home. Short and high *o*. Not ho-ame. Again, again!"

I struggled with the vowels that taxed my jaw, which was trained to speak Arabic. Elocution lessons were very useful in reminding me of the proper pronunciation, but I gained real experience through interactions with my friends and university colleagues in the years that followed.

My dancing lessons were a complete failure. I could not master the waltz, foxtrot, or any other dance style. Thankfully, that was not needed, as dancing soon became the practice of jumping up and down without any prescribed order, as long as you stomp your feet and wave your hands and do it alone.

Margaret and Ray had two children living with them. They—especially Margaret—adored André and Toucqué, two white poodles with aristocratic names. Their welfare and mood were matters of great importance.

I had a love-hate relationship with the poodles. When the three of us had our dinner trays in front of the TV in the evenings, André would jump on my tray and spill the food on my suit. "Naughty boy," Margaret reprimanded, and then she hugged the little beast lovingly.

When they went out, Margaret asked me to take the dogs for a walk on the heath. They behaved well. I kept a tight grip on their leash. If they ran away, the consequences would have been unimaginable. When I returned home and was alone with the dogs, they stared at me with obvious hatred. They gnashed their teeth and howled. I prayed for Margaret to come home quickly.

My hosts dubbed me PG (paying guest), a title previously awarded to the last occupant of my room. Peter, like me, maintained a long-term friendship with the family, and was a frequent visitor during his working trips to London. He was a country gentleman from Suffolk and an electrical engineer by profession. Peter's faded aristocracy was evident in his surname prefix, St. (saint) Leger. In spite of his upper-class origins, he was a mild revolutionary and a nonconformist. He told me a story about how he once emerged from the bathroom after a shower and went naked into his mother's drawing room, while she was having tea with her lady friends.

"Peter! Shame on you. Go and get dressed." Peter reemerged wearing only a hat. The old ladies left their tea and rushed home.

Peter played the piano in the house. His performance of "Für Elise" was one of the more memorable tunes in my mind at the time. Peter was set in his ways for a non-conformist. He took his tea by waving to Margaret and drawing T with his fingers. His omelette had to be the right shape and color with the right proportions of salt and pepper, two to one. I became familiar with Peter's ways as Margaret told me anecdotes about him during the evenings. By the time I met him, he was no stranger. We kept in touch for many years. Peter eventually took a job in the Middle East, and while I was in Beirut, I introduced him to a young Palestinian woman whom he later married. They have five children now, all in America.

I learned how fortunate I was to find housing with Margaret and Ray through the British Council, that it had saved me much humiliation. I was shocked to see in the advertisements: "No coloreds need apply." Who were these coloreds? Are they the people I met upon arrival, the Commonwealth subjects? Yes, the Africans are black, the Indians brown, and the Chinese are described as yellow. But, who are the whites then? White is the color of a sheet of paper. Nobody looks like that. The English are not white; they are red or pinkish. We used to call them *humran*, the red-faced. Nobody is white, unless he or she is dead.

I wondered what the fuss regarding the color of skin was about—apparently something that summed up your worth in England. We never had these distinctions and racial conceptions. As Arabs, we had black Sudanese and blue-eyed Syrians and everything in between. We measured people's worth by their pedigree and deeds or piety, but never by the color of the skin. It would have been as absurd as classifying people by the length of their ears, the roundedness of their face, or the size of their girth.

But that was England. Fifteen years after the Second World War, British society still had the marks of austerity, remnants of a food-rationing mentality, scarves and long overcoats for women, or caps, hats, or top hats for men, all signifying their class. The nineteenth-century racism justifying the British conquests of poor defenseless people in Asia and Africa was idealized as the white man's burden and carried out by Christian soldiers. It still lingered on in 1960s England (and some may argue even today). The looting, plunder, subjugation, and death of millions of people were the signs of an inherent British sense of supremacy.

Then again, British people themselves were similarly discriminated against according to class. They were expendable for a cause, as Alfred, Lord Tennyson wrote: "Theirs not to reason why / Theirs but to do and die."

Ray, for example, would never question his social rank, the working class. It would be like the Untouchables aspiring to be

Brahmins in the Indian caste system. In his family, there was not a single person who had a university degree or held a managerial job.

The FBI, the Federation of British Industries (not to be confused with the other one in the United States), now called the CBI (Confederation of British Industries), administered our scholarship. The trainees were assembled for the first time at FBI headquarters and were addressed by Vice Admiral Sir Sydney Raw. Sir Sydney Raw was a formally attired gentleman with a gentle but tired face. He welcomed us and extolled the virtues of British industry, which he said was "ideal to help build your countries." He expected us to remain friends of Britain and to be appreciative of the opportunity to catch up with the civilized nations.

At the reception, I met about half a dozen Palestinian engineers. Among these guests were Hisham from Jerusalem, who rose to be a government minister in Jordan, holding several different posts, and Khaled, also from Jerusalem, who was working on oil projects in Aden and later had his own company. Then there was Nigel, a British colonial born in Rhodesia (later Zambia). Nigel became a lifelong friend with whom I never lost touch despite years of interruption. He retired with a knighthood.

I was assigned to Sir Frederick Snow & Partners, Ltd. as a design engineer. The site of operations—a five-story building—was located at the poor end of Blackfriars Bridge. I joined Shackland's team. Shackland, I was warned, was a tough, no-nonsense taskmaster whom everybody avoided. He was a graduate of a technical school, not a university, but was a very good engineer with superb practical sense. He received me, the new foreigner, with grim acceptance. There were a few foreigners: an Indian I hardly saw and a Greek Cypriot called Harry Sophoclides. Harry was a delightful and cheerful young man. Culturally, the Greeks were the closest to Arabs in London.[65] We looked the same, ate kebab and hummus, and made fun of the British.

He showed me how to navigate the rough British waters. Through him, I learned how to take the Tube (the London Underground) and where to go for meals and entertainment. To show off, he told me that in his room he taped the flags of all the countries of the girls he had slept with. London was full of European girls who came to the city to work as au pairs and learn English. My work went reasonably well, in spite of my initial difficulty in using British specifications and units. I got used to the daily routine of work and going to lunch with the team in a dark little basement restaurant nearby, armed with luncheon vouchers. I worked with Shackland on an ambitious new project: the building of new-age hangars for BOAC (British Overseas Airways Corporation), the forerunner of British Airways. The work was demanding, new, and exciting. I learned a great deal about how to convert my theoretical knowledge from university to a practical scheme. Shackland, as a practical man, was masterful in creating workable solutions.

My first official six-month report was very positive, but much of this praise was probably due to lower expectations for the overseas engineer. The real test came three months after my arrival. As good an engineer as he was and as many years of practical experience as he had, Shackland had a technical diploma and, thus, did not have what was called "corporate membership" in an engineering institution, which enabled engineers to put their official stamp on design drawings. I heard about this membership and asked Shackland if I could sit for its exams.

"The next exam is in January, which will be only four months after your arrival here. You don't have much time left," he said.

"I'll take a stab at it. Maybe I'll get through one or more of the three exams."

"That is what I try to do each year. Good luck," he replied.

I took evening classes in Hammersmith in preparation for the exam. I took the three-day exams in January 1961. It was a tough exam; each subject took a whole day, from 9:00 a.m. to 5:00 p.m. nonstop, in order to complete the design of a whole project.

To the amazement of everyone, including myself, I passed the three exams. A few weeks later, a letter came with another surprise. I had won first prize in two of the three subjects from those sitting the exams in the United Kingdom and the British Commonwealth. The BBC Arabic Service reported the news, and that was the start of an association with the BBC that lasted for a few years.

The FBI director of studies was delighted that one of the engineers in their program did so well and congratulated me, saying, "My colleagues and I received the news with the greatest possible pleasure. Not only did you qualify . . . but you have won two valuable prizes, which I imagine must be a unique achievement for an FBI scholar and *particularly for one who is not English*."

I disregarded the final comment in the congratulatory note and chose to give him and his intention the benefit of the doubt. As always, my mind was in Palestine, not London. The BBC news reached Gaza. My parents were delighted but had different views about how to handle it: my father wanted to spread the news, whereas my mother was completely against it, superstitious about the evil eye.

What made me most proud was the talk from among the refugee community: "Here is 'one of us' right in Balfour's den, beating them in a fair competition. We can do it. We can succeed in restoring our right to return home." The Palestinian refugee question was at its lowest ebb then. We were not even called Palestinian, only Arab refugees. The name "Palestine" had been erased in Britain. Meanwhile, Gamal Abd al-Nasser, the hero of the Arabs, had declared candidly that he did not have a magic wand to liberate Palestine and restore Palestinians to their homes. Nevertheless, hope has no boundaries; the refugees never lost hope. These small stories of accomplishments from Palestinians around the world fueled determination back home.

At the end of my first year, I decided to terminate the two-year scholarship. "But we cannot pay you your airfare back," the FBI director said.

"Yes, I understand."

"And we will not pay you a salary."

"I'll manage."

Sir Frederick Snow and others gave me recommendations, and I was accepted as a postgraduate at University College London to do my master's degree in civil engineering. Money was a problem. Very little was left of the seven hundred pounds I had saved from selling my Volkswagen when I had left Kuwait. I kept my expenses to a minimum. My main expenses were the seven pounds a week for my lodging and the railway ticket to the university.

My research work was both theoretical and experimental and under the direct supervision of a Greek professor, called S.P. Christoulides, and the general direction of a senior British lecturer, named R.H. Elvery. I worked hard and late until the latest permissible hours, some days taking the last train home from Charing Cross at 11:00 p.m.

As the train sped into the night, I saw the top edges of rows of identical houses with protruding chimneys, all dressed in smoky black and gray. As midnight approached, the sight of these houses resembled tombstones in a large cemetery. When it was pea-soup foggy, the silhouette of chimneys looked like ghosts emerging from the darkness. It was not a pleasant end to a day of hard work.

My supervisor Elvery gave me a tutoring job for undergraduates, which helped defray some of my expenses. Of greater value, though, was the memorable lesson in humility that he gave me. Higher education in Britain has traditionally been a free and open quest for knowledge. Unlike education in the United States, education in Britain did not have standard courses that ended with an exam. We had to study, inquire on our own initiative, and even go to other universities to study a particular subject needed for research.

My thesis was about three-dimensional or space structures, a new subject that needed advanced math. These structures are very thin surfaces created in space by rotating a straight line or a curve along a given path in space. They are an imitation of the egg with its very thin skin and great strength. If we can define the curved surface we create in space mathematically, we can then arrive at the optimum surface to carry high loads at minimum stress. This way, half an acre of land or more can be covered without the need for columns in the center. This work needed rigorous mathematical analysis and experimental research.

I asked Elvery for advice, and he suggested that I attend classes given by a particular math professor. I sat in his class trying to follow his lecture. He was an old man, wearing a worn-out suit. His hand was shaking while he was writing on the board. He steadily wrote one differential equation after another in long lines until he filled the whole board. Unintentionally, he missed some superscripts that were easy to locate.

Elvery asked me how I found the classes.

"Very informative and very useful. But the professor made a number of mistakes."

His face turned red and he looked me straight in the eye and said, "He is one of the best maths professors in Britain. Although he is old, he has a great mind." Then he gave me a warning, "Do not let your arrogance get the better of your talent." I took this advice to heart.

Elvery later promoted me to a PhD student without having to sit for a master's exam. That added to my enthusiasm, but my financial problems became acute.

There were prominent Arab literary figures in the BBC Arabic Service, such as Hassan al-Karmi and Said al-Eissa.[66] A younger man, Ali Abu Sinn from Sudan, who interviewed me after I had passed my membership exams and later joined the Sudanese diplomatic service, suggested I work for the BBC part time.

Based on my early interest in journalism, I decided to write short pieces on science: the new inventions and fields of study such as the computer, cosmology, jet engines, and the like. It was not difficult. The references were readily available in English and I translated short pieces into journalistic Arabic. I broadcast seven minutes weekly for which I was paid seven pounds, all of which went to my landlady Margaret to secure my food and shelter.

I finished my voluminous thesis in about two and a half years, short of the required minimum of three and a half to four years.

Me in 1961 doing PhD research at University College London on space (3-D) structures imitating strength and the shape of an egg.

"You cannot submit your thesis now. Get yourself a job until the time comes," my supervisor advised. I found a job at a major power-generation government laboratory and bided my time. Finally, one year later, the fateful day of the exam came.

I sat in front of my external and internal examiners, notes in hand ready for questions on possible areas of weakness. We chatted in general on the subject and I was waiting for the tough part. With all the advantages of higher education in the United Kingdom, there is no indication until you sit the exam that you are anywhere near completion. As I wrung my hands, waiting, the tough part of questioning did not come. I inquired sheepishly if there were more questions.

"No," the examiners said. "Your thesis is a landmark."

"You made it tough for the next chap," one of the examiners said, smiling.

During the following days, I was in a daze. I did not know what to do with my days or nights, now that my work was finished. During my studies, my research fully occupied my mind. Now it was finished. I felt like, and the analogy may be appropriate, a pregnant woman who suddenly delivered her baby and felt empty.

The usual celebration and congratulations went on—in my absence—in Gaza. Some people even speculated that I had become *Inglizi*, adopted by the British.

But life in Britain gave me much more than a PhD. It gave me, as a young refugee, a much wider perspective about my Palestine, the nature of its enemies, and the intellectual weapons with which to fight for our rights. It also gave me the opportunity to be close to Britain's valuable records on Palestine.

After finishing my PhD I stayed in Britain, in the Power Generation Lab, and worked for the BBC on the side. The BBC milieu was cultured and worldly. During cocktails, functions, or parties, we had endless debates on a multitude of issues. Some people used convoluted words that I did not understand. I found out soon enough they did not understand them either, not clearly anyway. I turned this to my advantage to discover who was fake and who was genuine.

It was a simple trick. Someone would come up with a long, contrived, lopsided sentence studded with complex expressions. I would interject by saying, "Sorry, I am a foreigner and have just arrived here. What do you mean by . . . in simple terms?" In the majority of cases, I received a reply of "eh . . . umm . . . simple . . ." but no more. I had great pleasure in using this trick.

That was no consolation, however, for the culture shock I experienced when it came to understanding European perceptions of Palestine, Arabs, or Muslims. I was talking with Ali in the BBC club when an Italian on the staff, obviously drunk, came forward and told us what he thought of the Arabs. "I wish the Jews would exterminate all Arabs, reduce them to oblivion, and take over all their land. The Arabs are savage Bedouins, thieves, robbers, murderers. They kill and hate each other." Then he emptied his stomach on the floor.

It became clear to me, even in the first months after my arrival, that the current attitude to Arabs was derived from a bygone age, and that people were reading from books written in the twelfth century. Their ideas about us were frozen in time since the Crusades. Seven hundred years had not taught them anything new, nor had it improved their knowledge about us, it seemed.

The Victorian age, with its racist notions about the supremacy of the Europeans, only served to intensify their earlier beliefs. The subsequent occupation of Egypt in 1882 and Palestine in 1917 were seen as a restoration of the Holy Land to European Christendom. I was utterly shocked to find books in bookshops near the British Museum with titles such as *The Last Crusade*, *The Restoration of the Holy Land*, and *The Colonization of Palestine*. Worse still, Prophet Muhammad was depicted as an impostor and Islam as the idolatrous worship of a false prophet. In the epic French poem *La Chanson de Roland*, swine and dogs ate Muhammad. Francis Bacon, in his essay "Of Boldness," created the popular myth that Muhammad called the hill to him. When it did not move, he went to the hill. Of course, there is no basis whatsoever in Islamic literature for this story, and the now common proverb, "If the mountain will not come to Muhammad, Muhammad must go to the mountain," was a European invention.

Train journeys were my time to read great works in English—Plato, Aristotle, Machiavelli, and Nietzsche. I read about nineteenth-century European views of my Arab land in travelers' books such as Charles Doughty's *Arabia Deserta* in his quaint but eloquent English. Henri Pirenne beautifully described the history of the early Muslim–European encounter in *Mohammed and Charlemagne*. I had a keen interest in Bertrand Russell and acquired about a dozen of his books. Even now, I continue to follow his lasting legacy represented by the Russell Tribunal. Arnold Toynbee's *Study of History* in twelve volumes, his *Experiences* and *Change and Habit: The Challenge of Our Time*, were a constant source of inspiration. I never forgot the paragraph Toynbee wrote on Palestine:

> Of all the sombre ironies of history none throws a more sinister light on human nature than the fact that the new-style nationalist Jews, on the morrow of the most appalling of the many persecutions that their race had endured, should at once proceed to demonstrate, at the expense of the Palestinian Arabs whose only offence against the Jews was that Palestine was their ancestral home, that the lesson learnt by Zionists from the sufferings which Nazis had inflicted on Jews was, not to forbear from committing the crime of which they themselves had been the victims, but to persecute, in their turn, a people weaker than they were.[67]

Thirty years of British occupation and administration of Palestine had not given the British an updated understanding of Palestine. They retained that mental block and this was a painful experience to endure. Foreigners in Britain had to hold an alien card as a residence permit. When I went to pick up my card, I looked at its information before leaving the office. I went back to the clerk. "Excuse me, there is an error on my card. You wrote "uncertain" for citizenship. I am Palestinian." The clerk was in his forties. He could have served in Palestine ten years earlier. He gave me a look of understanding. "It is only a formality."

"What do you mean, formality? I *am* Palestinian. So were my father and my grandfather. The British came to Palestine to help it build its independence. Instead, they betrayed us. You know there is a Palestine. Now you deny it exists altogether?"

I had bottled up my rage, and there was no one nearby to help me release the frustration. It took a long time to find productive ways of transforming that emotion into action. In the meantime, such encounters were frequent. Another day I was standing in line in the Aliens Office again. A woman in front of me turned and said, "The line is long," in a heavy Eastern European accent.

"Be patient. It will soon move. Where are you from?"

"I am from Israel."

"You mean Palestine."

"There is no such thing. This is Israel. We have some Arabs; we treat them well. You know, we put drops in the eyes of sick Arab children."

"What about the people you expelled at gunpoint? Are you living in a Palestinian home?" She did not answer. The line moved on.

This was the first time in my life I had met a Jew who claimed to be Israeli. I must have seen many Jews in London but none who claimed to be Israeli. At least this woman was not wearing Haganah shorts and slinging a machine gun over her shoulder.

In the press, there were almost daily attacks on the Arabs, particularly in the *Daily Telegraph* editorials and on TV news. Nasser, the great hope of the Arabs, was a prime target, and refugees were not far behind. One evening, while I was having dinner with Margaret and Ray, the comedian Benny Hill was on TV impersonating an Arab refugee, looking ugly and savage.

"Do you want to see my children? Huh?" he asked. "Here they are." An image of Aborigine children from Australia with missing teeth, a ball of hair on their heads, and rings in their noses came on the screen. The audience roared in laughter.

I remember another similar instance when I was asked to represent our lab in an international conference on power generation. On my nametag was written "Great Britain." Jenkins, a colleague and a well-known engineer, was attending on behalf of one of the leading consulting firms. As we were talking in the evening, his daughter came over with a drink in one hand and the other hand tucked behind her boyfriend. She looked at me and then at my nametag for the leading laboratory and said, "Great Britain? You?" "My lab sent the best person they have," I retorted.

While the official or public side of Britain was not welcoming, the human side of my experience was. My life with Margaret and Ray as PG was pleasant, and I went on to have a lifelong friendship with Nigel.

Nigel Thompson was born in Rhodesia and lived with his widowed mother until he earned the FBI scholarship and came to England to study, work, and restore his connection to his English roots. John Havergal, a good friend of Nigel's to whom he introduced me, was the son of a navy admiral and wanted to prove himself. At eighteen, he took a train to Paris and Italy, and then a steamer to Libya. There he crossed the Libyan Desert on camelback and the African continent by truck, until he reached Cape Town. After a sojourn there, he started the return journey on a boat through Lake Victoria and the Nile River from its origins to the Mediterranean. He took a boat from Port Said to England, carrying with him hundreds of slides and a wealth of experience. John wrote beautiful poetry and was keen on philosophical thought, and he eventually joined a Scientology church.

By contrast, Nigel was as practical as an engineer could be, worldly, and able to maneuver his way around difficult situations. By necessity, he was cynical and appreciative of centers of power. He could have been a good politician.

The three of us spent hours debating a whole series of issues. Those discussions helped me to understand other points of view and ways to advance my own. They were armed with good English, somewhat highbrow reasoning, and the usual British dry sense of humor and understatement (which I love so much). I was armed with my knowledge of Arab history and culture, and of course, my personal experience in Palestine. John dubbed me "*the* cultured Arab"; I didn't take offense because of our close friendship.

John introduced me to British poetry. His Christmas gifts were invariably poetry books. One poem that we recited frequently and with more pleasure each time was by Yeats.

> When you are old and grey and full of sleep,
> And nodding by the fire, take down this book,
> And slowly read, and dream of the soft look
> Your eyes had once, and of their shadows deep;
>
> And bending down beside the glowing bars,
> Murmur, a little sadly, how Love fled
> And paced upon the mountains overhead
> And hid his face amid a crowd of stars.[68]

In turn, I introduced him to Arabic poetry, loosely translated. He had heard about al-Mutanabbi and his majestic prose, and Abu Alaa al-Ma'arri, especially his *Resalat al-ghufran* (the epistle of forgiveness), from which scholars surmise that Dante borrowed heavily for his *Divine Comedy*. Dante returned this literary favor by allocating the Prophet Muhammad to the eighth circle of hell, reserved for "sowers of scandal and schism."

John's favorite was Edward FitzGerald's translation of *Ruba'iyat Omar al-Khayyam*. I recited to him my English rendering of a verse by the Egyptian poet Ahmed Rami, made popular by the doyenne of Arab singers, Umm Kulthum.

> The heart is exhausted with the love of beauty,
> And the chest is too tight to take what it contains,
> Oh God! How can I be so thirsty,
> While the sweet water is running under my feet.

We spent many Sunday mornings reading newspapers on Hampstead Heath, not far from the apartment they shared. In that apartment, I met many of their friends and relatives. There was a long stream of single British girls coming from colonial Rhodesia, South Africa, and New Zealand to London to study and work. None established a long relationship with either of my friends.

We, the three of us, or mostly just Nigel and I, went to the theater and attended promenade concerts up in the gods, the highest, farthest, and cheapest seats for five shillings each. One of the most delightful experiences I had was seeing *My Fair Lady* in the theater after reading Bernard Shaw's *Pygmalion*. I have seen it dozens of times at the theater and the movies.

John took me to a Christmas midnight mass at St. Martin-in-the-Fields Church at Trafalgar Square. Reading the hymns and reciting words about Palestinian Jesus, I did not feel strange but found many of the lines to resonate with *suras* in the Quran.

Everywhere I turned, Palestine seemed to arise.

At that time, the iconic singer Fairouz, with her angelic voice and Haroun Hashim Rasheed's words, was enchanting the whole Arab world. She sang for Jerusalem and most memorably for return. Rasheed, a Palestinian poet from Gaza—himself not a refugee but working for a refugee relief organization—was moved by a little girl he heard one night asking her mother in a refugee camp: "When shall we return, mother? I want to return home."

I played the tape of Fairouz songs many times and one day John asked me to translate the words. Of course, poetry cannot be translated literally, least of all by an engineer. I did my best and hoped that perhaps the expressions on my face helped a bit.

In 1962 Fairouz came to London and sang at the Royal Albert Hall. We all went. That experience and the response of the public (which had a minority of Arabs) must have had a searing effect on John, the poet. He sent me his English rendition of Fairouz's song "We Shall Return" with this introduction:

> By sending these to Fairouz, you will be doing me perhaps the greatest honor I have ever had, so I hope all goes well. I really am extremely grateful for your interest and enthusiasm and hope you will accept the dedication at the first poem as a small token of my appreciation.
>
> To Salman
> The Refugee (from the Arab song "We Shall Return")
> By John Havergal
>
> One day
> We will return
> However late
> However long the way
> We will return home
>
> O wounded heart!
> Patience!
> And never forget
> The long road home
> How sad though
> How sad it is to see our native birds
> Flying there—
> While we remain, alone.
>
> When we met
> The nightingale and I
> At the steel shrubbery

The barbed wire at the border
He prophesies:
"We will return"
He says the birds are still in our trees
Among the rose bushes
And in the meadows
Waiting for us to come home!

O wounded heart!
How long are we to be blown
Like feathers in this cruel wind?
Come, my heart
Come, let us return home!

In the summer of 1962, Nigel and I decided to join a University of London students' trip to Scandinavia. About three dozen students took the train from Victoria Station to Dover by boat across the Channel and went north by train across Western Europe. We were joined by French students who kept singing, "Alouette, gentille alouette/ Alouette, je te plumerai" and "Frère Jacques, Frère Jacques, dormez-vous?" They were lovely melodies, and we all joined in and enjoyed.

We crossed the European countries one after another. The signs and languages changed as we proceeded through the journey. It struck me that despite the different languages, the different appearances of the stations, and, no doubt, different brands of Christian faith (or none at all), they maintained one adjective: European. By contrast, we, the Arabs, have the same language, history, geography, and culture, yet we could hardly travel freely like this since Sykes and Picot sat at a table with a map and conspired to cut us into pieces.[69]

In Copenhagen, I looked in old shops. To my surprise, I found a copy of George Sale's translation of the Qur'an.[70] I paid seven pounds for it, which made a big dent in my pocket. As I leafed through the worn-out pages of the book, I read that Sale, in his opening section "Preliminary Discourse," explained, as an apology to his readers, the need for this translation and listed several rules for how to refute Muslim arguments and to convert them to Christianity. His main thesis was that Islam was a heresy to the Christian faith. Sale said he was "obliged to treat both [good and bad views] with common decency." He went on that "however criminal Muhammad may have been in imposing a false religion on mankind, the praises due to his real virtues [as a temporal leader] ought not to be denied him."

Praises aside, the same dogma about Islam persists and seems to have grown in spite of unimaginable progress in the availability and transmission of knowledge. As I write this in the twenty-first century, I can hear the same message replayed, warning of Islam and "its terrorists." The French students on the trip taught me an apt expression for this chronic malaise: "Plus ça change, plus c'est la même chose," or the more things change, the more they stay the same.

A young American woman from New York sat next to me on the long journey. She told me she was Jewish and she had "nothing against the Arabs." Perhaps she needed to say that, though I certainly did not need to hear it. Neither of us mentioned Israeli crimes.

Scandinavia, as a whole, was delightful: its people, its landscape, its fjords, and its recent history. Scandinavians converted to Christianity at the time of the Crusades, and established their churches, which were made responsible directly to the pope, around 1150. Before that, their history as Viking people is scarcely known. I remember telling Nigel that the Vikings' earliest and only recorded history was written by an Arab ambassadorial envoy, Ibn Fadlan, in the year 921. How an Arab diplomat from Baghdad became the first chronicler of Scandinavian history is a strange story indeed.

Ibn Fadlan was a clever young man who made the best of his capture by the Vikings on the Volga and wrote a diary of what he saw and heard. He did not speak their language but understood it roughly through an interpreter. His observations were sharp and have stood the test of time. As they saw him writing, they thought he was "drawing their words."[71]

It was not all history on the trip. We had fun, talking, singing, meeting new people, and laughing at the cold water or lack of it altogether at the hostel where we stayed.

Meanwhile, our friend John Havergal met a country girl near his family home and was soon consumed by love, English style. I was reminded of the wonderful and hilarious book written by a Hungarian immigrant to England during the Second World War. The book, entitled *How to Be an Alien*, was a satirical take on restrained

English social behavior and the understated use of language. You can detect, within his book's satirical portrayal of the English way of life, a trace of jealousy and envy. The author proclaimed that "you can be British but you can *never* be English." He compared the Latin lover's devotion to his beloved to that of an Englishman. The former kneels before his beloved, expressing his undying love, and then proceeds to shoot himself on the spot to prove it. On the other hand, the young Englishman meets his girl month after month, probably year after year, and then announces casually, "You know, I think . . . eh, I think I rather like you."[72]

Of course, neither John, the poet and philosopher, nor his girlfriend, Philippa, were like the young English couple portrayed in the story. Philippa was vivacious, funny, and brimming with life. When I first met her, I was struck by her passion to enjoy life, to see its bright side every day.

When the time came, Nigel and I were invited to their wedding at the bride's family home in the country. Nigel was to be the best man. I consulted Nigel about the procedure and attire. It was a top-hat affair and I rented a suit from Moss Bros. I needed instructions on how to wear the hat. Margaret rehearsed the whole procedure with me.

There was a classic weather-permitting warning on the invitation, but the weather turned out to be perfect. The wedding took place in the spacious grounds of the family home next to a small lake. Guests milled around in the marquee, where there was lots of food and drink, and others used the many reception rooms in the house where older guests preferred to congregate. The guests were all English, mostly local residents. The majority were in the armed services, friends of the parents of the bride and groom; some had diplomatic careers, and others enjoyed life as landed gentry.

Among the sea of floating top hats, I was conspicuous as the only brown gentleman. In polite conversation during the lengthy event, those men who had international experience or knowledge praised the courage and fortitude of King Hussein, their son-in-law so to speak, as he had married Antoinette Gardiner. I was appended to Jordan as my "country of origin," for alleged easy reference when meeting wedding guests. None of these gentlemen, in their forties, fifties, and older, could have been unaware of the British role in Palestine. Some of those present must have known or heard of

British officers who had been hanged and British judges who had been kidnapped by Jewish terrorists.[73]

As praise was heaped on the "plucky little king," all kinds of abuse and contempt were heaped on Gamal Abd al-Nasser, the "Arab Hitler."[74] It had been less than a decade since the unceremonious British withdrawal from the Suez Canal in 1957, and the British public's vilification of Nasser had not subsided.[75]

Out of respect for the occasion and my hosts, I could not respond. Luckily, the spring garden, full of beautiful girls, the bride's friends, made for happy distraction. Not caring about politics, we had lots of laughs, flirtation, and dancing.

Nigel was keen on Philippa's younger sister, Nicola, or Nicky. She was even more vivacious and witty, and had a pleasant naughty streak to her. Nigel and Nicky got married some years later. I regret that I was not in England at the time. The couple bought a derelict house, an old water mill astride a stream. They slowly, over many years, built a decent home that included a barn, a stable for newly purchased horses, and then planted a vineyard and made their own wine.

When I got married and had children, we spent one Christmas with them in their house. We bathed our four children, two for each couple, in the same tub. We kept in touch as the years went by and our fortunes took us to many varied countries. Nigel rose in the same consulting firm from a junior engineer to a senior director and board member.

John took a serious interest in Scientology, and his interest in human rights remained as keen as ever. It was through him that, in 1965, I learned of a new organization called Amnesty International. It was very sad for me to hear later from Nigel and Nicky that Philippa and John had separated.

The lively social life at the BBC was felt especially by those who came from outside London and for foreigners who came from abroad. Most of them lived in BBC dormitories with separate floors for males and females. The living room where everybody met was on the ground floor.

Most of the English women in the dormitories came from the countryside. Unlike in Arab countries, where there is a vast difference in quality of life between urban and rural areas, no such sharp contrast existed in England. English country girls spoke and lived like city girls, with only a slight difference in sophistication.

I became friendly with one such young woman from Hurst, near Reading. She had the unusual name of Jillon (not Jill or Gillian) Sarsby. Jillon was quite adventurous and wanted to meet new people and see the sights and sounds of London. We did the usual tours together, from the Changing of the Guard ceremony at Buckingham Palace to Kew Gardens. We went to see many plays and musicals. Her younger sister, Jacquie, came to London a few times to join us. It was awkward for a young Arab man to deal with the friendship of an English girl. What does she expect? What was the proper way to treat her? What were the limits of acceptable or expected behavior? Her friendship was a training manual for both of us, but in different ways.

Jillon accompanied me to an annual dinner given by Sir Frederick Snow and Partners at the Connaught Rooms. It was my first experience of attending these formal dinners in my first year in England. The reception, the announcement of guests, the multi-course dinner, the Queen's toast and speeches were totally new to me and partly to Jillon.

Sir Fredrick, pleased by my engineering performance, and with a keen public-relations eye, spoke with me at some length in the reception line while a photographer took our pictures (which he sent to King Hussein with an appropriate letter). Jillon was thrilled with the photograph and sent it to her mother, ostensibly to tell her about what she was doing in London, but really more to respond to her mother's disapproval of Jillon going out with an Arab.

Jillon put it delicately to me, in a letter:

> I sent it to my mother just to PROVE to her that you ARE civilized, well-educated, good looking and charming into the bargain. At last she agreed with me; *some* Arabs are nice.

The adventurist spirit in both of us soon faded out, but the memory remains.

On regular working days, I got off my train at Westcombe Park in the evening. As commuters dispersed to their houses, I slowly climbed the hill, admiring these small beautiful houses with manicured gardens of flowers, grown on the tiniest patches of soil. In April, walking up the hill was like promenading in a festive symphony of colors and smells.

The house where I stayed with Margaret and Ray was on top of the hill. By the time I reached there, most of my fellow commuters had disappeared, but not all of them. There was a young lady who followed me, paces apart, up to the top of the hill, one evening after another until I decided to make those paces separating us be in front instead of behind me.

She turned to my street and entered the house smack opposite mine. We acknowledged each other's presence. It was not much of a surprise when I talked to her while we climbed the hill. She was a beautiful young woman with golden hair and blue eyes, radiating with health and as clear they make them in the Harz Mountains of Germany. Helga came to London to study English while she worked in a clothing store. She was keen to improve her fortune in life, armed with intelligence and German determination.

Helga and I saw each other frequently as neighbors. We took walks on the lovely Blackheath at dusk, sometimes in the company of Margaret's two poodles. Over a couple of years, this neighborly relationship grew to a keen attachment. Margaret liked Helga, and when Helga crossed the road to visit me one day, Margaret said, "This girl is clean and wholesome."

When Helga's mother was made aware that Helga went out with a man from the Morgenland, the Crusaders' name for the Holy Land, the exotic mysterious East, she was apprehensive: maybe this man was of Saracen origin. Helga would shrug it off and call me in German, "my beloved little monster." She sang delightfully, and encouraged me to sing with her, "Lili Marlene," which I learned by heart:

> Vor der Kaserne
> Vor dem grossen Tor
> Stand eine Laterne
> Und steht sie noch davor.

It was getting very serious with Helga. One night, she knocked on my window with tears streaming down her cheeks. "Peter wants to marry me. What do you think?" Peter was a decent English chap doing his PhD in physics. She had mentioned him regularly before, but only casually. I felt terrible and utterly limp in mind and body. Helga would have been a perfect wife, beautiful, decent, intelligent, and hard-working. Above all, our attachment to each other was very strong, cemented on our walks block by block over some years.

But I asked myself, "Would she be the perfect wife in thirty years?" Now we are both in a foreign country, but what about later? What does she know about Palestine? Would she sympathize with me, share my work? Would she cry when a disaster befell us? Would she get angry about the death and destruction meted out to Palestinians every day? Would she teach my children to love Palestine? Would she laugh at a Palestinian joke or even cook a Palestinian dish? Many non-Palestinian wives did so, but I had my doubts, and to be fair, that was probably because I expected much of her.

It was not without reason that I had doubts. One evening we went to the movies at Tottenham Court Road. The film was about the Boxer Rebellion in China in 1900. The purpose of the uprising was to overthrow the yoke of European domination in China. The British fought wars to keep their profitable business of selling opium to the Chinese. Other Europeans fought to keep their commercial interests at the expense of the Chinese, who were kept in unfavorable conditions. Every European country had its consul, merchants, and military regiments.

As the battle raged on in the film, I was on the Chinese side, defending their liberty. Helga was tense and worried. Finally, the European regiments entered the fray one after the other. "*Unseres* (ours)," Helga shouted in delight and pressed my hand as the German regiment appeared on the screen. Helga (and the cinema audience) applauded enthusiastically when their troops finished off the Chinese rebellion.

Peter married Helga and they moved to Boston, where he took a prominent position in physics research. Helga and I kept corresponding for several years and we met in London and in her Boston house, exchanging notes about our families and children. She is now a senior director in a publishing company and entirely happy with the choice she made for herself.

There were very few Arabs in England in the 1960s. Those I knew were mostly Palestinians living there and working for the BBC or studying for higher degrees. Of the latter, there were about a dozen with whom I met up once a month. They all assumed high positions when they returned to their countries of exile in the Arab world. They were a privileged few sent by their governments for political reasons or to secure their loyalty to them. One became a deputy minister of energy in the Gulf, and another became a minister of oil in another Arab country. These were exceptional circumstances for Palestinians, when their host governments became convinced of both their talent and their loyalty.

There were also those Palestinians who came on their own for higher education. Wajdi, a dermatologist, became a registrar at an Oxford hospital. Adel, a civil engineer, left his construction business to study for his master's degree. My own brother, Suleiman, came twice in this period—once for a diploma in tropical medicine and another time to attain his Membership of the Royal College of Physicians (MRCP).

In 1961, I had visitors from an unexpected quarter. Members of the first Palestinian refugee delegation on their way to the UN to plead their case stopped in London for a few days on their way to New York. The delegation consisted of Dr. Haidar Abd al-Shafi, Mounir al-Rayyis, mayor of Gaza, and my brother, Ibrahim, representing the Palestinian Lawyers Syndicate.

For those thirteen years since the Nakba, the voice of the Palestinian refugees had not been heard directly. There was a terrible need for the Palestinians themselves to describe the colossal plight of the refugees to the international community. Gamal Abd al-Nasser arranged the trip for this delegation in recognition of their rights and of his inability to do something about Palestine. I was astonished at how ill prepared the delegation was. To be sure, they had unshakable faith in Palestinian rights and they were prominent in their society. But they did not have proper documentation, a political program, or a lobbying strategy. They were relying on diplomatic help from the Arab League office in New York.

At our monthly Palestinian meetings, we discussed these issues. We all pointed out the importance of speaking to the west in its own language, as Fayez Sayegh had done so successfully.[76] We all believed in the armed resistance as the route to recovering our homes. It was aptly described by Abd al-Nasser in his famous line: "What was taken by force is to be restored by force."

We had an important visitor, Dr. Walid Kamhawi, a Palestinian from Nablus, whose seminal work, *al-Nakba and Reconstruction*, described his diagnosis and suggested solutions.[77] Armed resistance was on top of the list. We were all very conscious of the fact that the Nakba was directly responsible for the collapse of all neighboring Arab regimes: the fall of the monarchy and the rise of Arab nationalism in Egypt, the assassination of King Abdullah of Jordan, the frequent coups d'état in Syria, and the termination of Hashemite rule in Iraq. Transjordan was transformed by annexing eastern Palestine, dubbed "the West Bank" since 1948.

The problem was to find a way to take action when Arab countries, where the refugees were exiled, were either unable or unwilling to restore Palestinian rights. Worse still, they would not let Palestinians take action. It seemed Israel's occupation extended to all neighboring Arab countries.

The talks we had led to nothing. They were merely an expression of frustration and, of course, extreme concern. We always ended up eating a hearty kebab and hummus meal at a Greek restaurant, a sure expression of homesickness.

Adel was different. He was politically active. As engineers, we shared the experience of planning and undertaking practical action. Although he shared an office with me at University College while studying there, I did not see him very often. My schedule was tied up by my lab experiments and his was not. I sat with him over Sunday lunch at the usual Greek restaurant. I drafted a few lines of the principles of a new secret society and sounded him out on them. In the simplest terms, the society:

- has no allegiance to any Arab country or party
- derives its strength from God's justice, which never fails
- consists of a very small number of highly efficient members, organized in disconnected cells
- trains its members in grades from which they graduate up ward according to talent and experience
- creates and encourages a totally different group of people to act publicly within refugee camps for education of the young
- creates a similar or an extended group to act as the spoksmen of the society, who could or should be members of an Arab parliament.

That was in late 1963 and early 1964. As my days in Britain drew to a close, major changes in the Palestinian political scene took place in the Arab world by the end of 1964 and early 1965, namely the formation of the Palestine Liberation Organization (PLO) and the rise of Fatah. My life too entered a new stage.

15

Building the Country

In 1965, I received a job offer from the Kuwait City Municipality to act as a technical advisor to the municipal council, and primarily as a manager for a huge development project along Kuwait's shorelines. The offer was initiated by Tarek Bushnaq, a Palestinian town planner in Kuwait. He was asked by the mayor to suggest an Arab engineer with advanced education.

The offer was great news. My original excitement and the desire to learn in England were satisfied. It was time to move on. Here was an opportunity to use what I had learned to benefit an Arab country, now that Palestine was out of reach. Kuwait was a familiar place and had a large Palestinian community. Besides, I had three brothers working there.

The mayor, Muhammad Yousef al-Adsani, was a man of integrity and keen ambition to develop Kuwait. He was modest and austere but had an iron will. He rightly knew that the Kuwait City Municipality was really all of Kuwait, and he wanted to create a new country under one administration.

When he received me and explained his ultimate objectives, he asked me to identify the best ways to achieve these goals. There were three positions separating me from the mayor: Jassim, the general director of the municipality; Hamed, the Kuwaiti head architect and a friend since my first job; and Abd al-Haq, a Palestinian chief engineer and the brother of Dr. Haidar Abd al-Shafi.

My project, valued at fifteen million dollars, a huge amount at the time, was to fill the land along Kuwait's shorelines and build islands where marinas, entertainment and sports centers, restaurants, and shopping malls would be built. It was designed by a Canadian consulting firm with futuristic ideas. The project was very exciting. Although I did not have particular experience in this field, the training and education I had enabled me to tackle the task. We had constant meetings with the consultants and all the government ministries. In addition, foreign delegations visited Kuwait. Though the mayor's English was limited and he had invited me to attend the delegation gatherings and interpret, he was a very intelligent man and could see through his visitors' intentions in spite of the language barrier.

We often worked late, and when we left the office, I would drive my modern, government-issued car, and he would drive his battered old Volkswagen. When I inquired about that, he said that the car was his own property, while the others were public property.

"I'm going home; I am not on duty, so I use my own car." He stood next to his car for a while and said, "It is easy for me to get rich here. I just have to look the other way when I see some irregularity. But we have a difficult task, to serve our people and build their future."

He asked me once to review the cycle of applications and to suggest ways to improve the procedure. Almost everybody in Kuwait had some business with the municipality, whether it was building a house or a workshop, renting a piece of land, opening a restaurant, or selling vegetables.

I took a small team with me and traced the procedure of applications. It did not take long to find reasons for the delays and obstacles. The government made it a priority to give jobs to Kuwaitis—which was fair enough—but this also created unnecessary positions: one man's sole job was to write the date of incoming mail, and another, the date of outgoing mail. With better education and training, people could streamline their work: several tasks could be done by one person.

The bulk of the work was done by Palestinians, mostly 1948 refugees, who had left their families back in Gaza and the West Bank. They were terrified they might one morning receive a notice of *tafnish* stating that their services were no longer required, or "finished." After their exile, they feared more hardship and displacement for their families. The conclusions were obvious: more training for Kuwaitis and more job security for Palestinians.

I conveyed these two conclusions to the mayor. The Kuwaiti employees were quick to ask, "What is this restructuring your advisor wants to do?" The mayor thanked me for the report and hinted that I had more important things to do. That was the end of the matter for me. He dealt with it his own way instead.

Nevertheless, there were still happy endings to be found. I noticed a long line of Kuwaitis approaching the mayor for permission to build here and there. I observed once, gently, that he was wasting his time with those who wanted favors and exceptions. "My job is to serve the people," he said.

"But instead of resolving cases piecemeal, it can be done collectively."

"How?"

"By building a master plan."

"What will that do?"

"It divides the whole country into categories: commerce, industry, education, health, and residential. Each area will have standard regulations to follow, suitable for twenty or thirty years from now depending on population size and economic conditions."

"That sounds great. How can we proceed?"

"With your permission, I can contact Professor Colin Buchanan at University College."

"Go ahead."

In the mid-sixties, Colin Buchanan acquired great fame, as well as a great deal of criticism, over his plan to modernize Britain—with its narrow roads and old buildings—to meet the demands of rapid transport, the essential artery of development. Praise and criticism greeted his revolutionary book, *Britain 2000*.

I traveled back to the United Kingdom to see him. "I just graduated from the civil engineering department next door. Your reputation has reached far and wide. I am carrying a business proposal for you from Kuwait."

"Where is Kuwait?"

I explained.

"Ah! The oil sheikhdom!"

"Now it is more than that. A land of opportunity."

"No, thank you. I am not interested."

"Professor Buchanan, you have been severely criticized on the grounds that your proposal would pull down old buildings to make way for wide American-style highways and interchanges, devoring the English landscape. Now you have a golden opportunity to apply your ideas. This is a virgin country in need of a master plan."

"But it is so far away and I do not know it."

"Come for a week and see for yourself." He agreed, provided that he had time to buy a souvenir from the old *suq* for his wife and his secretary.

Hamed, the chief architect, and I took him on a helicopter ride all over Kuwait. A steering committee was formed and Hamed took charge of the project on behalf of the municipality. Buchanan's team grew to about two dozen architects and engineers. This became a Kuwaiti-run permanent department that exists to this day. The British expatriates were eventually phased out, and the staff, all Arab, grew at one time to almost one hundred.

I paid a visit to the British Council. Its director, Onslow Tuckley, received me warmly in his old house attached to the Council. It had all the trappings of the British Raj, complete with well-trained, turbaned Indian servants. He was a smooth talker with the upper-middle-class accent heard in the drawing rooms of the 1930s. Tuckley, it seemed, never married, and he had distinctively effeminate manners. Tuckley was pleased to hear my news and glad that I was succeeding.

Through him, I was introduced to the first secretary and other officials of the British embassy. They dropped by my office to see how things were going. Their main interest was the trade that resulted from the projects. I was invited to teas and dinners, and soon the invitations came from the American embassy as well.

I had a brief dalliance with a young American woman at the embassy. We had the occasional meal and went to the movies. Neither of us ever discussed our jobs, and looking back now, I think that the embassy perhaps considered me a potential asset. Ultimately, though, the chemistry was absent and the companionship ended.

Patrick Seale, the Middle East correspondent of the *Observer*, came to learn and write about my project. Kuwait had declared independence in 1961 and became a member state of the UN. It was a quiet, safe, and prosperous country under the rule of Sheikh Abdullah al-Salem. It was a working place where Palestinians took senior positions in education, health, and construction. Kuwaiti people were friendly to the expatriates and appreciative of their services, though social contact with Kuwaitis was very limited. Social activity among Palestinians was much higher. After all, young men who had come ten years earlier were married with children by now. Their children played together and created a new community, the first Kuwaiti-born Palestinian generation.

In this tranquil climate, working during the day and socializing with family in the evenings, who would have thought that Kuwait, like Beirut, Trieste, or Tangier, was a den of spies? There was no grand motive, except of course, the oil. But oil was safe and exports were steady. It must have been the western powers' fear of Arab national aspirations and their potential effect on oil supplies. Demands for a Middle East free from western colonialism and domination were inflamed by Gamal Abd al-Nasser and now by the growing Palestinian community.

I soon got my second job offer to be a spy, following my first offer in Cairo, this time in the usual subtle British manner. Sherrington was a young teacher at the British Council, a genuine and intelligent person. We exchanged invitations for dinner. I was a bachelor and he was newly married. Sherrington was well connected, and he introduced me to the small Kuwait English radio station, where I pursued my hobby of broadcasting a weekly program called "Science Diary."

Sherrington said that I had a good file at the embassy and I should enhance it further. I started to notice some suspicious British activities. I was meeting a friend at the airport on one occasion. While there, I just barely recognized the short, chubby Tuckley, who was wearing dark glasses and a long overcoat as he disembarked from a plane arriving from Qatar. What was he doing there, this English teacher? Later, while on holiday in Beirut, I watched a demonstration against western policies. I saw Tuckley again, sitting in one of the cars that kept circling the crowd. What was this English teacher doing in Beirut, milling around the demonstration?

These spottings made me reconsider the purposes of certain foreign people I had come across in Kuwait. There was also a French engineer who knew Tuckley well; he was married to an articulate American woman. We had dinner from time to time. Once, he insisted on taking a close-up picture of me. Another time, he rented a spacious office, but he had no staff and no work took place there. He traveled a lot; his English was no match for his wife's, even for small talk. A young English woman was a frequent guest of theirs; with no obvious means, she was living alone, claiming to be looking for her husband, a Palestinian student she had met in Britain.

Marshall, who was a senior officer at the embassy, frequently visited my office. When he knew I was going to Paris, he asked me to meet a Mr. X at the British embassy there and deliver a personal letter. I arranged to meet this man. He was cold, not friendly in the least. It felt more like a one-sided interview. If that was a secret mission, I must have failed.

Then there was Page, who became the architect of sheikhs' palaces and who was also closely connected to the embassy. Unlike most of us, he traveled regularly to the Trucial States (later the United Arab Emirates) and the Oman Sultanate, a forbidden land for Arabs at the time. The common contact for all those people was Tuckley. He seemed to act like the leader, and they all knew and visited him regularly.

The breakdown of my relationship with the British circle in Kuwait came soon after these connections became clear. Once, Sherrington gave me a ride in his car. On the way, he explained how the situation was deteriorating in Jordan, Yemen, Algeria, and other places, all because of Nasser and his extremism.

I do not think I was very diplomatic in my response, which was very different from the polite small talk that we were accustomed to. I told him about the shameful legacy Britain had left behind in Palestine, handing over the country to new colonists and transforming Palestinians into destitute refugees. I proceeded as if debating with an academic, which he was, ignoring any other occupations he may have had. News traveled quickly to Mr. Lamb, the first secretary at the embassy, whom I had invited with others to tea the next day. He caught a case of diplomatic flu and canceled our visit. Three years later, Archie Lamb became the British political agent in Abu Dhabi and had a hand in deposing Sheikh Shakhbout and installing the sheikh's brother Zayid. I was on a business trip to Abu Dhabi at the time of the deposing of the Sheikh and called and left him messages to enquire about business opportunities. He did not return my call.

Meanwhile, Palestinian political activity was not dormant. The search for the best way to recover our land slowly shifted from reliance on Arab countries, which had failed so miserably in 1948, to self-reliance. That required the acceptance by Arab countries of Palestinian operations in their territories. The Palestinians also hoped for material and political support from their Arab brothers.

The Gaza Strip was probably the best example of Palestinian independence. It was unfettered by an Arab regime's claim of sovereignty over the territory. Nasser had no claims on Gaza and his rule was generally administrative, provided our actions were not considered harmful to Egypt.

Thus, it was in Gaza that the first-ever Palestinian Legislative Council was convened in 1961. Previous attempts since 1920 had been nipped in the bud by the British Mandate, the so-called protector of Palestinian national rights. The All-Palestine government declared in Gaza in October 1948 had been stillborn, because of the Arab governments' reluctance to stand actively for Palestine after the 1948 defeat.

My cousin Hamed, the engineer, spent the 1950s in Saudi Arabia in the construction business. He acquired a small fortune by the standards of the era and he put it to use. He agreed with Ahmed Shuqayri (who was to become the first chairman of the PLO) that the pursuit of an independent Palestinian voice was the correct approach.[78] It followed that an independent Palestinian entity should be created. Hamed donated half his assets to this endeavor. He accompanied Shuqayri to Arab capitals from Kuwait City to Rabat lobbying for the idea. When Shuqayri came to Kuwait, I saw him with two members of my family, Abdullah and Hamed. As he spoke in his hotel room, not displaying the oratory he was known for, I found his arguments were made up more of wishes than plans. But he carried a long record of diplomatic experience and was acceptable to many Arab leaders.

The first Palestinian National Council (PNC) met in Jerusalem in 1964, passed the Palestinian National Charter, and created the Palestine Liberation Organization (PLO). Its members numbered one hundred, as selected by consultation between Shuqayri and the Palestinian communities he visited. It was perhaps the best representation of the Palestinian people seen yet. They represented all towns and villages, community leaders, leaders of the 1936 revolt, 1948 fighters, and notable political leaders.

King Hussein's supporters attempted to interfere in the PNC meeting. They insisted on adding some West Bank members who were loyal to him. In spite of this larger attendance, however the official record listed only one hundred.

There were three members of my family in the PLO: Hamed, who remained on the PLO executive committee for over forty years; Abdullah, who became the Palestinian ambassador to Qatar; and Ibrahim, the lawyer, who was on the first executive committee.

Back in Kuwait, Yasser Arafat was holding secret meetings that eventually led to the creation of the Palestinian National Liberation Movement, or Fatah by reverse acronym in Arabic. Though he had known me and my family since 1948, Arafat never approached me to join Fatah. Perhaps he had in mind fresh recruits from among the young teachers, lawyers, and engineers now working in Kuwait, Qatar, and Saudi Arabia.

No member of my family ever joined a narrowly defined political party, although we were always active in the political field. As far as freedom of our country was concerned, we had fought for it since the First World War, when my father fought the British at the Suez Canal in 1915. We had participated in all military and political activities since then. Abdullah, as you recall, was the leader of the resistance to the British in the 1936–39 revolt, as well as resisting the Zionists from 1947 to 1956 in southern Palestine. With or without political-party affiliation, we ensured that our participation and leadership continued as the national movement took shape again.

Yasser Arafat's clandestine meetings continued to collect recruits. One senior member was Khaled al-Hassan, from Haifa. As a secretary of the municipal council of Kuwait, al-Hassan held a very important position in Kuwait. He was clever and had a great ability to maneuver and bring together opposing views, a quality needed for any council member.

Although I saw the mayor of Kuwait City frequently, al-Hassan kept his distance from me for several weeks. Apparently, he needed a period of evaluation. He visited me at my home and we discussed the current situation. He was so cautious that he kept rubbing his hand behind the sofa and glancing at the table lamp to check if they were bugged.

I asked him if he knew anything about this mysterious organization called Fatah, which claimed to have made raids into occupied Palestine in January 1965. He was cagey but mentioned that in that raid, Israel had captured one of its fighters, by the name of Mahmoud Bakr Hijazi.

I thought of John Havergal, who had told me he had just joined Amnesty International, whose mission was to free prisoners of conscience. "Why don't we put Hijazi's case to them?" I wondered. Al-Hassan was intrigued and interested.

I took down all the information and flew to London, where, through John, I had an interview in Amnesty's very modest office. I handed over a lengthy memorandum making the case for the man. My theme was that he was a Palestinian expelled from his home by a foreign militia. He had tried to return, was captured, and then imprisoned.

I waited for an answer. It was an unusual case for Amnesty. Palestine, Palestinians, and the right of return were totally outside their vocabulary. The reply came at last on 11 October 1965, signed by Andre Mann, head of the investigation department.

> Our assembled information now permits us to come to some decision on this case. I am sorry to say that Hidjazi [*sic*] cannot be "adopted" as a "Prisoner of Conscience" by an AMNESTY Group, of which there are 400 spread around the world. You will understand that we cannot officially support the case of an individual who, according to his testimony and to the evidence reproduced in the Arab press, has crossed the frontier armed.

A letter was also sent to the Israeli Embassy in London, which operated without any opposition in the media, and it would have been most unusual for them to receive such a letter from Amnesty on behalf of a Palestinian. To their credit, Amnesty did not fully drop the case, but offered to send a British lawyer to attend the court proceedings and defend Hijazi. They also offered to cooperate with the Arab Bar Federation on the case. During the trial, Hijazi demanded to be recognized as a prisoner of war. The Israeli court turned down this request, and in May 1966, Hijazi was sentenced to thirty years in prison. Fatah, which celebrates its 1 January 1965 inauguration annually, lists Mahmoud Hijazi as its first prisoner.

The following year, I visited Jerusalem with my father for the first time. There I met Jum'a Hammad and Kamel al-Sharif, who had fought the Israeli occupation of the southern district in 1948. As Muslim Brotherhood members, they were accused of plotting against Nasser. They escaped to Jerusalem, where King Hussein of Jordan gave them shelter, protection, and opportunities for jobs and to express their views. I also met the mayor of Jerusalem, Rouhi al-Khatib, and he offered me the position of Jerusalem city engineer. It was a prestigious offer, regardless of the modest salary , meeting my ambition to help develop my country. There was also the added incentive of my intention at the time to meet a particular young woman from a well-known Jerusalem family, who might have been a good marriage match for me.

Unfortunately, matters did not work out on either count. I still hang on my wall a panoramic picture of Jerusalem, which the mayor sent me three months before the fall of Jerusalem in June 1967.

I flew to Beirut to meet friends of my family during my short summer holiday. One of them was a Palestinian banker who had made it in the tough Beirut market. He was on his way to meet a family, friends from Haifa who had moved to Cairo and Amman and then settled in Beirut. He asked me to join him, and I readily accepted, as he had hinted that there would be attractive eligible women present.

We had tea and I knew from the conversation that our hosts were a prominent Haifa family who owned much property in the city and surrounding villages. The grandfather was the mayor of Haifa at the beginning of the twentieth century. The father, our host, was now a bank manager. They had lost all their property, of course, and they lived on the father's modest bank salary.

Their eldest daughter, Najia, caught my eye. She was very pretty, petite, and delicate, with a smiling face. I managed to see her again, loosely chaperoned, and we corresponded for months after and met on my short visits to Beirut. In September 1966, we were married and she moved with me to Kuwait. She did not like it a bit. She started to experience physical pain, attributed to the weather, which must have aggravated other problems.

My work at the municipality project was progressing well, but came to an abrupt end. The government did not like the independence and ambition of Mayor Adasani and his forward-looking council. The council was disbanded by royal decree. The replacement mayor was a colorless man who lacked vision and was presumably ready to toe the government line.

The vacuum of leadership for the city-planning projects was filled by the minister of public works, Khaled al-Eissa. The ministry's job, of course, was to construct projects, not to plan them. He held a large meeting, attended by our side of the municipality and his engineers at the ministry, in order to discuss future plans. We were over a dozen engineers and architects. The new minister pointed with his hand that he wanted to open a new street here and there and to close this and that one. This could have caused significant changes to the major Kuwaiti shoreline project, a municipality responsibility. I objected on the grounds that it contradicted the whole scheme and it needed careful study to judge its feasibility.

He took this as an affront to his authority and remarked, "Your daily bread is in this project," meaning that if the project was canceled, I would have no job. I got very angry at the guarded threat and insult to my professionalism.

"Of all the fifteen engineers present, if we were outside the borders of Kuwait, I would be the first to get a job. No, thank you. I do not need your job."

As a result, there was a breakdown in communication between the ministry and the municipality, which lasted several weeks. The new mayor was lukewarm and ineffective. It was time to move on.

I enjoyed productive cooperation with the Canadian consultants. One of them was a soil engineer named Larry Soderman. Larry was a down-to-earth man, a senior in his consulting firm, and also a professor at the University of Western Ontario. Hearing the news that I was ready to move on from my current position, Larry suggested that I teach at his university, an offer I gratefully accepted. He arranged a contract for me, and we completed formalities as landed immigrants in Canada. It was a big leap into the unknown, but I had become used to such leaps. I did not heed the advice of my friends, who thought I was crazy to leave Kuwait and travel to "Eskimo land" to live in an igloo. A quarter of a century later, tens of thousands of Palestinians found that "Eskimo land" was the most warm and welcoming home for them after their expulsion from Kuwait, following its liberation from Saddam Hussein.

16

The Naksa and Eskimo Land

We started to pack for the journey to the New World. There were lots of good-byes to my brothers and friends in Kuwait. My colleagues at the municipality, its officials, and friends all attended a farewell party organized by my friend Nu'man. I planned to visit my parents in Gaza to say good-bye and to introduce my bride. It was May 1967 and the news was filled with headlines of imminent war. As it was revealed later, of course, it was Israel that was secretly planning the war. I received a terse telegram from my brother Ibrahim in Gaza, "Do not come. Situation tense." That was a good piece of advice.

We went to Amman instead and saw my brother Ali, and then we went to Beirut to spend a few days with my wife's family. Najia's family, her three younger sisters, her parents, and her grandmother, were very close, full of laughter, and seemingly without a care about the war looming on the horizon.

While not quite the final sailing of the *Mayflower*, our departure to the New World was to a place far away; it did not have easy telephone connections overseas and letters took more than a month to arrive. Our departure was punctuated by Najia's grandmother's tears, sobs, and pious prayers for a safe journey.

Early on the morning of 5 June 1967, Najia's father took us to the airport. We took our seats on the plane to London. We had no idea that this would be the last plane to leave Beirut that week, or even month. In London, we stayed at a small hotel in the West End. Knowing we came from Beirut, the proprietor was especially courteous.

"Did you know there is a war on?" he said slowly.

"Where? When? How?"

He answered our exclamations by bringing a TV set to our room. On its small black-and-white flickering screen, we watched in total disbelief the news of the destruction of the Egyptian air force and the Israeli advance into the Egyptian Sinai, the West Bank, Syria's Golan Heights, and of course, the Gaza Strip.

It was all unbelievable and incomprehensible. During the past twenty years, we had thought, dreamed, and planned for the advance in the opposite direction—to return to our homes and lands, to resume our peaceful lives, to terminate the shameful life of exile, and to restore our bond with our land, perhaps just in time to water the trees, repair or reconstruct the destroyed homes, and clean up the wells filled up by Israel. There was still a living memory that could trace places, fields, and roads, without the help of maps. For a year or two after the Nakba, people were able to sneak back to their houses in the darkness and find them as they had left them. Their horses could have returned to their stables by their own instincts. Birds, as the Fairouz song goes, did not leave and they would be waiting for us. Cactus trees, called *sabr* in Arabic, with the appropriate double meaning of 'patience,' would still be there; even if the trees had been cut down, they would grow again. The tracks, unpaved roads leading to the village or the fields, might still be traceable, although Israelis had plowed them in the opposite direction.

We had held our world in suspension over these years. We had taken a mental photograph, a still, of our life. Now the suspension ended and the photograph was forced to become a memory of a past reality.

In the following days, I hoped that I would wake up from this nightmare with a sigh of relief, that "it was only a dream." The terrible news of the Israeli occupation advancing on our land was like blood seeping over our wounded body, from limb to limb. Jerusalem, glorious Jerusalem, fell. The sight of Moshe Dayan at Haram al-Sharif (the holy site of the Noble Sanctuary) was difficult to believe. We found ourselves rubbing our eyes again and again. Historic al-Khalil (Hebron), resistant Nablus, defiant Jenin, all fell silently, without a crash, melting like an ice cube left in Kuwait's August sun.

And of course, the Gaza Strip, the largest refugee camp, fell; and because the memories of the horrendous massacres in 1956 were still alive ten years later, the Gaza Strip did not fall without resistance.

We switched TV channels from station to station. We had all the newspapers spread on the floor. On the third or fourth day, we went out to the street. We walked in a daze. The shops, the buses, the cars doing their daily routine, did not register in our minds. We did not see them. All we could see was the horizon where our homeland lay in captivity. We ran into one or two Palestinian friends visiting London at the time. We looked at each other, and each went on his or her way, speechless.

Then came another insult to follow the shameful defeat. The newspapers were full of stories: The glory of the small, righteous, defiant nation that resisted extermination by the massive hordes of savage Arabs with their lust for spilling blood. God has won. Civilization has won. Yet the victorious were magnanimous and had to administer the occupied territory as the "most humane occupation" in history. The news concluded that none of this would have happened if the Arabs had resorted to peace and accepted the occupation of 80 percent of Palestine and the expulsion of its people.

These stories were a facet of another war I did not expect, a war far away from the battlefield, in which I found myself defending my identity, my history, not to mention my country, as I listened to the radio, watched TV, or read the newspapers. Day and night, we paid the price of defeat again and again, vilified, scorned for being so evil, deserving what we got, and more. In one place, Israeli soldiers were treading over our soil in Palestine; in another, Israeli tongues and minds treading over our souls in London.

I rang Patrick Seale at the *Observer* to find out more news, perhaps less painful. He confirmed it all. My repeated calls afterwards were unanswered. There was no more to say. After a week of painful sojourn in London, we traveled to Canada.

The Canadian landscape that greeted us was a totally different experience. The expanse of land, as far as the eye can see, was lush green, dotted by trees bearing a full rainbow of colors, and by scattered houses and barns like sentries of this paradise. The serenity and peaceful surroundings were surreal, compared to what we left behind. It truly felt like a New World.

We had a very warm reception from Larry and Carol Soderman and their children. They insisted that we stay with them until we settled in. We were entertained daily with barbecues and outings. Larry introduced us to another family at the university, Alan and Sheila Davenport and their children. Alan was a brilliant engineer who made his mark by introducing a new field of aerodynamics in civil engineering. He was a pioneer in research work on the effect of wind on tall structures. His work aided in ensuring that very tall buildings, slender bridges, and three-dimensional space structures can withstand windstorms and earthquakes. Alan built a wind-tunnel laboratory, which grew in the following forty years to be the foremost wind-studies center. Alan himself became the world's leader in his field. He advised on the design of major structures around the world and won many awards, medals, and titles. I was to work with Alan on the Canadian National (CN) Tower in Toronto and other special structures, particularly cooling towers of power generation plants.

These two families were the closest to us. They made our stay in Canada pleasant. We keep in touch with them until this day. After two weeks of the Sodermans' hospitality, we moved to a new apartment, originally rented by another colleague in the university, Hugh Peacock and his wife, Jean.

Here we lived a life of schizophrenia. On the one hand, there was our outward life, with such good friends, interesting teaching and research assignments at the university, and barbecues and outings on the weekends. On the other hand, there was the world we had left behind; we were always wondering who was still alive, who had died, who was exiled, and where. What about my aging parents: how many Nakbas would they have to endure?

I recall Jean Peacock invited us to have lunch with her Irish parents. I poured out my heart to her father about the debris of life we had left behind. The poor man listened to me politely without any reaction. He knew nothing of my background and it dawned on me that I should not burden him with it. What did I know about the suffering of other people in the past? This was my cross and I had to bear it.

Soon the world we left behind caught up with us. Hazaa, my companion in the escape from Beersheba in 1948 and my sister's husband, wrote to me from Amman after escaping arrest by Israeli occupation forces in Gaza.

Amman, August 17, 1967.
I cannot believe I arrived in Amman, leaving my wife and children behind. Please ask my uncle [my father] to give them 30 pounds. They should eat every day and my children should have pocket money to buy sweets. I swear that the food sticks in my throat when I think of them.

I'll tell you what happened. On June 5, about 9:30 a.m., I was at the Beni Suheila roundabout near us when I heard bullets and bombs fly over my head toward Khan Yunis. The town was up in flames. I jumped over the [nearby] secondary school fence and hid for five minutes. I jumped from house to house until I reached ours. I found my wife and children and your parents in two pits we dug previously and covered with metal sheets. Your father was carrying the radio, listening to news, walking among the trees, not caring about the bombs.

At that moment, the Jews entered the eastern quarter, where I was, and killed all the young men they found. They occupied the secondary school and bombed our house. Your father was still walking with his radio. I told him that the soldiers he saw on the school roof were Jews and dragged him into the small pit where he sat and we were all lying down. We spent all Monday in the pit.

The Jews could not take the town, but they kept the school. They held the area between us and the school, but they did not dare to leave their tanks, out of fear of the returned fire from our side.

At dawn on Wednesday morning, we came out. The Jewish tanks withdrew but the soldiers on the roof remained. They saw us and fired mortar shells on us. I saw your father bleeding. We took him inside. Luckily it was only a shrapnel wound, which we bandaged. We had no water. The children had to wet their lips with yeast water we found in the kitchen.

On Wednesday, the resistance stopped. The Jewish infantry started to enter houses. We kept silent, our ears to the ground, as the tanks were under our window. There was a young man from Beni Suheila, hiding in the house across the street. They killed him. I heard him scream, "Oh! Father!"

About fifty men and women congregated at Abu Qasim's house because he had a basement. I heard the women screaming in this house. Then it was eerie silence. After sunset, I sneaked to their house. I found only women. They told me all of the men were taken captives, to dig pits and bury those killed in mass graves.

I inquired at the Canadian Red Cross about my family but they replied that they could not do anything, that it was not their jurisdiction, or some other excuse. Instead, my apartment became a sort of Red Cross center.

My extended family in Gaza, carrying the name of Abu Sitta, were about three thousand in number at the time. They knew my address, and Najia and I started to get letters from closer relatives, and then more distant relatives, inquiring about other family members with whom we had lost contact. Through Israel, mail came from the occupied territories to Canada. From my apartment, letters went out to the outside world, and vice versa. As word got around about our service, the trickle of letters became a flood from total strangers. My wife set up packs of envelopes and rolls of stamps. I redirected the letters as required.

Reading the letters was heartbreaking. You read about the old couple who became penniless as their son working in the Gulf could not send them money any more, the stranded student in an Arab country who did not know what had happened to his family, the sick who could not get medicine, the girl waiting for her fiancé to come and marry her as planned, or the people who had gone on vacation and could not return.

There was one case of a young man working in Abu Dhabi who implored me not to open his letter. When I insisted that I couldn't send a closed letter for an unknown person, he replied separately that he was one of three brothers who took turns, one to work, two to study. After graduation and work, they exchange places. There were delicate family matters of extreme hardship he did not wish to disclose. I sent his letter closed.

The flood of letters, with the addresses written in broken English and envelopes adorned with foreign stamps, surprised our simple Canadian postman, who saw a single foreign stamp as a curiosity. He must have thought I was running a secret ring of some sort. I explained as gently as I could.

This home post office took a toll on my health. You could not help but live each story, and frequently, the most help you could offer was the simple act of diverting the problem to someone else. My hair fell out and bald patches appeared. It took months of cortisone injections in the skull to recover.

The joy over Israel's victory that we had witnessed in the United Kingdom was even stronger in Canada—a spillover from a much more vicious propaganda campaign in the United States. I spoke at the Rotary and Kiwanis clubs, at churches, and at universities. An article I submitted to the *Globe and Mail* was turned down, in spite of a courageous protest letter by Alan Davenport. The *London (ON) Free Press*, published in this university town, printed a long article I had written—only after several lunch invitations to its editor.

Readers were mostly local people who cared only about their own affairs. I was reminded of this fact one weekend when we stopped at a grocery store several miles away to buy milk and bread. I saw the headline of the local newspaper, "John's Cow Hit by Speeding Car." I do not blame them in the least. It was not their fault that Balfour and Ben-Gurion did not have a plan to dispossess them.

The audience at the clubs I visited, a select group in society, wanted to hear the "other side." Israeli victory raised questions for them: who were the Israelis fighting and why? There must be another side to explain this big war. This curiosity, which extended to wanting to know about Arabs and Islam, opened the door for invitations to speak. Reverend A.C. Forrest of the United Church of Canada was familiar with Palestine, the Holy Land. He had visited Palestine after the 1967 war and was appalled to see the nature of "the humane occupation." He saw a brutal occupation, displaced people, and he wrote about it. Forrest was subjected to the usual ruthless chorus of defamation, but he would not budge and went on to write a book about the situation.

I received two invitations from the United Church. One was particularly interesting. It came from Reverend Stan Lucyk. He was an enlightened person, confident enough to listen to other views. I invited him for dinner with the local imam of the London mosque. He reciprocated by inviting me to speak at his church three times on Palestine and Islam. He was courteous enough to let me climb the pulpit next to him and answer questions he had prepared. The congregation was full of kind and simple people who came to learn. At the end, I stood with him at the door of the church saying good-bye to those who had attended. In the parlor afterward, I was even asked a question by a recent widow on why God had snatched away her beloved husband, which went beyond the political and cultural purpose for my visit.

My wife sat with the congregation and had bought a red hat for the occasion, which blended well with the church crowd. She was very sociable and had no problem chatting with people.

Mercifully, no one asked me questions like how I felt riding a car instead of a camel. But the moment presented itself soon enough. Stan invited us to Sunday lunch. His wife was fussing around preparing food for the foreign couple. At the table, she announced, "There is no pork. I knew you did not eat it."

"Thank you," we replied.

"Right here, this is a knife and a fork. Please feel free if you do not wish to use them." Immediately, I could see the great embarrassment on Stan's face. He was speechless for a moment; he remembered our dinner-table manners from when he was a guest at our house.

These activities to put forward the Palestinian cause were far too little to make an impact. I made contact with other Arabs in Canada who became lifelong friends. In Toronto, I met Jim Peters (Jamil Butrus) and Habib Salloum, whose grandfathers had immigrated to Canada at the beginning of the twentieth century or before. They had taught themselves Arabic. In fact, Jim was a teacher of Arabic, Turkish, and Farsi. I also met Ibrahim and Nuha Salti, recent arrivals from the American University of Beirut, both physicians doing advanced research in Toronto.

Arab communities at the time numbered around eighty thousand people in Canada, the majority being Lebanese. This community was dispersed all over the large country and its six time zones. They had dozens of clubs, societies, mosques, and churches. It was imperative to create a unifying structure to speak on our behalf. It was not easy, but the pull of the catastrophic results of the 1967 war was ultimately unifying.

In November of that year, we met again in my house and decided to form the Canadian Arab Federation (CAF). Dr. Salti was elected as the first president, and I was vice-president of information. Peters and Salloum took other positions. We started to contact all these Arab groups and we found a positive response, occasionally hampered by local differences of opinion.

I edited our new publication, *The Arab Dawn*, in English and Arabic and we held annual conventions in Toronto and Montreal. These actions, of course, attracted the attention of the Zionist groups, and consequently the Royal Canadian Mounted Police (RCMP), whom the Zionists pointed in our direction.

Me addressing the First Annual Canadian Arab Federation (CAF) Convention in Toronto, 1969. George Tomeh, UN Arab ambassador, sits on the far left, with Ibrahim Salti, CAF president, on the far right.

A member of the RCMP visited me at the university. I treated him as a student and I gave him a one-hour lesson in the history of Palestine. He did not visit again. I started to feel that my telephone was bugged. There were strange characters, certainly not the police, loitering around my house. The RCMP kept digging. In one of our annual conferences, the Jewish press announced that this was a conference aiming to destroy Israel and kill the Jews. I arrived early at the hotel reception desk to start preparations, my briefcase next to me on the floor. I looked around and the briefcase was gone. It had the list of addresses of all Arab societies in Canada. Nobody seemed to be bothered, except me. Half an hour later, the briefcase was "found."

Those of us on the executive committee sat in one room to go over the program. We asked for several rounds of coffee. The room-service attendant looked tall and athletic, but was clumsy in handling the coffee. His disguise was pathetic. More dangerously, we invited a speaker from the resistance movement party, Fatah. Hani al-Hassan was a long-time student leader in Germany, and he had just come back from an operation in the West Bank with a twisted ankle. We moved him from room to room every night.

Fatah and the June 5th Society, headed by Rosemary Sayigh, sent us numerous publications and newsletters about the conditions of the occupied lands. A big parcel sent to CAF was held by customs. Upon official inquiry, customs referred to a law prohibiting material described as "treasonable or seditious or immoral or indecent." That was the best definition the customs authorities could find, as if we were planning to split French Canada from the rest of the country or create an independent republic for the indigenous community, the First Nations. We wrote back in the most polite language to inquire which of these listed adjectives applied to our literature. I do not know what became of the letter.

During the same period, I went to pick up a parcel from Beirut at the London (Ontario) airport. The customs officer, who most probably hailed from a farming community nearby, looked at it and said, "No, you cannot have it. This is hate literature." For him it was a simple and understandable term.

I was prepared. "Officer, this is United Nations material. I do not think you wish to be responsible for violating international law."

"What?" He looked surprised.

"Look what is written here about violation of the Geneva Conventions. It is word for word what is in the parcel."

I showed him texts of ambassadors' speeches in the UN debates on the same subject, with the blue UN emblem on the letterhead of the documents.

"Sure?" he said sheepishly.

"Would I violate the law right here in your presence?"

"OK. Take it now. But next time I need *more* proof."

The federation expanded and young people like Khaled Mu'ammar joined and stayed with CAF for many years. French-speaking members, Louis Azzaria and Marie-Claude Giguère, took key positions, with Azzaria as the next president, after Salti.

We were able to submit an application to the Canadian Senate requesting an inquiry regarding media bias. The high point came on 15 December 1969 when we met as an official delegation with Minister of External Affairs Mitchel Sharp. He praised the "energetic, frank, and capable manner" of our presentation. He indicated that he would look into the Israeli violations of the Geneva Conventions. As soon as the word got out, he retracted his promise as being misunderstood.

The Arab League office, headed by Ibrahim Shukrallah, was interested in our activities and cooperated with us. As I was responsible for media and information, I maintained contact with Arab societies from Vancouver to Quebec. There was much to do and, as usual, we had relatively few resources.

Fatah had a larger media presence in the Middle East; other factions such as the Popular Front for the Liberation of Palestine (PFLP) were involved in more action on the ground in Palestine. CAF, as an independent entity, had to fill the role of an unofficial voice for all Palestinians. Fatah appointed an undeclared representative, Abdullah Abdullah, in Canada, attached to the Arab League office. He visited me to learn about the Canadian scene. Ibrahim Salti, CAF's first president, went to Beirut and made important contacts with resistance leaders.

The work with Arab communities in Canada was arduous. They were sparsely distributed, were of different backgrounds and political inclinations, and some representatives had the usual personal egotism. Generally, those who came forward were willing to do something for Arab causes, primarily for Palestine. Two-thirds of our time was taken up resolving and organizing the internal front and only one-third was given to addressing the Canadian public at large and the Canadian government.

My colleagues and I decided that this effort must continue. We had to persevere against the odds. While these small endeavors were an increase over the nonexistent action before CAF was formed, they did not leave any lasting impression on Canada's foreign policy, which is still predominantly influenced by the Zionist lobby.

In the United States, Arabs started similar activities. Professor Ibrahim Abu Lughod invited me to join the Arab-American University Graduates (AAUG), which I did. They produced well-researched books on Palestine that remain a valuable reference to this day. Other members included leading Palestinian professors such as Hisham Sharabi, Edward Said, Samih Farsoun, and Naseer Aruri.

Thirty-three years later and one year before his death, I visited Ibrahim Abu Lughod in his home in Ramallah. He had moved there to serve and spend his last days in Palestine. We spoke of our times in North America. During my time as his houseguest, he asked me to accompany him on a tour of Palestine for some of his engagements; I gladly accepted. We spent many hours on the road from Ramallah to Nazareth, then to Ras al-Naqura, at the Lebanese border, along the coast to Acre, Haifa, Jaffa (his birthplace), and back to Jerusalem and Ramallah. This long journey was the perfect time to listen to his many stories.

In 1948, having passed his matriculation exam, Ibrahim decided to go to the United States to study. The young refugee was penniless, but he hoped his brother there would help. Upon arrival, he found that his brother was similarly penniless. "We met another Palestinian, who invited us for coffee and cake, and discussed the Palestine tragedy," he recalled. "We were hungry, so we extended the conversation for another round of coffee and cake."

A new disaster struck. Ibrahim failed the tuberculosis (TB) test, which came back positive. A sympathetic professor directed him to another medical test. It turned out not to be TB but a birth defect in his lungs, which remained all his life. (While he was driving us around Palestine, he popped antibiotic pills to help his ailing lungs.)

In spite of massive financial hardships, he managed to graduate from the University of Illinois with a BA in 1951 and then a PhD from Princeton in 1957. He recalled one story in particular for me:

> I saw a notice about a play and I wanted to buy a ticket. I went to the designated room and found a young man, with his feet on the desk, American style.
> "I would like to buy a ticket for the performance," he told the young man.
> "What is your name?"
> "Ibrahim Abu Lughod."
> "Where are you from?"
> "From Palestine."
> The young man took his feet off the desk.
> "And I am too."
> "What is your name?"
> "Edward Said."

Ibrahim took a job in Cairo with the United Nations Educational, Scientific, and Cultural Organization (UNESCO) at Sirs al-Liyan. He moved there with his wife, Janet, who became an accomplished professor in her own right. Edward went to Cairo to visit his family, who were living there at the time. He invited Ibrahim to meet him and his family. They saw a lot of each other until the early 1960s, when each went his separate way.

When the Naksa, as the defeat of 1967 was called, struck, Ibrahim and colleagues planned to publish books to educate the American public about Palestine and the Arabs, the same public that was enchanted by the miraculous victory of the righteous Israelis over the savage Arabs.

"I thought of a subject: the portrayal of Arabs in western literature. Who would best write about it? Perhaps Edward could do it. He was teaching comparative literature at Columbia University. I wrote to Edward suggesting the topic," Ibrahim said. No reply came for weeks. One day he got a call from Edward. "I got your letter at my new address. I changed apartments. I shall write the piece."

Ibrahim showed me the main features and landmarks of Akka (Acre) and Haifa. As we sped on the coastal road to Jaffa, he continued, "Some weeks later, I received Edward's paper. It was the most excellent paper I have ever read." It must have excited something in Edward. Almost exactly ten years later, Edward published his seminal work Orientalism.

In Jaffa, Ibrahim showed me his school, al-Amirya, his street, his childhood playground, even one remaining manhole in the street, clearly marked Palestine Foundry Company, which his father had started in 1929, the year Ibrahim was born.

I spoke to him three days before he passed away on 23 May 2001, and he urged me, "Continue our work. We must go on struggling. They want to convert us to a nation of slaves."

The Israeli intelligence played a trick on his daughter. They told her that the permit for her father to be buried next to his father in Jaffa cemetery was revoked. The family did not take any notice and thousands of Jaffa residents attended the funeral as he was interred next to his father. With his death, he succeeded in fulfilling his wish to implement his right of return permanently.

My academic life in Canada was productive in such pleasant surroundings. Working with the world famous Alan G. Davenport was a privilege. He was brilliant, unassuming, and very friendly. In 1974, I took a sabbatical, and taught as a visiting professor at Southampton and Bochum universities in England and Germany. The lectures I gave were good enough to develop into chapters for the book I intended to write.

An American colleague I met at a conference, Phillip Gould, saw my lectures and suggested that he add some more chapters and prepare the book for publication, provided his name came first. I agreed. Gould wrote his dedication and I dedicated the book to my parents in Palestine. To my surprise, my co-author objected strenuously to my dedication. I did not know that he was Jewish, and even had I known, why should a respectable academic, of any religion, object to honoring my parents in Palestine? I was greatly upset and surprised at this blind prejudice, especially from a man like that. Finally, the book came out with my dedication: "To my parents, in their homeland Palestine, for their dedication to knowledge and truth."[79]

On the home front, my family life was bliss. London, Ontario, where we lived, was a pleasant, clean, and safe city, named "Forest City" for its many parks. It had a river, the Thames, a street called "Oxford," and a cathedral called "St. Paul's," in memory of the London that the early immigrants had left behind.

A year after our arrival, I bought a house in a nice neighborhood. The down payment consumed the last of the savings from my work in Kuwait. I walked on the green front lawn and the spacious backyard. Suddenly I found myself thumping the ground and jumping up and down on the grass. "This plot, this piece of the world, is MINE." It was the only land in the world, outside Palestine, which I could call mine, and here, I could do so unchallenged and unthreatened by guns or tanks. My father's comments came swiftly in a letter he sent me five months before he passed away, "By God's Covenant, you must give me your promise that you pledge before God Almighty that you will never abandon your country." These short words with boundless meaning were my father's last command.

My first cousin Ahmed was furious when he heard. "How dare you take root anywhere else but in Palestine! Do you not know our

Arab proverb: Build in foreign land and lose your self-esteem?"[80] Little did they know that this was merely a station on the long road of return.

Najia adjusted well to university social life. She made many friends among the professors' wives, and joined societies and activities. The dean called her "the princess." We hosted many dinners for our colleagues and they reciprocated. Our faculty members were largely Anglo-Saxon in origin, but there were also many of Eastern European origin. One was a scientist who had defected from Prague. Another was French with whose family we shared common Mediterranean culture, cooking, and olive oil. It is strange that at such distance from our old world, we created this relative affinity with each other.

Of the Anglo-Saxons, there were two Australians; one was a close associate of Alan, and the other did not stay long in London. Another colleague was a brash young English lecturer with unmasked racist tendencies. He soon left London and struggled to find a job until an Arab university in Kuwait took him, with a big salary and no tax, where he worked and lived for several decades.

All the wives got on well together, as did the children. We had car pools and pickups for birthday parties. Still, the two closest families were the Sodermans and the Davenports. Through them, we knew the meaning of Canadian weekends. We went out in the autumn to admire the symphony of colors painted by the trees' leaves. We went to apple farms, where we ate what we could for free and paid for the full baskets that we took and stored for the winter.

Alan took us with his family to his summer cottage by the lake. He loved to sail in his boat there and taught me the rudiments of sailing, and I learned what the term "turn about" means. They planned, in collusion with my wife, a surprise party for my first birthday in Canada. I went out of the door to get something and unexpectedly saw Alan coming toward me for the party. Surprised, he hid his face with his hand and looked the other way.

"Alan? Is that you?" Only five meters away, he kept walking, to keep up the disguise.

During the Christmas holidays, we took midnight walks with the Sodermans, even in sub-zero temperatures. If there was no wind and the chill was not too great, the weather was crisp and healthy. Larry Soderman died at age forty-two, without warning. It was a major shock to all of us. He was a good man, brilliant at his work, helpful to everyone. Without him, I would not have been there in London. He left behind a young widow, Carolyn, and three children. And here I thought I had left tragedy behind back home.

We were blessed with two beautiful daughters, Maysoun and Rania. We gave them Arabic names, but ones without guttural letters to make it easy for our Canadian friends to pronounce. As was the custom, Najia's mother came to help for their births. The welfare system in Canada, visiting and guiding young mothers, giving milk subsidies and medical checkups, was a replacement for our traditional family support system.

I took special delight in planting new trees and installed a new swing for my two daughters. I was not domesticated enough for my next-door neighbor, a German housewife, whose daily occupation was to watch who was coming and going. She complained that the grass on my lawn was not cut regularly and threatened to tell the city hall. More ominously, she was suspicious of those "Ay-rabs" who came to visit frequently for CAF meetings, and thought a terrorist cell was operating right next door. That said, she was not without a good side, but I was seriously afraid she would turn into a twenty-four-hour unpaid informer. I had to humor her; and my wife, with her good nature, did the rest. Our neighbor finally convinced herself (I think) that I was an oil-rich Arab who was regularly signing business deals.

In July 1968, the news came that my parents managed to get out of Gaza and reach Amman, taking advantage of the temporary policy initiated by Moshe Dayan of 'open borders.' They stayed with my brother Ali in Amman and we, their children, all flocked to see them. This was the first time they could breathe the fresh air of freedom since the Israelis occupied Gaza. I rushed to see them and introduce my wife, replacing the aborted trip of May 1967. We traveled quickly; our children were not yet born. My brothers, working in Kuwait, came too. Abdullah was already in Jerash, Jordan, commanding resistance troops in the south.

It was a tearful reunion. It was hardest on my father. Although the grand man had been a refugee for twenty years, he now lived under the shadow of the Israeli occupation. He could *see* Israelis in Gaza's streets in their jeeps, pointing their machine guns, treating people with cruelty and contempt.

I spent hours with him, a tape recorder on the side. I asked him about his life, and I stopped when he got tired. When he refused to talk, I hid the tape recorder and started a casual conversation. I asked him about his childhood; his father, who died around 1900; his participation with his uncle, Suleiman, in the war against the British at the Suez Canal in 1914–15; and his association with Esmet Bey, the Turkish garrison commander in Beersheba. He also told me how Winston Churchill asked him, along with other dignitaries, in Jerusalem in 1921 to keep peace in the land ("the authority was in our hands, not the British") when Palestinians were agitating against Balfour and his agent Herbert Samuel.

My father's face shone with pleasure when he talked about his pioneering in education, how he taught himself, how he built the first school in 1920 at his own expense, how his four children went to university, before the Nakba. He was sad when he talked about the struggle that had ended with our dispossession and exile, but was hopeful for the future.

After a long session, he turned to me with a renewed vigor and said in what seemed like a last will, "I say to my children and our people: keep your faith in God, keep your sight on your country which we shall recover, *inshallah*, no matter what hardships we face."

I sat with my mother too. She told me about her life in the shadow of her great husband, how she did her duties to match his position. She looked at me with sad eyes and said, "I am the mother of my children, who are like birds. I give them life, and then they fly away from the nest, leaving me alone. They became children of the world."

I sat with Abdullah for a short while. I wished it was longer but the house was full of well-wishers. He told me about his life as the leader of the 1936–39 revolt in the southern district and what it took to make ordinary people into patriots: education and a sense of belonging to the land of their birth and their death. "This bond to the land is what makes us Palestinians," he said.

Najia and I returned to Canada, invigorated by this trip in the wake of the 1967 tragedy. Two years later, in 1970, a series of tragedies struck that made me even more grateful for this time in Amman. I received a letter that my father had passed away. There was a huge funeral in which thousands marched. He was buried in Khan Yunis cemetery, eight kilometers away from his birthplace that sat just beyond the barbed wire. In the same month, Gamal Abd al-Nasser died, making millions of Arabs feel like orphans. A month later, Abdullah was murdered in Jerash.

Abdullah had another record, beside his thirty-five years of national struggle. He had considerable sway with East Jordanian sheikhs and he recruited many of their people to join "the Palestinian revolution" against the Israeli occupation. He was warned repeatedly to leave Jordan during King Hussein's war on the resistance movement; he refused. "I stay with my men," he insisted. Masked men from the Jordanian army and intelligence services (the *mukhabarat*) came to his house at night in the presence of his wife and his youngest son, Suleiman.

"Please come and have a cup of coffee with us at the headquarters."

After that, the stories vary about what happened. Some say they shot him a short distance away from the house. Others say they tied him to a car and dragged his body along with it. Until this day, no one has found his body. Fake investigation committees were formed with no result. Justice for his murder has yet to be served.

A few months later, another letter came from Gaza. My mother, the fountain of kindness, had also died. She could not bear life alone without my father. All this terrible news came to me in Canada in quick succession.

"I am now an orphan." My wife stood next to me with these letters spread on the table. Although I was ten when my parents sent away me to study, and I saw them only during holidays, their presence in my soul as pillars of support was the fuel of my life. To them I turned for advice. Every achievement I made was dedicated to them. Their pleasure at what I had done was the biggest reward I could have. When I was in London, England, I had nightmares about losing one of them. Now, at thirty-three, in a faraway land, with only a handful of Arabs around me to express their condolences, my grief was to remain inside my soul.

I went to the university, lectured, attended meetings, and had casual conversations. But my grief was made visible only to my wife and a few Arab friends. How difficult it was to live this schizophrenic life.

With my two children growing up and with no extended family around, nobody to call 'aunt' or 'uncle,' I thought a change in the course of our life was needed. Two things did it. First, my daughter Maysoun came in crying one day and said, "Tracy will not play with me. She says her grandmother is visiting. What is a grandmother?" Second, the 1973 war, with its decisive if limited victory, caused a rapid rise in oil rices. My Palestinian and Kuwaiti friends urged me to come back to Kuwait; there were many projects that needed to be built and the funds were available for them.

Some years earlier, the climate of business was not as good. While at the university, I went on a business trip in 1968 to explore prospects in the newly developing Emirates, but nothing panned out. I had returned to Canada with more promises than offers. It took ten years for some of them to materialize.

In 1975, the situation was very different. Oil wealth started to flow like a flood. A Kuwaiti friend, Salem Marzouq, who headed one of the major consulting firms, visited me and stayed for two nights. He invited me to return to Kuwait. And there were more convincing reasons for me to do so: I had three brothers, many contacts, and a decent record there. My daughters would find family, people to call 'uncle,' 'aunt,' and 'grandmother.' On the other hand, I was a tenured professor; I had a nice house and a lovely growing family. One night, after pacing around our sitting room hundreds of times until after midnight, I decided to go.

As a precaution, rather than leaving my job, I took one year's leave without pay.

17

Working with the Facts on the Ground

In 1975, I arrived in Kuwait for the third time. I found no major surprises, though one could begin to feel the impact of oil revenues. The first to smell the new aroma were western businessmen. They came to Kuwait in droves, wearing expensive suits and carrying elegant briefcases—everyone from the Swiss bank manager who wished to meet his client transferring millions to his account, to the manufacturing company's export manager who came to see the huge project for which orders were placed, to those who came to offer their goods or services. They spoke English with British, American, French, German, and Japanese accents. The dollar was the god to which they came to pay tribute.

My Palestinian colleagues who had remained in Kuwait received all these visitors and made their acquaintance on personal terms—a pleasant alternative to the telex messages, which previously had been the only medium of communication for these transactions. Many of my colleagues held key managerial positions earned over the course of twenty years of hard and productive work. Naïvely, western businessmen thought they could earn fast money, but negotiations with these managers in Kuwait proved to be a tough exercise. They realized that these Palestinians, previously known as Arab refugees, were their match.

I worked as an independent consultant with Salem and others. A real-estate tycoon in the Gulf asked me to act as his advisor on his projects. He rose from a humble government job to be the owner of real-estate assets worth hundreds of millions of pounds sterling.

He was sharp, clever in spotting opportunities and seizing them. More importantly, he was adept at giving a piece of the cake to those in the centers of power, who returned the favor by facilitating permits and approvals.

He needed a small contingent of lawyers, surveyors, and engineers to give shape to his ideas. There was no company structure, strategy, or debated policy. We were the extension of his hands and legs. I worked for him intermittently, but not exclusively, for two years, during which time I learned a great deal about a different world. He had two or three private planes. I traveled with him and his small entourage. We had lunches and dinners with sheikhs and princes, who, I often found, were very pleasant, gracious, ordinary people.

He conceived the idea of filling the sea along the shoreline on the Gulf and building luxury villas there. This project needed a permit, which was provided by one prince against a one-third share. He had no money to do the soil backfilling. He hired a European dredging company and secured a loan from a bank in that country to finance the project. The company and the bank were both eager to do the deal, but the bank required collateral—the land to be filled. The ultimate funding came from sales of luxury villas. The first batch was "sold" to famous people as an advertisement campaign, and a top marketing company was employed to sell the rest. Simple but risky. In reality, however, he let the various parties knock their heads together. The project had many hiccups, but eventually it was completed after many years of delay.

Before we landed in one capital, he handed me a plan of a building. "What do you think of this? I have signed a contract to buy it at four million."

I did my careful calculations. "It is only worth three million and the return is not worth the trouble," I announced.

"Keep your calculations to yourself. I already have a buyer for six million."

When we landed, there was a big limousine waiting, which whisked us to lunch with the happy buyer. It was a good lesson, but it was clearly not my line of expertise.

I decided to form my own construction-and-management company. But in addition to hard work, one had to have cash capital and good partners to succeed. I had saved some money, all of which I put in as capital. As for partners, I invited six to join me, hoping their cash would raise the capital. More importantly, their contribution in getting projects would help increase business, and above all, they would secure the needed financial facilities from the banks. We raised the minimum capital required, but as for the partners' contribution, it was next to nothing. I had to carry the whole burden on my shoulders while they waited for their annual check.

"There. It is all yours. We want to see people live here, children go to school, shoppers go to shops, patients go to the clinic, all in two years," the government official said.

I looked at the barren piece of land north of Aden on the edge of the inhabited area, with no infrastructure in sight. Could we do it in two years? We had to start from scratch. All I had with me was my briefcase. The Yemeni ministry official, who pointed out the site, and the Kuwait government representative, the donor, walked away to their cars and left me alone.

After about eight months of bidding and waiting for results, we had won this contract. We had plans ready. Our price was so low that when we won the bid, we received condolences for the early demise of the new company. I hired Palestinian engineers, all refugees. The first thing to be done was to build a camp for the laborers as well as offices, stores, and workshops. Most of this work was to be done in a month or two. The supply of materials had to be regulated carefully, as some ships docked at Aden only once every two to four weeks.

We sent one engineer to Egypt to arrange the recruitment of between three hundred and four hundred Egyptian laborers. Materials began to arrive from different ports around the world and pile up at the open space.

Aden was the capital of the People's Democratic Republic of Yemen, and the officials ran a tight ship. We were pleasantly surprised at the efficiency of the government. If you were ten minutes late for an appointment with the ministry, the appointment was canceled politely. There was absolutely no corruption. We were neither asked for nor offered to pay a single bribe. Our tons of materials lay in the open, without being touched. There was social liberty between the sexes, protected by law, and condemned by the conservatives as a brand of communism.

The country was poor, however. Hence, it welcomed unconditional financial support, particularly from Kuwait. Yemenis in the south were very courteous and hospitable. Our vehicles had special number plates for temporary operation in South Yemen. At the roundabout, Yemenis used to wave us through and give way for us to pass.

Soon after the Egyptian laborers arrived, supervised by Egyptian engineers, there were early signs of problems. Their production was lower than the stipulated rates they had agreed to in their contracts. After six months, it became clear we were sliding into a disaster. To make matters worse, there was a sudden epidemic of a strange strain of the flu. The whole site was paralyzed and we set up a field hospital with the government's assistance. When the Egyptian laborers had recovered, I chartered a plane to send them back home, leaving only the key Egyptian engineers. The site was totally idle for two weeks.

I flew immediately to China, and after two weeks of negotiations, recruited three hundred Chinese laborers. These negotiations were an exercise in endurance, as they used a tactic of introducing small items at the top of the agenda in order to drag the meeting out and exhaust us. They thought we would close on the remaining important items quickly, with agreement to their demands. This was not a strategy that worked with us, and we were ready to continue negotiations well into the night.

Another time-consuming practice was the use of an official interpreter. Usually their side was represented by a half-dozen people, at least. Although some of them knew English, they waited for the interpreter to finish and then started deliberations among themselves. They had plenty of time to think. We brought our regular work to the meeting and tried to finish it in the very long pauses between our questions and their answers.

As the Chinese labor arrived, we found that they needed to be trained: they were not familiar with what tiles looked like and their appreciation of the value of wasted material was different from our strict methods. With their agreement, we set up a training course on building trades for a dozen laborers, who then trained another group of their own. The Chinese laborers received no salary from us. We paid their management on a monthly basis for the work done and their government paid their salaries directly to their families. They had no currency in their hands except a small amount, usually used to buy a camera or radio. Our laborers in subsequent projects were Indian. They were familiar with building trades and were more capitalist than the Chinese, although much less disciplined. In the end, all projects were completed, but with much difficulty and only a small profit.

During this period, a political difference between the South Yemen leaders, Ali Nasser Muhammad and Abd al-Fattah Ismail, erupted and turned into a military confrontation in May 1986. There were many killed and wounded. All foreigners were evacuated. Every country sent ships to evacuate its nationals. The Queen of England even sent her private yacht, which was sailing nearby. Within a week, all labor left, including our Indian workers. All, that is, except the Palestinians. They had nowhere to go, and no one sent a ship to evacuate them.

I used to spend one week in Aden on the project site every month. When the disturbances started, I was in Kuwait at the time. Communications were cut—no telephone, no telex. I finally managed to find a line through a PLO wireless connection between Paris and Aden. The Palestinian staff who remained on site were safe; I just about managed to discern this through the crackling conversation.

Saleh, the project manager, was resourceful. He was a refugee from Kafr Ana, near Jaffa, and grew up in the Jalazoun refugee camp. Ghatees, the accountant, came from Jaffa city and was a refugee in Amman. Salah, the purchase manager, was from Beersheba and exiled to a Khan Yunis refugee camp. Sa'adi, the workshop manager, was from Isdud and a refugee in Rafah. And so on.

Some of them were fedayeen and had basic military experience. They dug trenches around the site in case tanks tried to enter, stored water in underground pits, painted one car white, hoisted an improvised Red Crescent flag, collected all medical-aid kits in one room for a makeshift field hospital, and collected all food available in a safe store, with perishable items placed in a refrigerator. With the main power cut, the key equipment was the power generators. They had four and moved them to dispersed locations underground in case one was bombed, extended the cables from the generators to the refrigerators, and closed the gate. They raised the Palestinian flag and stayed put. When the fighting was taking place in another quarter, they went out in their improvised ambulance and tended to wounded civilians in a neighboring area. They earned the respect and admiration of their neighbors.

As refugees, they yearned to return to Palestine not only as a national duty but as a necessity for life and stability. Ghatees, for example, carried a travel document that barely allowed him to go anywhere. Though he was married to a Palestinian woman carrying a Jordanian passport, his children were not considered Jordanian. He came one day, looking very depressed and carrying a letter. Their residence permit there had expired and they had to leave. The Jordanian authorities told his wife that the only way her children could stay with her in Jordan was if her husband was dead or if he divorced her. With these two alternatives, we sat in helpless silence. A solution was later found when he got a job in the Emirates, where he was united with his wife and children.

That said, these complications did not discourage marriage among Palestinians. While at Aden, another young site engineer asked for a long leave in order to get married. Upon his return, he had an engagement ring on his hand. He was a refugee from Yibna, living in the Jabaliya camp in Gaza. His parents told him of a nice Yibna family who lived down the street from where they used to live in Palestine. They followed their news and knew they had daughters of a marrying age. The young man searched for the family, with the help of their relatives and his parents, and found them in Jeddah. He introduced himself and was warmly received. He became interested in one of their daughters, an interest that was reciprocated, and they kept in touch for some time. He married the girl down the street from where both families lived before their dispossession, seemingly defying their geographic dispersion.

Working on international projects required a lot of coordination involving diverse groups. It was essential to develop teamwork skills. Frequently, the financing came from the Arab Fund in Kuwait or the World Bank in Washington. The supervising consultants were usually British or Arab. The labor usually came from the developing world. The materials came from Taiwan, Italy, Japan, and the United Kingdom on ships that came irregularly to Aden's poor port. The law was a combination of domestic and international laws. Banking, money transfer, and insurance laws were a complete jumble. Although the particulars varied for projects in Yemen, Saudi Arabia, Sudan, or Djibouti, the constant element for us was that the key staff was Palestinian. They would go anywhere, any time, and do a terrific job.

The babble of languages and accents among the labor from the developing world was diverse. We devised a system for tools, equipment, and materials in the form of a dictionary showing each item pictorially and its name in several dialects with a unique reference number. That was essential when you ordered an item from the head office (none was available locally) to be flown by air cargo for an idle machine. We flew nails, drills, and tires to avoid costly delays.

We learned a great deal from joint ventures with German, British, Italian, and Turkish companies and they learned from us how to handle overseas projects. The legal and logistical interaction between us was very rewarding. We were a modest medium-sized company, but we pulled our weight.

Our work and interactions were not only about construction. We were very aware of the politics that governed our lives and the region. In one instance, we refused to sign a contract on a strike day in protest against Israeli demolition of houses and expulsion of their inhabitants in Jerusalem. In doing so, we forced our foreign partner to respect the strike. We took it one step further and also encouraged them to contribute to aid Palestinians financially; some set up scholarships for Palestinian students to study in Europe. In the 1970s and 1980s, most companies, especially those with Palestinian management, practiced their politics through these activities. Neither we nor our joint-venture partners violated the boycott of Israel in our projects. All imports were thoroughly investigated.

In August 1985, Yasser Arafat asked me to take a team of engineers to Tanzania to see how we could help the country. I led a small team of Palestinian engineers with experience in buildings, roads, industry, and power generation. One member of the team was my friend Fathi al-Badri. Fathi was a brilliant project manager, with several landmark building in Kuwait and Saudi Arabia testifying to his skill.[81] We met the prime minister and various officials. When we toured the country, we found it was extremely rich, but its resources were neglected and its people untrained or uninterested.

In the nineteenth century, Tanzania was an ideal place for imperial colonization, fully exploited by the Europeans. We wanted to help Tanzania, which had stood by us at the UN and elsewhere.

The Palestinian ambassador was energetic. My team prepared a lengthy report outlining the potential of the country and the steps necessary to realize it: improving the infrastructure (expanding roads to remote areas), creating industrialized agriculture, and increasing power output. It was not difficult to see all these needs, but the solutions required huge finances and labor training. Unfortunately, nothing came of it. The capital for the projects was not available, and the training required a long time. The Tanzanian government offered us the opportunity to select and undertake private-investment projects, but we were not prepared for that.

As we flew toward Khartoum just before midnight, crossing the equator on our return journey, we sat in the almost empty plane talking about the beauty of the country, the vast fields, and the fruits left unpicked to rot on the trees, and how much of all that could be converted into real wealth for the people of the country.

These projects in Kuwait and elsewhere were filled with as many personal experiences as professional. When we moved from Canada to Kuwait, we settled down in a nice spacious flat. My children were overwhelmed by so many cousins, the children of my three brothers. The girls improved their Arabic, first understanding and then speaking. The first comment of my daughter Maysoun when we arrived in Kuwait was, “But there is nothing green here.”

The presence of my larger family and the wives of my Palestinian friends were a comfort to Najia, but the civil war in Lebanon was a cause of great concern regarding the safety of her parents and sisters. In fact, she was caught there for some time in 1982 during one visit, watching Israeli tanks rolling underneath their veranda after the occupation of Beirut.

We had a maid, a luxury unknown to us in Canada, but very common in Kuwait. The children went to good schools. It looked like life was going smoothly, but after two years there, my wife’s health deteriorated and she became unable to cope with looking after the children. We needed a governess or nanny and I resorted to my old friend Nigel for help. As usual, he rose to the occasion. Within two weeks, he had found some prospective nannies through *Lady* magazine. He interviewed candidates and called me to meet the one he had selected—Sheilagh— when she arrived at Kuwait’s airport.

I was waiting at the fence of the airport where passengers pass toward the passport control. There were no security barriers then. "Do you have a pen?" a woman approached me.

"Yes, of course."

It was Sheilagh. We took her home. She was in her forties, a little large and stern in her looks. The girls were watching her every move, fascinated, probably wondering how to deal with her. "I am thirsty. Do you have a glass of water?"

Maysoun rushed and brought her a glass. She looked around, inspecting the large salon with its paintings on the wall. Comfortable, but no prince's palace. Sheilagh was British and she was a godsend. She rescued me at just the right time. Her rough exterior hid a heart of gold. The children loved her. She made a list of what they were to do and when, with one copy posted in their bedroom and another in the bathroom. "Brush your teeth, then TV," was a typical instruction. She sat while they were doing their homework, checking and reviewing what they had done. Then they had to recite Quran. "Get me a Quran with English translation, so the children will not fool me," she requested. She also painted a Palestinian flag on their door.

Soon after her arrival, I had to rush to Riyadh to sign a contract. I stood at the stairs, hesitant. "Go! Go! They will be all right," she instructed.

My wife was relieved that the children were in good hands. My brothers' families liked her and she blended in well. She ate our foods, except *mulukhiya* (a type of specially cooked green leaves), proclaiming "I do not eat grass."

Her salary was a hefty portion of my income. What was worse was that I had sunk my savings into the capital of my new company. The first year or two of the company's operations were very trying; we were spending and hoping for eventual profit. Meanwhile, Najia was sick, the girls were growing, and I was paying Sheilagh's salary all at the same time. After a while, she became aware of all this, God bless her, and said, "Pay me when you can."

She received letters from *Lady* magazine with a questionnaire, asking her, among other things, about the wing allocated for her in the prince's palace and how many servants helped her. She did not bother to answer.

Sheilagh stayed with us for three critical years as the children grew. She eventually had to leave because her brother was sick and needed her. By that time, I could afford to pay her. After she had left and as the children grew older, they spent their holidays with her at her place in the Cotswolds, a lovely district in England. She showed off my daughters to her neighbors as the princesses she raised. She followed their graduations, their marriages, and the births of their children. An unbroken ritual is to wish her Merry Christmas every year.

18

On the Political Front

The Palestinian national movement, known as the "Palestinian Revolution," was at its zenith in 1974. Arafat made his famous speech at the UN in which he proclaimed, "Today I have come bearing an olive branch and a freedom fighter's gun. Do not let the olive branch fall from my hand."[82] UN resolutions clearly emphasized that the right of self-determination and the right of return were inalienable. Almost three decades after their dispersion, Palestinians was reassembling. The people were whole again, carrying their history with them, albeit severed from their geography. Syndicates, associations, societies for Palestinian lawyers, engineers, doctors, artists, laborers, women, teachers, and more were formed.

Newspapers, radio stations, centers of research, and dozens of media outlets were busy producing material in Beirut, Damascus, and elsewhere. Professors and students left their studies and joined the Palestinian revolution. Unbeknownst to their parents, young students studying in Europe surfaced in training camps in the south of Lebanon to be fedayeen, sacrificing their lives for their country. Grieving parents sometimes had to cope with the tragic and unexpected death of a son who, to their surprise, had died in Lebanon.

A brilliant Harvard professor, Hanna Mikhail, with the nom de guerre Abu Omar, and a friend of Edward Said, was lost in a naval mission. Edward's eulogy to him was as much a study of the quality of the people who dedicated their lives to the Palestinian struggle as it was an ode to Abu Omar.[83] King Hussein's 1970 crackdown on the resistance movement in Jordan and then the Lebanese civil war in the mid-1970s sapped the revolution's resources and perhaps disoriented its objectives.

It was not clear in June 1974, at its twelfth session in Cairo, that the Palestine National Council (PNC)'s adoption of the ten-point transitional program, thought to be politically pragmatic, was in fact the first of many calamitous concessions that were to follow. What every Palestinian knew—that his/her country started at Ras al-Naqura and ended at Umm Rashrash on the Gulf of Aqaba, that the Nakba was ethnic cleansing, that the Palestinian cause required the removal of the Zionist occupation—was inscribed in the Palestinian National Charter of 1964 and 1968. Now the Palestinians had started to talk about steps to achieve their goals, to start from accepting what was offered and to climb upward from there. It was a naïve, misguided policy, if not conspiratorial. We had known for so long that there is no place for Palestinians in the Zionist agenda "except as slaves," as Ibrahim Abu Lughod once said. That was now being challenged by the political choices of Arafat and other leaders.

In 1974, I had been selected as a member of the PNC, but I did not attend that Cairo meeting. Over the next decade, Arafat's position among various factions had wavered and he was under great political pressure. As the 1984 PNC session in Amman approached, he was desperate for votes. I could not attend, as I had to hand over a project in Yemen. He insisted that I should come and sent a private plane to collect me. I am sure he did the same for others who could not or would not come.

In spite of his antics and his lust for power, I thought he was a true patriot and would not sell out. Aside from George Habash, head of the PFLP, and Arafat's comrade, Khalil al-Wazir, many other leaders were of lower stature. The situation being what it was, and as an independent member in that crucial Amman meeting, I found it appropriate to vote for Arafat.

During that session, I was approached for election to the PLO executive committee, a sort of cabinet in exile, and to take up the position of director of the national fund, the equivalent of the Ministry of Finance, on account of my record, transparency, and business experience. I asked advice from my cousin Hamed, who had already been a member of the executive committee for a long time and held the position of director of the occupied homeland. He advised against it.

"When it comes to money," he said, "old bureaucrats in the PLO will fight you tooth and nail. You need to build a small army from within to fight them, and as you are an outsider, you will not have it."

He was right in more ways than he thought. He took me to his office for a cup of coffee. His office manager came with a pile of papers to sign. "We pay legal aid to defend Palestinian landowners whose land Israel confiscates under legal cover," he explained. I was watching as he signed one check after another.

"I saw the name of this landowner again, a moment ago," I observed. He checked and found this was the case. He put it aside. Another duplicate check for another person came up again. He put it aside as well. A check for a large amount was made out for a lawyer. "Who is that?" I inquired.

"He is the lawyer who has taken on several land cases," the office manager replied.

"How come the lawyer issues payments for himself? The application should come from the landowner. Do the owners know that the lawyer's bills are presented on their account?"

Hamed shouted at the office manager. "You are a band of thieves. This is people's money." He was angrier than I had ever seen him before. Hamed had a clean hand, a clean conscience, and as one Palestinian ambassador described him, "had a virgin patriotism." Not only did he donate half his savings in the early 1960s for the foundation of the PLO, he also did not receive a salary or travel expenses from the public purse for the forty years of his membership on the executive committee.

Despite the corruption even then, there were a great many who were dedicated, efficient, and honest. One of these was "the prince of martyrs," Khalil al-Wazir, or Abu Jihad. He was a survivor of the Lydda–Ramleh massacre, also known as the "death march" of 1948. At the age of thirteen, he became a refugee in Gaza. No doubt his experience must have left a strong impression on him, as he had become a freedom fighter from his early youth.

I met him a few times on the three-hour flight from Kuwait to Aden. He was going to see his small contingent stationed there, and I was going to see our construction site. We discussed many subjects related to Palestine. We were both engineers, and it was not difficult to agree on logic or planning. His death was a fatal blow to the resistance movement. He was murdered in his bedroom in Tunis on 16 April 1988, just after the beginning of first intifada. Today, it seems that many of those who were corrupt or unclean were the ones spared by the Israelis for future use.

At that time, my daughter Maysoun was a student at the University of Western Ontario. She presided over a small group of students in an organization named Concerned Canadians for the Middle East. They invited a number of speakers; one of them was the rising star Edward Said. The group also distributed posters showing the brutality of the Israeli occupation, which had fueled the first intifada. One poster showed a frightened Palestinian boy with Israeli machine guns pointed at him.

As usual, vociferous Zionist students complained to the university that the poster was fake, and it was an unfair comparison with the famous picture of a frightened Jewish boy with Nazi soldiers pointing their guns at him.

The university president took the bait, armed more with his prejudice than with his academic stature. He censured Maysoun and demanded she be taken for investigation. When she told me, I rushed to the archives of the prestigious Kuwaiti daily newspaper, *al-Qabas*, and retrieved the picture of the Palestinian boy on the poster. It was a genuine picture issued by Reuters.

Meanwhile, Maysoun received death threats by phone. "Watch out. You know what happened to Khalil al-Wazir. You may be next."

The university president's misguided judgment led to the case being put before the Human Rights Court in Toronto. Stewart Shackleton, a law student who saw the injustice of the situation as a matter of principle, took the case on behalf of Maysoun. The hearings took three years. At the end, not only did the president make an apology, but the university was strongly advised to start a course on human rights and the Palestine question. Shackleton became a renowned human rights lawyer.

The irony of course is that the offensive picture of the frightened Palestinian boy became very common. Dozens of similar pictures were taken over the following twenty years. Notable among them was the famous image of a boy (named Faris Odeh) standing defiantly in front of a huge tank with only a stone in his hand. What the picture did not show was that the boy was killed days later by another Israeli tank.

The nineteenth session of the PNC was held in Algiers in November 1988 in the wake of the first intifada. The atmosphere was filled with admiration at how this young generation that did not experience the Nakba, and was thought to be resigned to twenty years of Israeli occupation, could rise up in the intifada with bare chests to face Israeli tanks.

It was actually the first time that this news penetrated the wall of silence imposed on the western media by Zionist pressure. It exposed the truth behind the so-called 'humane occupation.' Arafat wanted to take advantage of this situation and advance the ten-point plan. His proposal was to declare an independent Palestine in the West Bank and Gaza Strip only—that is, in the lands Israel occupied in 1967—with Jerusalem as its capital. In his proposal, there was a reference to UN Resolution 181, which recommended allocating 54 percent of Palestine to the sovereignty of recent Jewish immigrants to the country, who, even with British collusion, had not owned more than 6 percent of the country at the time. Moreover, this allocation, which had no foundation in international law, meant that 467 Palestinian towns and villages (half the total Arab and Jewish population of that area) would find themselves ruled by a foreign minority. In fact, these areas had been ethnically cleansed before the State of Israel was declared.[84]

The PNC proposal did not clearly define the slice of Palestine on which the proposed state was to be declared. It invoked Resolution 181 and left the matter ambiguous. The Algiers session was attended by distinguished pro-Palestinian guests. There were also others, not so distinguished or pro-Palestinian. As I walked in the yard during the recess, I was accosted by an American "expert" on the Middle East who extolled the virtues of accepting a slice of Palestine, the expulsion of its people, and the rise of Israel on its ruins, as a fact of life which it would be a waste of time to challenge.

Then there was Trudy, the *Christian Science Monitor* correspondent living in Jerusalem, who mistakenly thought I was my cousin Hamed, and shadowed me for hours asking me about my views on every statement made. There was the learned Jerome Segal, whom I heard talking to a group of PNC members in the lobby about the only political option available: lie down and take it.

I had a reasoned chat with my friend Ibrahim Abu Lughod on the meaning of this proposal. He was standing with his friend

Edward Said, whom I had just met for the first time, and who was also in agreement with us.

We, the independent members, carried little weight in the deliberations. The bulk of the members were Fatah who were challenged only by members of the PFLP. The motion of declaring a state on the West Bank and Gaza was carried, with 253 votes for, forty-six against, with ten abstentions. It was a measure of those present, and not of a real constituency. I voted against the motion.

The first intifada, which erupted in 1987, gave us hope that the people would not surrender their patrimony. We in the *shatat* needed to do something about helping build our country.[85] I called for a meeting at my home in Kuwait to discuss this. About fifteen Palestinians answered my call. They were all distinguished in their fields: an economist who planned financial strategies and development plans for many developing countries, an engineer who was responsible for building major power-generation plants in the Gulf, and experts in agriculture, water, and international law.

We decided to form a development council to develop Palestine, even though it was under occupation. Our deliberations ended with a short but coherent blueprint of development under various scenarios. We needed leadership approval.

I flew to Tunis on 15 July 1990, to see Yasser Arafat. He saw me at 2:00 a.m., the next day, a time for clear thinking, he said. He seemed pleased and impressed. I emphasized that our group, collectively and individually, was willing to provide our services at no cost. He suggested I see a man by the name of Abu Alaa (Ahmed Qurei), who was looking after the PLO's projects. I had heard his name mentioned before as someone responsible for *sumud* (steadfastness) in his economic projects. I heard more news of failures than successes. When we were on our trip in Tanzania, we learned of his failing farm project, although the land was rich and water was abundant. Also, in Dar es Salaam, we met a man working for him who supposedly had experience in aircraft maintenance, but later learned he had very little.

I met Abu Alaa and explained our plan for the development council. He was not impressed. "We have already done all this planning," he said confidently.

I was extremely surprised. "You did? Did you have a similar team with leading professionals like this?"

"Yes, of course. We have had for years."

"Tell me more. I am fascinated." It turned out that he had consulted one or two experts from the United Nations Development Programme.

"If you have all the plans ready, can we help you with just one plan? Let us review it. Maybe we can give you some suggestions."

We argued. On 31 July, I received a packet with plans for the Gaza harbor. I sat with Ahmed Arafat, a colleague who built harbors in the Gulf, and he listed a number of suggestions. More importantly, he listed serious warnings about things not to do. We were preparing our report when other events overtook us. My office in Kuwait called. "Do not come to the office, sir."

"What is wrong?"

"The Iraqi soldiers are all over our building." It was Thursday 2 August 1990.

I made several calls to friends. It was true. The Iraqis had occupied Kuwait. I was alone in the house. Luckily, my daughters, both in university, and my wife were spending the summer in our house in London, Ontario. Maysoun called.

"How are you, Baba? We heard the news. I am coming to be with you."

"Listen to me carefully. The international lines may be cut off any minute. DO NOT come. Do not spend the money that I gave you for house repairs. You never know how long this will go on. Talk to my bank manager. He may let you draw some money." The line went dead.

After two days, I ventured out into the neighborhood. There was light traffic. Soldiers were at the main squares. I contacted my staff to meet at my house. I made sure that they had their passports and their share of the available cash and told them, "You are free. Stay or leave. Good luck."

I kept calling my relatives and friends. Every day the number of people answering the phone was fewer. They started leaving but no one came back to tell us of their experience. We did not know if they had arrived safely or had been killed or imprisoned.

The telephone rang at 3:00 a.m. "Are you awake?"

"Sort of. Who is this?"

It was Kariman, my sister-in-law's cousin. She was a dynamic, efficient woman who ran all her family affairs. Her husband was a dentist, and both of them had managed to leave Kuwait and reach Amman immediately after the Iraqi invasion. Three weeks later, she decided to return to Kuwait and collect her frail old father and her husband's sister. She had driven back all the way from Amman, packed her things, and had her passengers ready.

"Are you ready to leave at 7:00 a.m.?" she asked.

"Yes, I have only essential papers to carry." It was perfect timing. That week, the Iraqis had put out a notice that all holders of foreign passports should report to the police station. Those who had done that a few days earlier had not returned to their houses. Kariman's suggestion was the only option. I called Mahfouz, the brother of my very good friend Mustafa Nabil (my childhood friend from Cairo), and he joined us with his wife. He knew Iraq from his work there as an engineer.

On the morning of 21 August, we started out into the unknown in two cars; I was driving Kariman's Mercedes. Always prepared, she sat next to me with maps, passports, and a thermos full of coffee. As we headed north, the Iraqi soldiers at crossroads waved us through, as they thought we were heading to Baghdad. We cleared the city of Kuwait and started on the desert road.

At a military post, we saw a group of tanks changing direction with some others heading north. I heard a roar to my right. The tracks of a huge tank were higher than our car. The road could barely take both of us and I knew who would win. I kept to the far left, but the tank suddenly veered toward us and I heard the sound of a crash at our front bumper. I managed to keep going until we were waved over by a captain. I went out to inspect the damage with him. The front right edge was gone, and with it, the headlight. The captain apologized and asked if he could do anything. *Yes*, I said to myself, *let us go*.

At Safwan, the Iraqi border, there were thousands of cars milling around, trying to find their direction. Mahfouz suggested we take the road skirting Iraq from the west. When we started moving, we lost Mahfouz in the crowd. We kept going into the desert as the traffic thinned out.

Suddenly, we stopped. There was no traffic and no one in sight. Were we lost in the desert or were we on track? As the sun went down in the late afternoon, we waved at a lone passing car. The driver stopped and told us not to leave this road for any reason and not to stop for anyone. There were robbers and highwaymen. He was an Iraqi working in Kuwait. It was good advice.

We arrived at a gas station and pushed through the crowds to the pump. There, to our great delight, we found Mahfouz and his wife. We agreed to try not to separate again by staying close and signaling to each other with our lights. The August heat was intense and Kariman kept wiping my face, drying it with fresh towels, asking me constant questions to make sure I was not falling asleep. She supplied me with cups of coffee and observed the effects on my behavior.

About midnight, we reached a small town. We were very tired. While driving up and down the empty streets, we saw a hotel sign. The building was dark. We pushed the squeaky gate and rang the bell repeatedly. A man, half asleep, opened the door. He could tell we had money and asked for a high rate, which he knew we were powerless to refuse. He opened rooms, turned the air conditioning on, and prepared stale cheese sandwiches. The air conditioning in my small room was set very high. Although I welcomed it at first, it became so cold that I had to turn it off but I did not know how. The man had disappeared, so I walked through the dark corridors looking for the main switch. When I finally found it in the basement, I accidentally switched off the power for the whole building.

In the morning, we had fresh tea and coffee and some more cheese sandwiches, which this time tasted delicious. We proceeded on the desert road until we met the main road from Baghdad to Amman. As the only exit to Jordan, it was very crowded. We were low on gas. When we came near a station, we waited in a line two-to-three kilometers long.

I saw two Iraqi police patrol cars inspecting the line. I came forward and waved with papers in my hand. I told them I was a member of the National Council and I wished to have gas for my party of two cars. I do not know if he noticed the word "Palestine" rather than "Iraq" before National Council. He ordered a police car to escort us right to the pump. They pushed ahead of the people who had been waiting for most of the day and let us have a fill. I felt very awkward but relieved.

By late evening, we arrived at Trebil, the last Iraqi border point. Cars were parked as far as the eye could see under the lampposts of the huge yard. Kariman took the passports to be stamped. She came back hours later. She had asked the officer, hypothetically, what they did regarding holders of foreign passports. The reply was that they should not be here at all. They should have reported to the local police station (to be detained). If they were here, they should return to Baghdad immediately.

That was bad news, worse than we had expected. We debated what to do. Valid Jordanian and Egyptian passports were stamped, but my passport was Canadian. We decided to make a dash for it. Kariman hid my foreign (meaning western in this context) passport on her chest. We were six. She carried four Jordanian and two Egyptian passports. The fourth Jordanian passport, to account for the correct number of passengers, was an old one and was no longer valid. Kariman sat in the driver's seat, revved up the engine, and pushed forward in the darkness toward the direction of the exit.

It was a very tense moment. Our hearts were pounding, mine the loudest. What if I were discovered trying to leave the country illegally? I would have been thrown in jail for God knows how long. What about my family, who thought I was still in Kuwait? What about my company? What about my companions? They would be held as accomplices. Kariman's father was a frail old man, and he would not be able to take it.

We wove our way through thousands of cars until we cleared the yard without the sight of a soldier. Suddenly a soldier appeared in the darkness, waving a lantern. Kariman stopped. We tried to keep calm. Kariman was in control.

"Did you stamp your passports?"

"Yes, all of them."

"Show me."

He leafed through the top passport, hers, which also had the car permit.

"Please, sir. We are all very tired. We are all Jordanians and Egyptians going to our families in Amman. My father is a very old man. I am afraid . . . you know. . . . We cannot wait much longer." She kept talking and talking, while he was leafing through the passports. By the time he reached the third passport, he had probably had enough of her explanation.

"OK, go."

She moved slowly, and after one hundred meters pushed the gas pedal at full throttle until we disappeared into the darkness. We did not have the strength to congratulate ourselves. Five kilometers later, we saw a silhouette of a lone man waving a lantern.

"Iraqi?" No one dared to answer.

If he was alone and Iraqi, we decided we would dash at full speed. When we came close, Kariman uttered the words, "Look at his headgear. I think he is Jordanian." He was and we had entered Jordanian territory. We almost went out to kiss him. Kariman gave a short speech about happy Jordanians returning to their mother country. Now, we were all relaxed, actually tired after having used up all our adrenaline. I was not totally relaxed. There was no exit stamp on my passport. We arrived at the Jordanian border station. The sight of the big building, the shops, and the cafés was reassuring.

I went to the foreign-passports window. The officer looked at every page of my Canadian passport, now removed from Kariman's safe hideout.

"You are from Beersheba?"

"Yes?"

"A refugee in Gaza?"

"Yes. Now living abroad."

"Just a minute, please."

Kariman and the others got their passports stamped and were waiting at the door of that building, very thirsty. They would not leave. We huddled to think of the alternatives in case I had a problem. We would make a fuss and shout. Kariman could do this very well. No. Tell my embassy. That would take time. Accept my detention, but deport me to Amman. Last resort.

Five minutes had passed. Ten, fifteen, twenty minutes. No sign. The desk was cleared of officers, except one who was shuffling papers.

"Excuse me. Is my passport ready?"

"I do not know. You didn't take it? Just a minute. Is it this one?"

"Yes, thank you." I put it in my pocket and slowly walked to the door, where my party was watching. "It is done! DONE!"

We hugged each other and walked to the soft-drink stand. We bought the contents of his fridge and he charged us four times the regular price. But we didn't care. As dawn of the third day broke, we did not stop talking about every detail of the escapade. Over and over again. When we approached the outskirts of Amman at about midday, we asked for directions. They saw the number plates.

"How is Kuwait? Are you stashing away lots of money out there?" Their sarcasm was painful.

I went up the stairs of my brother Ali's house. He saw me coming through the glass door. He jumped up and down until I held him.

"Safe! You are safe!" he kept shouting.

There was barely enough time to sit down. I picked up the telephone and spoke to my family in Canada. I could not hear the words between sobs, laughs, and questions. For the next three days, the same length of time as my journey from Kuwait, I got some rest. I booked a flight to Aden to see my staff and laborers.

When I flew to Aden, I found the Indian laborers on strike. Quite rightly, they wanted to get their wages and leave. I could not pay them because our funds, like Kuwait's, were frozen. There was a scuffle, and we all ended up in the police station. I asked the Indian ambassador to intervene. He was an understanding man. I signed a two-page undertaking to pay all labor dues within a month. I borrowed some cash, gave the laborers pocket money, and purchased tickets from a travel agent on credit; the laborers left soon afterward. The Palestinian staff, who had nowhere to go, stayed put, with little money and much resilience.

I flew to London, England, and solved the financial problems by receiving part of our dues from the bank funding our project and settling some debts. What followed was the happiest holiday with my family in the other London, the Forest City of Ontario. Many Canadian friends came by; they could hardly believe my story.

"I am Palestinian. This is my umpteenth exodus," I reminded them.

19

The Invisible Face of the Enemy Takes Shape

Throughout the years since I had become a refugee as a child, the question that had plagued me about the invisible face of the enemy had never gone away. I decided to investigate. It took fifty years to find some of the answers I was searching for, and the investigation is still ongoing.

I started with my birthplace. In the early 1960s, in England, I pored over the maps and books in the Royal Geographical Society (RGS) library. I copied sheets from the reports of travelers, priests, spies, and surveyors. After I had left England, I returned frequently to spend many days at RGS until I had become a familiar face. I discovered the *Survey of Western Palestine* undertaken by the Palestine Exploration Fund (PEF) in the last quarter of the nineteenth century.

I often wondered about the daring and motives of those early nineteenth-century travelers who visited the Holy Land before we had even heard of colonial European Zionists. I could imagine one of them riding his horse, loading his belongings on a mule led by its owner, and being followed by a native guide. Others, like the Austrian Archduke Ludwig Salvator in 1879, traveled pompously with a large retinue and set up a camp of several ornamental tents when he stopped for the night. As to their motives, we knew nothing. We did not know that some of them were charting our land, preparing for taking it over by the end of the century.

And so it came about. Allenby's military plans, which I acquired (from national archives and specialized bookshops) and examined, were based on PEF maps and subsequent surveys. The maps showed first stations of his forces at Abu Sitta and Sheikh Nuran just before he made the breakthrough by conquering Beersheba.

During the Mandate, new maps showed Ma'in Abu Sitta, al-Ma'in, Karm Abu Sitta, our school, and many other details of our land. I read in some literature about British surveys that the British, before their hurried departure in 1948, took an aerial survey of many parts of Palestine. That was exciting; I might find valuable visual evidence there. I wrote several letters with no positive results until I found an obscure address of a place in the English countryside. I filled an application to receive an aerial photo of al-Ma'in. For weeks there was no reply. I phoned this department inquiring about my application. A formal voice came on the line.

"Why do you want them?"

"I am doing a university research project."

"Do you have a permit from the country concerned?"

"What is that?"

"Israel, I guess."

I gasped quietly. How can I ask the robber to give me permission? My long search had come to nothing, I thought. I recovered and tried to answer calmly. "This is the property of the British government, or, if you like, the government of Palestine, not Israel."

"Let me check with my superiors." It seemed like ages that I waited with the telephone on my ear and my heart pounding. Turning me down would close a treasure chest for me. The voice came on the phone. "Yes, you can have them."

When the photos arrived, I relived my childhood. Here was our house, our *karm* planted with almonds, apricots, figs, and grapes. Here was my old school and our motorized well and flour mill with its garden of palm trees and vegetables. From high up, the places looked like small dots, but I could see clearly the cultivated fields of wheat and barley, all the roads, seven of them in the center of al-Ma'in. Cultivated fields belie the Zionist myth, "We made the desert bloom."

The normal survey maps, made up of dots and lines, showed the correct details with scientific detachment. Photos showed life as it was lived. They do not lie.

I worked on every detail in the photos. My cousin, Dr. Muhammad, a surgeon and Hamed's brother, knew the land like the palm of his hand. From his father, he inherited the love of land and owning as much of it as possible. I sat with Dr. Muhammad for hours over several days until he identified each piece of our land and its owner. I made a large poster of the photo map and distributed copies among our family members.

Many Palestinians wrongly think that all documents of the government of Palestine during the Mandate are kept in one building in the United Kingdom. In reality, the documents were scattered. They were in two dozen locations, and none of the locations had complete sets. All public and private documents in Palestine were confiscated by Israel and kept in various identifiable archives. Still, it was possible to assemble the pieces and fill the gaps, just as archaeologists do with pot shards. It was arduous but doable.

I worked on the maps produced by Israel after 1948. These early maps in Israel were merely maps of Palestine (in English) overprinted in Hebrew for the changes they made. Israelis plowed over roads and tracks (except asphalt), cut and plowed over *karm* trees, and filled up or poisoned wells. Israelis marked destroyed villages as "abandoned," "debris," or "heaps." New kibbutzim, built on refugees' land, were marked by circles; these and the new roads leading to them were marked in purple. These were obviously prepared for the use of the Israelis, the newcomers, to show how to exploit the emptied land. In the early 1960s, maps in Hebrew showing only kibbutzim were produced.

The early maps were a very useful orientation for me. I had wanted to know, since the moment I had been hiding in the wadi with the women and children, who had done this to me, to all of us. I had read several Israeli books about the Nakba. They were full of stories of bravery and daring: how the veterans of the Second World War were able to capture the defenseless villages. That was four decades ago, when information was not as readily available as it is now on the Internet.

The names of the players in the tragedy began to emerge. First, the Negev Brigade that attacked us was led by Nahum Sarig (a.k.a. Nahum ben Shraga Weissfish). I obtained his photograph. Israeli literature indicated that Ben-Gurion saw him as an inefficient and sloppy officer. Perhaps he was just good enough to attack farmers.

The second player I could locate by name and photo was Benni Meitiv (Motilov). He was of Russian descent, born in 1926 in Palestine. He was the son of the *mukhtar* of the Dangur colony (previously

Nirim, now Nir Yitzhaq), near Rafah at the Egyptian border, fifteen kilometers away from us. He rode a horse and his dogs followed. With his broken Arabic, he fraternized with poor Arabs who lived in remote areas near his kibbutz. He probably fancied himself a sort of Jewish Lawrence of Arabia. He moved surreptitiously at night in an area close to the Egyptian border.

For the one and a half years before the al-Ma'in attack, he was spying on the Palestinians' strength. I studied his small book about the attack, in which he wrote:

> As an intelligence officer, I was given a white jeep to do my reconnaissance. As luck would have it, the leader of the Arab gangs [*sic*] was Sheikh Abdullah Abu Sitta. He was moving about in a white jeep too. His success was my failure and vice versa. We hated each other. . . .
>
> He lived in a two-story house of concrete and stone, decorated with marble columns of Byzantine origin, with a big garden and a water well. . . .
>
> He devoted all his time to fighting the Jews. His house became a command center and weapons depot, with armed guards defending the place day and night.[86]

The description of the house was exaggerated, a stretch of the imagination, in an attempt to show the grave dangers the Zionists had to face. Meitiv was the local guide for the Palmach; he was living in the area and knew people and places. He was the one who guided them to our house, school, and *bayyara*. He must have had an idea about our relative strength. Palmach soldiers, on the other hand, were mostly veterans of the Second World War; they had been released only three years earlier from service in Europe.

I wanted to know exactly what happened when they overcame our resistance in al-Ma'in. When they attacked us, Meitiv no doubt rushed to our house to find papers, weapons, and the like. I was always eager to capture that moment if I ever could. A breakthrough came when I received a most welcome e-mail from Tikva Honig-Parnass, of the Jerusalem-based magazine *Between the Lines*. She was a Hagana member in 1948, but turned sympathetic to the Palestinian cause. In her e-mail, she enclosed a quotation from a book by Arie

(Stinha) Aharoni. He was the battalion's cultural commissar and participated in the attack on al-Ma'in. He wrote:

> Tired and exhausted after three days of fighting [in Burayr] the soldiers of my battalion [*gdud*] were sent to accompany reinforcements which hurried to help Kfar Darom. The operation plan included an exciting temptation. The order said: to take over at evening Hirbeit [Khirbet] Ma'in, which overlooked one of the sandy roads to Kfar Darom. Part of the force was due to stay and hold Hirbeit Ma'in and the other party was due to accompany the reinforcement, and then come back and unite with the force which stayed in Hirbeit, and return together to the base.
>
> "Hirbeit Ma'in"—There was no one in the battalion who did not utter this name. This was the place in which Abdullah Abu Sitta, the organizer and commander of the gangs [*sic*] in the Negev, resided; the man whose forceful name spread fear all around; the name that every Bedouin had uttered in awe and reverence; the notable family who ruled the entire Negev, that had contact relations with the neighboring countries. To conquer the home of Abu Sitta was indeed a temptation.
>
> We went to Abu Sitta's home and were stunned: In the middle of the desert—unbelievable richness: luxurious furniture, plentiful oriental and European clothes, a radio, a truck, a beautiful Bedouin sword made of silver, a large important archive of photos and documents, letters from Emire Abdallah [of Transjordan] and Hassan al-Banna, the leader of the Muslim Brotherhood in Egypt; a lawyer's certificate of one of the family members, Shakespeare's *Othello* in English near Quran. Our happiness reached its climax when we found the weapons' store, although there was not much there: a number of ammunition boxes, a few guns, and two boxes filled with Italian explosive material. We were so happy [. . .]
>
> The battalion commander announced to us that the convoy to Kfar Darom—seven tanks—got stuck in the wadi near Kfar Darom. They were strongly attacked. The men withdrew by foot to Kfar Darom. Some of them were wounded. The battalion commander ordered us to leave "Hirbeit Ma'in" and return to our base in Tze'elim. The [collaborator] Bedouins came over to express their feelings: "If you could overcome Abu Sitta—there is nothing that can stop you."[87]

Aharoni's description of what happened at Wadi Selqa, after the attack on al-Ma'in, was brief and vague. He probably was not proud of the result. From my relatives I heard the detailed story, which had been told by eyewitnesses. As the Jewish convoy approached the Kfar Darom colony, Muslim Brotherhood members were waiting in Wadi Selqa. They destroyed all the tanks, except one, which managed to enter the colony. A gunner named Murjan created the most havoc and became a local legend.

The troops, which came to aid the colony in blowing up the railway line, barely had time to creep toward the colony for safety. From the wreckage of tanks came a strange stream of survivors: the chickens they had stolen from our houses. Kfar Darom soldiers dragged most of the dead and wounded away and took care of them. An overhead plane reported this defeat. The tanks waiting in al-Ma'in withdrew. The Muslim Brotherhood volunteers prepared for the assault on the colony the next morning. When the troops entered the colony, they found no resistance at all. All occupants, new and old, had fled during the night.

No other attack was attempted for seven months. Some men in my family returned to al-Ma'in. They harvested their crops and prepared for the next winter. Though the Zionists claim they controlled the Negev in this period, it is patently untrue.

Of the loot from our house, there was an item which my father greatly regretted losing. It was an inherited, historical sword, both valuable and meaningful. I hardly remember him without it during government and social functions. In all photos, he appears with it by his side. One day, when he was not around, I sneaked in and took the sword, unsheathed, and waved it in the air. My mother and my sister saw me. They rushed in, alarmed.

"Stop it! Stop it right now! Someone will see you. People will think we declared war. They will rush forward."

A friend of mine, Uri Davis, whom I met during campaigns for the right of return, was visiting friends at Nir Yitzhaq. Uri is a "Hebrew Palestinian," by his own description. I put the matter of my father's sword to him in case he could find its whereabouts. He took this request as a mission for a friend and started his detective work. This request triggered a long search, which he published under the title "In Search of the Abu Sitta Sword."[88]

He interviewed several officers of Battalion 8, whose commander was Haim Bar-lev. First, he started with Meitiv's French wife, Lina, living in al-Majdal/Asqalan. Meitiv died shortly before the interview. Meitiv had a long career in the Mossad, operating in Arab countries. His colleague and close friend Nahman became deputy director of General Security Services, the notorious Shabak, known for the torture of thousands of Palestinians.

Lina phoned Amnon Dagieli, living on my land in Nirim. Dagieli suggested talking to two officers, Adan and Aharoni, the author of the book. Lina arranged the meeting with Adan. From him, Davis discovered that:

> The 8th Battalion had three squadrons, two of which comprised three companies, and one, just two. Avraham (Bren) Adan was the commander of one of these squadrons. Adan was the commander of the company *(pelugah)* which occupied Khirbat Ma'in on May 14, 1948 as part of the Baraq Operation. They arrived at Khirbat Ma'in after a week of continuous fighting in the area, in the course of which Adan's troops conquered inter alia Burayr and Hulayqat, on the last day of the Baraq operation after which they returned to base. They were sent to al-Ma'in to back up an attempt to reinforce and supplement the besieged Kfar Darom.
>
> Upon arrival at Khirbat Ma'in, Adan and his men encountered significant resistance. Fire was showered at them from close quarters—a range of some 8 meters—by snipers behind a thick row of sabr cacti. Adan's unit overcame the resistance and took up positions on top of the hill. There they found a structure, a rather modest house made of mud bricks and a fairly large depot of weapons next to it. They blew up the house, lock, stock and barrel.
>
> Adan recognised the name, Abu Sitta, without difficulty. He actually had in his possession two photographs that were removed from Abu Sitta's house and were given to him as "souvenirs by Aharoni." Erroneously referring to Salman's father as Abdallah rather than Hussein Abu Sitta, he acknowledged his leadership of the Arab resistance in the southern region.

Adan arranged for Davis to meet Aharoni. Davis continued his narrative:

Aharoni had no idea where the sword or the library has ended up. The documents and files of al-Ma'in and Abu Sitta would have been appropriated by the Intelligence. Looting of moveable property by Israeli troops in the 1948–49 war was rife, and never properly reported.

The commander of the relevant battalion (no. 8) at the time was Haim Bar-Lev, now deceased. Battalion 8 Chief of Intelligence was Yair (Jerry) Boberman. He may have a clue.

Aharoni was willing to phone him and introduce me.

Boberman had considerable respect for Abdallah Abu Sitta as a formidable enemy. Was he still alive? What year did he die? He had a vivid recollection of Abdallah Abu Sitta's jeep, a white one with a machine gun mounted on it. The mobile machine gun represented a nightmare to the Israeli troops, until, in the course of an attack, it stalled and the occupants of the jeep had to abandon vehicle, machine gun and all.

Boberman took part in the attack on al-Ma'in and Abu Sitta (as did Aharoni), but when he entered the Abu Sitta home, it was empty, "as far as I recall," he said.

I challenged the statement. "Stinah [Aharoni] described the house in his memoirs," I said. "According to Stinah, the Abu Sitta home displayed unbelievable affluence."

"I never saw a sword," replied Boberman. I suggested at this point that I hand the receiver to Aharoni.

"But I think you had the sword in your hand," said Aharoni into the mouthpiece.

I urged Boberman for a lead, anything. Even a vague association would do.

"Haim Bar-Lev," he said, "had a passion for daggers, bayonets, and swords of all sorts."

The story came to a climax when Bar-Lev's wife, Tamar, agreed to meet Davis. The famous general's wife was sick and tired of the weapons her husband had acquired, actually looted. She was very glad to get rid of some. She gave Davis a sword answering to the description of my father's sword and they took a picture together with the sword.

On inspection and consultation, Davis found out this sword was not my father's. He continued the hunt, but received evasive answers such as, "I do not remember. Why do you delve into the past?"

Everybody was hiding in his own bubble of denial. That was the end of Davis's meticulous search. Although not complete, it revealed the face of the enemy.

By the spring of 1949, the invaders of my land decided to settle on the hilly spot of my childhood playground. Prefabricated huts were installed on this piece of land that was precious for me. They called it Nirim. A little to the north, on my father's land and my mother's family land, another kibbutz, Ein Hashloshah, was set up. Five years later, another kibbutz, Nir Oz, was set up on Hamed's land. Hamed devoted all his life fighting to recover this piece of land, as a symbol of all Palestine. The fourth kibbutz, Magen, was set up on the highest point of Abu Sitta land in al-Ma'in, at the site of the Sheikh Nuran shrine. From that vantage point, you could see the Mediterranean Sea on a clear day.

Many of the individual stories of atrocities in the early years of the Nakba were confirmed by Israeli memoirs and archives decades later. As I have related earlier, in the summer of 1949, two young men and a girl from a family whose land was located to the south of Nuran went to get supplies across that still porous armistice line. They were intercepted by a passing Israeli patrol. One man was killed, another escaped, and the girl was lost. The one who escaped saw her still alive and frightened, separated from him by the Israeli jeep. After a few days, she had not turned up and was thought to be dead. But she was still alive. Fifty-five years later, a soldier from the Nirim platoon revealed what happened to her and *Haaretz* published the gory details.[89]

The girl, between ten and fifteen, was captured by the Nirim platoon on 12 August 1949 and held captive in a hut. The soldiers, with the approval of the platoon commander, decided to rape her. They washed her, cut her long hair, and placed her on an army bed. Each of the three squads, A, B, C, and the drivers and medics, seventeen in total, would take her for a day.

She told the commander, Officer Moshe, that the soldiers "played with her." Either he did not know Arabic or he deliberately falsified the record because the expression sounded similar to "raped" or "assaulted me."

The platoon commander gave an order to execute the girl. The soldiers drove about five hundred meters from the kibbutz and dug a grave. When the girl saw them digging, she screamed, and ran for her life. She was machine-gunned down. The grave they dug was only thirty centimeters deep. They barely covered her with sand. Her hand was seen sticking out.

One officer collected a few items that were connected with the girl: the khaki shorts they let her wear, a bead necklace, a headscarf, rings, two bracelets, and tufts of hair that the company commander found hidden in the sand. The sergeant showed him the hut where the girl had been locked up and the torn bed on which she had lain. The company commander drew up a report summarizing his findings, and the sergeant and the three squad commanders signed it.

The report read:

> I killed the armed Arab and I took the Arab female captive. On the first night, the soldiers abused her, and on the next day I saw fit to remove her from the world.

For proper bookkeeping, there was a court case. The court's conclusion regarding the rape reads:

> We have before us no evidence capable of providing legal proof regarding the fate of the Arab woman [she was in fact a girl aged between ten and fifteen] during the night of 12 to 13 August 1949.

Several testimonies were collected by Haaretz reporters in 2003. Benni Meitiv, a founder of Kibbutz Nirim, wishing to remove the stigma of the crime, said,

> When people started to talk about it, I was one of those who made sure people knew it was the outpost, not the kibbutz. Our reputation was at stake.
>
> We tried to come across as just and innocent, to give the impression that we were in the right and good people. But if you look closely you will find a lot of sins, you will find that we looted, murdered, abandoned our God and committed all the transgressions that are written in the Torah.

Shaul Givoli, a settler–founder of Nirim, relates:

> A few years after the episode, I was wandering around in the abandoned outpost, when I suddenly saw, inside the outpost, that the desert winds had uncovered the bones of a very small hand, which looked like the palm of a boy or a girl.

According to *Haaretz*, Amnon Dagieli, another kibbutz settler–founder, living in Nirim in 2003, recalls:

> The talk was that they killed her and then tried to cover it up. Immediately afterward, there was also a reaction by the other side. At the time there was retaliation for whatever was done by either side, and a few days after what happened at the outpost, a car hit a landmine near [the kibbutz] Nir Yitzhak. One girl was wounded.[90]

I recalled the story of our good-natured schoolteacher, Abu Liyya. Earlier, I mentioned the devastating effect that the massacre in his village had on him. He did not know who the criminals were. He did not see the face of the enemy. We know now that it was the same Battalion 8 that attacked my birthplace two days later. Adan admitted as much to Uri Davis, when he said his battalion had just came from Burayr and Huleiqat.

The Burayr massacre was not reported in the Israeli narratives, of course. This massacre, like the one at Deir Yassin, took place before the state of Israel was declared and before any regular Arab army soldier set foot in Palestine. The Burayr massacre was reported repeatedly by the villagers to the international personnel in Gaza. A writer from Burayr wrote a book and listed the names of the victims. In typical Orientalist fashion, only when an Israeli historian told the story, or a truncated version of it, did the West listen. Even the supposedly meticulous Israeli historian Benny Morris did not mention it. The task was left to one of the perpetrators, Ziv Zipper, to talk about it fifty-five years later.[91] Two days after the Burayr massacre, Zipper wrote in his diary:

> May 15, 1948.
> The roar of the Egyptian plane howls over Nir Am, and the brown book is there. I am thinking of it and swearing at myself for thinking

about a silly lot of scribbling when today there is no meaning to life or creating or humanity, as the Arabs of Breire [a village that sat opposite the colony Brur-Hayil that was established on the village land] died like dogs. We broke their walls and incinerated their houses and broke and destroyed and smashed and killed that cold way, no thought at all about life or human beings or the meaning of feeling, as we watched the bullets smash skulls and saw the brain ooze out of a bleeding horror that had once been a man. But there was no feeling! No hate, or horror or disgust or pleasure or anything! Just killing stray dogs, say, or a sick donkey, or just squashing flies.

We kicked the doors open and smashed through dank-smelling holes that are their homes, and broke into their poor primitiveness of stupid savages that wanted war! (An Arab woman runs towards me, pulls a breast out of her dress and squirts milk on me, to prove that she is a young mother and wants to live. Nobody touches her.)

And today the nation became a nation. "Independence Day"![92]

On 17 June 2010, Zochrot, a small Jewish-Israeli group dedicated to educating the Jewish public about the Nakba, held a videotaped public hearing to listen to and question one of the soldiers who had participated in this massacre.[93] The soldier, Amnon Neumann, gave the usual story of heroism against what he admitted was a feeble resistance. When asked about Burayr village, he replied,

"There was a battle, there was slaughter . . . I do not want to go into these things, leave me alone! It's . . . it's not things we go into.

"Why?"

"Because I did it."

"Is that a good reason?" (Long silence).

Another question came up. "What did you do after that? Leave the village? Burn it down?

"In certain known cases, we burned the village. In others, we would leave it."

When asked about any rape cases, he replied, "Yes, there was *one* rape case. It was an Egyptian Jew; then he killed her."

The word "Egyptian" is meant to place the guilt on a Mizrahi. Of course, the Burayr rape, the Nirim rape case, and the multitude of cases in the north show that the crime was not an isolated incident, but part of the larger mentality encouraged when carrying out ethnic cleansing.

Time and again, we have acquired the names, faces, and photos of the perpetrators and their acts. And so often, there has been no remorse, no regret, no sadness, and certainly no admission of guilt. Perhaps the guilt remained ingrained in their souls, but they certainly do not wear it on their faces.

With every discovery, or perhaps more aptly, with every confirmation of an atrocity, I wondered how the culprits did not realize what they were doing to the history of Jews in the world. This history could no longer be solely marked by centuries of persecution, religious or otherwise. This history would, from now on, be indelibly marked by what the Zionists did to the Palestinians, constantly and remorselessly, failing to learn the lessons from their own past.

I continued with my search. I kept a close watch on the changes and conditions of our land from a distance, and as technology developed, I searched using more advanced means than libraries. In the 1980s, satellite photos became the latest in technology, but those were inaccessible to an individual and very expensive. Through intermediaries, I obtained four large photos of my home. I was mesmerized while observing every hectare, by how it looks now and the way I remembered it. After a while, it was not difficult to put everything in place.

I made maps of the old and the new and charted the changes made. Every kibbutz has two hundred to three hundred members, the four on my land totaling less than one thousand. The Palestinian owners of this land are now approaching ten thousand and living in refugee camps within easy reach.

When those kibbutzniks sit outside on a summer night, they can see the blaze of lights toward Gaza at the edge of the fields they plant; they hear the distant sounds of crowded existence; and they see the smoke rising on the horizon, its edges colored golden in the polluted glare, the sign of condensed life of 1.8 million people. They must know that their water system has siphoned off the good water upstream and diverted it from its owners in the camps. They must have heard of the Israeli sewage dam, which cracked and spilled its contents on Gaza's people.

I wondered what thoughts came to their minds, sitting there in the open fresh air, with a drink in hand and music playing in the background. Perhaps they have no feelings at all for the people they have made refugees, as they retreat to the safety of their bubble of denial, of their self-inflicted mass amnesia.

The searches in these archives, and the stories brought to light, show us that it is possible to give a face to the invisible enemy and to draw that face on maps, photos, and from testimonies—and give answers to those still crying out for justice from beyond the grave. What remains is to implant this record into the enemy's consciousness and achieve the justice that has long been denied.

20

Charting the Land

A man sipping coffee at a café in Vienna prophesied, "You will have a country in fifty years." This is what Theodor Herzl, the father of Zionism, told his fellow Zionists. An old man in a bunker in a Jaffa suburb got his generals in 1948 to understand that there was "no need to purchase an acre of land. The war will give us the land."[94] Ben-Gurion ordered the ethnic cleansing of Palestine. The same old man in his new, shiny office told his surveyors one year later to wipe Palestine from memory. That was the plan: to transform the myth that Palestine was a country without a people into a reality.

In 1949, in the week that Ben-Gurion signed the last armistice agreement (with Syria), he gathered a group of two dozen historians, surveyors, and Torah scholars and told them to wipe out any mention of Palestine or Palestinian names from the map.[95] If there were no Palestinians, how could there be Palestinian names? It was a simple logic, or so they thought. My mission is to defeat this logic and restore Palestine to its place in the records by accurately rendering the map.

My first shock was during the early 1960s when I was browsing maps in the Royal Geographical Society, the British Library, the National Archives (known as the Public Records Office then), the Palestine Exploration Fund (PEF), and other libraries. I did not find the name "Palestine" anywhere. It was barely over a decade since the Nakba, and Britain, of all countries, should have been fully aware of this name.

The librarians directed me to the name "Israel." There I found Palestine maps of the British Mandate with the name "Palestine" crossed out and "Israel" written instead. It was like an armed robber breaking into a house and then replacing the nameplate on the door.

It was an arduous task to collect maps of Palestine. They were scattered everywhere. As an independent researcher, I did not have the authority to request states to provide copies of maps they had. It had to be done slowly and persistently. I befriended many librarians over lunch or tea. I wrote dozens of letters to places that might have some data on Palestine. I visited bookshops, particularly those selling old books; some of these shops were tucked away in house basements in the suburbs. I bought thousands of books as they appeared in publication or older editions from rare-books stores.

At the Bibliothèque Nationale de France in Paris, I saw Jacotin maps of coastal Palestine, surveyed during Napoleon's campaign into the region in 1799. There were also volumes of *Description de l'Égypte*, which covered the area from Cairo to Damascus, including Palestine. In Leipzig, Munich, and Berlin, I found the German heritage of Palestine exploration. In Istanbul, a Palestinian friend helped me retrieve and translate some Turkish documents. In the United States, the Library of Congress was a good source. Yet it was in the UN that I obtained very valuable maps. I copied these while the librarian was having tea with a friend. There were detailed maps of the armistice line, now removed from Israeli maps. There were United Nations Truce Observers reports of Israeli atrocities, so many that the officers closed the file, writing that they had no time to investigate them all. In Egypt, there were records, some good, some mundane, of the Egyptian campaign to rescue Palestine in 1948.

This physically and mentally taxing search was done before the mid-1980s, when research was manual. I had to travel to libraries; now libraries travel to me. Technology has brought knowledge to our offices, thanks to the Internet, electronic libraries, and sophisticated search engines.

Still, the main source regarding Palestine was in Israel itself. The Israelis had not only taken over our country, but had also confiscated all its records: land registry, education, health, transport, banking, clubs, government papers (including city, municipality, and village councils), and private libraries and personal papers of leading personalities. The Survey of Palestine offices, located in Jaffa, were taken over by Israel. All maps, drafts, field papers, even printing plates, were confiscated by Israel. When the British decided to divide the maps between Arabs and Jews, the Haganah intercepted the trucks carrying the Arab share and moved it to their side. I could not possibly have access to these documents.

The accumulated material from diverse locations, however incomplete, was now on my table. What was to be done with it? Was it complete or reliable? Was it consistent and complementary? It took the better part of twenty years before the answer to this question was satisfactorily, not perfectly, resolved. When the technical work was completed, there was the problem of transliteration from Arabic into English, and vice versa depending on the source. Arabic guttural letters are not easily represented by Latin letters.

I obtained 150 village books from various Arab cities, written by Palestinians describing their village's geography and features in Arabic. To verify them, I sent place names to refugees living in their various places of exile. The results were recorded in Arabic and English, to the extent that regional variation in accent was preserved. The harvest of this work was fifty thousand names covering all of Palestine.

The history of these names goes much deeper. The *Survey of Western Palestine*, carried out by the Palestine Exploration Fund (PEF) in the last quarter of the nineteenth century, listed nine thousand names. It was essential to find them, compare them with the twentieth-century names, and note the differences. PEF survey officers collected these names by asking three different local guides in each village about the names common in their village. The names were then anglicized and sent to London for their Oriental scholar to verify them. He rewrote the Arabic names from the anglicized names.

I requested and received access to the original field notes. Boxes of papers that had not been touched for 140 years were brought to the PEF reading room. I found that quite a number of these transliterated names in London were misspelled. This was somewhat surprising as the original Arabic in the field register was preserved.

Who wrote the original Arabic? Certainly not the English team (one of them taught himself Arabic, but he died quite early). In the field notes of the PEF survey, there was a reference to an

"Oriental scribe." Who was this mysterious Arab? My search in the Arabic literature led me to a master's thesis from the University of Damascus. The scribe's name was Nu'man al-Qasatli, a Christian Arab from Damascus, who was an accomplished geographer and had written two books on the geography of Palestine and Damascus. At the University of Jordan, I found a manuscript in his handwriting describing his work with the PEF. In the journal, he described the field trips, their dates, and the name of the English surveyor he worked with. His record was identical to the PEF survey journal. Now I had the name of a scribe, his handwriting, and his journal. The question remained—did he have anything to do with the original Arabic names in London?

I had a look again at the field notebooks. The notebooks classified names in English and Arabic corresponding to each map. I stumbled upon a book with a list of names in which the Arabic handwriting looked familiar. I compared this with the Jordan manuscript. Lo and behold! They were identical.

The handwriting was clear. The Arabic names were correct both in spelling and in meaning. In the files, I also found an acrimonious exchange of letters among the members of the PEF team about the quality of their transliteration. Yet here was this important member of the PEF team, the only Arab, relegated to the position of an "Oriental scribe," unacknowledged for his contribution.

The PEF recently published an English translation of a book, originally written in Latin and ancient Greek, by Eusebius, the bishop of Caesarea in AD 313,[96] a contemporary of Hilarion, the saint said to have worshiped in the location of Sheikh Nuran in al-Ma'in. In this book, Eusebius lists Palestinian localities, states the distance between them, and he gives a small description of each, with references relating to the Bible. I compared the names and locations of these localities between the years 313 and 1948. The correlation was excellent. The differences were minor, mostly phonetic; interchanging the words kafr, bayt, and khirbet in the village and town names proved invaluable.

If these names were preserved for two thousand years, they may likely have existed one thousand years earlier. The continuity of life in Palestine through its people and their localities has been affirmed by serious research over many years, as the PEF survey also showed. The bishop's records were only further proof. Unfortunately, when I compared the names of localities in the years 313 and 1948, I found that 139 ancient localities were destroyed by Israel after its creation. This was a major blow to the history of humanity. Neither UNESCO nor the various bodies proclaiming the preservation of world heritage have protested.

What is the significance of place names and why are Palestinians eager to preserve them? These names are the vocabulary of Palestinian social history, carved out by Palestinians in their daily routine, describing their life, their history, and their land, speaking to them in Arabic. They were not names written by a committee at the order of a military commander.

Village names in Palestine often refer to the families that inhabit(ed) them. There are 120 names with the prefix *bayt*, the house of a certain family. There are fifty-one names which start with the word *kafr*, the village of a certain clan. There are 2,500 localities with the name *khirbet*, meaning 'hamlet' or ruin of an older place, which was or still is inhabited, but recognized regardless.

Place names etch the geography and history of the people, as the people saw them. These names honor family; they refer to 'Abu,' 'Umm,' 'Ibn,' 'Bint,' almost three thousand times. They relate to a place with particular features, such as 'Umm al-Shuqaf,' the place with pottery. They indicate ownership: Ali's garden, Hussein's field. They specify what is planted in the fields: olives, grapes, figs. They signify places where certain animals are common: horses, camels, gazelles, wolves, foxes, or birds—*hamam* (pigeons) and falcons. They paint the colors of the land and type of terrain: red, yellow, hills, cliff, and meadows. They point to the wells, springs, and ponds. The names inform us of the background of the farmer: 'Akkawi,' 'Ghazzawi,' 'Durzi,' and 'Nasrani.' They refer to the relative location of the village: lower, upper, or in-between *(tahta, fawqa, bayna)*. The names share special events: the horses' birthplace, the killing site of the chief, the hanging site, the battle scene. They have strange names such as 'going up and down,' 'the good name,' 'good morning,' 'the morning star,' 'shield protector,' 'wolf's face,' or 'dog's tail.'

In our records, there are five thousand names of holy places alone, the heaviest concentration anywhere in the world. They remained the subject of reverence by the Palestinians for centuries, even when their religion or language changed. People remained the same when they worshiped an idol, or prayed in a church or a mosque.

All these places, fifty thousand in all, have names of people, created by people, for people's recognition and use. That is what Ben-Gurion wanted to eliminate. This heritage that he tried to erase with his new maps and the villages he destroyed has been restored through the work for and publication of *The Atlas of Palestine*.[97]

What did he want to replace these names with? After much research, I discovered that the official Israeli Gazette produced only 6,800 names. These were names of Israeli settlements written in Hebraic fashion, changed names of a few remaining Arab villages, and mountains and rivers named after Zionist leaders. The number of Israeli names is less than that of the Palestinians by thirty-three thousand. Perhaps history was more difficult to invent than Ben-Gurion had anticipated.

I decided to visit my homeland and see for myself the land I knew and had charted over all these years. How does it look now? After spending years poring over its maps, I wondered if I would recognize it. What would be my reaction when I saw the same land I knew, but with strange faces and languages in our streets?

The time was right. Just after the signing of the Oslo Accords, there was a relaxation of Israel's oppressive procedures. I took my daughter Rania with me. My eldest daughter, Maysoun, could not come because she had a newborn to look after. After many preparations—a list of things to pack, a list of names and telephone numbers, a contingency plan to alert key people in case of trouble at the border or while there—we flew late at night, in October 1995, from Cyprus to Lydda airport.

"One more thing," Rania said as we prepared to land. "Be calm, please. I'll do the talking." I agreed.

From my window, I saw the darkness of the Mediterranean waters replaced by the sight of my homeland. The coastal lights of Palestine appeared, shattering the darkness. I knew we were approaching the coastal area, south of Jaffa. The concentration of lights drew a map of localities with which I was very familiar. As the wheels of the plane touched the ground, I felt the same jolt in my whole being.

Here I am, back in my country, but on what terms?

"What is the purpose of your visit?"

"Holiday . . . uh . . . tourism."

"You were born in Beersheba. Where is your ID?"

"I do not have one."

"Why?"

"It was a long time ago. Before your time." The young woman, with an Eastern European accent and with a cold face, handed the passport back.

"Good," I thought to myself. "We are done."

"See the officer," the girl said, pointing to a slip she had inserted in the passports.

The officer told us to get our bags. We got them cheerfully, talking and chatting. He must have been watching our reaction. He leafed through Rania's passport carefully.

"Why were you in Bahrain?"

"Wedding." A short and simple answer.

"Why were you in Beirut?"

"Visiting my aunt." He waved us to the exit.

The next morning, we woke up early and we went to the roof of one of the Arab hotels in Jerusalem to see the sights. The last time I was in Jerusalem was thirty years ago. The Dome of the Rock was shining in the first rays of light. The silhouettes of the closely packed houses in the Old City etched a line drawing of living history. Smoke rose from some houses and a few pedestrians and some people on bicycles started the business of life that morning. Rania was taking in the sights and sounds, comparing all this with what I have been drilling into my daughters' consciousness since their births.

Later in the day, we stood on the Mount of Olives, observing Jerusalem from the east, the same view immortalized in hundreds of nineteenth-century paintings. As we contemplated the significance of this sight, an Israeli guide started talking to twenty Japanese tourists about Jerusalem's Jewish-only history of three thousand years.

Why was there no Palestinian tourist guide, even in the occupied Palestinian territory? It was forbidden. For the next two weeks, we hired a car with a Palestinian driver who spoke Hebrew. He was used to accompanying Palestinians living abroad in the *shatat*, returning to visit their country. The next day we set off at 6:00 a.m., heading north.

How can you not stop at Nablus for a *kunafa* breakfast? Next was Jenin, the southern gate to Marj Ibn Amer. Here, we arrived at the Palestine occupied in 1948. The verdant plain stretched from Haifa to Beisan and is irrigated by the Muqatta' River (which they call Kishon) and a multitude of springs. Its fertile soil and varied plantation attracted the attention of the peculiar nineteenth-century English consul James Finn.[98]

We stopped at Mount Tabor, with a commanding view of the whole plain, Tiberias on one end, Acre (Akka in Arabic) on the other. Not far away lies Hittin, the site at which Salah al-Din (Saladin) decisively defeated the Crusaders. As we descended the mount, we saw Arabs wearing Israeli army uniforms and slinging Uzi machine guns, showing Jewish tourists a makeshift Arab tent and coffee-making pots. They looked pathetic—Uncle Toms catering to Zionist fantasies. They saw us photographing them, with obvious disdain on our faces. I heard one of them say in Arabic, "Yalla, let's go. Now our names and photographs will go to Arab countries."

We arrived at Tiberias and saw the devastated old city. There were remnants of a mosque, which we inspected. It sat amid stalls of fast food and *falafel*. A Moroccan Jew, by his looks, saw us carrying cameras and looking sad. He said something to his companion in Hebrew, which I did not understand. In my mind, I imagined he said, "Another Abdallah breathing his last sigh."[99]

In Safad, high on the mountain, I saw old Jewish and Arab houses intertwined, with the Arab homeowners no longer there. I thought of Moses Ibn Maimonides, the great Andalusian Jewish philosopher who wrote in Arabic and arrived here to seek refuge from Christian persecution but left for Cairo.

On the way I asked our driver to stop here or there, turn left after two kilometers or right at the traffic light. I wanted to show my daughter some sites or villages. Here was a massacre. There was a battle. This tank was destroyed on such and such a date.

"You have been here before?" the driver asked me. "I take a lot of visiting people. *I* tell them about places."

"Now you can learn more things to tell the next party," I said encouragingly. "In answer to your question, I never left. I am here every day." He looked perplexed. "Just drive on."

The spectacle of the fertile Galilee fields, their beautiful flowers and delicious fruits, was familiar to me. Now I saw them spread before me on the mountains, sprinkled with a few remaining Palestinian villages, so few that they paint, by their scarcity, a picture of the rich and ancient life that must have been flourishing here before their dispossession.

The beauty of the Galilee moved the heart of an ardent Zionist, Josef Weitz, whose life was dedicated to dispossessing the Palestinians. Shortly after the expulsion of the Palestinians, he toured the deserted Galilee villages and wrote this moving account:

> And the road continued eastward over mountains, and the Galilee is revealed to me in its splendour, its hidden places and folds, its crimson smile and its green softness and its desolation. I have never seen it like this. It was always bustling with man and beast. Herds and more herds used to descend from the heights to the valleys of the streambeds, their bells ringing with a sort of discontinuous sound, which vanished in the ravines and hid among the crevices, as if they would go on chiming forever.
>
> A strange stillness lies over all the mountains and is drawn by hidden threads from within the empty village. An empty village! What a terrible thing! Lives turned into fossilized whispers in extinguished ovens; a shattered mirror; a mouldy block of dried figs and a scrawny dog, thin-tailed, floppy-eared and dark-eyed.[100]

He did not suffer a twitch of conscience about the life he destroyed. Instead, he celebrated the expulsion by welcoming the new foreign occupants.

> At the very same moment, a different feeling throbs and rises from the primordial depths, a feeling of victory, of taking over, of revenge. And suddenly the whispers vanish and you see empty houses, good for the settlement of our Jewish brethren . . . War! That was our war!

I could instantly differentiate a Palestinian village from a kibbutz. The first, composed of stone houses, has the air of historical presence, spaced around in organic confusion as the houses aged and grew in number. The kibbutz is planned along straight lines, with square blocks made of prefabricated units—an artificial creation.

The roads we drove along were well built and well marked. Gullible foreign visitors were shown how Israel built a modern country. For me, an engineer and planner, I could see the propaganda aspect of over-praising them. All these roads were lower in quality than Kuwait's roads, and much shorter in length than the roads in Saudi Arabia. To the construction in both of these countries, Palestinian engineers made a major contribution. How long will it be, I thought, until we can plan and build in our own country?

In Nazareth, the only Palestinian city whose population was not expelled, we stayed at a small hotel. The Arab clerk on the night shift was not initially welcoming. The next morning he was more pleasant. "Sorry about yesterday. I thought you were from the West Bank. They come here without papers and the Israelis give me a hard time."

I knew why he became pleasant. "Can you find me a job where you live?"

This young man was denied a seat in an Israeli university. He went to Italy and earned a degree in medicine, "after a lot of dishwashing," to make ends meet. Now the Israelis would not give him a job—a common practice for Arabs in Israel, the "only democracy in the Middle East."

We arrived at Acre, the city where history learns, not teaches. I saw a sign, "al-Sa'adi," above a shop. I recalled that one of my colleagues, a distinguished engineer, Wa'il al-Sa'adi, was working in Beirut and the Gulf. I wondered if he was any relation. I went in and introduced myself, a Palestinian from the *shatat*. The al-Sa'adis were one family that was separated by the barbed wire at Lebanon's border. This Sa'adi and his daughter took us around to see the Jazzar Mosque, the Crusaders' crypt, and the multi-walled city. We were pleased to exchange experiences and to find that the family was indistinguishable from their Beirut branch. They told us how they were not allowed to repair their own house. If a Jewish settler is given the house, he is allowed to repair it and make any changes he wants. "Then they called our house uncared for," the man exclaimed.

Then we went to Haifa, the home of my wife's family. They owned a lot of property in Haifa and the coastal villages, which they had held for generations. I tried to extract detailed information from my father-in-law about his family house, but by then, he was old and incoherent. I took some notes and a small photograph of my wife, age two, perched on a stone staircase with her aunt and held by her aunt's husband.

We toured the streets to look for the house. We asked the remaining Palestinians in the Wadi Nisnas neighborhood about my wife's home. No clues. We saw the beautiful Ottoman-built municipality and the lovely houses around it. We drove around Hadar Carmel, slowly, with the photo in my daughter's hand, around and around, in wide and narrow streets, for almost three hours.

"Let's go. That's enough," I said.

"One more round, Baba," pleaded Rania. We drove slowly, gazing at the houses, imagining what they must have been. "Stop!" cried Rania. With the photo in hand, she said, "There it is. The stone stairs."

Indeed it was. We opened the small iron gate. The place looked deserted, the grass dry, and the trees reduced to dry branches. The door of the house was closed. We went around it. A window was open and we heard female voices. I was walking with my camera pointed at the house. I heard a scream as I pointed my camera at the only open window. There were about six women sitting at desks with calculators.

"You frightened me. We thought that was a gun."

"Sorry. I am just photographing lovely old houses."

We were about to leave. I came back, without pointing the camera. I could not deny my identity, especially in front of those occupants. "Actually, this is her house, her mother's house," I pointed to Rania.

"Ah! That is old history," the frightened girl said.

"What are you doing here?" I asked.

"We are an audit office. We are moving out soon."

"Can we see the house from inside, just to see the history?"

"No, that is not allowed."

As we prepared to leave, I saw a poisonous-material sign with a skull and crossbones. Could such materials really be stored here or was the sign a deterrent to intruders? At the gate, another girl followed us out and stopped us. "Please, you can come and see the house."

We entered. We saw the high ceiling, the wonderful ornamental tiles. The air was filled with memories. Just adding a few old-style sofas, a table with a Turkish cup of coffee, you could imagine my wife's Aunt Mariam emerging from another room to greet us. I remember her, tall and very beautiful. They called her "the Pasha's daughter."

Rania was overcome with emotion. She was initially calm and collected, but then she could not control herself. Her tears came streaming down her cheeks; she was sobbing uncontrollably. The girl brought her a glass of lemonade. Then she came back with an almost empty chocolate box. "Sorry, this is the only one left." She consoled her, saying, "You will be pleased. This house is on the preserved buildings list. It will be treated with extreme care."

We thanked her. The other girls were looking on with distant curiosity.

A mother and daughter separated by half a century: (left), Najia, my wife, a child of 2, with her uncle in his Haifa home, 1945; (right) Rania, our daughter, and me on the same staircase, 1995. The house has been confiscated by Israel.

We could not resist the temptation to take a picture of my daughter and me on the same staircase where her mother had been. We framed the two pictures, taken in 1945 and 1995, fifty years apart. Perhaps it was a small milestone, but nevertheless an important one on the long road we have to traverse, the road to return home. As we left the house, I looked at the new number on the gate: 15 Tiberias Street. New generations, take note.

We sped on the coastal road to Jaffa, noting mentally the erased names of the destroyed villages we passed and the land that Rania's grandfather owned in these villages. Another sight struck me—those blocks of dwelling units on both sides of the road, square ugly boxes with black holes for windows, built by Israelis after 1948. I saw similar houses when I visited the Soviet Union.

This hideous site was in stark contrast to the beautiful old stone houses in Palestinian cities and the Ottoman government buildings, which remain. Worse still, they looked so ugly in the midst of the beautiful Galilee landscape. I have not seen one new, decent architectural landmark that blends with the landscape. I am told that there are skyscrapers in Tel Aviv; I did not bother seeking them out. I have seen those, and even better, in New York and Dubai.

During this journey to my country, I thought abstractly of the motherland I had left. I saw her in my mind's eye in her traditional dress, living a traditional life, an oasis of tranquillity, always devoted to her children, at peace with her environment and her neighbors, her language and her culture. Now, as we drove around, it seemed to me that she, my motherland, was transfigured, in foreign dress and tongue. "No! No! This is not my motherland. This is a terrible nightmare. It cannot last."

Neither my daughter nor the driver was aware of my daydream. We all lapsed into a long silence, tired of constant movement. We continued on the long coastal road to Jaffa. The glistening Mediterranean waters at dusk peered at us on the right, from time to time, between the trees—a familiar and reassuring sign of my country.

At the outskirts of Jaffa, I told the driver to turn right and then left, then right again. We arrived at a moderately sized building with its own courtyard, surrounded by Jewish houses. The forlorn, isolated, and dignified building was the shrine and mosque of Sidna Ali or al-Haram. As I filmed the scene, I saw a couple with their children emerging from the building. "Do you come here often?" I shouted across the fence.

"Yes, every Friday, at least. Where are you from?"

"We are Palestinians like you, only living abroad, in the *shatat*."

I encouraged them to keep an eye on the site, a symbol of our heritage and right to be here. This Palestinian couple had made it their duty to take care of the mosque regularly. They assured me that they were well aware, and that they continued to fight for it against neglect, vandalism, and Israeli-government obstacles.

Years earlier, at an international conference that I was attending, an Israeli professor at Tel Aviv University asked me, "Sidna Ali. Is it not a mosque? Why do you show it as a village on your map?"

"It *was* a village. You expelled its population. It has a large cultivated land marked on British Mandate maps. Do you not teach this at your university?"

Ah, his university, another site of erasure. Not far from Sidna Ali, on al-Auja River (which they call Yarkon) , there was a village, Sheikh Mu'annis. It grew citrus fruit, the famous Jaffa oranges, and was owned by notable families, some of whom hailed from Jaffa. In 1948, the village was ethnically cleansed. Its population was expelled, but a minority moved to Lydda. Their houses were demolished in stages; the last was demolished only a few years ago. Israel built a highway over the village cemetery. Tel Aviv University was built on the village site. The *mukhtar* had lived in a nice house decorated with multiple arches at the entrance. After the village expulsion, the *mukhtar*'s house was preserved and repainted green. It was called the Green House and became the Faculty Club.

"Do you know that, when you have lunch at the Faculty Club, in the Green House, that the Club is a stolen house?" I asked the learned Israeli social studies professor.

"Stolen, you say. What do you mean?"

"The owner of this house is rotting in the Qalandiya refugee camp. Do you think it is fair?"

"Well, it was war, you know. But by negotiations, we shall reach a peace agreement."

We drove on and had a late lunch at Abu al-Afia restaurant by the sea in Jaffa. The food was good, as close to Palestinian food as the Israeli taste would permit. Two things spoiled my appetite. I asked the proprietor if he was Palestinian (there is a similar Arab-Jewish last name). When he replied in the affirmative, I asked, "Why the hell do you not have Arabic on your menu? Arabs are all around you. Why only in Hebrew and English?"

Uncle Tom smiled politely and said, "We are working on it."

As we ate delicious fish, I looked at the beautiful sea. There was this nice little mosque with its minaret shyly pointing to the sky. It was the smallest minaret I have ever seen. Next door, even probably in the same compound (I didn't have time or the wish to see), there were blazing lights in all colors advertising a nightclub and bar, probably an Israeli expression of "peaceful coexistence."

As night fell, I tried to locate Nuri al-Uqbi in Ramleh. After several phone calls to set a rendezvous, we arrived at his simple home. He treated us both to his great hospitality, as well as to a painful story of his extremely long struggle to restore his rights on his land. Al-Uqbi's name became well known recently when he and his countrymen in al-Araqib, an "unrecognized village," rebuilt their homes on their land after the Israelis had demolished them; in 1995, it was the thirty-third demolition. The number has continued to rise to double that.

Without any resources except his perseverance, al-Uqbi fought for years against the laws that said we did not exist. Since Israel considered that his land has no owner *(mawat)*, it thus became state land to be allocated to Israelis only and converted into Jewish-only private property. I knew the story very well, but to hear it from him, in his voice, seeing his facial expressions, was another matter. More than a decade later, in 2010, his case was brought to an Israeli court. He was helped by an Israeli professor who believed in equality among Israeli citizens. I sent him documents from the British Mandate and the Ottoman period, dating as far back as 1596. The Ottoman tax register of that year recorded the number of people who lived there, what they cultivated, and their tax that was due. The court ignored all this and accepted the opinion of the state expert, a Polish woman who did not understand Arabic. According to her, there were no Palestinians there, only shepherds who had come once with their sheep and then left.

I canceled a trip to Lydda nearby. I couldn't bear the thought of adding that to our day. I did not want to see Dahmash Mosque, where the worshipers who took refuge in it in July 1948 were mowed down by machine guns and by Davidka cannon; and where the death march originated and, in the July heat, seventy thousand people were expelled at gunpoint on orders of Yitzhak Rabin. Lydda, the home of the patron saint of England, St. George who slew the dragon, had its fair share of modern knights: George Habash, Khalil al-Wazir, Ismail Shammout, and Rajai Buseileh. I could not sleep that night. I tossed and turned in my bed in Jerusalem until I heard the muezzin calling for the dawn prayer.

After a few days of rest, we headed south. Ah! The south: my birthplace al-Ma'in and I were waiting to be united again. We took the highway to al-Majdal. On the way, we passed by Latrun, where the Jordanian army (known as the Arab Legion then) made a stand to defend Jerusalem against an Israeli attack. Yitzhak Rabin, one of the Israeli commanders, was personally defeated in one of the battles, which affected his spirits for a long time. The Israelis had left damaged tanks on the edge of a bluff opposite as an exhibit of the battle scene.

As we descended to the coastal plain, I saw that the countryside was sparsely populated, almost empty of Israelis. I noticed the same in many parts of the Galilee, which was still heavily populated by Palestinians. By contrast the coastal plain, primarily in the environs of Haifa and Tel Aviv, was now densely populated by Jewish settlers. Both of these metropolises swallowed up a half-dozen Palestinian villages.

When we arrived at al-Majdal's intersection, I told the driver to take a sharp left and then turn due east on the old road from al-Majdal to Iraq al-Manshiya. Halfway there, I got out of the car and viewed the landscape. At this intersection, the road going from north to south met the road we were on, going from west to east. This intersection, or zomet in Hebrew, was the scene of a decisive battle. The Egyptian officer in charge, Abd al-Hakim Amer, was on holiday that day.[101] That road was the northern border of the southern district, in which very few Jews lived before 1948. They had a few military posts, each manned by thirty soldiers. The land they owned was less than 1 percent of Beersheba district. The veteran Palmach soldiers broke the Egyptian defenses at the very spot where I was standing, and then they swept over half of Palestine without much difficulty.

As my daughter was filming, I showed her that three hundred meters to the east of where I was standing was the Iraq Sweidan police station, which repulsed the Palmach six times. They called it the "Beast" and they had to bombard it from the air until most of the defenders were killed.[102]

We drove south on the north–south road. A few more kilometers to the south, at the site of the destroyed village of Huleiqat, I saw a tall monument with inscriptions from Tanakh, extoling the bravery of the outnumbered Jewish soldiers and their victory over the numerous and murderous Arabs.

Once I had a chance to discuss the destruction of this very village with a Jewish soldier who participated in these events. In 2000, I participated in a UN-sponsored debate at the UNESCO building in Paris with the Israeli 'peace activist' Uri Avnery. We debated whether Palestinian refugees should be allowed to return to their homes. The debate went nowhere with him, but the audience got the point. He suggested we continue the discussion over dinner with his wife, Rachel. I agreed.

He told me he was a soldier with the terrorist organization Irgun, and was stationed on a hill in Huleiqat. He said he remembered seeing masses of wretched humanity, off to the west by the Mediterranean Sea, trekking to Gaza to seek refuge. He wrote a book about the heroism of the Jewish soldiers. The book was instantly successful and was translated into several languages. He became a celebrity. Encouraged by his success, he wrote another book, again from his war experience, on the atrocities that these same soldiers had committed. It was a mild criticism of the soldiers at best, and showed nothing of the savagery displayed in Deir Yassin, Dawayma, or Burayr. Even so, his second book, in a single Hebrew edition, was buried. He was ostracized and had barely escaped assassination.

I told him that the masses of humanity he saw that day had names, faces, and families. I told him about the large family in al-Jura (old Asqalan) having dinner in the first days of November when an airplane dropped a bomb on them, killing eleven members of the same family and leaving their limbs flying in the air and hanging on tree branches. I told him about children separated from their families, about the distraught mother who returned when she discovered in the middle of the night that she was carrying a pillow and not her newborn. I told him about my friend Abd al-Rahim Hussein, a boy of fourteen then, whose mother asked him to return and bring a sack of flour for them to eat. He carried it for forty kilometers, walking among the escaping refugees. At every large group of people, he shouted in the night, "*Yamma* (mother)." With no reply, he continued walking until he reached the next group. "*Yamma*." He repeated his cry of anguish. In Deir al-Balah, a voice came out of the darkness among palm trees, "*Na'am, Yamma* (Yes, mother)." Only a mother could know her son's voice. This boy is now retired with a PhD in Zionist history. Uri's wife, Rachel, was sitting opposite me. I saw her eyes moisten, fighting tears.

I told him about my life's quest, to know the face of that invisible enemy who made me a refugee. "Uri, what does the Huleiqat monument celebrate? The masses of wretched humanity?"

"You know, soldiers would like to celebrate their victories."

"Why did they not erect monuments for the massacres they committed, seventy of them?"

"I wrote about atrocities in my second book." There was a long silence.

I turned to Uri and asked, "Now that I know your background, would you agree that I should return to my home in Palestine, next to yours?"

"Definitely not."

"I'm saying, assume it is my own home where my family lived before 1948, but it is next to your home."

"NO!"

"We are in Paris now. Assume you wished to buy an apartment and a Frenchman objected to a Jew, not a French Jew, being his neighbor. What would you do?"

"We would raise hell, of course," Uri responded. That was the end of my conversation with an Israeli peace activist.[103]

My daughter and I left Huleiqat, continued south, and crossed the Gaza–Beersheba road. My heart pounded heavily. We were close to al-Ma'in. We crossed Wadi Ghazza and I climbed on the ancient Tell Jemmeh, witness to 3,500 years of Palestinian existence. If only it could talk. I reviewed the horizon before me and remembered the wheat fields of my childhood. Almost 150 years before me, an American priest, W.M. Thompson, exclaimed, "Wheat, wheat. An ocean of wheat." [104]

In 1883, Edward Hull, the head of the British Geological Survey in Palestine, observed that "[t]he extent of the ground here [near Beersheba] cultivated, as well as on the way to Gaza, is immense and the crops of wheat, barley and maize vastly exceed the requirements of the population."[105]

About one kilometer after Tell Jemmeh, I stopped the car, and we got out. "Rania, all you see before you belongs to you and your family." That was my first view of our land after forty-seven years of exile.

"All that? I was very happy we had this small, lovely house in Canada," she teased.

"Come. I'll show you." On our right, there was the new colony of Ein Hashlosha on my father's and my mother's family land. We crossed Wadi Farha, that expanse where my mother encountered her rival's messenger in the late 1920s and won a lasting victory!

"Slow down," I said, "slow down." I shouted. The rash driver wanted to complete his tour and return. I wanted to savor every minute and see every detail. On my right, the remains of our *karm* fence, the cactus, were clearly visible. Thank God for the cactus, our loyal sentry. There were no trees, no figs, grapes, or almonds. They were all gone.

"Turn right here. VERY slowly."

The house in front of the *karm* had gone. That was the house they robbed, where the sword was. But its memory did not die. I had already constructed a dimensioned plan of the house from memory and the aerial photos. "Turn left."

We drove on a narrow road leading to a cluster of trees. On my left, there were the remains of an unfinished house built by my cousin Ahmed when he got married. "Stop here."

Rania carried the camera and I looked around as if in a trance. Here was my school, now empty space. A few meters away to the south was the place where I was born. "This is my land, this is my home, this is my birthplace, this is my being, this is my identity that I carried with me everywhere. This will be my final resting place."

Overcome by emotion, I knelt on the ground for several minutes and I kissed it. Rania was filming. As I knelt for too long, she became worried. "Baba! Baba!" I stood up. She had one eye behind the camera, and the other was filled with tears.

"Rania, you are the twelfth generation in our family, the only one *not* born here. They robbed you of that natural right . . . they will not succeed. Your grandchildren will be born here."

I walked around what was left of the schoolyard and I found a familiar sight. The faithful eucalyptus tree was still there. Somehow, it had escaped the butcher's knife. I remember playing around it, climbing it, and getting scratched knees. During recess, it was the center of our activity. Now its branches were bare. It looked forlorn and abandoned. The whiff of its scent circulated in the air and reached me, as familiar as it was. Only this time, it seemed like a faint greeting from a long-separated family member who felt abandoned and longed for a warm reunion.

I saw, however, an unfamiliar sight: several graves with Hebrew inscriptions. The driver read the inscriptions on the tombstones to me. They were soldiers killed in the battle and honored for making me a refugee. The soldiers who survived must be old by now, the rapists of the teenage girl, those who killed my two uncles, those who killed over a dozen of my relatives . . . they must be around here or have been here. I decided I must go and see where they lived.

I took with me two handfuls of the good earth that fed us, witnessed our birth, and after a long life, becomes our eternal shelter.

We returned to the side road and headed north to the hill where I used to play. We decided to enter the Nirim kibbutz. I knew the site from my map very well. The gate was open. There was no one around, maybe because it was Saturday. Behind the gate, we turned right on a long loop. Prefabricated houses with small front yards were arranged in a semicircle. The circular road took us back toward the exit. On the right, there was a school and industrial buildings. In the middle of the road lay another memorial, one of the twenty-four tanks which had attacked us. There was a reservoir of the water siphoned from Tiberias Lake and the Upper Jordan River, channeled south by the National Water Carrier.

I thought to myself—was there anything here not stolen? Was there anything not an instrument of war and killing? How could these people sleep at night? Rania was no doubt contemplating the whole scene and comparing it in her mind with what I had told her since she was a child.

We went back to the main road, then headed south to the *bayyara*. There was no sign of it from the road. I guessed the distance and started to climb the little rise in the land where our horses and donkeys used to climb to fetch a drink of water. There was dried grass, and lizards leaping after the crushing sound of my feet. I told Rania to follow my footsteps in case there was a buried mine. Looking around at the neglected high grass, I saw the remains of the *jabiya*, the groundwater tank or reservoir. Gone was the flour mill. Nearby was a steel lattice covering the mouth of our ninety-five-meter well. That was what remained of our *bayyara*, blown up by the Palmach on the morning of 15 May 1948.

I was describing all this to Rania with some agitation. My voice was raised in anger. Suddenly a flock of pigeons nesting in the well flew in a beautiful formation, soared high in the sky, made a long loop, and returned slowly to their nest. What a message for us! That we fly away from impending peril, soaring in the skies, flying away in formations, and slowly turning back and gently landing in our nest.

Well, that is what I have done so far: flying all over the world, always with an eye to return to my nest. Fairouz's angelic voice in the song "We Shall Return" came to mind. The beautiful words of John Havergal echoed with the fluttering wings of the returning pigeons.

We crossed the road to see the remains of Abu Ibreisha's house. Abu Ibreisha, my father's cousin, was his partner in the *bayyara* and flour mill. The semi-destroyed house was roofless and blackened with smoke. It served as a newsletter for the returnees. Everyone who returned in the early 1950s, in defiance of Israeli machine guns and mines, scribbled a message on the walls: "Ahmed was here"; "Returning, God willing"; "See you soon"; "We will never forget you"; "Wait for me."

Not far to the southeast, another colony, Nir Oz, was planted on the land of Hajj Mahmoud, Hamed's father. Although Hamed later acquired land in Syria, Lebanon, Jordan, and Egypt, he would have gladly forfeited it all for his land in al-Ma'in.

On the main road heading south, we saw a sign leading to an ancient synagogue. An ancient synagogue here? I had never seen or heard anything of the kind. We went to investigate. There was a platform overlooking a mosaic floor ornamented with birds, animals, and plants. This was typical of Byzantine churches but with one addition, a menorah. I remember the floor very well. It was largely hidden by the soil. As children, we used to play marbles with the loose stones we could find.

My daughter took the risk and went down to the restored floor while I was filming. She found that the original stones—showing birds and plants—were of solid colors. The menorah stones were clearly painted. She found it easy to remove ten pieces of these stones. In the Byzantine era, there were three churches in our neighborhood, with almost identical design. None had menorahs. The first was at

Tell al-Far'a, nine kilometers southeast of us, the second in al-Ma'in, and the third at Tell Jemmeh, eight kilometers northwest of us.

After our trip, I visited the libraries of the Palestine Exploration Fund and the Royal Geographical Society and found images of the two other churches discovered by the Australians in 1917. Our church was in the middle of the other two. The three were all Byzantine Christian churches of the fourth to the sixth century, probably built by masons of the same tradition.

I redrew the plants, birds, and animals, their arrangements, and the ornamental frame around the floor. They were identical in character, varied only slightly by the hand and the design of the masons. Now a menorah had been inserted in that missing part of the floor. This insertion of the menorah with artificially colored stones was what attracted my daughter's attention. She took away a box of painted stones to prove it had been added.

We returned to the main road and headed south to Beersheba town, but not before we stopped at the fourth colony on our land, Magen. As I said before, it was built around a shrine, Sheikh Nuran, on a hill that commanded a full view of the area. The gate was guarded by a young woman in a booth. The taxi driver poked his head out of the window and shouted in Hebew, "Tourists." His taxi marking was supporting evidence.

"Visiting whom?" she replied.

He looked at me for an answer, "*Qubur* [graves]," he replied.

"OK."

"How do we get there?"

"Go straight to the end, by the swimming pool."

We found the lush garden with beautiful flowers and the swimming pool. By contrast, the shrine of Sheikh Nuran was derelict. The dome was partly destroyed, one half of the wall was missing, and the windows were gaping holes. A crude wooden observation post was still perched on the top since the days of 1948. What a fate for a fourth-century monastery, I thought.[106] In my time, the dome was perfect, the walls intact, and a green shroud covered the whole edifice.

I peered through the window and I got a big surprise. Within the rubble inside, I saw a stone Byzantine cross, intact. That confirmed what the PEF survey described about people in Palestine. The people who lived here were the same for centuries. They may have changed religion, but they revered the same holy places, made vows to their shrines, gave them offerings, and prayed for protection. As a child, I remember that Sheikh Nuran was visited by our women who wanted to have children or wish for a long life for their newborn. When they gave birth, they drew a white cross on their door. They hung small bells around the necks of their infants. Child mortality was high, and the grounds of Sheikh Nuran became a children's cemetery.

I told my daughter about this and we trod gently on the flat ground where little bones were buried. We did not see any grave markers because an Israeli bulldozer had compacted and leveled the ground.

We headed to Beersheba town along the same road that I had taken as a child with other children and my two young relatives, forty-seven years earlier. Back then, we were thirsty and hungry, and we were walking in the opposite direction, away from my school in Beersheba to my home. We were terrified of the Palmach jeeps with mounted machine guns. Now I was a much older man in a Jerusalem taxi with food and drink in my hands.

We crossed the bridge at Wadi Shallalah, where Hamed had planted mines and set up a forward position to warn and protect us from the invaders. We found a park complete with picnic tables. It was named after a Russian-born leader of the invading army, Levi Shkolnik (later named Eshkol). It would have been more fair to call it Hamed Park. When we arrived at Beersheba town, I saw to the left of the road a parade of high-rise flats covering the landscape. With difficulty, I found the old Gaza–Beersheba road. The first recognizable feature was the British war cemetery.

We walked along the rows of fallen soldiers from the Australian 4th Light Horse Brigade, which had conquered Beersheba on the evening of 31 October 1917. I recalled examining maps of the Allenby campaign in London and reading military reports describing his day-by-day progress toward Beersheba through my territory. I also saw a 1987 movie, a near replica of the campaign. It was entitled *The Lighthorsemen* and was about the breakthrough after two failures in Gaza. While walking between the lines of tombstones, I imagined hearing the thumping of the galloping horses.

Soon after the victory, the Palestinians were bitterly disappointed. When the news of Beersheba's conquest came to Allenby, Balfour sent a telegram to London: "We took Beersheba. Jerusalem will be your Christmas present." Arthur James Balfour, the British foreign minister, opened his drawer and took out a piece of paper, the contents of which was agreed upon with a group of wealthy Zionist Jews in Europe. In it, Balfour promised to "view with favour the establishment in Palestine of a national *home* for the Jewish people."[107]

As we left the cemetery, watched by curious Israeli settlers, dwellers of the high-rise boxes, I saw these words engraved in stone at the gate of the faded cemetery:

> The land on which this war cemetery stands is the free gift of the People of Palestine and it was given by the Municipality of Beersheba.

On 1 November 2010, Israeli newspapers reported that diplomats from around the western world were gathered in Beersheba to commemorate the ninety-third anniversary of Beersheba's conquest. A symbolic formation of the 4th Light Horse Brigade paraded in Beersheba's streets. The Australian ambassador said that her country has a special bond with the *Israeli* city. Who responded to these honors? It was *not* Sheikh Freih, who had made that victory possible, nor any of his Palestinian successors. It was a recent Jewish immigrant by the name of Ruvik Danilovich who had become Beersheba's mayor. He said that the event "symbolizes faith and ongoing struggle for freedom and independence." The coup de grâce came from Rabbi Raymond Apple, a senior rabbi to the Australian Defence Force. He said, without a hint of irony, "Israel deserves a Nobel Prize for unstinting dedication to humanity in the face of insults and untruths."[108]

We left the war cemetery, its history, and its ironies, and moved on to the old road toward my boarding school. We found the magnificent school building deserted, surrounded by barbed wire, but still intact. We sneaked under the barbed wire, taking a major risk. I was not in the mood to play it safe and miss visiting my old school. Next door, the government building had been converted into the notorious Beersheba prison where stories of Israeli torture are common. We entered the school building, now missing its doors and windows. I walked around, making a running commentary of my years there half a century earlier, only now it was with my daughter tagging along, filming, and listening.

"Here was my classroom. The first to the right as you enter. From the window, I could see my father coming to see me on most Mondays when he came to Beersheba court. I knew the *farrash* would call me in a minute to the headmaster's room where my father was waiting." I told her of our afternoon routines on his visits.

Rania was taking it all in. Too much to remember. Much she had heard before and now she was seeing it in stark reality. We went up the stairs to the dormitory. It was there, just as I remembered it, with two long halls separated by a corridor of lockers. Each hall was open, except for a room at the end for the supervisor. After our evening homework, the lights were switched off, and we were ordered to sleep. Whispering went on for a time and then it petered out and sleep became king.

It seemed there had been other, unlikely visitors to the school before we arrived. The walls were filled with graffiti in Cyrillic letters, Russian! I did not know what it said, but from the shapes and symbols, the words looked as if they were not exactly friendly.

We went out from the other side without being discovered. We saw another fine building, just as old. It was the Beersheba Mosque, in which the Israelis continue to deny Palestinians the right to worship. The mosque was also the place that the people who had escaped from the Beersheba massacre went to hide. They were then expelled to Gaza, together with the Egyptian soldiers who had surrendered. I saw pictures in the Israeli archives of the people hiding in the mosque and others who were carted away to Gaza. One of them was a child by the name of Iyyad al-Sarraj, an internationally recognized psychiatrist in Gaza, who passed away only recently.

In the old town, we saw the elegant house of Aref el-Aref, the district *Qaymaqam*. Opposite his house was the house of Sheikh Freih Abu Middein, the town mayor in 1922. The house had been converted into a restaurant.

I was anxious to cram as much as I could into this short visit, to see what I had not seen before, to walk on the blessed soil, to breathe the air, to see the trees that remained, and the signs, however derelict, of the landscape I knew. Yet there was one thing that defied the transformation of the landscape and the passage of time—the birds. Their numbers, their types, and their flights all remained an enduring symbol of our land.

Time was passing quickly. We rushed to the Gaza Strip. We stood in the line for foreigners at the Erez crossing point, the site of the depopulated and destroyed village of Dimra. Nobody mentions Dimra today, only Erez. The Hebrew word *erez* means 'the earth' or 'the land,' but in this case, it is *our* land without its owners.

I was ashamed that we had relatively easy treatment as foreigners at the crossing, while a hundred meters away, my people were being herded in long, caged corridors and subjected to long, humiliating interrogations.

In every country I have known, priority and better treatment are accorded to the citizens of the country; the foreigners face more scrutiny and suspicion. In Israel, it is just the opposite. Though I suppose it should not come as a big surprise; after all, it is the foreigners who are the citizens and the indigenous who have been made refugees.

Gaza, at first sight, looked poor, disorderly, and lacking modernity. I saw familiar faces. I heard a familiar accent. The sights, sounds, and smells were decidedly Palestinian. Here I saw my motherland, in her traditional dress and speaking her native Arabic. True, the dress was tattered, the streets were cluttered with wheeled carts and bicycles, and the roads were dusty, full of potholes. But it was home. No one was more surprised than Rania.

"They speak and look like us," she said.

We had a joyful reunion with my two brothers, who were there with their children, and the larger family in the four towns of the Gaza Strip. They took Rania with them for an initiation tour. I was sure, in a month or two, she would have no difficulty melting into *that* pot.

This visit to the Gaza Strip, my first refuge from al-Ma'in in 1948, came after an absence of thirty-three years. It had grown in population and the quality of life had deteriorated greatly. After the usual social rounds, I made a pilgrimage to my parents' graves. I went with my nephew, my niece, and Rania to Khan Yunis's old cemetery, not in use any more. The gate was closed. The rusty door squeaked as if it were crying with anguish.

I visited the tombstone of my father's grave. Words can hardly describe the life of this great man. I thought of his life, sheltering me in action and in thought. What was most heartbreaking for me was to think of his last days and his internment in exile. True, it is still a piece of our homeland, only eight kilometers from al-Ma'in, his birthplace, but his resting place was not his choice.

We went to the Beni Suheila cemetery, where my mother and my eldest sister had been laid to rest. The graves were simple and not clearly marked. I instructed my nephew to install a marble piece with proper writing. My niece sobbed at the sight of her mother's and grandmother's graves.

"Keep each other's company, like before. Speak to each other and chat, to while away the time," she said between tears.

Drained from this trip, but rejuvenated in other ways, we planned to leave. Again, in preparation for the Israeli Checkpoint Charlie, we had less luggage and much less paperwork. At Lydda airport, our luggage was checked in at the airline desk, but was marked with a sign. We were ushered to a separate desk.

"Where have you been?" the officer asked me.

"All over the country."

"Whom did you see?"

"A lot of people."

"What are their names and addresses?"

"Are you kidding? Do you want the name and telephone number of the waiter or the hotel clerk?"

"Do you have the hotel bill?"

"I do not have an expense account. I do not need to keep receipts. Hang on! I think I kept one."

"Do you have a card?"

"I am not on a business trip. Here is one in my pocket."

"How did you pay for your tickets?"

"Through my travel agent."

The girl, thoroughly indoctrinated, behaved like a robot. Another robot-like official came and started the same round of questions, cleverly observing our reactions.

"Look, your colleague asked the same questions," Rania responded.

"She is a trainee. I am the responsible person."

"Why did you send her then?"

My daughter got really angry and started to write down the questions.

"Why are you writing down the questions? It is not allowed."

"Why not?" Rania answered. "You are asking *me* these questions. It is not a secret. I could write them half an hour later from memory."

"Still, why are you still writing them down?"

"I shall ask my member of parliament to urge our government to make every Israeli visitor subject to the same questions and treatment."

"This is for your safety."

My daughter exploded. Brought up in a free society, conscious of her rights, not afraid to speak her mind, she retorted, "This is very stupid. I am *leaving* the country with *another* airline. What is it to you if we are blown up in another country?" And after a small pause, "Actually the real danger to our life was *here*."

They let us go. Orthodox Jews in black suits and curly hair were buzzing by with no hindrance. After the grueling interrogation, we had just enough time before departure to quench our thirst in the cafeteria. In the cafeteria, the Israelis were staring at us from every direction. Everyone must have seen us when we were taken aside for interrogation while they sped through without a problem.

As the dark Mediterranean waters appeared in the window, we both breathed a sigh of relief. Freedom again from seeing the overbearing Israeli presence on our land. How wonderful it was. Yes, it was a temporary relief. The real joy will come when we return permanently to my country, my motherland.

21

Wake-up Call

After six decades of Israel's wars against the Palestinians and Arabs, Israel waged a new kind of war against them. In previous wars, Israel attacked and expelled the Palestinians and destroyed their physical presence. But Palestinians remained much in evidence. Two-thirds of them are refugees away from their occupied homes. Half of the refugees are on Palestinian soil, under Israeli rule or under occupation; the other half are in exile along Palestine's borders and all over the world.

The new Israeli war targeted the Palestinians' inner self, their identity, their being. It aimed to pollute their minds like a Trojan-horse virus. This war did not bother to attack their hearts. Let them ache, dream, and remember, as long as they do not raise a hand or develop an idea.

In the half a century since the Israeli occupation of the West Bank and Gaza Strip, the western world has been the battlefield of this Israeli war. Israel has conducted the war beautifully, especially in some western quarters where truth was easily sacrificed. This war's aim was to produce and market a package representing the totality of the Israeli assets in the conflict and to push for its adoption. The package contains these essential elements: "There is no such thing as Palestine. There are no people called Palestinians."

From these elements, everything else follows. Those Palestinians who live in refugee camps belong to the countries where they live and shall die with their dream of the right of return. Those people who live under Israeli rule in Palestine are an Arab minority to be tolerated only if they remain subservient. Otherwise, they will be removed, under different code words. Those in the West Bank, if they claim sovereignty, land rights, water, freedom of movement, holy sites, and the like, will be bargained with, piece by piece, in marathon negotiations until there is nothing left to negotiate.

The Palestinian package was also based on essential elements: "Palestine is our country. We are Palestinians, rooted in this land. European Jewish colonizers came to our land, carried out the largest ethnic cleansing in Palestine's history, expelled us, took our land, and made us refugees. We are determined to return home."

The Israeli myth and Palestinian facts competed for ascendancy. New players came into this war. They were not only the usual pro-Israel Zionists, or the opportunistic western politicians, the best democracy money can buy. Some were recruited Palestinians.

After the Gulf War and Kuwaiti occupation, Arafat was exhausted in almost every field. His great lieutenants were murdered, one by one, and he was left only with those who did not pose much of a threat. Arafat, at his great moment of weakness, was faced with a diabolical war game: the 1993 Oslo Accords, the biggest hoax of the century.

An exiled government signing for occupied people and refugees, under the most severe duress, documents that never mentioned the words "Palestinian rights, international law, UN resolutions"—any of the staples of the Palestinian cause. No Palestine. No Palestinians, as we know them. With his foresight and eloquence, the celebrated Edward Said exposed the Oslo hoax just one month after it was signed in September 1993.[109] Now, after over twenty years of this deceitful charade, it is plain for all to see.

Fragmentation of the Palestinian rights' into five or six minor cases was designed to eliminate collective, all-encompassing rights. Signature by the weak party of a number of separate agreements written by the strong party completed the cycle of surrender.

I saw Arafat on TV, on the White House lawn and later in Cairo, speaking in meek, forgiving words, while Rabin stood by his side, pleading the case of the Israeli victims, crying in self-righteousness, "Enough, enough." I shuddered in disbelief. The tormentor and the victim had exchanged roles.

After watching the Cairo signing on 4 May 1994, I wrote a long letter to Yasser Arafat, delivered by hand:

I wished to hear you, Mr. President, say in your speech:

I stand before you today to remind you that, firty-six years ago, 85 percent of my people were uprooted by the force of arms and the horror of massacres, from their ancestral homes. My people were dispersed to the four corners of the earth. Yet we did not forget our homeland for one minute.

I remind you today that seventy thousand people from Lydda and Ramleh alone had been forced on a death march in the July heat. They were women, children, and old men, thirsty, lost, tired, and carrying nothing except the clothes on their backs. One of those children was my friend and comrade all those years, Khalil al-Wazir. The commander who expelled them is the one standing next to me now. He is also the one who ordered the assassination of my dear friend Khalil. Let us learn the lesson of history: Injustice will not last. Justice must be done.

I wished from my heart that you had said that. You know, Abu Ammar, that Palestinians have never before signed any agreement, armistice, or any accord of any kind, in which they agreed to forfeit any part of their country or their rights. You cannot do this today under any pressure.

Arafat replied to me ten days later, partly by handwriting:

These Accords are an important and necessary step toward the achievement of just, comprehensive, and permanent peace, which guarantees the restoration of our fundamental national rights, including the right of self-determination, and the establishment of our independent state with Jerusalem (al-Quds al-Sharif) as its capital *(and by hand)* particularly in light of local, regional, and international changes.

Sadly, there was no mention of the right of return in his letter.

"Realism" became the guiding mantra; "be realistic, we cannot beat Israel to deliver justice." The chorus on the Israeli side chanted: "Yes, yes, you cannot. Anyway, the country is already full; your villages were destroyed; to where will you be returning? We did not push you out; you left on Arab orders. Do you have any idea where those refugees who wish to return are today? Do you know where they come from originally? Do you know how many of them wish to return? How many wish to speak Hebrew and serve in the Israeli army? Do you think we would accept you undermining the Jewish character of Israel? Be realistic; be realistic."

The bazaar of compromises opened. Israelis gave the Palestinians one offer after another. Let us compromise. Compromise is the only way. Surrender to me half of your facts, packaged as my own, and I shall offer you half of my myths as yours. No. Here is a more *realistic* proposal to fit the situation on the ground: I'll take 80 percent of your facts and give you 80 percent of my myths.

Wait a minute. This is not fair. We cannot ignore the settlements in the West Bank. How about 90 percent, maybe 95 percent of your facts for me and the same percentage of my myths for you?

A plethora of mushroom-like growths sprang up on the face of the West Bank. All kinds of NGOs emerged, generously funded by the United States and the European Union, singing the praises of realism.

I pored over maps, statistics, and figures for weeks. There was a lot of data to sift through, analyze, and interpret. The interpretation led to a curious result. It must be wrong or at least largely wrong. I repeated everything again and got the same result.

I invited a friend, Abd al-Rahim Hussein, for coffee at Sultan Center, a seaside café by the Kuwaiti Gulf shore. Abd al-Rahim is the boy who cried "*Yamma*" looking for his mother on the refugee trek in 1948, who went on to become an expert on Zionism. I spread before him my maps and calculations.

"Israel is empty," I said.

"What?" he replied.

"Well, look here. Immigration and natural growth of Jews are settled around the same old colonies they acquired during the British Mandate."

"And what about our village sites, where we were born, from which we were expelled?"

"Empty. Practically empty. At least 90 percent of the sites are empty. Of course, there were lots of changes in the landscape, but this is the bottom line."

"My God, this is important, very important. It is DANGEROUS. Do not tell anyone," he said.

"I will tell the world."

The study took several turns and phases, and it developed over the years into a Return Plan. It covered other aspects like population, land ownership, water, agriculture, legal foundation, logistics, reconstruction, and rehabilitation. The blueprint of the Return Plan took shape.[110]

I spoke about my book, *Palestinian Right to Return: Sacred, Legal, and Possible* in almost every refugee camp in Palestine and in Arab countries and before dozens of Palestinian communities in the Arab world, Europe, and the United States. At first, Palestinians were incredulous; then they started to see the possibility of return as intriguing and hopeful. Since almost one and a half million maps of Palestine have been distributed worldwide, the young generation have become more inspired to think of their roots.

Many of the third and fourth generations of the refugees were born abroad, received an education, and had self-confidence and a defiant spirit. "How could you let Palestine, our homeland, slip from your hand?" they chided their parents, not taking into account the conditions of the time. This young generation is now found in many capitals of the world, at the major universities of the west, as students as well as professors.

In 1997, I was approached by two new non-governmental organizations (NGOs) dedicated to refugee issues and the right of return. The first was Badil in Bethlehem, run by Ingrid Jaradat Gassner, with good contacts in the West Bank, Gaza, and Europe. The second was the Palestinian Return Centre (PRC) in London, run by Majed al-Zeer, who established good contacts among Arab and Muslim communities in the United Kingdom and Europe. We cooperated well. Much of the work on the right of return and its implementation was disseminated by them. Yet it became obvious that people still needed to be mobilized.

The banner in Arabic reads: The Right of Return: Sacred, Legal, and Possible. A full house in Damascus, January 2004.

Me speaking at Capitol Hill, Washington, DC, in April 2002 with Hisham Sharabi listening. The audience was the faithful minority who believed in justice for Palestine.

After Oslo, the first to take initiative for popular action on the issue of the neglected right of return was Hisham Sharabi, a prominent Palestinian academic in the United States. In the early 1990s, he toured the Middle East in order to organize a people's conference to affirm fundamental Palestinian rights, particularly the right of return.

He had good intentions and solid objectives. Coming from the United States, he underestimated the latent force remaining in the Palestinian factions, which carried the day through armed struggle in the 1970s and part of the 1980s. In the 1990s, their power had eroded, and with the exception of two or three groups, they were reduced to a small office and a small staff. Yet they were still capable of thwarting any initiative to mobilize people they did not control.

On the fiftieth commemoration of the Nakba, I talked with Ibrahim Abu Lughod, who in turn talked with Edward Said. We agreed that there should be a declaration on the right of return signed by as many leading Palestinians as possible. The sponsoring committee consisted of the three of us, expanded to include two Palestinians of impeccable record, Haidar Abd al-Shafi and Shafiq al-Hout. Eventually the committee had twelve members. I wrote the first draft of the declaration, which was then edited and approved by the committee. It read in part:

> We the Palestinian signatories to this Declaration,
>
> Cognisant of the facts that . . . our people have endured 51 [now 66] years of exile, ravages of war, oppression, denial of national identity and racism and have been the victim of the largest meticulously planned ethnic-cleansing operation, unprecedented in modern history with the aim of replacing them with Jewish immigrants from all over the world.
>
> Hereby we affirm the following:
>
> The right of the Palestinian refugees and the uprooted to return to their homes is a fundamental right under the Universal Declaration of Human Rights, the International Covenant on Civil and Political Rights, the International Convention on the Elimination of All Forms of Racial Discrimination, the European, the American and the African Conventions on Human Rights and the Fourth Geneva Convention of 1949;
>
> The right of the Palestinian refugees and the uprooted to return to their homes is an inalienable right and has been affirmed by UN Resolution 194 over 130 times since 1948.
>
> Accordingly, we hereby declare that,
>
> We absolutely do not accept or recognize any outcome of negotiations which may lead to an agreement that forfeits any part of the right of return of the refugees and the uprooted to their homes from where they were expelled in 1948, or their due compensation, and we do not accept compensation as a substitute for return.

Ibrahim collected signatures from Palestine, and I from the rest of the world. The response was overwhelming, a sure sign that the Oslo Accords and what they stand for were rejected by the absolute majority of Palestinians. Refugees in camps, former ministers, and diplomats, lawyers, academics, activists, students, labor leaders, and housewives signed it. As an independent initiative, we did not seek, or include, any name of a person who had a position in any of the Palestinian factions.

It was published in all the Arab media. It was also delivered to the Arab League. We thought of delivering it to Kofi Annan, the secretary-general of the United Nations at the time. Certainly Edward Said was the best suited to do so, but Edward was sick. He was receiving harrowing chemotherapy for his cancer. During his illness, he never stopped writing and traveling for the Palestinian cause. Edward replied to my letter about meeting Kofi Annan:

> Dear Salman:
> I'm in the middle of round three of chemo but hope to make it to Boston. I think you and I should see Kofi, and can arrange it for the week after the conference if you can come to NYC for a day. Let me know right away.... As is, the petition seems fine.
> As ever, Edward

The Boston conference he referred to was the first major international conference on the issue of the right of return; it was held in April 2000 at Boston University. The conference was organized by Naseer Aruri, Elaine Hagopian, and Nancy Murray under the auspices of the Trans-Arab Research Institute (TARI). The conference was attended by over one thousand people, mostly from North America. Two dozen delegates arrived from the Middle East. It was the first public demonstration in which people saw through the Oslo hoax and refused to play the game.

The day after the conference, I saw a young man sitting quietly in the hotel lobby. He told me his name was Zahi Damuni and we had a chat. Zahi was meeting a group of young people to convert the words of yesterday into action. His group formed al-Awda in North America with links worldwide. Observing their record after more than ten years of hard work, I see they have made a strong impact on universities, unions, and human-rights groups. They convene a well-attended annual convention in which I frequently participate.

The 'realists' continued their efforts. They were made up of roughly four groups. The first is diplomatic. It consists of former diplomats who may genuinely or hypocritically believe in this kind of realism. Their objective is that Palestinians should forget Palestine and accept the crumbs Israel throws at them.

I accepted a lunch invitation from Richard Murphy, a career diplomat, with close knowledge of the Middle East. He was then director at the [US] Council on Foreign Relations. After the conference, my plane from Boston arrived late and I had to carry my heavy suitcase straight to the restaurant where we had lunch. My host was Henry Siegman, a former fellow at the Council and former director of the American Jewish Congress. Also present was Judith Miller, a pro-Israel journalist who later produced false reports on Iraq's nonexistent weapons of mass destruction. Auda Aburdeine, a Palestinian, facilitated this meeting. I described the Boston conference in glowing terms and explained how these young people, the third generation, demanded their right to return.

"Right to return where? Israel is full," Judith said, repeating the usual mantra.

"Not true. Even if it was, if a robber takes your home and brings in his relatives, does this make him the owner?"

"Let us not get into the past."

"But the past is the present. We are living it every day."

"Refugees will be paid compensation," Judith persisted.

"Let us pay this compensation to the Russian economic immigrants and with this money they can find jobs in Russia. They will be happy. Do you not know that the number of Russian immigrants to Israel is equal to the total number of registered Palestinian refugees in Lebanon and Gaza? With the refugees' repatriation and the Russians finding jobs in Russia, everybody will be happy. There will be no instability in either Lebanon or Gaza."

"Henry . . . say something!" Judith said desperately. Henry did not say anything. She called the waiter. "Double espresso, please!" She looked flushed and visibly uncomfortable. She left hurriedly.

The second group of 'realists' are the academic mediators. I was invited, by mistake it turned out, to attend a dialogue session between Palestinians and Israelis under the auspices of a leading United States university. One session was enough for me to see that the purpose was to tailor the suit of Israeli occupation to fit the occupied people—how to live with it, which gates to enter their enclave or leave, which goods to import or export. The attending Israelis were all past or present military officials. The Palestinians were security officials and businessmen who were eager to do business at any price. I heard one Israeli tell a Palestinian businessman that Prime Minister Netanyahu was so proud of his letter of support that he hung it on the wall of his office.

I prayed that no one would see me with this crowd. However, the American organizer, it was soon discovered, was Jewish with family in Israel. The event was not part of the famous university as he claimed; the venue was a rented room there. To boot, this organizer was caught with his hand in the till. He was accused of embezzling several hundred thousand dollars.

Another event was organized by a professor at the same famous university. The Israeli party again consisted of a group of intelligence and academic professionals (they are interchangeable). The Palestinian group was of mixed pedigree. It was one of them who invited me "because I had good arguments."

The Israeli party was discussing among themselves how much land, water, and air of the West Bank they are willing to give the Palestinians. The Palestinian party was silent, waiting for the generous offer. At the coffee break, I told one of the Palestinians, "What is this circus? Where are Palestinian rights?"

"Did you come from Mars? Be realistic," he said, surprised at my naïveté. This person heads a group that fabricates survey results on demand. Before becoming a realist, he was not able to pay his rent. He later received fees of tens of thousands of dollars per month.

I saw a former Mossad officer (by his own admission), during these lengthy one-sided conversations, making a flower out of paper. He looked at me and said, "I am very good at it." He picked up various markers from the table and painted some leaves red and green, leaving the paper white. "Look. Is it not beautiful?" he said.

"Make it more beautiful. Try this one." I threw a black marker toward him and he painted some leaves in black.

"Now you have a Palestinian flag," I said.

He looked as if he had been bitten by a snake and threw the flower back toward me. I put it in my buttonhole. After the single session I attended, I wrote a long, critical letter to the organizing American professor. I saw him months later. He was apologetic explaining the failure of his initiative. The group was disbanded.

The third group of 'realists' has populated the mushroom field which grew in the West Bank and less so in Gaza. So many NGOs preaching their self-styled peace sprouted in the occupied Palestinian territories. Their literature was promoting a new virtual map of the region. There was no mention of the right of return or Palestinian land occupied in 1948, no reference to the six hundred or so depopulated towns and villages, no maps showing Palestine in full, and a reluctance to teach Palestinian history in schools.

Following these rules of omission, the NGOs earned a good living. This new industry was preaching a kind of hired neo-patriotism. Your fees rise as your patriotism sinks. The acceptable packaging of their new mission was to market it as new political thought, a realistic strand of politics. As the veteran Fatah leader Salah Khalaf (Abu Iyyad) put it, "Treason became a matter of political *opinion*."

To their credit, many NGOs refused to fall into this trap. I recall the case of Mashriqiyat, a women's group in Gaza teaching women to be aware of their rights. They were doing a good job teaching women their rights within society, in marriage, in education, in housing, and so on. When their empowerment extended to housing rights, demanding the right of return to the house from which the family was expelled in 1948, the European Union cut their funds. The group worked for free for one year and then had to disband.

The fourth group of 'realists' is alien to the history of Palestinians. Never before have we had Palestinians publicly advocating the forfeiting of Palestine and our homes as a public policy. I say never before, because those odd individuals who did that before 1948 were summarily shot. In the nineties, this group signed secret or public agreements. They held public meetings in five-star hotels. They appear on talk shows. They are courted (and paid for) by western officials. They do not dare enter a refugee camp, ever. They drive around in armored cars with bodyguards. A case in point is the ill-fated and much derided so-called Geneva Initiative organized by the Palestinian Yasser Abed Rabbo and the Israeli Yossi Beilin. Its primary aim was to forfeit the right of return in all but name. It died unceremoniously.

We started preparing for the next conference after Boston, this time in the Middle East where more Palestinians could come.

My dear friend, the great patriot and great mind, Ibrahim Abu Lughod, passed away on 23 May 2001. I spoke to him two days earlier and asked him how he felt. He sounded frail and weak, but remained in high spirits. "Never mind about me. How are the preparations going? We must continue. Do not stop."

I tried to obtain permission to hold the conference in Cairo in 2003. It is closer, cheaper, and likely to accept the variety of passports that Palestinians carry. Through an Egyptian friend, I inquired about this possibility. The news was initially encouraging. Yet a week later, the friend called: "Sorry, higher authorities refused." I went to see the Yemeni ambassador. He was welcoming. Weeks passed without an answer, the Arab way of saying no. Friends tested the mood in some Gulf countries. All answers were evasive. What about London? It was a strange idea. Many of the participants, especially from the refugee camps, had travel documents only, not passports; some had a past that was unpalatable in the West.

We gave it a shot. I wrote letters to the British consulates in the Middle East, helped by recommendations of friends in Britain, with a list of invited participants in their region to "a conference on the refugee situation." To my surprise, all but one arranged visas, some at the last hour. The one exception was our designated chairman of the conference, Shafiq al-Hout, a true patriot and a founder of the PLO. The usual trick for refusal is to grant a visa after the conference date, which also happened in this case.

As an independent group, we would not receive any funds except from like-minded Palestinians. Many paid their own airfare. Edward, on his sickbed, was following the progress of preparations. He wrote,

> Dear Salman,
> I was so pleased to hear from you. Where are you now? I'm home or in hospital, quite ill and undergoing treatment and having a bad time, though I can still write and, I suppose, think. As for the meeting you mention a hundred Pals—can't we get it going? I think it's massively important. Shall you and I and one or two others constitute ourselves as a committee and set about having that meeting despite all the difficulties. I think Europe would be a good site and in addition to obvious WB and Gaza people we have to have at least 50 percent from the shattat, which is mostly unorganised and inactive collectively. For a new civil order in Palestine, for resistance, for our self-salvation. Do let me know what you think Salman please?
> With warmest wishes, as ever,
> Edward.

Sadly, it was the last letter I received from him.

We have lost those giants, Ibrahim, Edward, Haidar, and Shafiq (who passed away later), but their mission is carried on.

The conference was held in London in October 2003, attended by one hundred Palestinians who came from refugee camps and university campuses. Shafiq al-Hout spoke to the conference by phone. His unforgettable remark was, "It is a shame that the Palestinians cannot find an Arab home for their conference. We found it only in the land of Balfour."

The outstanding result of the conference was not only the affirmation of the right of return, but the understanding that the best way to defend it, achieve it, and implement it was the democratic election of a new National Council for all Palestinians worldwide. This became our constant theme after the Oslo hoax.

The United States, Israel, and client Arab leaders resisted the call for democratic elections of a new PNC. Official Palestinian leaders were lukewarm about it, quoting difficulties and objections. We wrote many times to and had one meeting with Mahmoud Abbas, the successor to Yasser Arafat as PLO chairman. I met Salim Zanoun, the PNC speaker, many times. The lame excuses were always the same: objections by governments, lack of knowledge about Palestinians and their locales. All excuses were meant to maintain power.

We decided to hold another conference in Beirut in May 2007 for this specific purpose alone: to defend the right of return by demanding the rebuilding of the PLO on a democratic basis. Given that PLO departments were essentially idle, we planned on organizing popular activities to fill the void until a proper PLO functioned, sort of shadow PLO departments. Since the 1990s, the PLO had become an empty shell of its former self, doing nothing. The burden of defending the Palestinian cause was left to dedicated groups in the occupied territories, young Palestinians in the *shatat*, and their supporters in countries where they reside.

The archaic PLO skeleton rose to life to attack our conference with outrageous accusations—accusing us of everything from being agents of the European Union to agents for Iran. They could not conceive of the idea that independent Palestinians could rise up, fund their own conference, and demand democratic representation.

Still, there was plenty of hope. Our youth who have yet to see their homes in Palestine are 70 percent of Palestinians. They gave the world a wake-up call. They have formed right-of-return committees in almost every place where Palestinians are found.

They continue to hold demonstrations at every possible square and campus. They write poems, sing songs, and produce movies. They launched the Boycott, Divestment, and Sanctions (BDS) campaign. They sent flotillas with their foreign supporters to break the illegal and inhumane blockade on Gaza. They have brought their foreign friends in droves to protest the Apartheid Wall that cuts deep into the West Bank.

Ben-Gurion must be turning in his grave to lament his failing forecast that "the young will forget." The wake-up call was sounded and no one can block the ears of the youth to its call. In mid-May 2011, thousands of young people gathered at the barbed wire of Palestine's borders, in Lebanon, Syria, Jordan, and the armistice lines in the West Bank and Gaza, and stretched their necks to see and to reach their homes within sight. They were met with Israeli tear gas and bullets, but also with eager Palestinian compatriots who remained, meeting them on the other side of the fence, supporting each other's effort. It is only a sight today; it will be an entrance tomorrow and a permanent abode the day after.

22

The Last Mile

My long journey on the road to return is not by any means unique. Almost any Palestinian can describe a similar, if not more painful journey. Almost seven million Palestinians, dispossessed of their patrimony, yearn to sleep in their own beds like normal human beings.

Many fighters returned to Palestine to fight the occupier on our land. Hundreds of those who made the return journey stayed permanently at a numbered cemetery kept by Israel. Some Palestinians became the incarnation of sailors in the legendary *Flying Dutchman*, a ship that was never allowed to land at any port, doomed to navigate the oceans forever. Some Palestinians spent weeks and even months in transit lounges of various airports. When their residence permits expired where they were working, they were deported and told to "go home." They were put on the first flight leaving the country. They were shunted from airport to airport. They continued wandering on these eternal journeys. If the *Flying Dutchman* was a product of seventeenth-century folklore, this Palestinian journey is the product of a *real* colonial project.

Even on the territory of Palestine itself, the Palestinians who were expelled but could remain within Israeli-occupied areas were not allowed to cross a short distance and return home. Those who were expelled from their villages and ended up in a refugee camp never arrived at their camp of exile in one straight journey. They hovered around their village trying to return. They sought refuge in a safe village nearby. When that village was attacked, the host and the guest tried to find another nearby temporary refuge while they waited to return. They were always intent on return.

When they finally settled in an UNRWA exile camp to escape death, death did not spare them. Israeli tanks and planes showered them with their rations of bombs. Nobody can ever forget the sight of pools of blood, demolished homes, and women sitting on the debris in Jenin, Gaza, Rafah, Sabra, Shatila, and many other camps. The barbed wire, the machine guns, and the wall between us and our homes have prevented us, so far, from making our return.

My friend Ibrahim Abu Lughod made it in two trips. The first journey occurred when he returned from the United States and served at Birzeit University to help compose a Palestinian curriculum. The second was when he managed to obtain "permission" to be interred next to his father in a Jaffa cemetery.

I followed this news with the greatest satisfaction—Ibrahim *could* do it—and with the deepest sadness that this great man could not *live* in Jaffa with all his family, friends, and students in his remaining days. He made sure it was the place where he would rest.

The pursuit of the return, at their assembly on the barbed wires separating them from their homes on 15 May, Nakba Day, by those wonderful young people, will continue. New ideas are developing, such as building villages of return in the West Bank. The will of millions of helpless people is always bigger than a single power, no matter how mighty.

We at the Palestine Land Society and our partners are going one logical step further. We plan for the reconstruction of destroyed Palestinian villages. Our plans are derived from a massive database. We are charting the original houses of every refugee in his or her village, the land he or she owns—he and she and their *hamula* (extended family). We are recording his place of exile today, how far it is from his home, whether he can reach it by foot or by bus.

We are creating a file for every village, its house plans before 1948, its features and characteristics, its crafts, its economics, and its status of education. Now that the number of those who are educated has shot up to meteoric proportions, the villages' economic parameters have changed dramatically, except that land and agriculture remain vital assets. Young architects are now working on the reconstruction of these destroyed villages, to be built in the same locations with the same beautiful old features, but with modern amenities. Pictures of old villages, of their remains, sketches of their dreams are spread on the table before them.

As for my birthplace, my niece Layla and my late brother Ali's granddaughter Serene, both architects and planners, are now working on the town plan of al-Ma'in, zoning for commercial, industrial, and residential areas and reserving the choicest pieces for the university campus. Its centerpiece is the reconstruction of the school that my father had built in 1920.

In spite of a nine-fold increase in the Palestinian population since 1948, the number of required houses upon the return of the refugees is only 1.5 million units, a small fraction of similar projects built in the Gulf and Saudi Arabia with the help of the Palestinians.

The welfare of the population is linked to its economy, of course. The Palestinians are clever and hard-working. When they are spared the suffering of exile and can return to their homes, and when they enjoy their freedom in their country under good governance, they will work wonders. Upon return, they could be employed in services, light and specialized industries, and trading, to compensate for the shrinkage in agriculture. The workforce needed for all this is already available. Very little capital, except in the initial stages, is needed.

Our studies have shown that the rehabilitation and repatriation of the Palestinians will cost much less than the large sums paid by the United States to support Israel and the injustice in Palestine. It is also much less than the full compensation for what they lost, if Palestinians decided to abandon their country and sell it, God forbid.

Return is cheaper, just, peaceful, and lasting.

The present occupants of my land are very well known to us. We know their numbers and their occupations. I have maps of how they divided our land among them, approximately 20,000 dunums (4,750 acres or 2,000 hectares) each, at the rate of 300 dunums (72 acres, 30 hectares) for each of the seventy families there. That means the density of the settlers on my land is fifteen people per square kilometer at most. Those of my family, the least privileged who still live in a refugee camp in the Gaza Strip, live at a density exceeding five thousand persons per square kilometer. Yet they live only a few kilometers away from their homeland.

Some years ago, one of our young family members wanted to pierce the bubble of denial and bring those people living on our land at Kibbutz Nirim into the realm of reality. He sent an email explaining to them that the land is ours and had been ours for generations and that we had not seen Jews before their conquest of May 1948. He concluded by saying that we must return, and as a "moderate" Mapam (Workers' Party) kibbutz, Nirim members should support it.

A reply came to our young man from behind the wall of denial. "You do not really expect us to believe your statement, as you know too well that many Negev kibbutizim, including Nirim and ten others, were established in 1946 alone, two years before 1948."

The author of the reply was referring to the eleven military posts erected at night in 1946 to influence the hand of the Partition Plan committee. Nirim, on our land, was not one of them. This Nirim was built in the spring of 1949 after the conquest of al-Ma'in.

In his answer to our young man's question about why he was not allowed to return, the voice came back with this logic:

> Let us say that we reach an understanding and members of the Abu Sitta family return here. I can visualize that day and can imagine your joy, but I can also see your first disappointment, when you see how little of your former land will be returned to you.
>
> Your status as lords of the land will of necessity also be different, since the way of the world is for refugees and immigrants to fill the lowest rung of the economic and social ladder of the society they have been "accepted" into, with no chance of rising above it for a few generations, if at all. The Jews around you will show little empathy for your distress, just as the government shows little to our Arab-Israeli citizens, to our sorrow and shame. At first a wave of criminal violence will erupt, which will be followed by one of nationalist feelings. Each side will stand behind the insult it feels, real and imagined—it really doesn't matter—and dig in to its own side's arguments, beliefs, claims, and whatever.

He, of course, assumed that we would return under the rule of racist Zionism, not to a free, democratic country.

Our young man sent an almost humorous note of defiance from a popular song by The Police: "Every breath you take."

Such a condescending tone came from our "friendly settler" in the neighborhood. He considered himself a liberal. He was not a Jewish fundamentalist or a right-wing Netanyahu follower. If we returned, he advised, we would face the unpleasant specter of living among the racist Israelis he does not agree with, but would nevertheless defend and support.

That was the extent of the vision of those Israelis who claim to see through their bubble of denial. There was no mention of our ethnic cleansing, massacres, and theft of land. There was no sense of reality that, a few kilometers away, the owners of the land are crowded in a refugee camp.

Planning and working on the return plan gains more urgency and more potency every day. For wherever events will take us in the future, return is coming, no doubt about it. That, of course, will require, as a basic principle, the fall of racist Zionism. The plan of return can accommodate all the circumstances in which this may come, whatever they are.

Yes, Zionism will fall. Just consider what happened to the world's regimes and leaders in the eighty years after the 1930s, when the British opened the floodgates of Palestine to Jews from around the world. And just consider, in the same period, the resistance movements that suddenly rose up.

There are, however, ingredients in Zionism which could determine its fate sooner rather than later. First, Zionism is based on certain misconceptions traded as facts. Lies do not have a long shelf life. Palestine and Palestinians do exist. Ethnic cleansing took place in 1948 and is still taking place today in a variety of forms. Second, Zionism marches against history. European colonial soldiers, after three hundred years of colonization in Asia and Africa, packed their bags and returned to Europe in the mid-twentieth century. Third, the Zionists still go by the creed of the Zionist ideologue Jabotinsky, "Live by the sword alone." Their motto became: Let your sword be the biggest, sharpest, and the most effective that modern technology can provide. Do not let morality, legality, or lessons of history stand in your way. That doctrine cannot last. Fourth, we live in a big neighborhood, in which there are over 190 nations. Many, more than 150, believe Zionist ways are not good for the world.[111] That leaves Israel with one, the last, the most powerful, the richest, the staunchest supporter: the United States. But, as events in Vietnam, Iraq, and Afghanistan have shown, all powers have their limitations. Riches dwindle and its politicians have to one day face the wrath of their genuine constituency.

These philosophical thoughts and historical lessons may sound too idealistic; they do not move armies or make headlines. Yet they most certainly reassure the human spirit and guide it in its long, slow path to change.

We do not need to consider only the external forces that could demolish racist Zionism. Let us look at the positive forces that may build justice. There lies my real and earnest hope.

My faith is first and foremost in our young people, whom I have seen and worked with in the last two decades. This faith in return grows deeper in them; their parents and grandparents did what they could in their time and have passed the message to them.

Then there is the growing international indignation about the injustice in Palestine. In recent years, we have seen masses of previously (assumed-to-be) helpless people, with their sheer will, topple mighty dictators who had ruled for three or four decades.

It is the determined will of people that counts. It must of course be accompanied by vigorous planning and action. An iron will does not bend in the face of obstacles or challenges, failures or disappointments. These challenges only sharpen it. Its ultimate reward is to enforce justice, to return home. The fuel for this long journey is the sheer limitless will of those seven million Palestinian refugees. And I am proudly one of them.

On that fateful day in mid-May 1948, riding behind my brother on the horse, I turned my head and looked back at my birthplace for one last glimpse. I looked at the smoldering remains of our houses, the debris of the school, the demolished mill. The receding meadows and the tips of the date palm slowly sank into the horizon.

The pain engulfed my young heart. However, I did not despair. No. I felt as if I had been set on a path of a rescue mission, a lifelong mission to return. I left behind, squatting on my land, the Russian Sarig, the Ukrainian Meitiv, the German Boberman, and the South African Zipper. I spent the next seven decades putting faces and names to those "invisible" enemies. It was *my* al-Ma'in that was held captive in their hands, but it was never theirs to own.

To rescue al-Ma'in is to rescue a small, precious piece of the whole of Palestine's mosaic. Reassembling that larger mosaic has been the task taken up by Palestinians for over sixty-seven years. It took them through the fedayeen, the PLO, the PNC, the Palestinian Revolution, the UN, and more intifadas. The road is indeed long.

My task took me to nine skies and nine flights and I am still flying. We are still homing in. Every day will ultimately bring us closer, although our modest advance is the sum of a few successes and many failures. Like the pigeons in our well, flying away, doing a loop in the sky, and homing back to their nest, I will be carried by my own wings on my return. If that will not be possible, I will be carried for at least three more flights. The tenth flight will be from Kuwait to Amman to be buried in our family cemetery, next to my brothers. It is accessible to many of my family.

The eleventh flight, when the time comes, will take me from the Amman cemetery to a spot in Abasan village in the Gaza Strip near the barbed wire and machine guns, separating it from my birthplace—only one mile away.

The last mile.

It is my wish to be temporarily interred in a plot facing al-Ma'in, waiting for the last journey home. It is my wish to make the journey of the last mile—from Abasan's barbed wire to the spot where I was born, just a few meters from our school—accompanied by family and friends on foot, feeling every grain of the soil denied to us for over half a century. It is the same spot where I knelt and kissed the ground when I visited it with Rania in 1995. My soul will rest in peace when I feel I've made that journey of the last mile. In my mind, I can see the engraving on the tombstone: "Born here, torn away from his home at a young age, he spent the rest of his life flying in the skies of the world on the long, arduous journey to return home—and he finally made it."

The twelve flights have more symbolism. My daughters are the first generation not born at home, in twelve traceable generations of my family. Perhaps they can restore the severed bond through their children and grandchildren.

I believe, even amid all of our political realities, that our family's motto, "We Persevere," will be vindicated, that human spirit and determined will can triumph in the end.

Afterword

Writing an afterword to my memoir while in Gaza, as the blood of over 200,000 Palestinians is being spilled and the dust from the destruction of buildings fills the skies, seems callous and out of touch with reality. How can I talk about the hopes and aspirations of the past while the ugly present is staring me in the face? How can I talk with nostalgia while I am gripped with utter rage and helplessness?

But the descriptive journey of a refugee over the last seventy-six years, like mine, could serve to teach another lesson—the long journey is here to haunt us; it is here to say that the journey has not ended. It is not a story of the past but of the present. If you dismiss the odyssey of seventy-six years as an old story, it is here now to destroy our present and to mobilize millions of young people around the world who have never heard of us before. The death they see on TV would not have happened had they known or even heard of the Nakba. They would have then stood up, shouted, and cried until the bloodshed of innocent lives had stopped and the criminals had been brought to justice.

A simple unsolicited story illustrates this. A group of young Americans in the countryside, neither professionals nor researchers, host a book club to discuss domestic matters of interest to them. They stumbled upon *Mapping my Return* and discovered, among other things, that "Israel was carved out of Palestine." I connected with them on Zoom. Their questions and the exchange of information I had with them was more valuable to me than ten university lectures.

The period that elapsed since this book was first published in 2014 has added more chapters to the same story.

The quest of the Palestinian people for their legal representation since 1948 has continued. This was made more urgent after the Oslo hoax, when the occupier sat with the unelected representatives of the occupied to split the latter's patrimony (see page 298). It was a false promise of restoring justice to Palestinians. The effort to hold Palestinian conferences described in the book continued. In October 2017, we convened the Popular Conference for Palestinians Abroad, in Istanbul. It was attended by 6,000 Palestinians from fifty countries. I was elected president of its general assembly. To hold this conference in the first place was a heady achievement. It is functioning today under a different leadership. Still, it has a long way to go before it can secure wide support for our national rights. The enemies of the Palestinians are too numerous. But that is no reason to give up.

In Chapter 11, "The Funeral Town," I described the tragic end of the life of my friend Nadid, in 1956. He was murdered at the door of his home by Israeli soldiers, in view of his pleading mother and weeping sisters. This was in the early days of November 1956, following the occupation of Gaza by Israeli forces as part of the tripartite attack on Egypt, secretly hatched by the governments of Britain, France, and Israel.

As narrated in Chapter 11, the carnage took place over several days in Khan Yunis, with Israeli soldiers going from house to house, mainly targeting males aged between fourteen and fifty—those with the potential to mount resistance—and mowing them down with machine guns in front of their female relatives or in public squares.

The massacre was repeated steadily in the nearby towns and villages where we had contacts, since Khan Yunis was where our family had moved after we were driven away by Israeli forces, in late 1948, from our house and lands in al-Ma'in, Beersheba district. I can only imagine what happened in Gaza City and other parts of the Gaza Strip, as everything was hushed up and hardly ever mentioned in the western media.

Magically, for the besieged people of the Gaza Strip, the carnage came to a sudden end when they woke up to find that Israeli forces had pulled out of the entire Gaza Strip, thanks to the presence of a principled president by the name of Dwight D. Eisenhower in the

White House. This pattern of Gestapo-like mass expulsion started in 1948: Once Israeli forces overpower local armed resistance, they open fire on civilians to ensure that they run away from their homes and take refuge in unoccupied areas, never to return. Then they turn their attention to decimating the men still remaining.

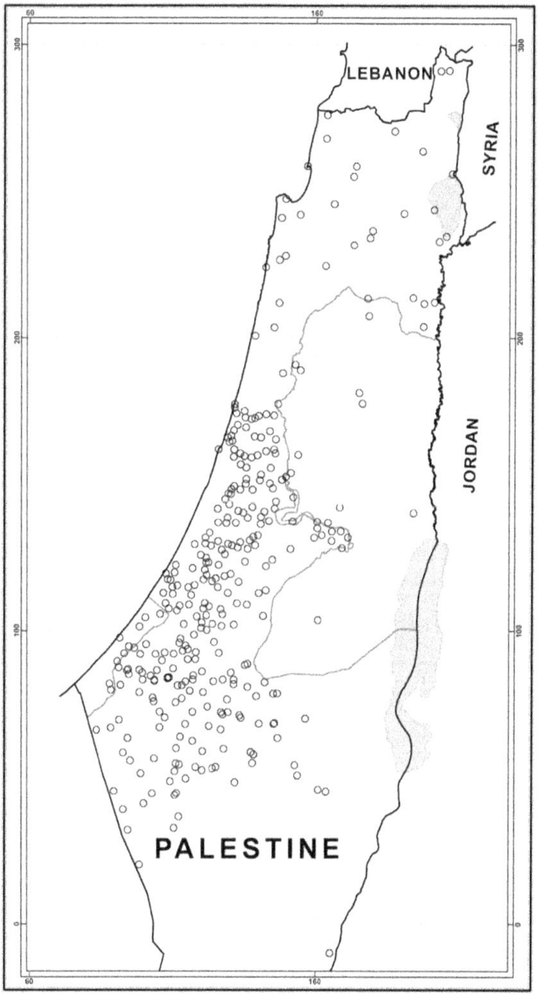

Map 1
Villages of Origin of Gaza Refugees. In 1948, Palestinians in 247 villages in the southern district of Palestine (area 12,500 km2) were attacked by Israel and driven through a series of massacres to the Gaza Strip, which was reduced two years later to an area of 365 km2. Palestinians never gave up their right to return home.

In retrospect, this story, as well as the stories of dozens of other massacres committed by the Israelis during and since the war of 1948, portended the blood-thirsty genocide that the 2.3 million people, my people of the Gaza Strip, are subjected to today as I write.

Israel attacked the Gaza refugee camps constantly, especially in 1953, 1967, 1971, 1987, 2008–2009, and 2014. The attacks culminated in the bloody shooting of the protesters in the Great March of Return in 2018–2019. That was when the young men and women, the third and fourth generation of refugees, risked their lives and stood by the barbed wire, along the Temporary Armistice Line of 1950 (see page 114), demanding to return to their homes which were within sight. The Israelis mowed down hundreds of them with machine guns. Particularly gruesome was the intentional shooting of their knees, creating a generation of amputees, a burden to their families. In the Great March of Return in Gaza, Israel injured 35,600 protesters. Of those, 6,750 were shot by Israeli snipers, deliberately shattering their knees.

In November 2021, I decided to go to Gaza.

Crossing the Sinai desert brought to mind the trek I had made with my sister in October 1948, when we escaped the explosive barrels Israel dropped on us from the sky.

I arrived in Gaza with a mixture of joy and pain, seeing my people after decades of absence, finding no fields, just a continuation of camps stretched side by side, and without the familiar agricultural stretch between Rafah, Khan Yunis, Deir al-Balah, and Gaza City. The Gaza Strip (with an area of 365 square kilometers as of 1950, after Israel reduced its area from 555 square kilometers, the original area of the Armistice Agreement of February 1949) is the temporary refuge of the people of 247 towns and villages in the southern district of Palestine (area 12,500 square kilometers) who were expelled by Israel in 1948 and crammed into camps at a density of 8,000 people per square kilometer. The Gaza Strip is the largest concentration camp in the world.

My priority was to catch a glimpse of my birthplace, al-Ma'in Abu Sitta. I traveled as close as possible to the barbed wire where the demarcated Temporary Armistice Line of 1950 was located. Against the warning calls of the Palestinian guards and my companions, I advanced close to a mound with machine-gun nests, poised ready to kill anyone trying to return home.[112]

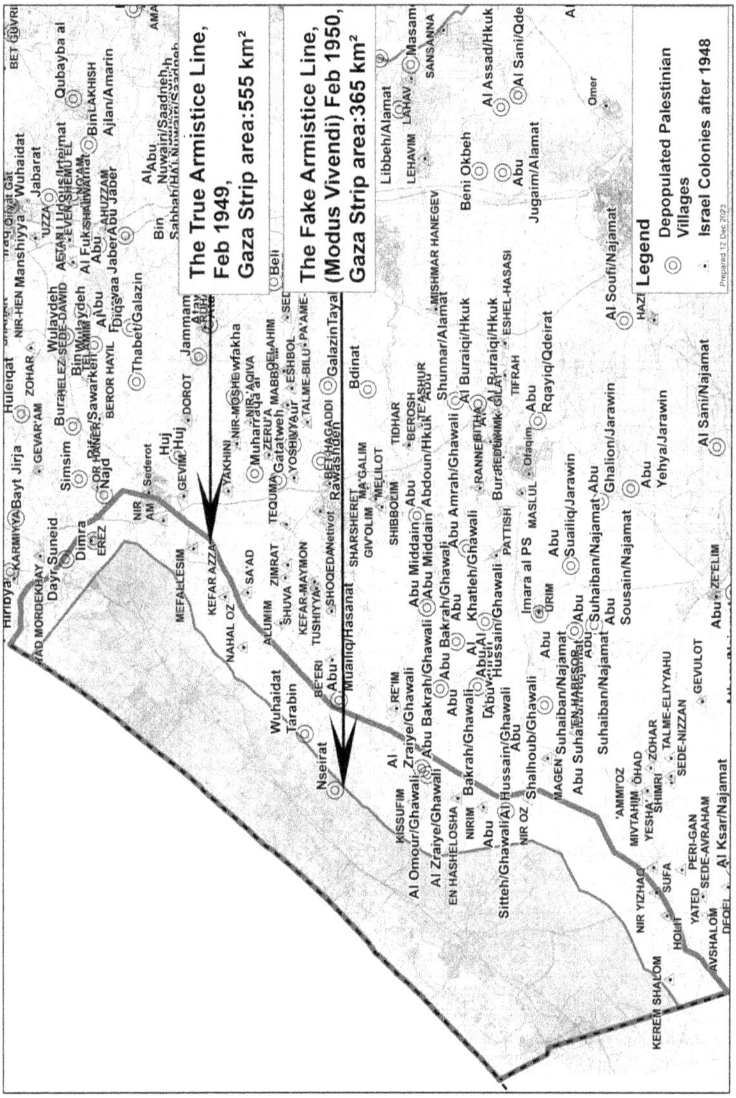

Map 2
The True and Temporary Armistice Line. On 24 February 1949, under the supervision of the UN, Egypt and the Haganah forces, representing the state-to-be Israel, signed the Armistice Agreement that created the Gaza Strip (area 555 km2). Under the pretext of clashes resulting from returning refugees, a temporary agreement (*modus vivendi*) was signed in February 1950, creating a buffer zone that reduced the area of the Gaza Strip to 365 km2. The original agreement was to remain in force. Israel has never withdrawn to the original line and instead built several kibbutzim in the area, which was attacked by Hamas on October 7, 2023.

I saw the tips of the trees in my birthplace, now inhabited by Ashkenazis from Poland, Ukraine, Romania, and Germany. They had built four kibbutzim—Nirim, Nir Oz, Ein Hashlosha, and Magen—on my land. There are about 1,500 of them, squatting on the land belonging to 11,000 members of my family, now in refugee camps.

Driving around the Gaza Strip, I saw resilience, determination, and resourcefulness, despite the extreme hardships imposed on daily life. Every space was used for living, working, or planting, like when vegetables were planted in a two-story shed occupying a small space. The rubble of destroyed residential buildings was converted into a breakwater, creating a makeshift harbor. School buildings were used in double shifts to increase the number of students eager to learn. Cemeteries were full, with signs that read "No more burials allowed." Every family without exception is bereaved. As you enter any residential quarter, you see street signs showing the names and pictures of the martyrs from that neighborhood.

I visited the graves of my parents and recited prayers. I visited the Citadel site where the Israelis in 1956 dragged hundreds of ordinary people from their homes and shot them against its ancient wall.

But the warmth of the people in the face of unimaginable adversity is boundless. The reception of an exiled Palestinian returning to visit was very hospitable. I met family members, neighbors, students, teachers, civic leaders, and many others. The house was full of visitors and well-wishers daily, and they were welcoming and eager to know what we tell the world about them.

To help our people we must do much more than express good wishes. In previous chapters of this book, I described how I collected documents about Palestine. Since then, we have produced *the Atlas of Palestine 1917–1966* in English, Arabic, Spanish, and Russian. We have also produced *the Atlas of Palestine 1871–1877*, largely based on the Survey of Western Palestine by the (British) Palestine Exploration Fund with corrections and additions, not to mention several poster maps of Palestine.

What to do with this data? It must be put to use. Through the Geographical Information System (GIS) and demographic data, we conducted a study with much more detailed results than the first study of 1994. We traced the origins of the refugees and their land ownership. We found who the Israeli squatters on their land were, and when and where they had come from.

Photo 1
A Glimpse of Home. In November 2021, I returned to Gaza after a long absence. I came as close as possible to my birthplace al-Ma'in. Over the last seven decades, I toured the world, pursing my right to return home, and here I am, one kilometer away from my home and cannot return. No matter what, we shall not give up our Right of Return.

This study yielded startling results. We found that 87 percent of Jews in Israel live in fifty-five localities out of 924, or only five percent of the total number of localities. The area they occupy is only 1,400 square kilometers or 6 percent of Israel's area. This means that Israel is practically empty save for three cantons: Tel Aviv, Haifa, and West Jerusalem. It also means that Palestinians can return home without major displacement of Jews willing to live in peace in a free Palestine.[113]

This Return Plan is supported by maps and figures, including the identification of the villages of the refugees' origin in all camps, the length of the road of return from all refugee camps to the village of origin, and the time taken for return. This showed that the return trip varies from zero kilometers—as in the Gaza Strip, South of Lebanon, and the Jerusalem district—to a maximum of thirty-five kilometers. The Right of Return is not only sacred to Palestinians and legal under international law, but it is also practically feasible.

When refugees return, they will find their homes destroyed, thanks to a massive destruction plan undertaken by Israel in its first fifteen years of existence. The destruction idea is based on the assumption that the refugees will neither find a home to return to nor even locate its original location. It is both a deterrent and a scheme to erase the place. The sites of the destroyed villages were covered with European trees planted by the Jewish National Fund (JNF). Today the JNF has created over one hundred parks or forests on the lands of destroyed villages.[114] These parks are named after Western leaders who assisted the Zionist colonial project and made the Palestinians refugees.

But this destruction will not deter Palestinians from returning home. The history and geography of their villages are well recorded in Palestine maps, in the archives of the Palestine Land Society,[115] in over four hundred "village books" written by the people of each village and by various other means.

We collected much of this data and created an inventory of about 550 villages. We started a competition for Palestinian architectural graduates to select one Palestinian village as their graduation project and produce a full reconstruction plan for it, based on the pre-1948 house plan and project it into the future with an increased population and complete modern amenities.

Now the competition is in its ninth year, with up to twelve universities and about sixty students participating each year. In the past years, 270 graduates have participated and completed winning designs for fifty villages representing various regions of Palestine.[116]

The Plan of Return is now complete. It has been presented in many fora.[117]

Of their own volition, some young people in Gaza tried to return home. On October 7, 2023, a small number of young people, the third- or fourth-generation descendants of 1948 refugees, broke through the well-fortified fence of the Gaza concentration camp and started the journey to return home. They reoccupied about 1,500 square kilometers of their homeland in one morning. For a while their dream of returning home almost came true.

It should have. They had come from 247 towns and villages in the southern district of Palestine. They are the bulk of the Gaza Strip population today.

I could have been one of them.[118] I was born in my father's land where Nirim Kibbutz was built.

The vilification of refugees trying to return home and the sympathy for the squatters on their land in Western colonial circles is a sure sign that the perpetrators of the Nakba are still at work today. Unlike any other ethnic cleansing endeavor, the campaign against Palestinians continues to this day, from 1948 to 2024, and has turned into a full-scale genocide in 2023, in defiance of the United Nations, the international courts, the International Court of Justice (ICJ) and the International Criminal Court (ICC), in front of TV cameras and with complete disregard for the world's rage against Israeli crimes.

Israel has elevated its original crime of ethnic cleansing in 1948 (expelling people and taking their land) to full extermination (killing the people who demand the right to return home).

The ferocity of the genocide since 2023 is unprecedented, both in its scope and in the extent of its visibility for all the world to see. The figures of the dead quoted by the medical journal *Lancet* in July 2024 came close to 200,000 and were rising rapidly at the time of writing. In addition, about 380,000 buildings had already been destroyed in less than a year, including 405 schools and universities, 700 hospitals and health facilities, 290 mosques, and three churches. Based on an estimate by the United Nations monitoring group OCHA (Office for the Coordination of Humanitarian Affairs), twelve buildings are destroyed every hour in Gaza. Essential figures in the society are deliberately targeted and killed: professors, doctors, nurses, teachers, journalists, aid workers, and technicians. With hundreds of thousands of family members murdered, orphans, widows, and others are left to face life on their own.

What kind of memoir can portray all this? The news, though censored by Israel and its allies, leaks into social media and shocks the world.

On the morning of October 8, 2023, I received a call from my nephew, Dr. Ghassan Abu Sitta, the surgeon and son of my late brother Soleiman, the pediatrician. He told me, "I am going to Gaza." I was not surprised. Since his days as a medical student, Ghassan has rushed to help the injured in Palestine, initially during the First Intifada in 1987 and then during subsequent intifadas and all Israeli attacks on Gaza since 2006. He also treated the injured in conflicts in Yemen, Syria, and Iraq. Ghassan has been committed to fighting for just causes since he was a high school student. He keeps his family's legacy alive.

At the time of the phone call, he was a few kilometers away from his homeland, al-Ma'in, where his father was born. Ghassan's saga as a war surgeon, his rush to help, and his immense devotion to his people are now known around the world.

What would the particular settlers in al-Ma'in make of this history when they made us refugees in 1948? Some of them are still "hostages" in Gaza today, as propagated by the western media. What about us, 2.3 million hostages in the Gaza concentration camp, who have been waiting to return home for seventy-six years? This figure includes 11,000 members of my family.

We have neither forgotten nor forgiven. Al-Ma'in is my family home. We documented every member of our family who lived in or owned a piece of it. We traced its history over a period of two hundred years. We gathered maps, photographs, oral histories, and official records about it.

But what gripped me for years was the desire to know how they destroyed our landscape in 1948: Who looted our property? Who demolished our houses and burned our homes? Who stole the valuables, particularly my father's sword in Abdullah's house? Who blew up the school that my father built in 1920? What did they make of its historical stones? Who stole the engine at the ninety-five-meter deep well? Who stole the motor and the four silos of our flour mill? Who uprooted the trees in our *karms* (orchards)? (Part of the cactus fence is still there, defying them.) Why did they dig and scrape the seven roads leading out from al-Ma'in to Beersheba, Gaza, Khan Yunis, Rafah, and other places?

Moreover, I wanted to know how they built their landscape on our ruins. Why did they build new roads different from ours? How did they select the location of the new kibbutzim? What are the first installations they made? Barracks? Water tanks? Fortified fences? Prefab accommodation? How did they select the new immigrants to settle there?

These and many other questions occupied my mind. At the time of writing, I am glad to say that I made substantial progress in answering them. But that is only a start. A master plan is being prepared for al-Ma'in, as mentioned in Chapter 22, page 313.

We shall build Sheikh Hussein University around the location of the school my father built and construct a replica of the one-room school at the center of the campus. The university will have faculties of engineering and architecture (to rebuild Palestine), agriculture (to make use of our historical wheat fields), law (to reclaim our rights), and humanities (to preserve our heritage). This will occupy about one quarter of al-Ma'in in the northwestern side.

On the hill (height 115 meters) to the west of the campus, a Sheikh Hussein Conference Center will be built, where annual and quarterly conferences are to be held to discuss the issues of Palestine, in particular those of interest to Gaza and Beersheba.

At the center of al-Ma'in, we shall rebuild the seven roads leading to so many places and build a big square, actually a circle, or a plaza, with a statue for the martyrs. On its northern side, we shall build a mosque. Its minaret shall be 150 meters high with a light to be seen at least in Gaza and the cities of Beersheba. On the center southern half, we shall build a big commercial center, largely for the products and the needs of the area. Next to its east and south, we shall build a light industrial area to produce and market local needs.

The *maqam* (shrine) of Sheikh Nuran (originally that of the fourth century monk and mystic St. Hilarion) shall be renovated with a tiled courtyard and a small museum. The infants' cemetery around it, now bulldozed, shall be adequately marked. The Byzantine church (claimed to be a synagogue) shall be renovated, in a style similar to other existing Byzantine churches southeast of al-Ma'in at Tel al-Fara'a, and north of it at al-Breij (recently discovered) and further than that, in the south and north of Gaza City.

Four residential areas shall be allocated beyond the center from all sides for the branches of the family: two for Saqr descendants in the western half of al-Ma'in, one quarter for Husseinat, and another quarter for Awaydhah east of that. Houses in these residential areas shall be widely spaced, located around the fields of each family, similar to Texas ranches, not a replica of closely spaced village houses.

I hope that *Mapping my Return* will not remain at the mapping stage but will move on to the stages of implementation and realization. Recent destruction of Palestine's history and geography must and shall be rectified.

It is inconceivable that such a precious part of the world as Palestine would be hijacked by East Europeans driven by Western colonial schemes, its history taken as their own, its geography emptied of its people, and its names replaced by newly carved names, its heritage obliterated, its people killed, dispersed, and vilified as criminals, while the criminals are hailed as the righteous, the brave, and the just. The history of mankind has never known such perversion.

Let us hope that the blood of hundreds of thousands of Palestinians killed and injured, the cries for justice of thousands of orphans and widows, and the rage and anger of millions of people around the world, would be enough to bring justice to the people of Palestine. Justice means only one thing: return to their homeland in a free Palestine.

Notes

1 The Arab Revolt (also known as the Arab Rebellion) took place between 1936 and 1939 in protest against the British admission of thousands of Jewish immigrants to Palestine. This influx of immigrants undermined Arab rights in the country. The British sent the Palestine Royal (Peel) Commission of Inquiry following the six-month-long Palestinian general strike. On 11 November 1936, the Commission arrived in Palestine to investigate the reasons behind the Rebellion and returned to Britain on 18 January 1937.

2 The Maria Theresa Thaler (MTT) is an Austrian silver coin that has been used in world trade continuously since it was first minted in 1741. The MTT is found throughout the Arab world.

3 The folkloric poet (probably Hajj Mustafa Zabin al-Ugbi]) said, "And Al Mughasiba boys descended like wolves / Dashing to the battle field / with the swiftness of young camels." Cited in Clinton Bailey, *Bedouin Poetry* (Oxford: Clarendon Press, 1991), 259.

4 Originally *tawashi* meant a castrated servant in the sultan's hareem palace. Perhaps one of his ancestors was *tawashi*.

5 Laylat al-Qadr, the Night of Destiny, Night of Power, Night of Value, Night of Decree, or Night of Measures, is the anniversary of the night we Muslims believe the first verses of the Qur'an were revealed to the Prophet Muhammad. It occurs usually in the last ten days of Ramadan.

6 The verse is by Quintus Ennius (239–169 BC), considered to be the father of Roman poetry and whose influence on Latin literature is great. It means, "The war trumpet with terrifying sound blew *taratantara*."

7 These horrid memories came vividly to mind when, twenty years later, I saw the play *Oliver Twist* set in an orphanage.

8 The nature of this link is unknown, although the German scholar Oppenheim lists details about that link he heard from al-Saqr in the

1920s. Max von Oppenheim, *Die Beduinen*, vol. 2, reprint (Zurich: Georg Olms Verlag, 1983), 101, 108. My nephew Fawaz, studying at Leipzig University, Germany, sent me a photograph, the earliest I had ever seen, of my father. It was in a book by the Orientalist professor Oppenheim, the emissary of the Kaiser to Islamic Arab countries.

9 I would not have known where Qanan al-Saru was had I not stumbled on it in the maps prepared for the occupation of Palestine in 1917. I found the location while searching in the map library of the Royal Geographical Society.

10 Lt. Col. Frederick Peake was the commander of Transjordan forces before John Bagot Glubb. See Peake Pasha, *A History of Jordan and Its Tribes* (Florida: University of Miami Press, 1958), 200; Arabic translation: *Tarikh sharq al-Urdun wa qab'iliha*, trans. Bahaa eddin Touqan (Amman: Arab House for Publishing and Distribution, ca. 1935), 514.

11 When Muhammad Ali assumed power in Egypt in 1805 he had the ambition to expand the territory of Egypt. The natural extension of Egypt was al-Sham, or Greater Syria. He sent his son Ibrahim Pasha north to occupy as much land as he could where "people spoke Arabic." Ibrahim actually conquered territories up to southern Turkey. The sultan, aided by European powers who feared this new state, forced Muhammed Ali to withdraw his army. According to the London Treaty in 1840, he withdrew on the condition that Egypt's rule would be reserved for him and his descendants. This dynasty remained the rulers of Egypt until it was abolished by Nasser in 1952.

12 Naum Shuqair, *Tarikh Sina* [The history of Sinai] (Beirut: Dar al-Jil, 1991), 583.

13 Victor Guérin, *Description de la Palestine*, 7 vols. (repr., Amsterdam: Oriental Press, 1969), 2:266.

14 *The Survey of Western Palestine, 1882–1888*, 10 vols. and maps (London: PEF and The Royal Geographical Society; reprinted by Archive Editions with PEF, 1998).

15 Philip J. Baldensperger, "The Immovable East," *PEF Quarterly* 57, no. 2 (1925): 90.

16 In the 1980s the grandson of Qutna was the Jordanian ambassador in Kuwait. My brother, Suleiman, then a pediatrician in Kuwait, renewed the old contact with him.

17 Alois Musil (1868–1944) was an Austro-Hungarian and Czech theologian, orientalist, explorer, and writer. In the years 1895 to 1917, he traveled extensively throughout the Arab world, collecting a huge body of scientific material.

18 Sheikh Nuran was revered by the people during all ages. Musil dated the Nuran site to the fourth century, when Christians escaped with their religion to what was then wilderness.

19 Alois Musil, *Arabia Petraea*, 3 vols. [German] (Vienna: Kaiserliche Akademie der Wissenschaften, 1908), 2:226, vol. 2, part 1.

20 Muhammad Ali, ruler of Egypt (r. 1805–48) built railways and Nile barrages and sent scholars to study abroad. Abd al-Rahman al-Kawakibi of Aleppo and Muhammad Abdu of Cairo were noted political reformers. Many Syrians in Egypt, such as Jurji Zaydan, had made great advances in modernizing Arabic literature, theater, and finance.

21 Bailey, *Bedouin Poetry*, 352.

22 The Imperial School for Tribes was established by Sultan Abd al-Hamid II in 1892 to train the sons of Arab notables from Syria, Iraq, the Arabian Peninsula, and Libya in preparation for self-government. They were trained as military officers and civil administrators.

23 See Yigal Sheffy, *British Military Intelligence in the Palestine Campaign 1914–1918* (London: Frank Cass, 1998).

24 In return for services rendered, Sheikh Freih was made a Member of the Most Excellent Order of the British Empire (MBE).

25 Henry Cattan, *The Palestine Question*, 2nd ed. (London: Saqi Books, 2000), 13–15. See also Sami Hadawi, *Bitter Harvest: A Modern History of Palestine* (London: Scorpion Publishing Ltd., 1989); W. Khalidi, ed., *From Haven to Conquest: Readings in Zionism and the Palestine Problem until 1948*, 2nd ed. (Washington, DC: Institute for Palestine Studies, 1982). For an analysis of the Balfour Declaration and international law see Henry Cattan, *Palestine and International Law* (London: Longman, 1973); Francis A. Boyle, *Palestine, Palestinians and International Law* (Atlanta: Clarity Press Inc., 2003); W.T. Mallison, *The Legal Problems Concerning the Judicial Status and Political Activities of the Zionist Organization/Jewish Agency*, Monograph No. 14 (Beirut: Institute for Palestine Studies, 1968); W.T. Mallison and S.V. Mallison, *The Palestine Problem in International Law and World Order* (Essex: Longman, 1986); Musa Mazzawi, *Palestine and the Law* (Reading: Ithaca, 1997); and Jonathan Schneer, *The Balfour Declaration: The Origins of the Arab–Israeli Conflict* (New York: Random House, 2012).

26 Public Records Office, CO 733/2/21698/folio 77, 29 March 1921; McDonnell, *Law Reports of Palestine, 1920–1923*, 458. Available by inspection in the National Archives (previously Public Records Office), Kew Gardens, London.

27 "Report of the District Commissioner's Office, Southern District (Jaffa) 5 October 1938," in *Political Diaries of the Arab World: Palestine and Jordan, 1937–1938*, ed. Robert Jarman, (Cambridge: Cambridge University Press, 2001), vol. 3, 359.

28 Aref el-Aref, "Gaza Diary, 1938–1939" (unpublished manuscript), Oxford University, St. Antony's College, Middle East Centre.

29 My father attended the fifth (1922), sixth (1923), and seventh (1928) National Conferences, the National Arab Conference in Bludan (1937), and the very important National Committees Conference in Jerusalem (1936). He was also a member of the Arab Higher Committee and the Higher

Islamic Council of Gaza. See Bayan Nuwayhid al-Hout, ed., *Documents of the Palestinian National Movement 1918–1939: From the Akram Zu'aytir Papers* [Arabic], 2nd ed. (Beirut: Institute for Palestine Studies, 1984); Bayan Nuwayhid al-Hout, ed., *The Palestine National Movement—Diaries of Akram Zu'aytir, 1935–1939* [Arabic], 2nd ed. (Beirut: Palestine Research Centre, 1992). My father made the statement that "the jihad cannot be postponed" at the National Committees Conference in Jerusalem on 7 May 1936. See al-Hout, *From the Akram Zu'aytir Papers*, 428.

30 This became the first line in history to dissect Arab land, and it became an international boundary between Israel and Egypt after the controversial Camp David Accords in 1978.

31 "Fortnightly Report 110 16, 31 July 1945," in R. Jarman, *Political Diaries of the Arab World* (Cambridge: Archive Editions, 2001), vol. 4, 198.

32 President Roosevelt asked King Abd al-Aziz for advice on European Jews who had suffered at the hands of the Nazis, obviously hinting that Palestinian doors should be wide open for them. The king replied, "Give them the choicest lands and homes of the Germans who oppressed them. Make the enemy and oppressor pay. Amends should be made by the criminal, and not by the innocent bystander. What injury have Arabs done to the Jews of Europe?" The president assured the king that he would never do "anything hostile to the Arabs." This is related by an eyewitness, Col. William Eddy, *FDR Meets Ibn Saud* (Washington, DC: America–Mideast Educational & Training Services Inc., 1954), 32–33. FDR died shortly afterward, in April 1945, clearing the way for extremely hostile American presidents.

33 Kermit Roosevelt Jr., *Partition of Palestine: A Lesson in Pressure Politics* (New York: Institute of Arab American Affairs, 1948).

34 As late as 1946 there were hardly any Jewish settlements in the Beersheba district. Because of that, the July 1946 Morrison-Grady plan for the division of Palestine actually took the Negev out of the borders of the Jewish state, and Jewish settlement was prohibited in this whole area. In response to the plan, the Jewish National Fund, the Jewish Agency for Palestine, the Haganah Defense Forces, and the Mekorot Water Company decided to extend Jewish settlement in the Negev very significantly, to insure that the area would remain part of the Jewish state. See "The Negev's 11 Points," Palyam.org [Hebrew], http://www.palyam.org/About_us/displaySOHarticle?name=The%20Negev%27s%2011%20Points&id=t00035&bl=b00035

35 On 29 November 1947, the United Nations (UN) narrowly passed Resolution 181 proposing the division of Palestine into an Arab and a Jewish state. The labels "Arab" and "Jewish" did not mean ethnic or religious entities; that would be against international law. The labels refer to a region where a government based on the majority of the population is likely. The Palestinians formed a majority in the Arab state with

practically no Jews there. In the Jewish state, Arabs were almost equal in number to Jews. The Jewish state would control 54 percent of Palestine, with Palestinians living in 467 towns and villages being placed under the rule of Jewish immigrants. The Partition Plan was a mere suggestion and had no binding value. The Jews embraced the plan and the Palestinians refused to give up half their country.

36 Benny Morris, *The Birth of the Palestinian Refugee Problem Revisited* (Cambridge: Cambridge University Press, 2004), 76.

37 We heard firsthand from Hamed about his burning of books. The story about Yasser Arafat's involvement was related by Hamed to Alan Hart, *Arafat: A Political Biography* (Bloomington: Indiana University Press, 1989), 74–78.

38 This detailed information was collected by Aref el-Aref, a copy of whose unpublished papers I obtained. His notes illustrate the pathetic state of our defenses against the Palmach battalions, who were superior in arms and training.

39 Arab regular forces were outnumbered during the initial and subsequent phases of the war. Lebanese forces, for example, which started at 700, and reached a maximum of 1,000, had no military impact. They even lost a dozen Lebanese villages to the Israeli forces. Syrian forces (about 2,000) tried and failed to capture two Israeli settlements south of Tiberias. The well-trained Iraqi forces, which started at 2,500 and expanded later, arrived without orders *(mako awamer)* to defend the villages. They was able to defend Jenin against Israeli attacks but lost the surrounding villages. Iraqi forces were subsequently withdrawn at the request of Transjordan. The Arab Legion of Jordan, with a maximum force of 4,500 well-trained and armed men, and led by British officers, maintained defensive positions in the Old City of Jerusalem. The brunt of the fighting after 15 May was taken up by Egyptian forces. In the beginning, they numbered 2,800, and were expanded rapidly to 9,292. In October, the size of the force increased to 28,500, in addition to 1,109 Saudis, 1,675 Sudanese, and 4,410 volunteers, mostly Palestinians. As a force of 35,662 men under one command, it was by far the largest Arab force. Its task was to defend a large Arab area, over half of Palestine, with very few Jewish settlements in it. Like other Arab forces, at no point did it attempt to enter the designated Jewish state. Under the inept leadership of General Mawawi, however, Egyptian forces lost all of this territory, with the exception of the tiny Gaza Strip, defended by Mawawi's successor, General Ahmed Fouad Sadek. See Salman Abu Sitta, *Atlas of Palestine 1917–1966* (London: Palestine Land Society, 2010), ch. 3, 85–106.

40 The report of the International Committee of the Red Cross described the attack as "a scene of horror." It gave the fatalities figure at 150. Eyewitnesses gave the figure of 225 killed, twice the number who were butchered at the infamous Deir Yassin massacre. The Red Cross is known

for its reluctance to describe the extent of wars they witness for fear the local authorities might prevent them from operating in their territory. That the Red Cross used such language in describing Deir al-Balah's carnage, coming only three years after their experience in the Second World War, is significant. See ICRC archives in Geneva: ICRC Report G59/I/GC, G 3/82, January 1949 Report, dated Gaza, 4 February 1949.

41 David Ben-Gurion, *Yawmiyat al-harb (1947–49)* [War diaries (1947–49)], translated from Hebrew by Samir Jabbour (Beirut: Institute for Palestine Studies, 1998.) Ben-Gurion was the head of the Jewish Agency beginning in 1935 and became the first prime minister of Israel in 1948. In the entry for Monday 6 December 1948 (p. 651), he wrote: "We took over Egyptian defenses in al-Ma'in, Sheikh Nuran, Tell Far'a." On 26 December (p. 677), he wrote briefly, "Battalion 13 losses at Hill 86 were 13 dead, 10 missing, 35 wounded, and many weapons lost." There was no mention of outright defeat.

42 Morris, *The Birth of the Palestinian Refugee Problem Revisited*, 258. He mentioned that Israelis "apparently execut[ed] dozens of army-age males . . . [and] appear[ed] to have raped and murdered a teenage girl." There was no mention of mass murder, lobbing grenades into houses, and torching the village. In Ben-Gurion's *Yawmiyat al-harb* [War diaries], in the 14 May entry, he wrote, "Nahum Sarig occupied Burayr village. Sixty Arabs fell."

43 The full text of the Declaration is given on the Israeli Knesset website (http://www.knesset.gov.il/docs/eng/megilat_eng.htm). In his *Yawmiyat al-harb* [War diaries], Ben-Gurion mentions the conquest of Burayr, entry of 14 May, pp. 320, 377. The official Israeli narrative of the 1948 War called Burayr the 'Butchers' Village' on account of their defense of their village with their limited means. See *Harb Filistin, 1947–1948* [The Palestine war 1947–48: the official Israeli narrative], translated from Hebrew by Ahmad Khalifah (Beirut: Institute for Palestine Studies, 1984), 324.

44 More accurately, the International Committee of the Red Cross (ICRC). The ICRC set up offices in Palestine in January 1948. Their arrival was initiated by Jewish organizations to inspect the camps of Jewish terrorists held by Britain and the camps of illegal immigrants flooding Palestine.

45 See Americans for Middle East Understanding: http://www.ameu.org/The-Link/Archives/The-Lydda-Death-March.aspx

46 Lie, the first secretary general of the United Nations, supported the foundation of the State of Israel. His passionate support for Israel included passing secret military and diplomatic information to Israeli officials. See Hilde Henriksen Waage, "The Winner Takes All: The 1949 Island of Rhodes Armistice Negotiations Revisited," *Middle East Journal* 65, no. 2 (2011): 105.

47 Resolution 194 (A/RES/194 (III) 11 December 1948), para 11 called for the return of the refugees, which is the foundation of all relevant United Nations resolutions. Full text available at: http://unispal.un.org/UNISPAL.NSF/0/C758572B78D1CD0085256BCF0077E51A

48 See "The Origins of Sharon's Legacy," *Al-Ahram Weekly*, Issue No. 779, 26 January–1 February 2006, http://plands.org/articles/018.html
49 Interview, October 1995, at his home in Abasan.
50 See Salman Abu Sitta, "Isra'il al-dawla al-sariqa abadan: kayfa qadamat Qita' Ghazza fi ittifaqiya sirriya" [How Israel contrived to shrink the Gaza Strip], *Al-Hayat*, 28 March 2009, 15, http://plands.org/arabic/articles/050.html; Abu Sitta, *Atlas of Palestine*, 98.
51 Ben-Gurion, *Yawmiyat al-harb* [War diaries], 22 August 1949. The entry reads, "A shameful atrocity . . . 22 men from Battalion 22, Carmeli Brigade, mass raped a girl." On 2 April 1950, he wrote, "Again our soldiers caught 2 Arab girls, raped and murdered them." Quoted in Benny Morris, *Israel's Border Wars, 1949–1956* (Oxford: Clarendon Press, 1993), 167.
52 On 28 and 29 August 1953, Unit 101, led by Ariel Sharon, carried out this attack. Foreign observers called it "an appalling case of mass murder." See Morris, *Israel's Border Wars*, 242–43.
53 On 31 August 1955, Israelis attacked Khan Yunis police station with orders to "kill as many enemy soldiers as possible." They killed seventy-two and wounded fifty-eight. Morris, *Israel's Border Wars*, 350. See also Joe Sacco, *Footnotes in Gaza* (London: Jonathan Cape, 2009).
54 See the full report: Survey Report, Northwest Sinai Project, Republic of Egypt at: http://unispal.un.org/unispal.nsf/0145a8233e14d2b585256cbf005af141/243565397043 98a785256f400057d90c?OpenDocument, and http://unispal.un.org/unispal.nsf/0145a8233e14d2b585256cbf005af141/24356539704398a785256f400057d90c?OpenDocument#sthash.Fxu399Tb.dpuf
55 Mahmoud Fahmi Howeidi is one of the most prominent modern Islamic writers, widely respected and with a large constituency of readers. The Howeidi family was active in politics and government during Nasser's regime.
56 Benny Morris states that the Israeli government objective on 29 October 1956 was "to eliminate the Egyptian fedayeen bases in the Sinai Peninsula" as the main cause of the offensive. See Morris, *Israel's Border Wars*, 403. There were no such bases in Sinai. Sinai was defended by the Egyptian army. Fedayeen launched their attacks from the Gaza Strip and Jordan. Morris goes on to say, in footnote 2 on the same page, "Both the radio and the FM statement were deliberately misleading on a number of counts. The units [the Israelis] attacked at Ras al Naqb and Kuntilla [in Sinai] were Egyptian army, not Fedayeen."
57 The name of the commander of the battalion that attacked Khan Yunis is Doron.
58 The Khan Yunis and Rafah massacres are illustrated by Sacco, *Footnotes in Gaza*.
59 Ihsan Khalil Agha, a Khan Yunis native, wrote a lengthy book about this: *Khan Yunis wa shuhada'iha* [Khan Yunis and its martyrs] (Cairo: Markaz Fajr Publishing, 1997). UNRWA figures for those killed in Khan Yunis:

275 (140 refugees, 135 locals); in Rafah: 111 (103 refugees, 8 locals). See "Special Report of the Director of UNRWA" covering the period from 1 November 1956 to mid-December 1956, UN 11th Session, Supplement No 14A (A/3212/Add.1), New York 1957, pp. 3, 4.

60 Abdel Bari Atwan, *A Country of Words: A Palestinian Journey from the Refugee Camp to the Front Page* (London: Saqi Books, 2008), 29–30.

61 David Hirst, *The Gun and the Olive Branch* (London: Faber and Faber, 2003), 328.

62 The only notable exception was Joe Sacco, the celebrated journalist and cartoonist. He discovered this massacre fifty years later while reporting on the siege of Gaza. He retraced the massacre day by day through survivors, and then he published and illustrated it. See Sacco, *Footnotes in Gaza*.

63 The story of Beni Hilal—the adventures on their long march from Arabia to North Africa—is a popular narrative.

64 Omar Nashabe, "Israel's Killing Spree on Verdun Street," *Al-Akhbar*, 10 April 2012.

65 A popular party of the period, the Syrian Social Nationalist Party, founded by Antoine Saadeh, actually called for Greater Syria and Cyprus to be united as one people.

66 Hassan al-Karmi had a famous weekly radio program on Arab culture and poetry. He also wrote several dictionaries. His daughter Ghada is an accomplished writer and political activist. Said Jiries al-Eissa was a well-known poet in the Arab world.

67 Arnold J. Toynbee, *A Study of History*, abridged ed. (Oxford: Oxford University Press, 1957), vol. 2, 199.

68 William Butler Yeats (1865–1939) was an Irish poet and playwright and one of the foremost figures of twentieth-century literature. In 1923, he was awarded the Nobel Prize in literature, the first Irishman to receive the award.

69 While the Arabs were fighting in the First World War with their allies, the British and the French, to remove Turkish rule and become free and independent, the British Sykes and the French Picot were conspiring to divide the Arab world between them. This conspiracy, with variations of players and methods, is still going on a century later. There is an abundance of literature on this subject; see, for example, George Antonius, *The Arab Awakening: The Story of the Arab National Movement* (New York: Capricorn Books, 1965).

70 George Sale, *The Koran, or Alcoran of Mohammed* (Bath: Hazard, 1795). Sale's translation was the first from the original Arabic. Earlier English translations were made from Latin or other languages. Sale (1697–1736) spent twenty-five years in Arabia and completed his translation in 1734.

71 Ahmad ibn Fadlan ibn al-Abbas ibn Rashid ibn Hammad was a tenth-century envoy of Baghdad (of the Abbasid caliph) to the king of the Volga Bulgars. His party was captured and some were killed. He survived and

wrote the description of the Viking trading posts at the Volga and beyond. His interesting story has been the subject of books and films. See, for example: *Ibn Fadlan and the Land of Darkness: Arab Travellers in the Far North*, translated by Paul Lunde and Caroline Stone (London: Penguin Classics, 2012).

72 George Mikes, *How to Be an Alien*, 1st ed. (London: André Deutsch, 1946). The original is a hardback with illustrations by Nicolas Bentley.

73 The Jewish terrorists' deeds against the British in 1945–48 are described by British officers in: Edward Horne, *A Job Well Done: A History of the Palestine Police Force 1920–1948* (Sussex: The Book Guild, 2003); and R. Dare Wilson, *Cordon and Search: With the 6th Airborne Division in Palestine, 1945–1948*, repr. (Nashville: Battery Press, 1984).

74 For a sympathetic account see Avi Shlaim, *Lion of Jordan: The Life of King Hussein in War and Peace* (London: Penguin Books, 2007).

75 Anthony Nutting resigned his post as minister of state for foreign affairs in protest against British policy. See his book, *The Arabs* (London: Hollis and Carter, 1964).

76 Doctor Fayez Abdallah Sayegh (1922–80) was for years the leading political consultant for the Palestinians at the United Nations. He was also the chief architect of the 1975 UN resolution on Zionism and racism. He was a member of the Palestine National Council. The Association of Arab-American University Graduates (AAUG) was founded at a 1967 meeting in Sayegh's home in Washington, DC.

77 Walid Kamhawi, *al-Nakba wa-l-bina fi-l-watan al-'arabi* [The nakba and reconstruction in the Arab world], 2 vols. (Beirut: Dar al 'Ilm li-l-Malayin, 1956). Distinguished Palestinians wrote about the Nakba in the following decade or two. See, for example: Constantine Zureik, *Ma'na al-nakba* [The meaning of the nakba], in *Complete Works of Constantine Zureik* (Beirut: Centre for Arab Unity Studies, 1994), 1:195–260; and Aref el-Aref, *al-Nakba wa nakbat Bayt al-Maqdis wa-l-firdaws al-mafqoud, 1947–1952* [The Catastrophe and catastrophe of Bayt al-Maqdis and of paradise lost, 1947–52], 6 vols. (Sidon: al-Maktaba al-'Asriya, 1956).

78 Ahmed Shuqayri was the first chairman of the PLO. He fought for its formation against Arab governments' objections until they agreed. He had a distinguished diplomatic career representing Arab delegations at the UN.

79 Phillip L. Gould and Salman H. Abu Sitta, *Dynamic Response of Structures to Wind and Earthquake Loading* (London: Pentech Press, 1980; New York: Wiley, 1980).

80 The proverb in Arabic says: *Man bana fi gheir daru, galla miqdaru.*

81 Fathi al-Badri is a refugee from Beersheba town, exiled to the Gaza Strip. His family barely survived the Beersheba massacre when the Israelis occupied the town on 21 October 1948. His family and others were loaded on trucks and dumped at Gaza's gates. Fathi was always a staunch patriot. At Cairo University, he was close to our colleague, Kamal Adwan,

a founder of the Fatah movement, who was assassinated by the Israelis in Beirut in 1973 by a team that included Ehud Barak dressed as a woman. (See, for example, Omar Nashabe, "Israel's Killing Spree on Verdun Street," *Al-Akhbar*, 10 April 2012.)

82 Full text available online at *Le Monde diplomatique*, https://www.monde-diplomatique.fr/cahier/proche-orient/arafat74-en

83 "Edward Said: A Tribute to Abu Omar," *Hanna Mikhail Abu Omar*, n.d., http://www.abu-omar-hanna.info/spip/spip.php?article103&lang=ar

84 See Abu Sitta, *Atlas of Palestine*.

85 The most accurate translation for *shatat* is actually 'dispersion in exile.' The common translation of 'diaspora' does not apply to Palestinians because it does not take into account the forced cause of their dispersion.

86 Benni Meitiv, *Sowers of the Desert*, 4th ed. [Hebrew] (Merhavia: Kibbutz Ha Avtze Hashomer Hats'er, 1972), 49.

87 Arie Aharoni, *Diary of a Candidate for Treason* [Hebrew] (Tel Aviv, Israel: Sifriat Poalim Publishing House, 2000).

88 This and the following two extracts are both published in *Left Curve*, no. 32 (2008).

89 Aviv Lavie and Moshe Gorali, "I Saw Fit to Remove Her from the World," *Haaretz*, 29 October 2003.

90 That was not the only rape case in Negev. Ben-Gurion jotted in his diary eight months later that Batallion 22 caught two Arab women, raped them, and killed them. The nearby villages of Abasan and Khiza'a ambushed an Israel Defense Forces (IDF) command car ten kilometers inside the occupied land and killed five. These are two examples among many cases. See Morris, *Israel's Borders Wars*, 166.

91 Ziv Zipper was born in Germany in 1925. When he was thirteen, his family moved to South Africa and a year later to Rhodesia (now Zimbabwe). In 1945, he immigrated to Israel, together with his collection of jazz records, and he joined Kibbutz Shoval. At first he served in the Mobilized Guard in the Negev. The unit was made up of Palmach members who were drafted into the British settlement police force. They were issued weapons and uniforms, and they guarded the water pipeline.

92 "The Zipper Diaries," *Haaretz*, 5 May 5 2003.

93 See Zochrot's website: http://zochrot.org/index.php?id=844

94 See, for example, Meron Benvenisti, *Sacred Landscape: The Buried History of the Holy Land since 1948* (London and Los Angeles: University of California Press, 2000), 120.

95 See, for example, Benvenisti, *Sacred Landscape*, 11.

96 G.S.P. Freeman-Grenville, Rupert L. Chapman III, and Joan E. Taylor, *The Onomasticon by Eusebius of Caesarea: Palestine in the Fourth Century* A.D. (Jerusalem: Carta, 2003).

97 See Abu Sitta, *Atlas of Palestine*; and www.plands.org.

98 He was an evangelist determined to convert Jews to Christianity. His response, when he saw the fertile land and the people who cultivated it, was that he wished those people to perish and the Jews to replace them.

99 Abu Abdallah, a legend in Arabic history, was the last Arab king in Spain. He left in 1492, after seven centuries of Arab rule. He uttered his famous farewell words with "a sigh" when he looked back at al-Andalus for the last time.

100 Benvenisti, *Sacred Landscape*, 155.

101 Abd al-Hakim Amer was the Egyptian field marshal under Nasser during the 1967 war and was blamed for the defeat.

102 It was also called the "Monster on the Hill." See Chaim Herzog, *The Arab–Israeli Wars* (Bath, UK: Book Club Associates, 1982), 96; Dan Kurzman, *Genesis 1948: The First Arab–Israeli War* (New York: Da Capo Press, 1992), 585.

103 This conversation was played out again in widely published correspondence with Avnery. See Uri Avnery, "The Moral Right of the Refugees to Return," *Counter Punch*, 16 May 2014, http://www.counterpunch.org/2014/05/16/the-moral-right-of-the-refugees-to-return/

104 W.M. Thompson, *The Land and the Book* (London: Thomas Nelson and Sons, 1911), 556.

105 Edward Hull, *Mount Seir; Sinai and Western Palestine* (London: Richard Bentley and Son, 1885), 139.

106 The Austrian-Czech scholar Alois Musil visited Nuran in 1898 and 1900 and he believed Nuran, or possibly Nurban, was Lychonos, (also seen as Lichonos or Lichognos), which was mentioned in the *Life of St. Hilarion*, a Palestinian saint. According to Musil in *Arabia Petraea*, vol. 2, part 1, p. 244, note 3.2, the historian Sozomenus, the grandson of Hilarion, wrote in *Historia Ecclesiastica* (5.15) in the sixth century that his grandfather "with all his household" settled on a ridge overlooking the whole place. According to the same work (5.15, 14–17), Hilarion settled in the wilderness near Gaza in 306 and practiced the monastic life until ca. 353. He did so because "Gaza had a history as a place hostile to the early Christians. Several had suffered martyrdom there. . . . The people of Gaza were so hostile to the Christians that the Christian church had been built outside the walls, at a safe distance." It is known that early Christians practiced their religion in places away from the coast.

107 For the text of the Balfour Declaration, see the discussion and references in Abu Sitta, *Atlas of Palestine*.

108 Greer Fay Cashman, "Int'l Participants Mark 93 years since Battle of Beersheba," *The Jerusalem Post*, 1 November 2010, http://www.jpost.com/Local-Israel/Around-Israel/Intl-participants-mark-93-years-since-Battle-of-Beersheba

109 Edward Said, "The Morning After," *London Review of Books* 15, no. 20, 21 October 1993.

110 For full review see: Salman Abu Sitta, *The Palestinian Right to Return: Sacred, Legal, and Possible*, 2nd ed. (London: The Palestinian Return Centre, 1999); "The Feasibility of the Right of Return," in *The Palestinian Exodus, 1948–1988*, ed. Ghada Karmi and Eugene Cotran (London: Ithaca, 1999), 171–196; *The Palestinian Nakba 1948: The Register of Depopulated Localities in Palestine*, 2nd ed. (London: The Palestinian Return Centre, 2000); *From Refugees to Citizens at Home: The End of the Palestinian–Israeli Conflict* (London: Palestine Land Society and The Palestinian Return Centre, 2001); "The Implementation of the Right of Return," in *The New Intifada: Resisting Israel's Apartheid*, ed., Roane Carey (London: Verso, 2001), 299–319; *The Return Journey* (London: Palestine Land Society, 2007); *Atlas of Palestine*. For all works: www.plands.org.

111 One hundred and fifty is the number of UN members who have voted along these lines.

112 My trip to Gaza was reported in Mondoweiss. Salman Abu Sitta, "Return? To Gaza," *Mondoweiss*, January 28, 2022, https://mondoweiss.net/2022/01/return-to-gaza/.

113 This study was mentioned in several reports and lectures. See for example: "The Right of Return: The Only Key to Peace," Palestine Land Society, https://www.plands.org/en/articles-speeches/speeches/2019/the-edward-said-memorial-lecture-australia.

114 For a study of eighty-four parks and the lands seized by the JNF, *see The Atlas of Palestine: Land Theft by the Jewish National Fund* which can be downloaded for free here: https://www.plands.org/en/maps-atlases/atlases/atlas-land-theft-by-the-jewish-national-fund.

115 The archives of five hundred villages are catalogued here: https://www.plands.org/en/villages-database.

116 The news of the previous seven years is reported here: https://www.plands.org/en/competition-news.

117 The Return Plan was presented at the University of Pennsylvania in September 2023: https://www.plands.org/en/articles-speeches/speeches/2023/return-plan-2023.

118 The article published in Mondoweiss caused an uproar in the Zionist camp. It revealed many facts that they wanted to hide, reversing the roles of criminal and victim. Salman Abu Sitta, "I Could Have Been One of Those Who Broke Through the Siege on October 7," *Mondoweiss*, January 4, 2024, https://mondoweiss.net/2024/01/i-could-have-been-one-of-those-who-broke-through-the-siege-on-october-7/.

www.ingramcontent.com/pod-product-compliance
Lightning Source LLC
Jackson TN
JSHW011056180425
82865JS00002B/2
9781649034359